ROYAL HISTORICAL SOCIETY
STUDIES IN HISTORY 58

PROTECTING THE PUB

Reproduced from a contemporary trade journal
Courtesy of the British Library

PROTECTING THE PUB

Brewers and Publicans Against Temperance

David W. Gutzke

THE ROYAL HISTORICAL SOCIETY
THE BOYDELL PRESS

First published 1989

A Royal Historical Society publication
Published by The Boydell Press
an imprint of Boydell & Brewer Ltd
PO Box 9   Woodbridge   Suffolk IP12 3DF
and of Boydell & Brewer Inc.
Wolfeboro   New Hampshire 03894-2069   USA

ISBN 0 86193 215 3

ISSN 0269-2244

British Library Cataloguing in Publication Data

Gutzke, David W.
  Protecting the pub : brewers and publicans against
  temperance. — (Royal Historical Society Studies in
  history ; ISSN 0269-2244 : 58
  1. Brewing industries & trades, history
  I. Title   II. Series
  338.4'7'663309
  ISBN 0-86193-215-3

Library of Congress Cataloging-in-Publication Data

Gutzke, David W., 1949-
  Protecting the pub : brewers and publicans against
  temperance / David W. Gutzke.
     p.   cm. — (Royal Historical Society studies in history,
  ISSN 0269-2244 ; 58)
  Bibliography: p.
  Includes index.
  ISBN 0-86193-215-3 (alk. paper)
  1. Brewing industry—Great Britain—History. 2. Liquor
laws—Great Britain—History. 3. Prohibition—Great
Britain—History. I. Title. II. Series: Royal Historical
Society studies in history ; no. 58.
HD9397.G69G88   1989
338.4'766342'0941—dc20   89-31973
                                                              CIP

⊚ The paper used in this publication meets the minimum requirements of American National Standard for Information Sciences —
Permanence of Paper for Printed Library Materials, ANSI Z39.48-1984.

Printed in Great Britain by The Ipswich Book Company

TO MY PARENTS

Contents

The Society records its gratitude to the following whose generosity made possible the initiation of this series: The British Academy; The Pilgrim Trust; The Twenty-Seven Foundation; The United States Embassy's Bicentennial funds; The Wolfson Trust; several private donors.

Tables

Preface

This book could not have been written without the help of many organizations, and I am grateful to the following for permission to quote unpublished material for which they hold the copyright: Mr. Burns and A. G. Tilbury (Brewers' Society); John C. Overton (National Union of Licensed Victuallers); John Ingolby (Allied Brewery Traders' Association); A. D. Harris (Yorkshire Brewers' Association); K. G. W. Steven (East Midlands Brewers' Association); Keith Bacon (Western Counties Brewers' Association); M. H. Baker (South Wales Brewers' Association); W. R. S. Forsyth (North East Brewers' Association); M. P. Ingle (South Eastern Brewers' Association); C. Kilshaw (North West Brewers' Association); R. Pryor (Brewers' Company); M. A. Telfer-Smollett (Northern Home Counties Brewers' Association); the Guildhall Library; and the Staffordshire Record Office. For permission to quote correspondence, I am thankful to the following owners of the copyright: Mr Mark Bonham Carter; the Earl of Balfour; the Bodleian Library; Sir William Gladstone; the British Library; the Marquess of Salisbury; the Clerk of the Records of the House of Lords; the Kent Archives Office; the Lambeth Palace Library; the Trustees of the National Library of Scotland; and the Wiltshire Record Office.

I have incurred many debts in completing this book. Trevor Lloyd not only supervised every stage of research and writing, but gave shrewd advice, encouraged personal initiative and showed unfailing interest. John Beattie, Richard Helmstadter, the late Stephen Koss, David Fahey and David Healy read various drafts and made helpful suggestions. I also benefited from the advice of Craig Horle and Dominic Capeci, Jr. I am indebted especially to the University of Toronto for three research fellowships, and to Mr Robert Webber (Brewers' Society), Mr Keith Bacon and Mr C. Kilshaw (North West

Brewers' Association) whose kindness can be acknowledged but never repaid.

Finally, I want to thank my wife, Jessica Gerard, for her patience and support, and for willingly reading and commenting on numerous drafts. She will forgive me for dedicating this book to my parents, whose faith, optimism and assistance helped sustain me during the many years of research and writing.

David W. Gutzke
May, 1989

Abbreviations

Abbreviations used in footnotes are placed in parenthesis.

ABTA	Allied Brewery Traders' Association (ABTA)
Alliance/UKA	United Kingdom Alliance (UKA)
Association	National Trade Defence Association (NTDA), formerly the National Trade Defence Fund Brewers' Company (Br. Co.)
BS	Brewers' Society (BS)
C	Conservative (C)
CBS	Country Brewers' Society (CBS)
CETS	Church of England Temperance Society
Council	United Parliamentary Council of the Retail Licensed Trade (UPC)
Federation	National Federation of Off-Licence Holders' Association
Fund	National Trade Defence Fund (NTDF)
L	Liberal (L)
League	Licensed Victuallers' National Defence League (LVNDL)
LPDL	Liberty and Property Defence League (LPDL) London and Provincial Licensed Victuallers' Defence League (LPLVDL)
Society	Licensed Victuallers' Protection Society of London (LVPSL)
U	Unionist (U)

Introduction

'We have been borne down in a torrent of gin and beer', observed W. E. Gladstone, the defeated Liberal prime minister after his party lost the 1874 General Election. Thereafter, the electoral power of the drink interest itself became a controversial issue. Yet seldom has a British pressure group aroused such contemporary antipathy but so little scholarly scrutiny as late Victorian brewers and retailers. Historians have preferred investigating groups which wanted specific disabilities removed (Corn Laws, Anglicanism's privileged status and female disfranchisement) or some immoral aspect of society reformed (slavery, insobriety and compulsory examination of prostitutes). Anti-reformers have been largely neglected, in part because they usually aligned with Conservatives whose pre-war electoral vitality seemed secure. It was R. C. K. Ensor who was responsible for linking the Conservatives' strength with the brewing industry, and for re-establishing its reputation as an awesome political power. In his survey of England published in the 1930s, he pointed to limitless donations from brewers and the enormous influence of drink retailers on working-class customers as fundamental to explaining 'why conservatism was so much more successful in the forty years after 1871 than in the forty years before that date'.[1]

Accepting Ensor's verdict and conscious of the Labour party's post-war rise to prominence as the alternative to Conservatism, historians have been more intrigued with the decline of Liberalism. To many late Victorians even more disturbing was the growth of a corrupt political machine subverting popular opinion, democratic institutions and parliamentary laws. In

[1] W. E. Gladstone to Robertson Gladstone, 6 Feb. 1874, quoted in John Morley, *The Life of William Ewart Gladstone*, 3 vols. (1904), 2: 495; R. C. K. Ensor, *England, 1870 – 1914* (Oxford, 1936), p. 22.

1

1894, Liberal prime minister Lord Rosebery expressed these fears, declaring that 'if the State does not control the liquor traffic, the liquor traffic will control the State'. Amid the distractions of a world war two decades later, another Liberal and future prime minister, David Lloyd George, did not forget to identify Britain's chief obstacle to victory: 'We are fighting Germany, Austria and Drink, and, as far as I can see, the greatest of these deadly foes is Drink'.[2]

This is a study of the power of beer, mobilized by the brewing industry to resist government support for anti-drink legislation. This book examines how sophisticated, wealthy and astute businessmen and shopkeepers protected themselves against ruinous legislation, and their immensely difficult task of unifying into a national pressure group. It is by no means a definitive treatment; much more needs to be known about the major temperance societies and changing drinking habits. This study explores the economic and political context of attempts by beer producers and sellers to cooperate on behalf of common threatened interests. Had attaining such solidarity not been so contentious, so protracted, or offered so many insights into a divided industry operating as a pressure group, other dimensions of the drink debate would have warranted greater attention.

Nineteenth-century brewers specialized in different kinds of beer. London brewers, centrally located within England's largest urban market, became the first large-scale producers through their sale of porter, a bitter, heavily hopped, thick dark beer. It replaced other types including stout, a darker, stronger and dearer beverage, as the country's leading beer during the late eighteenth century, and remained popular well into the Victorian era. Elsewhere brewers continued to make ales, usually somewhat lighter in body and flavour, though still far more potent than continental or American lagers which appeared late in the nineteenth century and which even then created more curiosity than converts.[3]

---

[2] *The Times*, 24 May 1894 and 30 March 1915.
[3] E. M. Sigsworth, 'Science and the Brewing Industry, 1850–1900', *Econ. Hist. Rev.*, 17 (1965), 543–6; H. D. Watts, 'Lager Brewing in Britain', *Geography*, 60 (1975), 140–1; *Evid. Royal Com. Arsenical Poisoning*, 1904, 9 (Cmnd. 1845), p. 264; Oliver MacDonagh, 'The Origins of Porter', *Econ. Hist. Rev.*, 16 (1964), 530–5; Jonathan Brown, *Steeped in Tradition: The Malting Industry in England Since the Railway Age* (Reading, 1983), p. 20.

Beer drinkers began abandoning porter in the 1840s and 1850s for pale ales, widely distributed by the new railways. Already established as a lucrative export commodity, this distinctive beer was brewed with gypsum flavoured water at Burton-on-Trent. Generous hopping still made it quite bitter and strong but nevertheless lighter than porter. By the 1860s and 1870s many London brewers had conceded that pale ale had displaced porter as the preeminent beer, and set up branches in Burton.[4] Pale ales certainly dominated the market, but did not monopolize it. Whether brewed locally or imported from the Guinness brewery in Dublin, stout also had its advocates. London's continuing importance as a brewing centre and the emergence of Burton and Dublin as strong rivals was reflected in the geographic origins of the first ten brewer millionaires who died in the years 1868–1904: four came from London, three from Burton and one from Dublin. These brewers sold beer through thousands of intermediaries, retailers, but it could still be obtained privately. Engaged in what was commonly known as the 'family trade', firms like Stansfelds, Fremlins and Davenports ran small breweries supplying customers direct.[5]

By the end of the century public taste altered once again, discarding heavy pale ales for those with fewer hops and a glittering, bright appearance. Although still distinctly bitter, the new ales were perceptibly lighter, somewhat less alcoholic, usually bottled, and increasingly consumed at home.[6] In discussing the advent of bottled beer and the concomitant shift to off-consumption, scholars assume that this new beer primarily attracted middle-class drinkers. As chapter 7 argues, however, many working-class drinkers also adopted a new drinking pattern which provoked controversy within the brewing industry over home delivery.

[4] Sigsworth, 'Science and Brewing', pp. 540, 543–5; C. C. Owen, *The Development of Industry in Burton Upon Trent* (Chichester, 1978), pp. 75–7, 79–82.
[5] Patrick Lynch and John Vaizey, *Guinness's Brewery in the Irish Economy, 1759–1876* (Cambridge, 1960), pp. 199–201; W. D. Rubinstein, 'British Millionaires, 1809–1949', *Bull. Inst. Hist. Res.*, 47 (1974), 208–12; George Bruce, *Kimberley Ale: The Story of Hardys & Hansons, 1832–1982* (1982), p. 50; James Stansfeld's obituary, *Halifax Evening Courier*, 17 Feb. 1898; Charles Booth, *Life and Labour of the People in London*, vol. 7: *Population Classified by Trades* (1896), pp. 125–7.
[6] Brown, *Malting Industry*, pp. 21–2; Sigsworth, 'Science and Brewing', p. 546.

Most brewers sold their beer through retailers, to whom magistrates granted an annual licence specifying what, how and when liquor could be sold. The most prestigious and biggest group of retailers, publicans or licensed victuallers, possessed the most comprehensive licence permitting the sale of beer, wine and spirits for consumption either on or off the premises during most hours of the day. Earlier in the century most publicans would have brewed their own beers, but now fewer did so each decade as commercial brewers expanded production.[7] Beerhouse keepers, the second largest group, acquired inferior privileges under the 1830 Beer Act, which made retailing beer far easier by setting merely nominal qualifications but which prohibited sale of other liquors. In addition, beerhouse licences had shorter licensing hours, and received either on- or off-consumption rights, unless the applicant applied for both. It was not, therefore, beerhouses but rather pubs which competed with the third group, off-licences, created early in the 1860s to sell bottled wine and spirits solely for domestic consumption. In off-licences, drinking and sales of open bottles were forbidden, which meant they never seriously rivalled pubs where customers could enjoy a glass of wine or shot of spirits. Over three-quarters of these licences were held by small tradesmen who also stocked groceries, and late Victorians not surprisingly .often used the terms licensed grocers and off-licences interchangeably.[8]

As retailers ceased brewing, their exclusive role as sellers of beer, legally restricted numbers and certain factors inherent in brewing itself gave brewers powerful motives for purchasing licensed premises outright. Former independent retailers then leased the pub or beerhouse from the brewer becoming his tenants. Since they had often received financial assistance in purchasing the outgoing tenant's custom and fittings, they signed a contract agreeing to carry only their creditor's beer and typically bought other items from him as well. Started late in the eighteenth century, the tied house system covered at least

---

[7] A good overview of this shift and other major nineteenth-century changes in brewing is provided in Ronald B. Weir's 'The Drink Trades', Roy Church (ed.), *The Dynamics of Victorian Business: Problems and Perspectives to the 1870s* (1980), pp. 212–35.

[8] Walter Gilbey to Herbert Gladstone, 19 Apr. 1899, Brit. Lib., Herbert Gladstone Papers, Add. Ms. 46,057, fos. 154–7.

seventy-five per cent of all English pubs and beerhouses by 1900.

According to the standard interpretation, it spread rapidly early in the nineteenth century, stagnated after the anti-gin Beer Act of 1830 encouraged new licences and so thwarted prospects of cornering markets, and then, with stricter licensing policies reimposed by the 1869 Wine and Beerhouse Amendment Act and per capita beer consumption declining after 1876, resumed growth in the 1880s and 1890s.[9] Chapter 1 challenges this view. In the so-called 'free licensing' era (1830 – 69), many brewers, while no longer frantically acquiring licences, expanded their tied estate and later received further incentive, not from legislation, still less from national drink trends, but from the railway's opening of hitherto inaccessible markets. Exploiting the commercial opportunities of fast, cheap transport, Burton and certain northern brewers achieved phenomenal growth at the expense of smaller firms, whose inability to brew the popular ales created fear of these larger intruders. Local brewers then retaliated, and purchased licences as an alternative to intensified competition. Historians also misdate the renewed scramble for licensed property; brewers were already buying sizeable numbers of pubs and beerhouses late in the 1860s and mid-1870s.

Urbanization had made brewing as lucrative in large provincial cities as in London, but the social and economic consequences — excessive drinking, disease, poverty and sheer squalor — provoked disquiet. Nineteenth-century reformers addressed these problems in four ways.[10]

---

9   John Vaizey, 'The Brewing Industry', P. Lesley Cook (ed.), *Effects of Mergers: Six Studies* (1958), pp. 401 – 7; K. H. Hawkins and C. L. Pass, *The Brewing Industry: A Study in Industrial Organisation and Public Policy* (1979), pp. 18 – 19, 25, 27 – 8, 34; Kevin Hawkins, 'The Conduct and Development of the Brewing Industry in England and Wales, 1880 – 1938' (Univ. of Bradford Ph.D. dissertation, 1981), pp. 62 – 3, 71; P. L. Payne, 'The Emergence of the Large-Scale Company in Great Britain, 1870 – 1914', *Econ. Hist. Rev.*, 20 (1967), 530 – 1; E. M. Sigsworth, *The Brewing Trade During the Industrial Revolution: The Case of Yorkshire* (York, 1967), p. 32; Richard G. Wilson, *Greene King: A Business and Family History* (1983), pp. 103 – 4; T. R. Gourvish and R. G. Wilson, 'Profitability in the Brewing Industry, 1885 – 1914', *Bus. Hist.*, 27 (1985), 146; see also John Lowerson and John Myerscough, *Time to Spare in Victorian England* (Hassocks, 1977), p. 70.

10 The following 4 paragraphs are based on Brian Harrison's *Drink and the Victorians: The Temperance Question in England, 1815 – 72* (1971), chs. 3 – 5, 7, 9.

Free trade advocates, alarmed at rising gin consumption among the working classes and disgusted at the pubs' privileged status, initially dominated the debate, securing parliamentary approval of the 1830 Beer Act which instituted a *laissez-faire* attitude towards beerhouse licences. Local magistrates, regulators of these licences, had no choice but to licence qualified applicants, and beerhouses (especially in northern cities) and pubs proliferated until free licensing ended in 1869.

Even before free traders transformed the licensing system, Evangelicals, industrialists and others inspired an anti-spirits campaign late in the 1820s. With support drawn primarily from the social establishment (aristocrats and Anglican bishops) and from Quakers, this second stage espoused abstention from spirits as a means of popularizing middle-class values. Their concern was to reaffirm the virtuous abstainer's belief in abstention, not to redeem the drunkard.

Far more radical and less socially deferential was the third temperance phase, total abstinence or moral suasion, begun early in the 1830s. Teetotalism emphasized the vital importance of reforming drunkards, and, as a movement largely of middle-class dissenters and respectable working-class labourers, merged political and religious radicalism so that these Liberal nonconformists came to regard social mobility as their objective.

The fourth temperance stage developed when militants advocated prohibition in the 1850s: they now concentrated on cutting off the supply of alcohol rather than on suppressing its demand. Only then did temperance activists politicize the issue with a proposed legislative solution which began polarizing political parties in the 1870s. Prohibitionists, with their persecuted nonconformist mentality, preference for popular control and instinctive dislike of monopolies, naturally found Liberals more sympathetic to their goals than Conservatives. Prohibitionists ensured Liberalism of working-class and nonconformist votes, particularly in northern cities where intemperance flourished and industrialization's blight was most conspicuous. Their attacks on brewers and retailers quickly escalated into a campaign: prohibitionist MPs repeatedly introduced legislation banning sales of alcohol, while local supporters publicized abuses in legal enforcement as evidence of the impossibility of regulating such an immoral 'traffic' without corrupting those engaged in it.

In response, the drink interest started organizing a national pressure group, commonly known by members and critics alike as 'the trade'. In its broadest sense, it comprised wholesalers (brewers, whisky distillers and wine importers), retailers (publicans, beerhouse keepers, off-licence holders, licensed grocers as well as wine and spirit merchants), traders in hops and barley, together with pottery bottle makers, glass blowers, coppersmiths, cork and sugar merchants, coopers and stave makers, and finally drink shareholders — indeed, everyone with an interest in alcoholic beverages. The reality of 'the trade' was somewhat less exalted. Clearly brewers and the two leading retail factions, publicans and beerhouse keepers, developed the strongest identity with the trade, and displayed the strongest political commitment to its defence. As members of the propertied classes, brewery shareholders had strategic importance in the drink debate, and one which justified devoting considerable efforts to mobilizing them as an effective political force. Few other potential members of the trade actually joined it. Distillers never overcame their reluctance to protect brewers who alone owned the large number of tied houses which drink detractors loathed as a monopoly. The ancillary trades had enormous propaganda value, but remained unorganized until 1907, doubtless because economic grievances made some groups like hop growers uncooperative. Economic as well as political cleavages rendered off-licence holders and licensed grocers even harder to incorporate into the trade, frustrating brewers who appreciated that these retailers had two key traits, nonconformist sentiments and Liberal convictions, useful to augmenting the trade's electoral appeal. Whatever the political rhetoric, therefore, brewers, publicans and beerhouse keepers constituted the major groups within the trade, and provided the crucial funds, activism and leadership for its defence.

The conventional interpretation argues that early in the 1870s brewers and retailers quickly expanded or founded new organizations to form the trade, the monolithic pressure group which successfully defied temperance reformers and Liberal antagonists until 1914. Its immense financial resources, even larger than those of political parties, established it as a formidable late Victorian pressure group on behalf of Conservative candidates, feared for its unique influence with working-class voters through pubs and beerhouses. Granted its long-sought objective in 1904, the reimbursement of licences abolished at the behest of magistrates, the trade in 1914 knew the heavy Liberal taxes of the 1909 People's budget would be repealed, and 'looked forward with confidence to the return of a favourably disposed Conservative government'.[11] Such a view implicitly assumes that brewers and retailers subordinated internal conflicts to mutual political goals, and receives indirect support from the two economic studies of the Edwardian brewing industry, one written by John Vaizey, the other by K. H. Hawkins and C. L. Pass. They contend that the trade avoided price competition, emphasizing that breweries vied for customers strictly on the basis of product quality and public-house amenities.[12] Recently, David Fahey and R. B. Weir have disputed part of this argument. The larger incomes of temperance organizations, retail apathy, economic changes and ultimately competition from the Labour party convince them that the trade has been overrated as an attractor of working-class votes for Conservatism.[13]

This book, the first systematically to use fourteen trade newspapers and minute books, and the annual reports and correspondence of over thirty trade societies, maintains that historians have misjudged the brewing industry's role as a pressure group. Placed in both an economic and political context, brewers and retailers are depicted as businessmen and quasi-independent shopkeepers with threatened common interests, but not always with common priorities or even reconcilable objectives. Brewers and retailers organized themselves nationally much later than scholars have recognized, and well into the 1880s were still implementing organizational reforms and collecting less funds than prohibitionists. The trade, far from being monolithic, was often disrupted by debilitating quarrels. Initially geographic rivalries, jealousy, different legal privileges, conflicting economic functions and diverging political affiliations caused discord which brewers and retailers did not

[11] Ibid., pp. 226, 266, 342 – 3, 347, 373; John Turner, 'State Purchase of the Liquor Trade in the First World War', Hist. Jour., 23 (1980), 592 – 3; W. R. Lambert, Drink and Sobriety in Victorian Wales, c.1820 – c.1895 (Cardiff, 1983), pp. 166, 208; Peter Mathias, 'The Brewing Industry, Temperance and Politics', Hist. Jour., 1 (1958), 113.

[12] Vaizey, 'Brewing Industry', pp. 409 – 10 and The Brewing Industry, 1886 – 1951: An Economic Study (1960), pp. 17 – 18; Hawkins and Pass, Brewing Industry, p. 39.

[13] David M. Fahey, 'Brewers, Publicans, and Working-Class Drinkers: Pressure Group Politics in Late Victorian and Edwardian England', Histoire sociale/Soc. Hist., 13 (1980), 94, 98, 100 and 'The Politics of Drink: Pressure Groups and the British Liberal Party, 1883 – 1908', Soc. Sci., 54 (1979), 80 – 1; R. B. Weir, 'Obsessed with Moderation: The Drink Trades and the Drink Question (1870 – 1930)', Brit. Jour. Addiction, 79 (1984), 98.

surmount until late in the 1880s. National organization came even more slowly, so it was not until the 1890s that the trade's popular but hitherto exaggerated reputation as a collective political force was fully deserved.

Historians have also consistently overlooked the fact that the trade was preeminently a group in which unequal economic relationships between employers and employees could provoke friction sufficiently intense to undermine the solidarity necessary for pursuing long-term political goals. From the late 1890s, tied house practices, private clubs and direct home delivery of beer by brewers fostered acrimony between brewers and retailers, which escalated into overt hostility as trade leaders and protective societies repeatedly failed to reach acceptable solutions. Retailers often found their position as brewers' tenants objectionable, and some even joined an organization dedicated to abolishing the tied house system. There were two other specific brewers' policies which put tied tenants at a competitive disadvantage and aggravated discontent: by providing capital for working-class clubs and in facilitating the shift from heavy to light pale ales with home deliveries of beer, they alienated many retailers whose nearby pubs and beerhouses lost custom. These divisive economic disputes not only belie the assertion that the brewing industry suppressed fierce competition, but merit consideration when assessing the trade's effectiveness as a pressure group.

For all these reasons the trade's political power fluctuated between 1875 and 1914. Four distinct phases, paralleling trends in gross expenditure, are identified. Throughout the 1870s and early 1880s, the trade was poorly organized, chronically underfunded and just sporadically aroused to action. Extensive changes in both organization and expenditure vastly enlarged its power in the years 1883 – 91, but it was not until the 1890s with full-time electoral agents, more funds than opponents and support drawn from across the class spectrum that the trade gained its greatest influence. Disunity re-emerged at the 1900 Election, and increased progressively in the Edwardian era. Legislation in 1904 instituting an insurance scheme for revoked licences had contrary effects on brewers and retailers. On one hand, it led grateful trade leaders to become avowed Unionist allies; on the other hand, many of the rank and file, embittered at the denial of compensation, repudiated partisan politics, and took revenge on official trade candidates, whom they refused to support or even voted against at the 1906 Election. These angry brewers and retailers were disheartened by the Liberals and their 1909 People's budget which heavily taxed the brewing industry. Meanwhile, retailers revived old quarrels, income fell short of rising but essential expenses, and both the industry's prestige and membership in protective societies declined. Business grievances heightened tensions and helped undermine trade unity, as some disaffected societies sought legislative redress, not so much for what opponents had inflicted but for alleged economic injustices caused by greedy brewers.

This study argues that geography, competing economic functions and long traditions of autonomy promoted sectionalism, which persistently thwarted efforts to consolidate authority at the national level. Relentless threats gradually induced the trade to recognize the need for one representative national organization, but regional associations acknowledged neither their subordinate status, nor national priorities as paramount to local concerns. Paradoxically, while the trade was seemingly becoming more unified nationally, sectionalism and disunity also increased, discrediting the Unionist party as a staunch ally, demoralizing the rank and file, and denying brewers and retailers the much vaunted solidarity and confidence in 1914 which some scholars have mistakenly attributed to them.

1

The Brewing Industry Transformed

As a pressure group, the trade arose from the common economic interests of brewers and beer retailers; their relationship was primarily an economic one. Thus it is essential to examine how their respective positions changed as the structure of the brewing industry and its distribution network evolved over the nineteenth century. Late in the previous century specialized functions developed in brewing and retailing, replacing publican-brewers by commercial brewers and publicans. Large-scale brewing also allowed brewers to gain direct control over drink shops through the tied house system. By the late Victorian period, brewers had purchased large numbers of pubs and beerhouses, serving mostly working-class drinkers, but had invested little in wine or spirit retail shops, catering to middle- and upper-class patrons. Conflicting economic interests and awkward financial relations would create deeper trade schisms than any political controversy.

For more than a hundred years publican-brewers (sometimes called 'handicraft brewers'), who acted as both brewers and publicans by brewing beer at their pubs and selling it to customers, had been yielding to commercial brewers, the producers and sellers of beer for wholesale distribution. Better techniques, cheaper but superior beer, and, wherever coastal access permitted, shipping facilities gave commercial brewers decided advantages, thus eclipsing publican-brewers. Even before the mid-1830s, these small-scale entrepreneurs had disappeared in London and most of Ireland, though elsewhere they still produced almost half of all beer. Three decades later, however, it was the brewers who claimed three-quarters of total output. Handicraft brewers, primarily in Birmingham, Leeds, Ripon, York and much of Shropshire and Worcestershire, brewed only one out of every five barrels in the 1870s, and less each subsequent decade.[1]

The commercial breweries which superseded them can be divided into four classes according to size and product. First was the leading stout and porter beer producer, Arthur Guinness, Son & Co., which sold 700,000 barrels in 1876, nearly eight times more than at mid-century. Dominating the Irish market and developing a lucrative, though subsidiary, English trade, this Dublin firm had assets of £6 million by 1900, and outsold all other producers of British beer.[2]

Of equal stature and almost equal size was the second class, large brewers of pale ale. In Edinburgh such breweries as William Younger & Co. brewed 400,000 barrels in the 1890s, while in Burton-on-Trent Bass, Allsopps and Worthingtons among others used the distinctively flavoured local waters, so that Burton soon displaced London as the chief brewing centre. Unrivaled in Britain, Bass's extraordinary growth (60,000 barrels in 1847, over 900,000 in 1877 and 1.5 million in the 1880s) reflected the rapid shift in public taste from porter to pale ale. Allsopps, Bass's closest competitor, also reached 900,000 in 1876, but thereafter sales plummeted. In 1900, Bass and Allsopp together had shareholdings of nearly £11 million. To remain competitive, Trumans, Charringtons and Manns, three big London breweries, set up Burton branches early in the 1870s.[3]

Located in London or major provincial towns was the third group of brewers, producing between 100,000 and 600,000 barrels. In London, Truman, Hanbury, Buxton & Co. ranked first with 600,000 barrels in 1876, followed by Watneys, Combes, Reids and Barclay, Perkins which sold 300,000 – 550,000 barrels.

1 Vaizey, 'Brewing Industry', pp. 399 – 400; Sigsworth, *Brewing Trade of Yorkshire*, pp. 3 – 8; Peter Mathias, *The Brewing Industry in England, 1700 – 1830* (1959), p. 552; Lynch and Vaizey, *Guinness's Brewery*, p. 40; Brown, *Malting Industry*, p. 17 – 18; George B. Wilson, *Alcohol and the Nation: A Contribution to the Study of the Liquor Problem in the United Kingdom from 1800 to 1935* (1940), p. 368.

2 Mathias, *Brewing Industry*, pp. 3 – 27; Lynch and Vaizey, *Guinness's Brewery*, pp. 89 – 90, 199 – 201, 260; Vaizey, 'Brewing Industry', p. 398. Shareholders in 1900 are drawn from T. Skinner, *The Stock Exchange Year-Book and Diary for 1900*.

3 Sigsworth, 'Science and Brewing', pp. 540, 543 – 5; Hawkins and Pass, *Brewing Industry*, p. 21; Vaizey, 'Brewing Industry', p. 398; David Keir, *The Younger Centuries: The Story of William Younger & Co., Ltd., 1749 to 1949* (Edinburgh, 1951), p. 75; T. Skinner, *The Stock Exchange Year-Book and Diary for 1900*.

Few provincial breweries approached this scale; closest were Ind Coope (Romford and Burton), Peter Walker (Warrington and Burton) and Joshua Tetley (Leeds) with 340,000 – 400,000 barrels late in the 1880s.[4]

Finally, small provincial firms like Greenall Whitley (St Helens and Warrington) Samuel Smith (Tadcaster) and Greene King and Sons (Bury St Edmunds), brewing under 100,000 barrels, made up the fourth and numerically largest group.[5]

Throughout the nineteenth century both the network for distributing beer and brewers' relationship with retailers changed considerably. Commercial breweries deprived publicans of their function as handicraft brewers and with it their independence. Insufficient capital prompted publicans to accept brewers' money. When a brewer lent publicans money to purchase or lease pubs from him, a 'tied' contract was signed by which they agreed to sell only his beers. Brewers knew their beers did not always reach customers in prime condition: it was perishable and so easily spoilt; it was delicate and so susceptible to damage; it was unlabelled on draught and so misrepresentation was encouraged. Brewers therefore wanted to supervise closely the sale of their beer, and resorted to the tie as a practical means of safeguarding their reputation and profits. In addition, tied houses let them more easily anticipate demand.[6]

Eighteenth-century brewers had resisted such incentives to buy numerous pubs until the evolution of larger breweries and a new policy on the part of magistrates transformed the industry in three other ways: retail shops emerged devoted to selling alcohol, brewers acquired surplus capital to supply publicans on credit, and the number of outlets for beer contracted. Only in the 1790s did the last and final factor appear. In enforcing stricter licensing requirements which reduced the number of

---

[4] Hawkins and Pass, *Brewing Industry*, p. 21; Hurford Janes, *The Red Barrel: A History of Watney Mann* (1963), p. 133; Alfred Barnard, *The Noted Breweries of Great Britain and Ireland*, 4 vols. (1889 – 91), 1:272, 296, 302 and 2:65, 73, 98; Vaizey, 'Brewing Industry', pp. 398 – 9; Sigsworth, *Brewing Trade in Yorkshire*, p. 13.

[5] J. Norman Slater, *A Brewer's Tale: The Story of Greenall Whitley & Company Limited Through Two Centuries* (Warrington, 1980), p. 139; Sigsworth, *Brewing Trade of Yorkshire*, p. 12; Wilson, *Greene King*, p. 272. Of the 2,270 commercial brewers who produced 1,000 or more barrels in 1880, for example, 2,243 fell below 100,000 barrels (Wilson, *Alcohol and Nation*, p. 49).

[6] Vaizey, 'Brewing Industry', pp. 400 – 1.

licences, magistrates created an artificial scarcity making surviving ones more valuable. As beer consumption fell and competitors threatened to monopolize markets, disquieted brewers started purchasing houses, which soon provoked bidding rivalries, escalating prices, and a speculative licensed property boom until 1830. Incoming publicans had generally paid the former occupant £100 or less for 'good-will', but, as competition drove prices up into the £500 – £2,000 range, they exchanged their autonomy for indispensable loans from brewers. By 1830, brewers, largely in the home counties and Hampshire but not in London, owned well over half of all pubs.[7]

In that year Evangelical concern over gin's rising popularity, pressure from free trade advocates and disenchantment with restrictive licensing inspired the Beerhouse Act, which allowed unfixed numbers of taxpayers to acquire a licence for selling beer only.[8] Public houses had hitherto monopolized sales by offering beer as well as small quantities of spirits, wine and liquors to customers drinking at the bar or wanting to take their purchase away. To acquire or keep these tightly-regulated privileges, an individual approached local magistrates, meeting in what were aptly termed Brewster Sessions, who could issue a certificate which he would then submit to excise officials for a licence. Magistrates thus granted no liquor licences. But as only they could sanction the prerequisite certificate and as all public-house licences came before them for annual renewal, which various offences might jeopardize, the magistrates' power was in fact paramount.

Accordingly, the legislation creating beerhouses diverged from conventional practice: excise officials, not JPs, conferred these beerhouse licences; licensing became free rather than restricted (a change which fostered the rapid growth of all licences, especially those for beerhouses); statutory closing hours were imposed; two separate categories, for consumption on and off the premises (previously united in pub licences)

---

[7] Lynch and Vaizey, *Guinness's Brewery*, pp. 226 – 7; Mathias, *Brewing Industry*, pp. 117 – 34, 228 – 43; Francis Sheppard, *Brakspear's Brewery, Henley on Thames, 1779 – 1979* (Henley on Thames, 1979), pp. 23 – 30; Peter Clark, *The English Alehouse: A Social History, 1200 – 1830* (1983), pp. 254 – 60, 263 – 7, 283 – 4. Country brewers acquired direct control over pubs through owning the leasehold or freehold, whereas those in London relied more on informal loans.

[8] Harrison, *Drink and Victorians*, ch. 3; Clark, *English Alehouse*, pp. 295 – 6, 334 – 5.

appeared when the act was slightly amended in 1834; and spirit sales were disallowed. Other later types of licences circumscribed pubs' dominant position as retail outlets for wine and spirits, but none had so great or enduring an impact on sales as beerhouses. Before Parliament finally gave magistrates some discretion over these licences in the 1869 Wine and Beerhouse Act, almost 53,000 beerhouse and 18,000 additional public-house licences had been granted, more than doubling the aggregate number of licences since 1829.[9]

Historians share three assumptions about the tied house system's subsequent development. First, that brewers, now thwarted by free licensing from cornering retail markets, stopped buying drink shops. Second, that new legislation (1869 – 72), extending magisterial control over beerhouses and generally upgrading standards for all licences, stabilized the number of drink shops, and revived fears of market exclusion. Finally, that two related changes, private brewing partnerships being converted into public companies and rising drink shop prices, meant that brewers had only just resumed buying houses in the 1880s.[10]

For only the third assumption do historians cite apparently persuasive evidence. In 1886, Arthur Guinness, Son & Co. floated £6 million of public stock, becoming the first of 260 firms which sold about £185 million of share capital before 1900. Public investors, impressed by Guinness's outstanding reputation and resurgent beer consumption, engendered a boom in which virtually all huge breweries participated. With this money, brewers quickly acquired numerous pubs and beerhouses. Newcastle Breweries bought 170 of its 300 tied houses between 1890 and 1897, while Yate's Castle Brewery (Manchester) purchased all but forty of its 175 houses in the years 1888 – 96. Even more dramatic were the acquisitions of Georges & Co. of Bristol, owners of seventy houses in 1888 but 350 four years later. Allsopps exhibited this trend best by buying some 1,200 houses in the fifteen years after 1887, for which it paid well over £3 million. 'The buying of public houses developed from a competition to a war, and from a war to a panic', one scholar of Victorian pubs concludes. Licensed property prices soared especially in London, where three pubs which sold for £2,000, £7,000, and £17,500 prior to 1884 now

9   Wilson, *Alcohol and Nation*, pp. 102, 395 – 6.
10   See p. 5, n. 9.

brought £86,000, £52,000 and £95,000 respectively late in the 1890s. Few brewers, whatever their private means, could purchase public houses without recourse to public capital.[11]

Scholars, though accepting this chronology, vigorously dispute what provoked brewers' renewed purchase of licensed property in the 1880s. John Vaizey regards fewer licences and growing beer consumption as the principal factors which enhanced the intrinsic value of drink shops. Because magistrates withdrew licences and granted few new ones when beer production was rising from 28 million (1884) to 37 million barrels (1900), brewers felt compelled to vie aggressively to control diminishing numbers of retail shops. Brewers themselves recognized that selling stock to an enthusiastic but unwary public proved both immensely lucrative and helpful in amassing funds for licensed property investments.[12] P. L. Payne, too, emphasizes the role of licensing restrictions, but also stresses that larger breweries, owing to better transportation, bigger cities and mechanization, likewise intensified demands for a network of secure outlets. Anxious to protect markets, brewers bid competitively against rivals, forcing up prices.[13] For K. H. Hawkins and C. L. Pass, bigger breweries were also significant, but for wholly different reasons. To the estimated £30 million invested in licensed property in 1869, brewers added another £170 in the next three decades, not so much because magistrates repudiated free trade in beer as because per capita beer consumption, steadily increasing in the 1860s and early 1870s, declined sharply and unexpectedly after 1876, and then settled at a lower level. Brewers, who had meanwhile enlarged plant capacity to meet projected market growth, feared losing traditional outlets. According to Hawkins and Pass, these two factors hastened purchases of licensed houses by provincial

---

11   Vaizey, 'Brewing Industry', pp. 403–4; John Pudney, *A Draught of Contentment: The Story of the Courage Group* (1971), p. 115; *Evid. Royal Com. Liq. Licensing Laws*, 1898, 36 (Cmnd. 8693), p. 367; Alan Gall, *Manchester Breweries of Times Gone By* (Swindon, 1982), p. 4; Mark Girouard, *Victorian Pubs* (1975), pp. 78, 80; Hawkins and Pass, *Brewing Industry*, pp. 32, 34. Hawkins and Pass (pp. 29–30) do provide some examples of how quickly brewers of moderate size acquired tied houses. Greenall Whitley surpassed them all, purchasing almost 500 houses between 1882 and 1892 (Slater, *Greenall Whitley*, p. 139; John Baxter, 'The Organisation of the Brewing Industry' (Univ. London Ph.D. dissertation, 1945), pp. 219–20).
12   Vaizey, 'Brewing Industry', pp. 403–7 and *Brewing Industry*, pp. 7–8; Wilson, *Alcohol and Nation*, p. 370.
13   Payne, 'Large-Scale Company', pp. 530–1.

16

brewers from the 1880s. But Richard Wilson finds this unconvincing: while per capita consumption did decline, total beer production continued rising until 1899. Pressure for acquiring drink shops generally came from licensing restraints except in Suffolk, where total licences remained unchanged well into the mid-1890s. There brewers were an anomaly, buying pubs and beerhouses earlier than elsewhere as a means of suppressing competition.[14]

By neglecting the 1830 – 69 period, all these studies overestimate the importance of stricter licensing or beer consumption trends. Free licensing and the vast numbers of beerhouses it promoted certainly prevented the licensed property boom, but not brewers' desire for increased tied holdings. Popular tradition has it that Reading brewer Blackall Simonds, apprised of imminent government legislation in 1830, discreetly noted likely sites near his brewery while hunting, and on learning of the Beerhouse Act shrewdly acquired fifty of them for building new beerhouses. T. A. B. Corley's recent study of the brewery discounts the story as apocryphal, but still confirms that Simonds vastly enlarged his tied house estate with eight purchases per decade. Of his seventy-nine houses in 1872, forty-two had come into his hands since 1837. In Oxfordshire, William Brakspear at least tripled his tied houses with twenty-nine purchases between 1825 and 1868, the same number as Robert Lindsell and William Hogge were buying in Bedfordshire.[15] Similarly, the number of free licences declined steadily in Norfolk, with tied tenants employed in over half of the drink shops in such towns as Great Yarmouth, Norwich and Lynn by the mid-Victorian era. Two local breweries, Steward, Patteson, Finch & Co. and Youngs, Crawshay & Youngs, so quickly predominated that both together had already gained control of over forty per cent of the licences (672) they held in 1892. In another East Anglian county, Suffolk, John Cobbold was busily purchasing unoccupied mansions, and converting them into

---

14 Hawkins and Pass, *Brewing Industry*, pp. 25, 27 – 30, 36; Wilson, *Greene King*, pp. 117 – 18, 141.
15 Pudney, *Courage Group*, pp. 86 – 7; Sheppard, *Brakspear's Brewery*, pp. 55 – 8, 67; T. A. B. Corley, 'Simonds' Brewery at Reading, 1760 – 1960', *Berks. Arch. Jour.*, 68 (1978), 80, 83; Ken Page, *Greene King: Biggleswade Brewery, 1764 – 1984* (Sandy, Beds., 1984), pp. 2 – 3; see also David W. Backhouse, *Home Brewed: A History of Brewing and Public Houses in North Wiltshire* (Swindon, 1984), p. 8; Kenneth Neale (ed.), *Victorian Horsham: The Diary of Henry Michell, 1809 – 74* (Chichester, 1975), pp. 39 – 40, 43, 54 – 5, 57, 59 – 64.

inns or pubs. With some 200 houses in the mid-1870s and his supremacy in Ipswich ensured, Cobbold and his sons had what outlets they required for the next two decades.[16]

Midland and northern brewers also exploited the Beerhouse Act to expand holdings. Within a three-year period, one Birmingham brewer's representative took out some 200 beerhouse licences. Even Michael Thomas Bass, whose Burton ales retained widespread popularity, began buying Stafford-shire houses from 1860. Newly established breweries, having few or no tied houses, lacked much capital, and so often postponed making financial commitments. Thomas Chesters, a Manchester brewer since 1842, purchased his first public house in 1856, but then went on to buy sixty-four more over the next fourteen years. Most historians believe that the shortage of licensed houses prompted mergers of breweries from the late 1880s. Greenall Whitley, however, had systematically absorbed smaller rivals since the 1860s, and boasted 195 houses in 1882, years before amalgamations supposedly replaced piecemeal purchases. Within one decade this Lancashire brewery achieved primacy in England and Wales with 681 tied houses, reflecting its avowed objective of securing growth by eliminating competitors.[17]

Brewers purchased large numbers of pubs and beerhouses after 1830 for five major reasons: unstable beer demand, lower licensed property values, speculative rewards, local rivalries and competitive disadvantages. Because brewers could max-imize profits only with constant output, tied houses insulated them against erratic beer demand, which declined seventeen per cent in the years 1836 – 43 and fourteen per cent in 1853 – 5. Reduced pub prices also attracted many brewers with uncertain markets. Compared with the £500 – £2,000 level of the pre-1830 boom years, licensed property outside London seldom rose much beyond £700 and often fetched as little as £200 in the 1830s – 40s. By the 1850s and 1860s prices moved upwards into

16   *Evid. Sel. Comt. Public Houses*, 1852 – 3, 37 (855), pp. 123 – 5; Terry Gourvish, *Norfolk Beers from English Barley: A History of Steward & Patteson, 1793 – 1963* (Norwich, 1987), pp. 35, 39, 47, 56 – 7; Baxter, 'Brewing Industry', pp. 219 – 20; Michael Jacobson, *The Cliff Brewery, 1723 – 1973* (n.p., 1973), p. 20; Agreement between John C., Thomas C. and Felix T. Cobbold, Suffolk R.O., Cobbold & Co., HA/231/1/3, 8 May 1876.

17   Wilson, *Alcohol and Nation*, p. 102; Owen, *Industry in Burton*, p. 95; Frank Cowen, *A History of Chesters Brewery Company* (Manchester, 1982), pp. 4 – 6, 33; Slater, *Greenall Whitley*, pp. 23, 144, 147.

the £700 – £800 range, thereby eliminating this incentive.[18] The third motive actuating brewers' control of houses was exemplified by Peter Walker, founder of a Liverpool brewery in 1846 and owner of over fifty local tied houses in 1868. ' "If the magistrates continue the free trade system" ', he predicted in the mid-1860s, ' "I shall double the number of my [tied] houses, and if they stop it will double the value of the houses I have" '. Heeding his own advice, Walker acquired about forty more Liverpool houses alone during the next decade.[19]

Halifax brewers invested in tied houses not because of speculative gain but because of local rivalries and competitive disadvantages. Initially they avoided buying drink shops, having none as late as 1837, but by 1876 owned almost two-fifths of the town's houses. Eight firms then owned seventy-seven (thirty-three per cent), showing brewers' monopolistic traits in the so-called 'free trade' era. In fact, Halifax brewers purchased more licensed premises in the pre-1876 years than in the following two decades. Impetus came in part from two of the oldest and largest breweries, and in part from upstart competitors. The former's acquisitions of houses alarmed local firms which adopted retaliatory tactics. Recently-founded breweries wanted tied houses, in contrast, to counter their more established rivals' two distinct advantages, beers with established reputations and loyal customers. With these outlets, new brewers ensured uniform sales, prevented mishandling of beers and obtained a 'shop window', aimed at persuading free house retailers to stock unknown brands.[20]

Neither tighter licensing legislation nor falling beer consumption can satisfactorily explain why breweries engaged in what Vaizey calls the 'Brewers' Wars' from the mid-1880s. Both he and Payne assume that local magistrates utilized greater powers to reduce licences universally after 1880. But in nineteen English counties between 1855 and 1886 the average number of on-

---

18 Wilson, *Alcohol and Nation*, p. 369. For licensed premise values after 1830, see: Neale, *Victorian Horsham*, pp. 39 – 40, 43, 54 – 5, 57, 59 – 62; Sheppard, *Brakspear's Brewery*, pp. 55 – 7; Wreglesworth, Richardson and Gall, *Pubs of Macclesfield*, p. 29; Douglas J. Elliott, *Buckingham: The Loyal and Ancient Borough* (Chichester, 1975), p. 194; Gourvish, *Steward & Patteson*, p. 48.

19 *Evid. Sel. Comt. on Sale of Liquors on Sunday Bill*, 1868, 14 (402), pp. 47, 50, 54, 56; *Evid. Sel. Comt. of the House of Lords on Prevalence of Habits of Intemp.*, 1877, 11 (418), pp. 193 – 5; Baxter, 'Brewing Industry', pp. 219 – 20.

20 P.W. Robinson, 'The Emergence of the Common Brewer in the Halifax District', *Trans. Halifax Antiquarian Society*, (1981), 76 – 8, 93 – 4.

licences, far from declining as these scholars claim, actually increased by ten per cent. In Gloucestershire, Sussex, Essex and Hampshire, all significant brewing areas, the number of on-licences grew between twenty and thirty-four per cent, though many native breweries still became leading owners of tied houses. In the eighteen counties where licences decreased, five (including Somersetshire, Cornwall and Leicestershire with small breweries) accounted for almost seventy-five per cent of the total. In addition, brewers competed most intensely for houses in counties where the number of licences remained unchanged or rose. This is clearly evident in the 1892 parliamentary return identifying on-licence owners. Of the sixty-five English country breweries (i.e. those outside London) which ranked among major tied house purchasers with 10,817 on-licences, forty-eight were located in these counties and held 8,515, or four-fifths of the total.[21] Nor is the Hawkins and Pass thesis more plausible. They merely speculate that brewers responded to lower per capita beer consumption, and, preoccupied with the post-1880 period, mistakenly conclude that 'deterioration in the brewers' market environment' caused the accelerated expansion of the tied house system.[22]

Brewers' rationale for rapidly accumulating tied houses emerged earlier, exhibited greater diversity and owed more to long-term changes than historians have hitherto recognized. By 1868 the railway had created national markets, stimulated larger breweries and transformed Burton into England's premier brewing centre. Its brewers then accounted for nearly eight per cent of England's total beer sales, almost a four-fold increase, and thereafter continued to outstrip aggregate beer output, with a market share of almost twelve per cent late in the 1880s.[23] Other breweries had meanwhile achieved impressive but slower growth. In Lancashire Peter Walker & Son produced 340,000 barrels just four decades after being founded, and in Yorkshire Henry Bentley's Breweries had expanded from under 10,000 to 100,000 barrels. The railway's impact, however, was uneven. Only certain breweries, especially brewers of pale ale, which travelled better and paid higher profits, exploited burgeoning

---

21 Compiled from Wilson, *Alcohol and Nation*, pp. 379 – 80; Baxter, 'Brewing Industry', pp. 219 – 20; *Home Office Return of the Number of On-Licences*, 1892, 68 (294).

22 Hawkins and Pass, *Brewing Industry*, pp. 27, 36.

23 Owen, *Industry in Burton*, p. 79, 229; Wilson, *Alcohol and Nation*, pp. 369 – 70.

beer consumption in the 1860s – 70s. Their movement into new distant areas antagonized local firms, which sought tied outlets as an alternative to larger outsiders gaining access to markets, a tactic precipitating other regional breweries' reciprocal acquisitions. This was analogous to the pre-1830 years when England's biggest breweries, then in London, had also encroached on the markets of smaller provincial firms. In each instance, country brewers reacted immediately and in a similar way. 'Tied houses', Peter Clark comments, 'were used to freeze out the London firms, to stop them gaining a strong foothold in the provincial trade'.[24]

Contrary to received historical opinion, competition had already heightened in the mid-1870s, and escalated, with available free houses depleted in the 1880s, into another boom, sustained by capital from the sales of public stock for buying chains of houses from smaller, unsuccessful firms. Throughout the country the proportion of tied houses advanced appreciably, despite varying licensing trends. Although the percentage of Oxfordshire's licences declined as Nottinghamshire's increased, breweries in each still bought houses. Hunt's Banbury Brewery purchased sixty-four tied houses in the mid-1870s, whereas Hardy's Kimberley Brewery acquired six houses during the decade.[25] Whether in Portsmouth, Chester, Newcastle-on-Tyne, Ely, Sheffield, Liverpool and Cardiff or more generally in Durham, Kent, Norfolk and Staffordshire, brewers' licensed properties multiplied before per capita beer consumption fell in 1877. Most informed observers shared the view of Chester's chief constable in April 1877 that 'brewers . . . buy them [licensed premises] up as fast as they can'. Near his town, Macclesfield brewers were already purchasing as many houses as they would in the 1880s.[26]

But in some counties pressure came from regional, not national, firms which saw enlarged sales as a means of

24 Sigsworth, *Brewing Trade of Yorkshire*, p. 13; Clark, *English Alehouse*, p. 266; Barnard, *Noted Breweries*, 2:98; Vaizey, 'Brewing Industry', p. 398.

25 *Victoria County History of Oxfordshire*, 10: 66 – 7; Bruce, *Kimberley Ale*, p. 46; Wilson, *Alcohol and Nation*, p. 379.

26 *Evid. Lords Comt. Intemp.*, 1877, 11 (171), pp. 313 – 14, (271), pp. 5, 42 – 3, 93, 102, 158, 293, 300, 359, (418), p. 172; *Evid. Royal Com. Liq. Licensing Laws*, 1898, 36 (Cmnd. 8693), p. 415; Cowen, *Chesters Brewery*, pp. 5 – 6; compiled from Wreglesworth, Richardson and Gall, *Macclesfield*.

suppressing competition. Two Suffolk brewers illustrated such rivalry. With five houses between them in 1869, Greene and King vied for supremacy in the 1870s, each buying at least forty houses before the latter's interest abated, though his opponent's avidity for undisputed control persisted.[27] As this struggle suggests, momentum once acquired became self-sustaining.

Licensing legislation did influence proliferating numbers of tied houses, but not as historians have depicted. The 1872 Licensing Act increased the likelihood of a licence being endorsed and thus possibly forfeited, and so many retailers, unable to afford costly appeals, brew profitable beers or meet stiffer competition which reduced profits, found offers by brewers irresistible.[28]

In London, the licensed property boom developed not merely later than in the provinces, but for different reasons. There only in the mid-1890s, long after country brewers had inaugurated bidding wars, did firms become frantic buyers of outrageously priced licensed houses. London's higher property values, its larger numbers of drink shops with leaseholds and its traditional arrangement of a brewer lending prospective licencees money to purchase a pub or beerhouse in exchange for stocking their benefactor's beers, primarily explain this delay. As the 'London system' worked well and the alternative, outright purchases, seemed uneconomical, London brewers continued to act as retail creditors in the 1870s. Problems arose, however, in the following decade: falling beer consumption and rising overhead costs bankrupted numerous drinksellers, many of whom defaulted on their loans. Retailers and brewers alike increasingly considered customary loan-tie methods outmoded. Retailers sought other financial backing to avert economic difficulties blamed on London brewers, who themselves grimly saw mortgage outlays mount while beer sales declined. Relations between them rapidly deteriorated when Burton brewers,

[27] Wilson, *Greene King*, pp. 104–5.
[28] Scotland's dissimilar licensing system and magisterial hostility prevented brewers there from purchasing licensed premises (Ian Donnachie, *A History of the Brewing Industry in Scotland* (Edinburgh, 1979), pp. 154–5, 194–6, 206–14; Rudolph Kenna and Anthony Mooney, *People's Palaces: Victorian and Edwardian Pubs of Scotland* (Edinburgh, 1983), p. 30).

coveting London markets, not only financed some publicans (as did agencies like the Licensed Victuallers' Mortgage Association), but actually began acquiring houses. Pressure equally came from inside the city. Small London firms used public debentures as a substitute for limited capital, buying reversions of unexpired leases or competing for those formerly controlled by larger rivals. To avert further losses, leading metropolitan breweries therefore became owners of licensed property after 1895.[29]

Competitive bidding ensued, prices soared and by 1900 tied houses had supplanted the 'London system'. Charrington's experience in which licensed property sales approached £3 million during a three-year period probably typified other major London breweries. No pub, however meagre its taking or unimpressive its surroundings, seemingly discouraged brewers. For one located in impoverished Kensal town, for instance, the Cannon Brewery Co. paid £97,000 in 1896, almost seven times its 1891 value. But such exorbitant figures hardly reflected average prices; between 1893 and 1898 this firm spent on average roughly £11,000 apiece on 125 licensed premises. Moreover, while Mark Girouard cites six London pubs going for an average of £74,000 in the years 1896 – 8 and two contemporary temperance advocates publicized another five realizing between £46,850 and £112,000 in 1897, pubs or beerhouses outside the central perimeter rarely commanded such prices.[30] Even with attached property, two Sutton pubs in northern Surrey sold together for £6,000 in 1897. London prices, always the country's highest, rose briefly far above the £2,700 commonly paid for licensed premises elsewhere, though when the

[29] D.M. Knox, 'The Development of the Tied House System in London', *Oxford Econ. Papers*, 10 (1958), 68 – 9, 73 – 4, 77 – 8; Girouard, *Victorian Pubs*, ch. 4; Edwyn Barclay, 'The Future of the Public-House', *Nineteenth Cent.*, 65 (1909), 997 – 8; Walter Pearce Serocold, *The Story of Watneys* (St Albans, 1949), p. 25; Pudney, *Courage Group*, pp. 31 – 2, 34 – 5; *A Hundredth Birthday: Reviewing a Century of [Joshua Tetley & Son's] Progress, 1823 – 1923* (Leeds, n.d. [1923?]), p. 18; Hawkins, 'Development of the Brewing Industry', p. 309.

[30] L. A. G. Strong, *A Brewer's Progress, 1757 – 1957: A Survey of Charrington's Brewery on the Occasion of its Bicentenary* (1957), pp. 38 – 9; *Licensed Trade News*, 6 June 1896; Girouard, *Victorian Pubs*, pp. 78, 80; Joseph Rowntree and Arthur Sherwell, *The Temperance Problem and Social Reform* (1899), p. 341.

boom collapsed soon after 1900 the differential in prices dropped.[31]

Tied houses dramatically altered the relationship between brewers and retailers. Independent and semi-tied drink sellers prevailed at mid-century: tied tenants and managers in 1900. In that year free retailers, who ordered beer from the distributor offering the best discounts, ran about one-quarter of all pubs and beerhouses. For those not holding their own freeholds, this helped offset their heavy rents and responsibility for repairs. Less autonomous, indebted to a brewer and tied for beer, retailers under the London system still possessed higher status than the mere tenant, who neither owned his lease nor had much prospect of repaying his loan and achieving independence. They, like free retailers, had decreased markedly in the 1890s, with most becoming tied tenants, now the predominant group. In brewer-owned houses, tenants signed a covenant which required them to stock their landlord's beer at prices slightly above those paid by free retailers. However, what tenants sacrificed to non-tied retailers in price they recovered in lower rents and free maintenance. Whether tied or not, all these retailers operated on a profit basis denied to the last group, managers who received salaries or sometimes commissions. Many magistrates disliked the manager who often misrepresented himself on the licence as a genuine tenant to forestall opposition. Northern and midland brewers in particular hired managers because of greater profit, flexibility and security against forfeited licences. At least half of the houses in Manchester and Liverpool and about one-fifth of those in Birmingham were employing managers in the 1890s.[32]

31 A. J. Crowe, *Inns, Taverns and Pubs of the London Borough of Sutton: Their History and Architecture* (1980), pp. 63, 76. For licensed premise values after 1870, see: Sheppard, *Brakspear's Brewery*, pp. 74–8; Wreglesworth, Richardson and Gall, *Macclesfield*, pp. 5, 12–13, 25, 27–9, 36; Elliott, *Buckingham*, pp. 192, 195, 197–8; Wilson, *Greene King*, pp. 105, 120, 138; Bruce, *Kimberley Ale*, p. 62; Fred Luckett, Ken Flint and Peter Lee, *A History of Brewing in Warwickshire* (Warwick, n.d. [1982?]), pp. 16–18; Backhouse, *Home Brewed*, p. 10; see also Avner Offer, *Property and Politics, 1870–1914 : Landownership, Law, Ideology and Urban Development in England* (Cambridge, 1981), pp. 264–5.
32 Barclay, 'Future of Public-House', p. 996; Knox, 'Tied House System', pp. 66, 68–71; *Brewing Trade Review*, 1 Apr. 1887, 1 Nov. 1895 and 1 July 1896; *Evid. Royal Com. Liq. Licensing Laws*, 1897, 34 (Cmnd. 8356), pp. 232–3, 243, 35 (Cmnd. 8523), pp. 415–20, and 1898, 36 (Cmnd. 8693), p. 4; Hawkins, 'Development of the Brewing Industry', p. 208.

The primary purpose of issuing public shares, the vertical integration of brewers with licensed property, had another entirely separate yet unforeseen consequence. With stock now widely diffused beyond the families directly engaged in brewing, brewers could enlist several hundred thousand shareholders, interested in lucrative dividends alone, against temperance legislation imperilling the industry's prosperity. The families originally owning ten of England's largest brewing companies, for example, sold virtually all their £6.3 million of preference shares. Many purchasers of this and other brewery stock were moreover extremely prominent. The *Daily News*, publicizing official shareholding lists in 1903 – 4, calculated that twenty per cent of the MPs and over twenty-five per cent of the Lords held stock, acted as trustees or themselves produced alcoholic drinks. Half Balfour's cabinet were so connected, including such well-known politicians as Walter Long, Alfred Lyttelton, St John Brodrick and Lords Lansdowne, Londonderry and Selborne. Altogether some 1,100 members of what the paper termed the 'governing classes' — MPs, peers, baronets, knights, privy councillors and lesser titled persons — had between them invested £9.5 million, surpassing the share capital of all but one brewing company.[33] Shareholders' vast financial interests immensely influenced Liberal perceptions of prohibition. Concluding that such a policy had become politically untenable, Liberals instead espoused licensing reduction after 1899, and came to see limited compensation as an unavoidable part of subsequent temperance legislation.

Tied houses gave brewers an unfavourable image in the press, which portrayed them as ruthless businessmen whose virtual monopoly of retail outlets restricted competition, provided inferior beer at high prices and reaped excessive profits. Public hostility changed the brewing industry's defensive organizations quite as decisively as its political tactics. Forced to mobilize ancillary industries, brewers helped establish the Allied Brewery Traders' Association in 1907, designed to give substance to the industry's ubiquitous propaganda — the injustice of penalizing groups which depended in some cases entirely on brewing for their existence.

Tied houses also embittered many retailers against brewers, jeopardizing the industry's political influence. By using

---

33 'Brewery Companies' Shareholders', *Brewers' Journal*, 15 Dec. 1894, 15 Jan. and 15 Feb. 1895; *Daily News*, 20 Apr. 1904.

managers and mistreating tenants, brewers angered retail leaders, whose trade associations could only recruit sympathetic *bona fide* licensed victuallers or beerhouse keepers. With managers disqualified by official policy, and dissatisfied tenants by private prejudice, numerous retail societies lost not only members but electoral power. Altered drinking patterns furthermore affected relations between brewers and their tenants. Edwardian beer drinkers, increasingly abandoning their traditional habits of on- for off-consumption, stimulated fierce rivalry, leading some brewers to adopt home delivery which deprived tied house tenants of custom and thus impaired the industry's unity.

Although brewers chiefly acquired pubs and beerhouses during the tied house boom, there were other types of retail outlets. Several new categories of licences reflected mid-Victorian class-segregated drinking patterns. As Peter Clark points out, even before 1830 Evangelical attacks on public drinking, medical criticism of insobriety, ideological emphasis on the virtues of domesticity, and incipient class consciousness had discredited pubs for upper- and middle-class patrons, who then lacked a respectable alternative for purchasing alcohol.[34] To encourage wine consumption early in the 1860s, W. E. Gladstone helped enact two bills permitting shopkeepers and wholesale spirit dealers to obtain wine or spirit licences respectively for consumption off the premises. Both did much to popularize domestic consumption, except among beer drinking urban and rural labourers, who still frequented public houses.[35] Because so many grocers took out off-licences for wine and soon

---

[34] Clark emphasizes that the respectable classes began withdrawing from pubs before temperance reformers became organized. Thus, the temperance movement accelerated rather than inaugurated this protracted process, which continued into the mid-Victorian period. Nottingham pubs, for instance, retained respectable female customers until the 1850s (Clark, *English Alehouse*, p. 307; J. J. Rowley, 'Drink and the Public House in Nottingham, 1830 – 60', *Trans. Thoroton Society Notts.*, 79 (1975), 81). Other reasons for the development of class drinking habits are discussed by Girouard (*Victorian Pubs*, p. 12) and Brian Harrison ('Pubs', H. J. Dyos and Michael Wolff (eds.), *The Victorian City: Images and Realities*, 2 vols. (1973), 1:166 – 7).

[35] Harrison, *Drink and Victorians*, pp. 248 – 51. Asa Briggs rightly notes that some local off-licences attracted working-class customers, but there is little evidence for his belief that they consumed large amounts of wine rather than beer (Asa Briggs, *Wine for Sale: Victoria Wine and the Liquor Trade, 1860 – 1984* (1985), pp. 44, 47 – 9, 63, 85).

afterwards for spirits, these traders became known as licensed grocers, of whom 2,700 existed in the mid-1870s. Spirits sold only in quart bottles, shorter licensing hours, Sunday closing and higher licence fees placed licensed grocers at a competitive disadvantage to publicans in working-class areas so off-licences came to be situated predominantly in affluent urban areas. It was in these prosperous neighbourhoods that W. & A. Gilbey, London's leading wine and spirit merchants, made a fortune. In such working-class districts as St Giles or Whitechapel, 'our agencies have been tried', lamented one Gilbey partner in 1878, 'but the trade is not sufficiently remunerative to enable them to be retained'.[36] Working-class drinkers preferred draught beers and small quantities of spirits enjoyed in their local pub's congenial atmosphere.

Acrimony between off-licence holders and other retailers derived in part from their different status under licensing laws. Intended for the respectable classes and loosely regulated, off-licences were meant to multiply steadily as demand increased, whereas magistrates cited adequate working-class drinking facilities as the reason for increasingly denying new public-house licences. Yet publicans exaggerated their legal disabilities, for in 1896 only 12,100 (9.5 per cent) of the 128,300 licences were solely for off-consumption of wine and spirits. Uneven magisterial supervision did cause genuine economic grievances. Publicans, on the one hand, acquired or leased pubs, which had risen markedly in scarcity value following stricter licensing policies; licensed grocers, on the other, unencumbered by expensive beer pumps or other pub accessories, kept overheads low on readily obtained less costly sites. Grocers further applied their typical low profit margins to the alcohol they now sold. 'The grocers' trade', explained John Betts, chairman of the Tea Dealers' and Grocers' Association, 'is conducted at a very much smaller rate of profit than many other trades, and the wines and

---

[36] *Evid. Lords Comt. Intemp.*, 1877, 11 (171), p. 155, (418), p. 298, app. b, and 1878 (338), pp. 509 – 10; *Evid. Royal Com. Liq. Licensing Laws*, 1898, 36 (Cmnd. 8693), p. 19; Harrison, 'Pubs', pp. 167 – 8; Kenna and Mooney, *People's Palaces*, p. 35. For information on W. & A. Gilbey, see Alec Waugh, *Merchants of Wine: Being a Centenary Account of the Fortunes of the House of Gilbey* (1957); Herbert Maxwell, *Half-a-Century of Successful Trade: Being a Sketch of the Rise and Development of the Business of W. & A. Gilbey, 1857 – 1907* (1907).

spirits have been sold at that rate of profit'.[37] Not surprisingly, publicans wanted full magisterial control extended to all off-licence holders, whose stagnant numbers of licences would then have acquired scarcity value largely nullifying this competitive advantage.

Politics also promoted economic rivalry. On-licence retailers detested grocers for consistently supporting Liberals, a voting pattern already pronounced in the mid-Victorian period. As J. R. Vincent notes in his study of poll books, 'over generations, Tory butchers have been locked in combat with Radical grocers'. Licensed grocers, grateful to W. E. Gladstone for introducing them into the liquor business, saw tradition, loyalty and prospective financial gain as sufficient justification for being steadfast Liberals. So did more influential Liberals like the Gilbey, Gold, Grinling and Blyth families, united by marriage as well as by business interests in W. & A. Gilbey. Two of its directors were Charles Gold, Liberal MP for Saffron Walden (1895 – 1900), and Sir James Blyth, whom Sir Henry Campbell-Bannerman ennobled in 1907.[38] During the 1895 Election when Gold suggested authorizing localities to prohibit liquor licences, brewers, publicans and beerhouse keepers conveniently opposed him for political and economic reasons. The Liberal party appreciated such devotion, usually exempting grocers from harsh provisions in its temperance proposals.[39]

Over the nineteenth century the brewing industry became large-scale and commercialized, vertically integrated as brewers gained control over beer retailing. The closer link between brewer and retailer through the tied house system altered their activities as a pressure group, hurting the brewers' public image and threatening trade unity, but broadening the base of public support, thereby weakening Liberal zeal for prohibition and

---

[37] Wilson, *Alcohol and Nation*, p. 397; *Evid. Lords Comt. Intemp.*, 1877, 11 (418), p. 287.

[38] For a list of MPs with drink connections who sat between 1874 and 1914, see David W. Gutzke, 'Rhetoric and Reality: The Political Influence of British Brewers, 1832 – 1914', *Parl. Hist.*, (forthcoming), apps. 1 – 3. John Vincent, *The Formation of the British Liberal Party, 1857 – 68* (Aylesbury, 1972), pp. 152 – 3 and *Pollbooks: How Victorians Voted* (1967), pp. 16, 61 – 3; see also Richard W. Davis, *Political Change and Continuity, 1760 – 1885: A Buckinghamshire Study* (Newton Abbot, 1972), pp. 179 – 80; T. J. Nossiter, 'Shopkeeper Radicalism in the Nineteenth Century', T. J. Nossiter, A. H. Hanson and Stein Rokkan (eds.), *Imagination and Precision in the Social Sciences: Essays in Memory of Peter Nettl* (1972), p. 415.

[39] NTDF 1895 Report, B.S., p. 22.

more generally retarding temperance reforms. Yet for many, the brewing industry's expansion was not welcomed as a profitable source of investment, but abhorred as a menace of unmitigated horror, exacerbating human misery and undermining Britain's strength and stability. Drink has hitherto been examined from an economic perspective, but to other Victorians its social and moral dimensions were far more significant.

2

Critics of the Pub

Brewers formed a pressure group to counteract temperance reformers' escalating attacks on drink as the chief cause of poverty and other social problems. There was persuasive evidence of rising beer consumption and of more conspicuous drunkenness, both exacting unacceptably high costs not merely from the individual but from society. Convinced that larger numbers of licences had increased insobriety, many drink critics advocated licensing reduction, while others, scornful of any panacea for alcohol's inherent iniquity, saw prohibition as the only practicable solution.

Brian Harrison, in his meticulous study, *Drink and the Victorians*, examines four remedies for intemperance proposed during the years 1815 – 72: free trade in beer, abstention from spirits, total abstinence (or moral suasion) and prohibition. Each succeeding solution was more extreme than its predecessor, alienating upper-class patronage as working-class supporters pursuing respectability campaigned with middle-class nonconformists against an Anglican landed elite. From an attempt to legitimize the early Victorian class structure in the anti-spirits movements, temperance reform became a means of articulating political and religious radicalism and of seeking social mobility, and finally, once moral suasion seemed ineffective, of asserting claims for group recognition through prohibition. During this period, membership in the temperance movement was chiefly urban, flourishing in northern English manufacturing towns but not in London or the agricultural south-east, and linked with nonconformity, especially in Wales where nationalism reinforced religious dissent. Clergymen or industrialists predominated as leaders, men whose nonconformist convictions gave them a Liberal outlook.[1]

---

[1] Harrison, *Drink and Victorians*, pp. 64, 90 – 1, 107, 113 – 15, 117, 133 – 4,

By the 1870s insobriety had perhaps diminished somewhat. Harrison attributes this not so much to the efforts of temperance agitators but to those he calls counter-attractionists, who concentrated on modifying the environment as a means of ameliorating poverty. New dietary habits, recreations and leisure patterns, all initially unassociated with public drinking, played instrumental roles: non-intoxicating beverages like cordials and ginger beer became popular; coffee shops and free libraries opened; popular sport attracted vast crowds and numerous participants; and railways afforded readily accessible, cheap transport, notably for seaside outings. Of these, none had so great an effect as railways, for arduous coach travel had required frequent stop-overs at inns.[2]

However much had been accomplished, counter-attractionists were neither completely successful nor solely responsible. They did cooperate in establishing parks, libraries, museums and music halls. But late nineteenth-century Liverpool, Manchester, Sheffield and Preston closed two or more such facilities on Sundays, and Stoke-on-Trent had yet to contemplate planning, much less opening, any public parks. In other respects, the

---

137 – 9, 143, 214, 348, 352 – 3 and 'The British Prohibitionists, 1853 – 72: A Biographical Analysis', *Internat. Rev. Soc. Hist.*, 15 (1970), 380 – 2, 386, 398 – 9, 405 – 8, 410; see also Lilian Lewis Shiman, *Crusade Against Drink in Victorian England* (New York, 1988), chs. 2 – 4 and 'Temperance and Class in Bradford: 1830 – 60', *Yorks. Arch. Jour.*, 58 (1986), 174, 177 – 8. The Anglican church's response to pressure from working-class temperance reformers is explored in Gerald Wayne Olsen's 'From Parish to Palace: Working-Class Influences on Anglican Temperance Movements, 1835 – 1914', *Jour. Ecclesiastical Hist.*, (forthcoming). I want to thank Professor Olsen for letting me see his article.

2 Harrison, *Drink and Victorians*, pp. 33, 51, 334 – 6 and ch. 14; John K. Walton, 'The Demand for Working-Class Seaside Holidays in Victorian England', *Econ. Hist. Rev.*, 34 (1981), 249 – 65; Lambert, *Drink and Sobriety*, p. 15. In a much broader survey, Elizabeth Malcolm, however, credits temperance reformers with helping promote sobriety in Ireland (Malcolm, *'Ireland Sober, Ireland Free': Drink and Temperance in Nineteenth-Century Ireland* (Dublin, 1986), pp. 329 – 31). For the role of coffee houses in encouraging sobriety among skilled workers, see Clark, *English Alehouse*, p. 308; J. Othick, 'The Cocoa and Chocolate Industry in the Nineteenth Century' and D. J. Richardson, 'J. Lyons & Co. Ltd.: Caterers and Food Manufacturers, 1894 to 1939', Derek J. Oddy and Derek S. Miller (eds.), *The Making of the Modern British Diet* (1976), p. 86, 162 – 3; Robert Thorne, 'The Movement for Public House Reform, 1892 – 1914', Derek J. Oddy and Derek S. Miller (eds.), *Diet and Health in Modern Britain* (1985), pp. 238 – 9.

57948

pub's traditional functions persisted, as chapter 8 indicates. Some friendly societies and trade unions rented rooms under church or chapel control, but most, rebuffed by Anglican vicars or nonconformist ministers who often monopolized public spaces, used public-house accommodation until Edwardian Labour MPs addressed this issue.[3] Other salutary changes, owing little to counter-attractionist exertions, only had similar influence decades later. Safe beer had seemed preferable to bad water. Some large cities now had uncontaminated public water; yet most tolerated defective, restricted or interrupted water supplies into the 1880s. In rural areas, in contrast, working-class prejudice against water frustrated reforms well after the turn of the century. Doctors did begin devaluing alcohol's medicinal uses, but most continued prescribing it for some diseases, and for breast-feeding mothers.[4]

By the late Victorian period insobriety had at least become less visible, reflecting decreased public drunkenness among the respectable classes. Temperance propaganda had already discredited pubs and beerhouses as drinking places for upper- and middle-class men who from the mid-century had resorted to merchants, off-licence shops, private clubs or restaurants for wine and spirits.[5] Drink shops thus drew their beer-consuming male clientele almost exclusively from working-class and, to a much smaller extent, lower-middle-class men who began weekday drinking sometimes in the morning or at lunch but

---

[3] Harrison, *Drink and Victorians*, pp. 322 – 3, 336, 339 – 40; *Evid. Lords Comt. Intemp.*, 1877, 11 (171), pp. 54 – 5, 114, 152, 308 and (271), p. 64.

[4] David W. Gutzke, ' "The Cry of the Children": The Edwardian Medical Campaign Against Maternal Drinking', *Brit. Jour. Addiction*, 79 (1984), 73, 76; Anne Hardy, 'Water and the Search for Public Health in London in the Eighteenth and Nineteenth Centuries', *Med. Hist.*, 28 (1984), 271 – 5; Amy A. Pruitt, 'Approaches to Alcoholism in Mid-Victorian England', *Clio Medica*, 9 (1974), 99; Harrison, *Drink and Victorians*, pp. 298 – 9, 307 – 8; Christopher Holdenby, *Folk of the Furrow* (n.d. [1913?]), p. 89; H. Keeble Hawson, *Sheffield: The Growth of a City, 1893 – 1926* (Sheffield, 1968), pp. 4, 7; Eglantyne Jebb, *Cambridge: A Brief Study in Social Questions* (Cambridge, 1908), p. 94; Robert Newton, *Victorian Exeter, 1837 – 1914* (Leicester, 1968), p. 255; *Evid. Lords Comt. Intemp.*, 1877, 11 (418), p. 114 and 1878, 14 (338), p. 233.

[5] Harrison, *Drink and Victorians*, pp. 45 – 6, 319 and 'Pubs', pp. 167 – 8; Girouard, *Pubs*, pp. 12 – 13; *Evid. Lords Comt. Intemp.*, 1877, 11 (271), p. 105; Robert Thorne, 'Places of Refreshment in the Nineteenth-Century City', Anthony D. King (ed.), *Building and Society: Essays on the Social Development of the Built Environment* (1980), pp. 231, 233.

usually after 4 p.m.[6] Pubs became quite crowded several hours later, and busiest between 8 and 11 p.m. On Saturday, drinking started much earlier, typically about noon, and often continued into Sunday, the two heaviest days for drinking and drunkenness, largely because employers paid wages at the end of the week. The social class of arrested drunkards confirm that skilled working-class males now consumed less alcohol. Of those charged with drunkenness in Manchester, Liverpool and Leeds in 1872, for instance, ninety-five per cent or more were semi- or fully illiterate. Magistrates who heard drunkenness cases concurred, commonly describing offenders as 'amongst the lowest class of working men'.[7]

Female drinking habits correlated more closely with social status. Middle- and upper-class women, emulating their male counterparts, purchased or ordered wine or spirits from off-licence shops, though some in the late Victorian era visited London's more fashionable pubs where separate 'ladies only' bars provided privacy.[8] Religious scruples and drink's disreputable image alike deterred lower middle-class women not from drinking gin or beer, but from doing so regularly in pubs. Even in rural areas or small towns, wives accompanied their

---

6 From the late 1870s and into the early 1890s, many lower-middle-class males participated in the Gospel temperance movement (Lilian Lewis Shiman, 'The Blue Ribbon Army: Gospel Temperance in England', *Hist. Mag. Prot. Episcopal Church*, 50 (1981), 406 – 7).

7 Harrison, *Drink and Victorians*, p. 397; B. Seebohm Rowntree, *Poverty: A Study of Town Life* (1901), pp. 314 – 26; Arthur Sherwell, *Life in West London: A Study and a Contrast* (1897), pp. 8 – 9, 130 – 6; *Evid. of the Sunday Bill Comt.*, 1867 – 8, 14 (402), pp. 4, 8, 11 – 12, 21, 33 – 4, 49, 57, 97, 143 – 4, 149 – 50, 231, 238; *Evid. Lords Comt. Intemp.*, 1877, 11 (171), pp. 16, 73, (271), pp. 47, 141, 241, 253 and (418), app. c; V. A. C. Gatrell and T. B. Hadden, 'Criminal Statistics and their Interpretation', E. A. Wrigley (ed.), *Nineteenth-Century Society: Essays in the Use of Quantitative Methods for the Study of Social Data* (1972), p. 380; John Burnett, *Plenty and Want: A Social History of Diet in England from 1815 to the Present Day* (1985), pp. 199; David Jones, *Crime, Protest, Community and Police in Nineteenth-Century Britain* (1982), pp. 102, 164; Lambert, *Drink and Sobriety*, pp. 48 – 9.

8 Rowley, 'Public House in Nottingham', p. 81; Noel Buxton and Walter Hoare, 'Temperance Reform', Bentley Gilbert (ed.), *The Heart of the Empire: Discussions of Problems of Modern City Life in England* (1901; reprint edition, Brighton, 1973), p. 177; Thorne, 'Places of Refreshment', pp. 246 – 7; Gutzke, 'Edwardian Medical Campaign', pp. 71 – 2.

husbands only on Saturday nights.[9] Respectable working-class women in industrial cities often avoided pubs, too, but below this rank drinking increased as income declined. Pub-going women, like men (whom they rarely outnumbered), chose lunch and evening hours for drinking, usually beer or stout, sometimes gin but seldom spirits. Some simply called at neighbourhood pubs to fetch beer in jugs for their husbands' lunches or dinners. Collectively the proportion of working-class pub patrons which was female probably averaged between twenty-five and thirty per cent, and increased slightly or decreased abruptly in differing residential areas.[10] Women differed from men not only in frequenting drink shops less often, but in one other crucial respect: going on drunken sprees. John Burnett's study of nineteenth-century working-class autobiographies rather surprisingly points out that many children recalled reclaiming their fathers but not one mother from binges at pubs or beerhouses. Unlike German urban labourers who drank continually but moderately throughout the day, British working-class drinkers normally drank heavily in short periods, making them more prone to drunkenness.[11]

Drunkenness among the masses was hardly a novel phenomenon, but only in the nineteenth century did it inspire successive campaigns aimed at reducing drink consumption. Middle-class businessmen, evangelicals and nonconformists,

---

9   Hugh McLeod, 'White Collar Values and the Role of Religion', Geoffrey Crossick (ed.), *The Lower Middle Class in Britain, 1870–1914* (1977), pp. 71, 75; Gutzke, 'Edwardian Medical Campaign', p. 72; Michael Winstanley, 'The Rural Publican and his Business in East Kent before 1914', *Oral Hist.*, 4 (1976), 73; Pamela Horn, *Labouring Life in the Victorian Countryside* (Dublin, 1976), p. 153; Brian Harrison and Barrie Trinder, 'Drink and Sobriety in an Early Victorian Town: Banbury, 1830–60', *Eng. Hist. Rev.*, Supplement 4 (1969), 8–9.

10 Rowntree, *Poverty*, pp. 314–26; Sherwell, *West London*, pp. 8–9, 130–6; *Return of Women and Children in Public-Houses: Information Obtained from Certain Police Forces as to the Frequenting of Public-Houses by Women and Children*, 1908, 89 (Cmnd. 3813); *Evid. Sunday Bill Comt.*, 1867–8, 14 (402), pp. 48, 50; Gutzke, 'Edwardian Medical Campaign', p. 72; Lady Bell, *At the Works: A Study of A Manufacturing Town* (1907; reprint edition, London, 1985), p. 132; *Daily Paper*, 4 Jan. 1904; Thorne, 'Public House Reform', pp. 236–7.

11 James S. Roberts, *Drink, Temperance and the Working Class in Nineteenth-Century Germany* (Boston, 1984), pp. 45–7; John Burnett (ed.), *Destiny Obscure: Autobiographies of Childhood, Education and Family from the 1820s to the 1920s* (1984), p. 237.

finding the pervasive influence of drink intolerable, founded
various temperance organizations. What were their motives?

J. B. Brown's argument that prohibitionist leaders as self-
made midland and northern businessmen equated social
mobility with teetotal or temperate habits, applies equally to
moderate temperance officials.[12] In fact, their animus against
drink was often inspired less by self-appraisal than by self-
interest. John Taylor, perennial chairman of one national
temperance society, for example, boasted of his abstemious
workers' higher productivity. Similarly, Robert Whitworth, a
Manchester cotton manufacturer, collier owner and secretary of
a Sunday closing society, thought shutting drink shops on
Sunday would reduce absenteeism and so improve efficiency on
Monday.[13] The prospect of greater profit turned this busi-
nessman into a zealous reformer, deeply envious of the pub's
privileges. He saw that working men who spent money on
drink had less to spare for manufactured goods, especially as
only drink shops opened on Sunday, just after pay day. His
colleague, Edward Whitwell, spoke for them both: 'It is . . . an
anomaly that this [drink] trade should on Sunday have the
monopoly of the opportunity of swallowing up the ready money
which ought to go to other businesses'. Exasperated at the
inability of a Gateshead submarine cable manufacturer and
Sunday closing advocate to grasp why drink retailers alone
could legally do business on Sunday, one unsympathetic
government commissioner exploded: 'A man does not want to
get a marine cable on a Sunday, whereas he does want to get
some beer'.[14]

Prominent prohibitionists like W. S. Caine disingenuously
supported communities banning drink as a ploy for enhancing
their own control over employees. He complained that the
nearby pub 'enables my men to slip in during business hours,
and to waste time there', undermining factory discipline at his

---

[12] J. B. Brown, 'The Pig or the Stye: Drink and Poverty in Late Victorian
England', *Internat. Rev. Soc. Hist.*, 18 (1973), 383. Harrison's *Drink and the
Victorians* (pp. 152, 155, 207, 221) examines the nonconformist background of
temperance leaders connected with business.

[13] *Evid. Lords Comt. Intemp.*, 1877, 11 (418), p. 221 and 1878, 14 (338), pp. 3–4;
see also *Hansard*, 3rd ser., 253 (25 June 1880), cols. 897–8; Lambert, *Drink
and Sobriety*, pp. 37–8.

[14] *Evid. Lords Comt. Intemp.*, 1878, 14 (338), pp. 6, 18; *Evid. Sunday Bill Comt.*,
1867–8, 14 (402), p. 239; see also Lambert, *Drink and Sobriety*, pp. 36–7, 204.

ironworks. Local manufacturers cited their indirect and unwilling contributions to the pub's custom as justification for wanting to close it. Chiefly concerned with obedient workers, not the provision of working-class amenities, these paternalists held views as blatantly self-serving and unsavoury as those they imputed to their opponents.[15]

Less easily dismissed, however, is the moral dimension of the anti-drink indictment. Mindful of middle- and upper-class scepticism, temperance reformers frequently exaggerated the evils of drink, but were genuinely sincere, basing their indictment on first-hand knowledge of the sheer wretchedness inflicted by alcoholism. Archdeacon Frederic Farrar, Dean of Canterbury, exemplified these attitudes: 'The catastrophe and devastation of homes, the abnormal debasement of souls, the chronic and revolting squalor, . . . and . . . human misery in its most unmitigated forms . . . have their source and origin in the . . . gin-shops and public-houses'.[16]

He saw ubiquitous public houses as the source of immense temptation. Drunken labourers who physically abused wives and children convinced Farrar that alcohol must be banned not universally but only among the lower classes where its misuse was so frightful. Labourers' wives knew only too well what to expect from inebriated spouses: ' "Our husbands return home the worse for liquor after 10 or 11 o'clock" ', and then ' "we . . . get our eyes blacked" '.[17] Even those with incomes from drink such as F. N. Charrington, son of a large London brewer, sometimes found its social consequences intolerable. A man emerging from a Charrington pub in Mile End became enraged at his wife's plea for money, and so severely struck her that she crumpled to the ground. Charrington, witnessing the incident, promptly disclaimed all financial interest in the family business, and instead undertook philanthropic work. He, Farrar, and

15 *Evid. Lords Comt. Intemp.*, 1877, 11, (171), p. 66.
16 F. W. Farrar, 'Mistakes about Abstainers', *Contem. Rev.*, 65 (1894), 552; see also A. E. Dingle and B. H. Harrison, 'Cardinal Manning as Temperance Reformer', *Hist. Jour.*, 12 (1969), 496.
17 Archdeacon Frederic W. Farrar, 'Lord Bramwell on Drink: A Reply', *Nineteenth Cent.*, 17 (1885), 877 and 'Drink: A Last Word to Lord Bramwell', *ibid.*, 18 (1885), 86; *Evid. Lords Comt. Intemp.*, 1877, 11 (418), p. 135; see also David Woods, 'Community Violence', John Benson (ed.), *The Working Class in England, 1875–1914* (1985), pp. 189–90; Burnett, *Destiny Obscure*, p. 230; Nancy Tomes, 'A "Torrent of Abuse": Crimes of Violence between Working-Class Men and Women in London, 1840–75', *Jour. Soc. Hist.*, 11 (1978), 331–4.

many others argued that drink's deleterious consequences went far beyond individual demoralization: 'The stream of horrible profits which drunkards pour into . . . the drink trade . . . everywhere leaves the slime of its overflow over devastated areas of society'.[18]

Insobriety was regarded in the 1870s and 1880s as the chief social evil because of its unquestioned role in causing poverty. For late Victorians who commonly held the individual, not society, responsible for human distress and blamed moral failings, notably intemperance, for economic inequalities, the doctrine of self-inflicted poverty naturally possessed widespread appeal. Drink 'leads to the bad home rather than the bad home . . . to the drink', declared one respected Anglican temperance official late in the 1880s. These sentiments, promulgated largely by temperance activists, influenced official thinking about social issues. Testimony from medical, legal and penal authorities convinced the 1872 parliamentary committee probing habitual intoxication that 'drunkenness is the prolific parent of . . . poverty'.[19] Indigence caused by squandering money on drink was the recurring theme of countless periodical articles.[20]

Other significant factors, such as low wages, cyclical unemployment or dismal housing, stimulated little interest and less scrutiny before the late 1880s. Although subsequent social investigators provided statistical evidence of impoverished families in 'chronic want' spending virtually nothing on drink, the conventional orthodoxy persisted, especially among prohibitionists. In 1908, Thomas Whittaker, for example, could still contend with more conviction than accuracy that 'the number who drink because they are poor is small compared with the

---

[18] Harrison, *Drink and Victorians*, p. 341; Farrar, 'Abstainers', p. 549.

[19] *National Temperance League Annual for 1889*, p. 103; Peter Mathias, 'Brewing and Politics', p. 108; Brown, 'Drink and Poverty', pp. 380–1; *Report Sel. Comt. Habitual Drunkards*, 1872, 9 (242), p. iii. The background of this committee is discussed in Roy M. MacLeod's 'The Edge of Hope: Social Policy and Chronic Alcoholism, 1870–1900', *Jour. Hist. Med. and Allied Sci.*, 22 (1967), 218–20.

[20] For typical periodical articles blaming excessive drinking for poverty, see Francis Peek, 'Intemperance: Its Prevalence, Effects, and Remedy', *Contem. Rev.*, 29 (1876), 31–2; Sir Wilfrid Lawson, 'The Drink Difficulty', *Nineteenth Cent.*, 5 (1879), 405–6.

number whose poverty is due to drinking'.[21] Like his predecessors, he felt abstinence would solve numerous social problems, ranging from drunkenness, slums, insanity, disease and premature death to crime, vice and depravity. Non-prohibitionists demanded less but expected as much from sobriety.[22]

Temperance proponents, quite confident of drink's evil effects and preoccupied with costly public agitation to justify donations, were likewise uninterested in determining what proportion of working-class budgets went towards drink. Not until the turn of the century did reliable data replace speculation as the basis for informed discussion. Charles Booth, in his massive inquiry into East London's poverty, concluded in 1902 that moderate drinkers spent roughly one-quarter of their incomes on drink.[23] Two contemporaneous studies disagreed, offering somewhat lower estimates. According to Rowntree and Sherwell, three-quarters of the British population accounted for two-thirds of all drink expenditure, and spent 6s 5d of average weekly earnings of 35s on alcohol, over one-sixth of their aggregate budgets. Seebohm Rowntree's study of York working-class families contained similar findings. Even this more conservative figure still meant that British working-class families spent one-third more on drink than their German counterparts in these same years.[24] Such averages disguise the fact that some British working-class families spent nothing whatsoever on alcohol, while others perhaps as much as one-third or half of

---

21 Thomas P. Whittaker, 'Will the Licensing Bill Promote Sobriety?', *Nineteenth Cent.*, 63 (1908), 708; see also Rev. Henry Carter, *Liquor versus Life* (n.d. [1908]), Univ. of Wisconsin, Guy Hayler Temp. Collection, p. 7; Brown, 'Drink and Poverty', p. 392; Booth, *Life and Labour*, vol. 1: *East London* (1889), pp. 147 – 8; James H. Treble, *Urban Poverty in Britain, 1830 – 1914* (1983), chs. 1 – 2, pp. 110 – 11, 117 – 19.

22 *Temperance Record*, 4 (1906), p. 578; W.S. Caine, 'The Attitude of the Advanced Temperance Party', *Contem. Rev.*, 63 (1893), 48; *Evid. Lords Comt. Intemp.*, 1877, 11 (418), p. 131; *Evid. Sunday Bill Comt.*, 1867 – 8, 14 (402), pp. 37, 92; Whittaker, 'Sobriety', pp. 707 – 8; Peter McCandless, ' "Curses of Civilization": Insanity and Drunkenness in Victorian Britain', *Brit. Jour. Addiction*, 79 (1984), 49 – 50; Lambert, *Drink and Sobriety*, pp. 27, 66.

23 Harrison, *Drink and Victorians*, pp. 371, 379 and 'The Rhetoric of Reform in Modern Britain: 1780 – 1918', *Peaceable Kingdom: Stability and Change in Modern Britain* (Oxford, 1982), pp. 408, 414; Booth, *Life and Labour, Final Volume: Notes on Social Influence and Conclusion* (1902), p. 70. Similar amounts were spent by rural labourers (Francis George Heath, *Peasant Life in the West of England* (1881), p. 375).

24 Rowntree, *Poverty*, pp. 142 – 3; Roberts, *Temperance in Germany*, pp. 109 – 10; Rowntree and Sherwell, *Temperance Problem*, pp. 8 – 11.

their earnings. Occupation and education heavily influenced the category into which a family fell. A survey of budgets in over 1,000 British working-class families in 1889 – 90, mostly with skilled jobs in the cotton, wool, steel, coal, coke and glass industries, discovered that about half avoided drink altogether, and the other half spent well under five per cent of their total income on it. Frequent purchasers of books and newspapers, they attest to the strong relationship between literacy and sobriety.[25]

Polemicists in the drink debate did embellish their arguments with statistics revealing broad consumption trends. The whole discussion was conducted in terms of per capita consumption, though Rowntree, Sherwell and others noted that this approach had its shortcomings. Beer consumption, having declined to 18.6 gallons in 1843 (about half the amount in 1800), advanced slightly in the 1850s, and thereafter rose sharply from 23.9 gallons (1859) to 34.4 gallons (1876). Wine consumption virtually stagnated until the 1860s and 1870s when it more than doubled, peaking at 0.56 gallons (1876). Spirit consumption, however, grew rapidly in the 1820s, levelled off in the 1830s at 1.23 gallons, and repeated a more moderate cycle of slump, expansion and slump between 1842 and the early 1860s before also increasing rapidly to 1.3 gallons in 1875. In Scotland and Ireland whisky outsold its rivals, but beer persisted as the customary English and Welsh alcoholic beverage, still comprising about sixty per cent of consumers' drink expenditure in 1876. Never again did these three drinks attain the levels of the mid-1870s. Consumption of beer, like wine and spirits, fell steadily, and, except for a partial recovery in the 1890s, reached 26.7 gallons in 1914.[26]

Whether this trend in per capita consumption was accompanied by a decline in insobriety provoked lively disputes. Joseph

---

25 Burnett, *Plenty and Want*, p. 199; *Sixth Annual Report Com. Labor*, 1890 – 1, U.S. Congress, House Executive Document, 51st Congress, 37; *Seventh Annual Report Com. Lab.*, 1891, *ibid.*, 52nd Congress, 2; Lynn Hollen Lees, 'Getting and Spending: The Family Budgets of English Industrial Workers in 1890', John M. Merriman (ed.), *Consciousness and Class Experience in Nineteenth-Century Europe* (1979), pp. 169 – 86.

26 Wilson, *Alcohol and Nation*, pp. 9, 331 – 5; A. R. Prest and A. A. Adams, *Consumer's Expenditure in the United Kingdom, 1900 – 19* (Cambridge, 1954), p. 85; *Evid. Lords Comt. Intemp.*, 1877, 11 (418), pp. 299 – 300; Ian Donnachie, 'Drink and Sobriety, 1750 – 1850: Some Aspects of the Scottish Experience', *Jour. Scot. Lab. Hist. Society*, 13 (1979), 8 – 9.

Rowntree and Arthur Sherwell, who co-authored *The Temperance Problem and Social Reform*, rejected the per capita figure of 31.8 gallons in 1899 because it included two large but abstinent groups, teetotalers and children, who together made up about forty per cent of the population. After recalculation, beer consumption in 1898 reached 55 gallons, and, when apportioned by gender, 73 gallons for males. Thus, the average late Victorian male alcohol drinker still consumed large amounts of beer — about 1.5 pints daily.[27]

Temperance advocates pointed to soaring arrests for drunkenness which had more than doubled between 1860 and 1876 as further proof of greater working-class drink consumption. This rate apparently meant drunkenness was expanding nearly ten times faster than the population. But an overall statistic concealed much geographic variation. Metropolitan London, where the level of arrests had grown by seventy-eight per cent, was easily overtaken by industrial cities. In Liverpool, infamous for its unruly seamen, arrests rose eighty-seven per cent, while the quip 'drink is the fastest way out of Manchester' gained substance there with an over 300 per cent increase. The latter, however, was not England's most drunken city. Based on arrests per 1,000 in 1876, the leading cities were: Liverpool (42); Newcastle on Tyne (37); South Shields (33); Durham (30); Warrington (29); Birkenhead and Gateshead (both 28); and Manchester (27). By way of comparison, Norwich and Cambridge, much smaller southern cities, had 1.6 per 1,000. Adjusted for population, English and Welsh drunkenness peaked in 1876, before dropping abruptly in the next two decades. Pessimists stressed that there were still more arrests in the 1890s than in the mid-1860s.[28]

It was not just rising arrests for drunkenness, but widespread insobriety in society generally that disturbed temperance reformers. In denying that official statistics accurately measured the amount of overindulgence, they received persuasive

---

[27] Wilson, *Alcohol and Nation*, p. 333; Rowntree and Sherwell, *Temperance Problem*, pp. 5-6. Evidence from one York working men's club strongly suggests that regular drinkers drank somewhat higher amounts. Assuming 90% of its receipts came from drink and taking into account club prices one-third less than at pubs, the typical member consumed nearly two pints daily (Rowntree, *Poverty*, p. 330).

[28] *Report and Evid. Lords Comt. Intemp.*, 1878-9, 10 (113), p. xxxiv and 1877, 11 (171), apps. b, c, e and f, 14 (338), p. 586; Rowntree and Sherwell, *Temperance Problem*, pp. 86-7.

support from the committee on Habitual Drunkards in 1872. 'There is a very large amount of drunkenness . . . which never . . . is dealt with by the authorities, but which is probably even a more fertile source of misery, poverty, and degradation than that which comes before the police courts'.[29] How police interpreted or enforced the law was partly responsible, but countless drunks escaped prosecution for other reasons — shortage of manpower, limited police authority or inadequate jail facilities.

There were three separate categories of drunkenness: drunk and disorderly, drunk and incapable and simple drunkenness. Those arrested for drunk and disorderly conduct were noisy and unruly, 'reeling and knocking people off the pavement', or guilty of defying repeated warnings to move on.[30] Whether the law was rigorously enforced depended primarily on local circumstances. Metropolitan police merely connived at keeping the peace, watching abstainers dragging their besotted friends out of brawls and taking them home. Sometimes police themselves, as in Manchester, broke up fights between inebriates without making arrests. Elsewhere constables simply overlooked flagrant offenders. In Norwich, recollected magistrate Simms Reeve, 'the police do not care particularly to see drunken [and disorderly] people, unless they come right in their way'.[31]

Officially those who could not find their way home, personally endangered themselves or lay prostrate, stupefied by drink, all qualified for arrest under the second category, drunk and incapable. A Cumberland barmaid, an unofficial but tested authority, more bluntly defined a drunk as someone who ' "falls down and cannot get up again" '. Specially excluded were trespassers, drunks asleep on private property and those still mobile but obviously quite intoxicated. 'A man or woman drunk in the street with a crowd of people round about, is a demoralising spectacle', lamented John Jackson, chief constable of Sheffield, but one which neither he nor his subordinates

---

29 *Report Sel. Comt. Habitual Drunkards*, 1872, 9 (242), p. iii.
30 *Evid. Lords Comt. Intemp.*, 1877, 11 (171), pp. 9, 198 and (271), pp. 108, 250; *Evid. Sel. Comt. Habitual Drunkards*, 1872, 9 (242), pp. 91, 96, 121; *Evid. Sunday Bill Comt.*, 1867 – 8, 14 (402), p. 149.
31 Booth, *Influences and Conclusion*, pp. 110 – 11; *Evid. Lords Comt. Intemp.*, 1877, 11 (271), p. 84 and 1878, 14 (338), pp. 6, 10; Wilbur R. Miller, *Cops and Bobbies: Police Authority in New York and London, 1830 – 1870* (Chicago, 1977), pp. 124, 126.

could prevent. Yet, police lacked the will as much as the power to make arrests. ' "We do not take them in if we can avoid it" ', one London policeman confessed, expressing the implicit universal rule. George Turner, police superintendent of poverty-stricken Stepney, explained official attitudes by identifying three intoxicated stages: influenced (walking unaffected); staggering (often known as tipsy); and helplessly drunk (immobile and befuddled).[32] Police most certainly apprehended drunks reaching phase two, those unsteady afoot, but rarely in large numbers. To have arrested more was clearly foolhardy, claimed the chief constable of Leeds in the 1870s: 'We should not have cells enough to hold them all'. Even the paralytic escaped if aided by friends or indulgent policemen. Drunks thus often enjoyed immunity from arrest, though bystanders sometimes asked who benefitted. Robert Whitworth, having helped a drunk lying on a Manchester pavement onto his shaky feet, asked a nearby policeman to place him in protective custody. The policeman refused. He 'got up and staggered off', but Whitworth knew then and remembered later that the man 'was not fit to go alone'.[33]

Two other factors, both related to police perceptions, further reduced the number of drunks apprehended. Conflicting responsibilities often put the policeman in a quandary. Unwilling to leave his beat while accompanying inebriates to jail, he arrested just the worst cases. Such action was tacitly endorsed by his superiors partly because they thought property and lives deserved precedence, and partly because they regarded drunkenness as but a nominal offence.[34] Many of those who were arrested, moreover, never figured in official returns. There existed in Leeds, Liverpool, Manchester and probably elsewhere a separate, unreported category: drunks arrested but later released uncharged at the jail once named in a 'refused

---

32 *Evid. Lords Comt. Intemp.*, 1877, 11 (171), pp. 310 – 11, (271), pp. 250, 252 – 3 and (418), p. 134; *Evid. Sel. Comt. Habitual Drunkards*, 1872, 9 (242), pp. 97, 103, 105, 134; *Evid. Sunday Bill Comt.*, 1867 – 8, 14 (402), pp. 49, 70; George W. E. Russell, *Sir Wilfrid Lawson: A Memoir* (1909), p. 124.

33 *Evid. Lords Comt. Intemp.*, 1878, 14 (338), pp. 6, 10; *Evid. Sel. Comt. Habitual Drunkards*, 1872, 9 (242), p. 132; *Evid. Sunday Bill Comt.*, 1867 – 8, 14 (402), p. 10; Booth, *Influences and Conclusion*, pp. 105 – 6; Miller, *Cops and Bobbies*, pp. 68 – 9.

34 *Evid. Lords Comt. Intemp.*, 1877, 11 (171), p. 22; *Evid. Sunday Bill Comt.*, 1867 – 8, 14 (402), pp. 7 – 8, 16.

charges book'. Liverpool's chief constable, though unauthorized by the watch committee, used this system, freeing individuals who had sobered up, appeared respectable or whose friends or a spouse escorted them home. Had these drunks not been so reprieved, apprehensions in Manchester would have risen by forty per cent in the 1860s and in Liverpool by thirteen per cent in the 1860s and early 1870s.[35]

Of the three types of drink-related offences, simple drunkenness was the easiest to detect but hardest to prosecute because the law directed that offenders be summonsed, not arrested. In cities like Newcastle with vast numbers of visitors, police had no straightforward way of discovering the names and addresses of drunks. Officers also disliked being inquisitive, lest they themselves provoke more serious trouble. 'If you stop a man . . . and ask him where he lives', stated Sheffield's chief constable, 'you will very soon . . . turn the quiet drunkard into the disorderly drunkard'.[36] One alternative, having police shadow roaming drunks about the city, would produce addresses, but at the expense of neglected beats. Birmingham's constabulary had experimented with a modified policy in which detectives discharged these functions, but lengthy surveillance proved prohibitively expensive. It also proved extremely unpopular. Newspaper denunciations of alien police tactics, together with public hostility, led the town council to discontinue covert activities and dismiss pending charges. For these reasons, large urban police forces merely ignored semi-intoxicated but inoffensive drunks going home after a drinking bout.[37] The greater intimacy between authority and populace in small county towns facilitated police control of drunks, whom constables assisted home before posting a summons.[38]

[35]   *Evid. Lords Comt. Intemp.*, 1877, 11 (171), pp. 5, 57, 164 and apps. b and e; *Evid. Sel. Comt. Habitual Drunkards*, 1872, 9 (242), pp. 120, 133; *Evid. Sunday Bill Comt.*, 1867 – 8, 14 (402), p. 45, and app. 2.

[36]   *Evid. Lords Comt. Intemp.*, 1877, 11 (171), pp. 308 – 9 and (271), pp. 12 – 13; *Evid. Sunday Bill Comt.*, 1867 – 8, 14 (402), p. 277.

[37]   *Report and Evid. Lords Comt. Intemp.*, 1877, 11 (171), pp. 195 – 8, 213 – 14 and 1878 – 9, 10 (113), p. xxxiii; *Evid. Sel. Comt. Habitual Drunkards*, 1872, 9 (242), pp. 101, 132; *Evid. Sunday Bill Comt.*, 1867 – 8, 14 (402), pp. 7 – 8; Barbara Weinberger, 'The Police and the Public in Mid-Nineteenth-Century Warwickshire', Victor Bailey (ed.), *Policing and Punishment in Nineteenth Century Britain* (1981), pp. 85 – 6; see also Miller, *Cops and Bobbies*, pp. 33 – 4. In 1871 Bruce's proposed creation of public house inspectors caused vehement hostility (Harrison, *Drink and Victorians*, pp. 266 – 7).

[38]   *Evid. Lords Comt. Intemp.*, 1877, 11 (271), pp. 279, 288.

The shortage of manpower decreased arrests in all three categories. In particular, established practices collapsed when heavy drinkers flooded large cities, especially in seaports like Liverpool where the population fluctuated dramatically. Once numerous sailors landed, a local JP related, 'the strain upon the police of taking drunken people to the bridewells is so great, that a great number . . . do not then fall into the hands of the police, who would unquestionably do so when they were less busy'. Such problems in Liverpool, which had proportionately more policemen than most other industrial cities, reveal the degree to which drunks evaded prosecution.[39] In some cities, furthermore, constables were overburdened with huge beats. Sharply contrasting experiences of two similar industrial cities partly clarifies otherwise baffling statistics. In the 1870s, each Manchester policeman patrolled 5.3 acres, and apprehended one out of thirty-seven persons for drunkenness, whereas each Birmingham constable covered 17.5 acres and arrested only one out of 131 persons. Thus, small police forces dispersed over large areas apprehended fewer drunks than larger, more concentrated ones, but probably encountered just as much insobriety.[40]

No one in the 1870s knew the exact discrepancy between registered and actual drunkenness at the local, much less the national, level. Estimates of those who eluded prosecution ranged between thirty-four and ninety-eight per cent.[41] Support for the higher one came from Joseph Chamberlain, Birmingham's temperance-minded Liberal MP, who publicized a crude but disquieting study which dramatized pervasive working-class insobriety. At 8 p.m. on Saturday, 3 March 1877, prohibitionist volunteers began a vigil outside thirty-five of Birmingham's busiest pubs, where during the next three hours they counted over 14,000 departing customers, including some 800 legally categorized as drunk. Yet the city's energetic constabulary arrested only twenty-nine as drunk and disorderly in the whole twenty-four hours. Chamberlain did concede that correspondingly fewer drinkers visited Birmingham's other

---

[39] *Ibid.*, (171), pp. 22, 127 – 8; see also Carolyn Steedman, *Policing the Victorian Community: The Formation of English Provincial Police Forces, 1856 – 80* (1984), pp. 50, 154.

[40] *Ibid.*, 127; *Report Lords Comt. Intemp.*, 1878 – 9, 10 (113), p. xxxiii; see also Miller, *Cops and Bobbies*, pp. 124 – 5.

[41] *Evid. Lords Comt. Intemp.*, 1877, 11 (418), p. 134 and (271), p. 245; *Evid. Sel. Comt. Habitual Drunkards*, 1872, 9 (242), p. 97.

licensed shops. His revised figures were nevertheless startling: drinkers numbered about 100,000 (over one-quarter of the city's population), 5,000 of them guilty of simple drunkenness. This graphic survey vividly illustrated the late Victorian legal system's failings — understaffed urban police forces, forbearance towards mere drunks and ineffectually controlled streets overflowing with heavily intoxicated, lurching or lingering drunks, some falling upon private property for unmolested sleep.[42]

Temperance and religious leaders, magistrates, police constables and doctors came to see fewer licences as the best remedy for seemingly rampant insobriety. In multiplying drink shops, the State, they believed had unwittingly multiplied lower-class temptations. This attitude derived from convictions of inferior working-class morality and of drinkers' impaired powers of resistance. One Brighton magistrate, betraying his own social prejudice, pointed to education in explaining why 'persons in our class are able to restrain themselves . . . in the presence of liquor; whereas those [working-class] people cannot'. Diminished responsibility as the result of alcohol made labourers with deficient characters particularly liable to drunkenness. 'Men are inundated by these very conspicuous temptations; a weak-minded man going out of a public-house and turning right or left, finding another public-house staring him in the face, is unable to withstand the renewed temptation', argued Samuel Nicholls, chief constable of Newcastle. Numerous doctors concurred. Almost half the medical officials of lunatic asylums who responded to a temperance questionnaire in the 1870s, for instance, attributed increased insanity cases to more liquor licences.[43]

Certainly the number of licences had burgeoned in the previous four decades: 19,200 more publican spirit licences and 47,600 new beerhouse licences had been granted, more than

---

42 *Evid. Sel. Comt. Habitual Drunkards*, 1872, 9 (242), p. 91; *Evid. Lords Comt. Intemp.*, 1877, 11 (171), pp. 205 – 6, 241 – 3; see also Newton, *Victorian Exeter*, p. 270.

43 *Evid. Sunday Bill Comt.*, 1867 – 8, 14 (402), p. 83; *Evid. Lords Comt. Intemp.*, 1877, (271), p. 16 and (418), p. 56 and app. c; see also *ibid.*, (271), pp. 35, 175, 231, and (418), pp. 3, 38, 76, 89 and (171), pp. 46, 144 – 5; *Hansard*, 3rd ser., 196 (12 May 1869), cols. 651, 672 and 253 (25 June 1880), col. 900; Steedman, *Police Forces*, p. 152. Medical assumptions about the relationship between alcoholism and insanity are explored in Pruitt, 'Alcoholism in Mid-Victorian England', pp. 96 – 7.

doubling the total number of such licences. The distribution of on-licences, thickest in urban areas, appeared as provocative as sheer numbers. Of the northern and midland industrial cities with 50,000 minimum inhabitants in 1876, two possessed one on-licence per 100 – 150 persons, seven one per 150 – 199, and an equal number one per 200 – 249. Metropolitan London, in contrast, ranked lowest with a ratio of one per 379, but even here on-licences saturated specific localities, like the Broadway/ Hammersmith intersection in affluent Kennsington where forty-one drink shops stood within 500 yards. Working-class districts especially abounded in them; the notorious area including Soho, St James, had 798 per square mile.[44] Pubs and beerhouses had proliferated in virtually every late-Victorian city. One half mile in Birmingham's labouring quarter contained over 100 on-licences. Where sailors collected wages in Liverpool, forty-six liquor sellers eagerly awaited business within a 200 yard radius. Nor was Wales any better. Arrayed along Swansea's High Street were thirty licensed houses in a 900 yard span, and on the Strand seventeen more in 700 yards.[45]

Advocates also saw licensing reduction as a way of eliminating objectionable retail practices which aggravated insobriety. Licence holders were criticized for illegally countenancing music, singing, dancing, popular games (cards, dominoes and dice) and serving drunks alcohol, less because of lucrative profits than because of the 'great struggle to get a living'. Quite simply, superfluous licences had heightened commercial rivalry, compelling wrongdoing from hard-pressed retailers.[46]

Beerhouses, created in 1830 and permitted cheaper premises than pubs to stimulate competition, were often denigrated as the worst offenders. They expanded most rapidly in northern industrial cities. In England and Wales altogether there were one-and-a-half times as many pubs as beerhouses, but

---

[44] *Evid. Lords Comt. Intemp.*, 1877, 11, (171), app. c and p. 335 and (418), pp. 179 – 80; Wilson, *Alcohol and Nation*, pp. 335, 395 – 6; Rowntree and Sherwell, *Temperance Problem*, p. 493.

[45] *Evid. Royal Com. Liq. Licensing Laws*, 1898, 36 (Cmnd. 8693), p. 448; *Evid. Lords Comt. Intemp.*, 1877, 11 (418), p. 22; J. Chamberlain, 'Municipal Public-Houses', *Fort. Rev.*, 27 (1877), 154.

[46] *Evid. Lords Comt. Intemp.*, 1877, 11 (171), pp. 237 – 8, 314 and (271), pp. 175, 210, 376; James B. Brown, 'The Temperance Career of Joseph Chamberlain, 1870 – 7: A Study in Political Frustration', *Albion*, 4 (1972), 37.

beerhouses easily outnumbered pubs in Manchester, Birmingham, Salford, Sheffield and Barrow-in-Furness, and fell just short of a majority in Newcastle.[47]

But abolishing beerhouses, however appropriate in these instances, would have left unchanged pubs' pernicious influence elsewhere, so reformers assailed evils common to them both. By general consent, Liverpool, England's most drunken city, where pubs accounted for all but fifteen per cent of the on-licences, provided ample material for caustic debate. Critics regarded its high turnover of retailers, nearly one-third in some years, as conclusive evidence of excessive drink establishments. With the advent of tied houses, detractors accused brewers of employing tenants who survived only by misconduct. Faced with prosecution and the possible loss of their licence, brewers acted swiftly, firing the hapless tenant and hiring a replacement. Law-abiding retailers, on the other hand, went bankrupt or, if salaried employees, were discharged. The tied house system and its treatment of servants had other adverse consequences, critics maintained. It not only discouraged high quality prospective tenants from applying, but, in separating legal obligations from ownership, nullified threats of a licence being revoked, formerly a powerful stimulus to good conduct.[48]

Liberal licensing bills early in the 1870s were less important for embodying the temperance critique of poverty than for clarifying subsequent trade/temperance conflicts. Indeed, three contentious subjects, monopoly value, compensation and time limit, then introduced into the licensing debate recurred in most proposals until 1914. In markets like the late-Victorian licensing system, analogous to present-day radio stations, premises doing legitimate, state-regulated business, whether pubs licensed to sell alcohol or radio stations licensed to broadcast, acquired a value greater than otherwise warranted. One Rugeley public house, for example, sold for £3,000 in the 1870s, considerably more than the £600 it had fetched unlicensed three years

---

[47] *Evid. Lords Comt. Intemp.*, 1877, 11 (171), apps. b, e, g, i and (271), apps. b, c, k, n; Wilson, *Alcohol and Nation*, p. 396; W. L. Clay, *The Prison Chaplain: A Memoir of the Reverend John Clay* (1861), p. 510; Shiman, *Crusade Against Drink*, p. 101.

[48] *Evid. Lords Comt. Intemp.*, 1877, 11 (171), pp. 58 – 9, 77 – 9, 305 and (271), p. 293; see also *Evid. Sel. Comt. Public Houses*, 1852 – 3, 37 (855), pp. 116 – 17.

earlier.[49] This disparity, called monopoly value, had been created by the state's restrictive policies. Withdrawing licences as a matter of policy rather than on grounds of misconduct would raise the issue of compensation: should the government reimburse owners of abolished licences, and if so, on what basis? Whether every individual or just those given short notices deserved compensation became the focus of political dispute. Restricted compensation, the latter approach, was known by the term 'time limit'. These three topics shaped the licensing controversy for the following half century.

In 1871 Henry Bruce, Gladstone's home secretary, sponsored a Licensing bill designed to change radically licensing, supervision methods and opening hours. His proposal linking licences with population, substituting ratios of one per 1,000 in towns and one per 600 elsewhere for the overall average of one per 201, conceivably meant suppressing well over half the existing on-licences. Compensation took the form of guaranteeing renewal of licences for ten years, but they would be treated thereafter as new licences, with likely higher licence duties levied to give the state much of the monopoly value. Ratepayers then wanting fewer licences could approach magistrates about reducing numbers until reaching the minimum ratios. Bruce also envisaged more rigorous legal surveillance by creating separate public-house inspectors with extensive powers. Finally, he sought much shorter opening hours, eliminating discretionary pub hours outside London, imposing at least five closed hours after midnight and somewhat reducing Sunday hours. Like later licensing measures, Bruce's bill antagonized both sellers and detractors of alcohol. Disgruntled prohibitionists had not achieved their goal, while the trade denounced him for attempting to usurp property. Bruce, denied popular support, ultimately dropped his bill, but in 1872 obtained parliamentary approval for several of its clauses — magistrates' undisputed authority over licensing, fewer opening hours and stricter penalties, though only by abandoning the contentious question of licensing reduction.[50]

In 1879 the House of Lords Committee on Intemperance, which had sat for thirteen months interviewing 100 witnesses and amassing almost 1,700 pages of detailed testimony,

[49] *Evid. Lords Comt. Intemp.*, 1877, 11 (418), p. 10.
[50] Harrison, *Drink and Victorians*, pp. 262–78; Wilson, *Alcohol and Nation*, pp. 106–7.

repudiated the anti-drink critique that had partly inspired Bruce's abortive bill. The Lords' Report, while admitting that certain areas had increased drunkenness, dismissed claims that insobriety was either pervasive or related to licence density. In drawing these conclusions, it argued that several factors discredited total statistics of arrests as an index of intemperance: unequal sizes of police forces, the limits on legal authority and the general neglect to issue summons. Two important changes, better-run licensed houses and a thirteen per cent decline in the number of beerhouses since 1860, probably had a salutary impact on drinking habits. Accordingly, the Report ascribed larger per capita beer consumption to increased wages and more drinking by moderate, not by immoderate, individuals.[51]

Three authorities undermined the thesis of growing insobriety. First came Professor Leone Levi, well-known statistical and liquor specialist. He emphasized that drunkenness, far from being distributed randomly, predominated in densely populated urban areas in six counties in northern England with manufacturing, industrial or mining economies. Sharply rising committals for drunkenness, he contended, reflected greater abuse of alcohol, not universally but by one small group, as well as more strictly enforced laws by policemen, responding to growing public intolerance of insobriety.[52]

John Dendy and J. H. Poynting supplied further proof of marked regional variations. Using ratios for per capita drunkenness, they divided English and Welsh towns and counties with a line from Grimsby, Lincolnshire to where the Severn and Wye merged in Gloucestershire. Northern towns and counties had over three times as many apprehensions as their southern counterparts. Five counties (Lancashire, Durham, Cheshire, Yorkshire and Cumberland) contained sixteen of the twenty major cities with the highest per capita arrests, seaports being the worst, followed by coal mining, manufacturing and finally market towns.[53] However methodologically dubious these

---

51 *Report Lords Comt. Intemp.*, 1878–9, 10 (113), pp. xxxi, xxxiii–iv, xxxviii.
52 Weinberger, 'Warwickshire', p. 86; *Evid. Lords Comt. Intemp.*, 1877, 11 (418), pp. 203–5; S. J. Davies, 'Classes and Police in Manchester, 1829–80', Alan J. Kidd and K. W. Roberts (eds.)., *City, Class and Culture: Studies of Social Policy and Cultural Production in Victorian Manchester* (Manchester, 1985), p. 36; Steedman, *Police Forces*, p. 155.
53 *Report and Evid. of the Lords Comt. on Intemp.*, 1878, 14 (338), app. r and 1877, 11 (418), app. g; see also Rowntree and Sherwell, *Temperance Problem*, p. 88.

findings seem retrospectively, they convinced many contemporaries and a reputable committee conducting the most exhaustive inquiry into intemperance until the late 1890s.[54]

Citing these three men's testimony, the Report likewise relied on per capita figures in rejecting the licensing reductionists' central thesis that more licences had caused more insobriety. Since 1857 apprehensions for drunkenness had increased 115 per cent, but meanwhile the proportion of licences had actually fallen by eight per cent. Higher ratios of licences per population occurred, moreover, not in less sober northern but in less drunken southern towns and counties.[55] The Report duly refuted the related point, linking licence transfers with excessive drink shops. As magistrates regained authority and greater power over licensing in the years 1869 – 72, three developments had ensued: approval of new licences virtually ceased; many beerhouses closed, unable to meet higher rating qualifications or to comply with harsher laws; and licence prices correspondingly rose. In response, brewers had purchased dearer houses in which they installed a tenant who fully knew offences would jeopardize the licence and his tenure. Frequent transfers thus represented tenants penalized for risking sizable investments. The Report itself credited fear of dismissal with promoting better licensed-house practices.[56]

This compelling testimony nevertheless did not overcome the committee's natural misgivings about continuing high intemperance, which many communities regarded as an immense evil that debased citizens and caused poverty, crime, rising female drunkenness and possible economic malaise. Its Report consequently endorsed a radical scheme of licensing reduction, initially limited in scope but potentially far-reaching in impact, in which the government would allow localities to emulate the Swedish Gothenburg system. Like other municipal

---

54 For scholarly criticism of apprehensions as a measure of insobriety, see Gatrell and Hadden, 'Criminal Statistics', pp. 358 – 60; Harrison, *Drink and Victorians*, pp. 278, 315 – 16; J. J. Tobias, *Urban Crime in Victorian England* (New York, 1972), pp. 10, 19 – 21, 264 – 6.

55 *Report and Evid. Lords Comt. Intemp.*, 1878 – 9, 10 (113), pp. xxxv – viii, and 1877, 11 (418), p. 206. Faster growing cities in the north, together with magistrates' restraint on new licences, produced a situation in which the population 'outgrows its numbers of public-houses', Dendy and Poynting speculated (*ibid.*, 1878, 14 (338), app. r, p. 583).

56 *Report and Evid. Lords Comt. Intemp.*, 1878 – 9, 10 (113), pp. xxxi – ii; see also *ibid.*, 1877, 11 (271), p. 19, (171), pp. 312 – 14 and (418), p. 55.

programmes, some agency under local auspices monopolized liquor sales, run on a non-profit basis with fewer retail outlets. One such ambitious approach already espoused by Joseph Chamberlain for Birmingham projected the abolition of over half the city's licences within one year.[57] By urging an unorthodox remedy to a long-established social problem of indeterminate origin, the committee underlined how seriously it viewed intemperance.

Temperance reformers demanded licensing reduction because they hated the brewing industry's supposedly vast political power mobilized through pubs and beerhouses as ardently as drink's role as a social evil. Influenced by nonconformists' convictions and persecuted outlook, temperance leaders discerned a conspiracy in which Britain's Anglican landed governing elite sanctioned drink shops as a means of ensuring that government revenue came from indirect taxes on working-class drinkers, not from direct property levies. The resulting enrichment of aristocrats and brewers at the expense of permanently impoverished labourers, exacerbated class tensions and threatened social revolution, temperance advocates contended. With this argument they won over many late Victorians otherwise uninterested in anti-drink rhetoric. According to this gloomy diagnosis, brewers had formed a huge state monopoly of formidable political power and commensurate wealth, which had thoroughly corrupted British republican institutions.[58] Joseph Chamberlain, expounding local municipalization of licences in the *Fortnightly Review*, condemned the brewing industry for 'the serious degradation of public life and the lowered tone of political morality'. Drink opponents recounted with much relish an episode in the 1870s when two licensed victuallers were ejected from the House of Commons after incautiously sitting on the bench reserved for MPs. Overhearing their conversation with attendants, Jacob Bright, MP, his voice filled with sarcasm, protested their eviction: 'Why should they not come in? They knew it was their own House'.[59] Later in the

---

[57] *Report Lords Comt. Intemp.*, 1878–9, 10 (113), pp. xxxviii, xlv; Brown, 'Temperance Career of Chamberlain', p. 38.

[58] A. E. Dingle, *The Campaign for Prohibition in Victorian England: The United Kingdom Alliance, 1872–95* (New Brunswick, New Jersey, 1980), pp. 19–20; Brown, 'Drink and Poverty', p. 385; Dingle and Harrison, 'Cardinal Manning', pp. 492, 504–6, 508; Harrison, *Drink and Victorians*, p. 222.

[59] Chamberlain, 'Public-Houses', p. 157; Russell, *Lawson*, p. 104.

century Rowntree and Sherwell elaborated on this theme, devoting twenty-six pages of their book to assailing the trade as a 'social and political menace' which so successfully manipulated national and local government that they became merely nominally democratic. By then frequent analogies were drawn with European and American political corruption. In 1901 the Reverend T. C. Fry virulently castigated brewers and retailers, characterizing them as 'wealthier and stronger than any continental Mafia'. Similarly, prohibitionist Thomas Whittaker reviled the trade for becoming 'a kind of British Tammany, a widespread source of political corruption, a distinct danger to the state, and a menace to the purity of our . . . public life'.[60]

Such powerful but unscrupulous businessmen who intimidated cabinet ministers and MPs as ruthlessly as they manipulated magistrates and town councils, meant that meaningful reform, though vitally necessary, was exceedingly unlikely. 'The influence of the brewers', one temperance official plaintively remarked in 1877, 'is so large that I almost despair of seeing any measure passed through the Legislature in opposition to it'. Vital to surmounting this insidious influence was the reduction of its source of power, thousands of licensed houses.[61]

Prohibitionists had meanwhile reformulated the theory of self-induced poverty to account for the so-called 'Great Depression'. They viewed rising drink consumption as the chief cause of Britain's faltering economy. Drink-sodden workers prevented economic growth in countless ways: in lowering productivity and profits, they raised export prices and competitive barriers; in dissipating wages on alcohol, they bought fewer goods; in becoming paupers, lunatics or criminals (all demanding some form of state care), they increased local taxes.[62]

Unreliable wage earners, in fact, prompted much strident protest late in the 1870s. Urban labourers going to work

---

[60] Rowntree and Sherwell, *Temperance Reform*, pp. 91–117; Rev. T. C. Fry, 'Temperance Reform: What Blocks the Way?', *Econ. Rev.*, 11 (1901), 153; *Hansard*, 4th ser., 89 (19 Feb. 1901), col. 558; see also Russell, *Lawson*, p. 229.

[61] *Evid. of the Lords Comt. on Intemp.*, 1877, 11 (418), pp. 106, 110, 231.

[62] Brown, 'Drink and Poverty', pp. 381–3, 388–9; A. E. Dingle, 'The Rise and Fall of Temperance Economics', *Monash Papers in Econ. Hist.*, No. 3, (1977), 5–7.

detoured at the pub for their morning 'nip', which detained them several hours or even the entire day. Such behaviour was hardly work time. One typical Lancashire cotton manufacturer grumbled at witnessing '40 or 50 looms stopped on a Monday morning through the workmen being off drinking'.[63] Those attacking absenteeism blamed licensing hours quite as much as drink habits. With London pubs and beerhouses open daily from 5 a.m. to 12:30 a.m. and provincial establishments (except rural areas) from 6 a.m. to 11 p.m., working-class drinkers had vast opportunity for over-indulgence. Shorter Saturday shifts had simply promoted insobriety. 'A man has time now on Saturday to get drunk twice before he goes to bed', complained James Wetherell, chief constable of Leeds. Somewhat shorter Sunday hours, two near lunch and four or five after dinner, inconvenienced only publicans and beersellers. Once Saturday's labour ended, uninterrupted drinking lasted allegedly through much or all of Monday.[64]

Yet in this instance, detractors mistook moral failings for Saint Monday, the traditional but then declining working-class custom of rejecting surplus money earned under regimented capitalism for subsistence incomes with leisure time. In South Yorkshire collieries, Stoke potteries or Sheffield iron works, all areas where full Saturday shifts, higher-paid piece rates or unmechanized labour still thwarted industrial discipline, workers continued to extend their weekends, often but not always by drinking. Disgruntled employers naturally criticized Saint Mondayism, but so did indignant Sunday closers like the Rector of Christchurch who insisted that 'Saint Monday is the legacy of drunken Sunday'. Whatever motivated celebrating

---

63   *Evid. Lords Comt. Intemp.*, 1877, 11 (418), p. 68, (271), pp. 46, 59, 171, 316 and (171), pp. 56, 145, 233; *Evid. Sel. Comt. Habitual Drunkards*, 1872, 9 (242), p. 136.
64   *Evid. Sel. Comt. Habitual Drunkards*, 1872, 9 (242), p. 137; *Evid. Lords Comt. Intemp.*, 1878, 14 (338), p. 5, 1877, 11 (271), p. 29 and (418), p. 185; Harrison, *Drink and Victorians*, p. 329. Scottish licensed houses had been closed on Sunday since 1853, and similar restrictions applied later to those in Wales (1881). Irish drink shops, except in five cities, were closed temporarily on Sunday between 1878 and 1905 and permanently from 1906 (Malcolm, *Drink and Temperance in Ireland*, pp. 238 – 9, 245, 257, 273; Wilson, *Alcohol and Nation*, pp. 170 – 2).

Monday as a holiday, entrepreneurs rightly suspected it reduced output: one survey showed one-fifth fewer colliery and iron workers on Monday produced almost one-quarter less tons.[65]

While temperance societies saw restrictive legislation as a partial solution for poverty, economic stagnation and the brewing industry's pernicious power, their dissimilar objectives and priorities led to divergent programmes. The National Temperance League (NTL), established in 1855 and dedicated to total abstinence, redeemed drunkards by moral suasion. League supporters did seek bills curbing the number of licences, licensing hours and methods of selling alcohol, but felt cooperating with other sympathetic groups outside politics more appropriate for securing long-term gains.[66]

While politically less important, the Church of England Temperance Society (CETS), was numerically much larger, with 150,000 – 200,000 members in the 1890s. Founded in 1861 as an expression of the established church's concern, it became the biggest U.K. temperance organization by admitting both abstainers and non-abstainers. Viewing intemperance less in moral than in social terms, the CETS much preferred moderate drinking; it still recognized teetotalism could be useful as an example for drunks to emulate. Anglicanism and a broader scope distinguished the CETS from rival national bodies as much as its allies and specific policies. Of all temperance organizations, the CETS alone worked closely with Conservatives, and lobbied for locally elected boards with control over licensing as well as sweeping reduction of licensed premises, based largely on Bruce's abortive bill. It was on his proposed method of compensating dispossessed brewers and retailers that the CETS most steadfastly disagreed with him, and with

---

[65] Douglas A. Reid, 'The Decline of Saint Monday, 1766 – 1876', *Past and Present*, 71 (1976), 78, 86, 91 – 2; *Evid. Lords Comt. Intemp.*, 1878, 14 (338), pp. 3 – 5, 24, 1877, 11 (171), pp. 112 – 13 and (271), p. 59; *Evid. Sunday Bill Comt.*, 1867 – 8, 14 (402), pp. 26, 148 – 9, 219, 267; see also Booth, *Influences and Conclusion*, pp. 73, 118; Harrison, *Drink and Victorians*, p. 40. W. R. Lambert ('Drink and Work-Discipline in Industrial South Wales, c.1800 – 70', *Welsh Hist. Rev.*, 7 (1975), 289 – 306) discusses to what extent the inculcation of capitalist work norms changed Welsh drinking habits.

[66] *Evid. Lords Comt. Intemp.*, 1877, 11 (418), pp. 221, 226 – 9, 231.

the third prominent temperance organization, the United
Kingdom Alliance.[67]

Averse to futile government regulation of drink, impatient
with the NTL's moral suasionist approach, determined to
politicize the temperance question, and heartened by Maine
prohibitionist legislation, temperance enthusiasts formed the
United Kingdom Alliance (UKA) in 1853. Borrowing ideas
suggested by a London brewer, the UKA soon adopted local
veto, a strategy in which a two-thirds majority of local
ratepayers could by referendum prohibit drink shops after a
grace period of three years. Liberals initially disliked its political
implications. Its extension of government intervention seemingly conflicted with their traditional concerns for moral
progress and free trade. To allay such fears, the UKA argued
that in abolishing the monopolistic licensing system, in curtail-
ing police requirements and in encouraging local self-govern-
ment, prohibition would actually reduce state interference. It
was not prohibitionist reasoning, however, but economic
changes in the brewing industry late in the 1880s that converted
Liberals to greater state regulation, unacceptable in other
spheres. Their mistrust of monopolies had intensified when
breweries acquired numerous tied houses and substituted
corporate for proprietary management. In this altered context,
Liberals felt popular control was essential.[68]

Prohibition became Liberal policy as part of the famed 1891
Newcastle programme, but never won parliamentary approval.
Introduced in 1893 to the Commons, a Local Veto bill only
received its first reading. Equally unpopular was the veto's
successor, which gave ratepayers three alternatives; withdraw
some licences, prohibit them entirely or oppose any change.
Liberals proposed it in 1895, but resigned from office before the

---

67 David M. Fahey, 'Drink and the Meaning of Reform in Late Victorian and
Edwardian England', *Cithara*, 13 (1974), 52–3; *Evid. Lords Comt. Intemp.*,
1877, 11 (418), pp. 82–3, 89, 92, 95–6, 98; Shiman, *Crusade Against Drink*,
pp. 99–109; see also Gerald Wayne Olsen, 'The Church of England
Temperance Magazine', *Vic. Periodicals Newsletter*, 11 (1978), 38–49. Factors
which restricted CETS influence with politicians and militant temperance
reformers are discussed in John R. Greenway's 'Bishops, Brewers and the
Liquor Question in England, 1890–1914', *Hist. Mag. Prot. Episcopal Church*,
53 (1984), 63–5, and in Gerald Wayne Olsen, 'Anglican Temperance
Movements in England, 1859–73: An Example of Practical Ecumenism',
Study Session (Can. Cath. Hist. Assoc.), 40 (1973), 44.

68 Harrison, *Drink and Victorians*, ch. 9, and pp. 291–6; see also Dingle,
Campaign for Prohibition, ch. 1.

bill's second reading. This approach, resurrected in the 1908 Licensing bill and backed by a commanding Liberal majority, again failed when rejected in the Lords. Only Scotland belatedly acquired such powers in 1913. Details of UKA proposals changed therefore between 1893 and 1914, but prohibitionists' commitment to their objective remained as tenacious as public hostility to its realization. They could not claim that inadequate organization had defeated them. The UKA possessed district agents who set up local constituency machinery, harassed parliamentary candidates, arranged public meetings, collected petitions and never raised less than £13,000 annually in the 1870s. By 1873 it was employing a full-time organizing secretary and paying him £200 yearly.[69] No comparable organization, activity or concern then characterized the brewing industry.

National organization, money, enthusiasm and later Liberal allies, however, were insufficient partly because people liked beer, and partly because the UKA implacably resisted compensation. Brewers and publicans alike insisted that licences, granted for one year, became 'property' when repeatedly reissued, revocable only with fair compensation unless lost through misconduct. 'Long usage and established custom', avowed the *Brewers' Journal*, 'have given licence holders a right to renewal practically constituting a vested interest, and carrying with it a just claim for compensation'.[70] Even the CETS agreed. Compensation also followed Parliament's precedent of recompensing former slave owners. To these arguments the UKA retorted that acknowledging licences as property would not only thwart further reforms by inflating the value of surviving pubs and beerhouses, but penalize taxpayers, the providers of the money. In response, Salisbury's Government supported two proposals drawing funds from the industry itself by either higher licence or beer duties, but prohibitionists repudiated each as morally unacceptable. It was, therefore, neither the amount, nor the length or even the source of compensation, but rather the principle that antagonized extremists.[71]

---

[69] Harrison, *Drink and Victorians*, pp. 230, 239–40; Dingle, *Campaign for Prohibition*, p. 192; Henry Carter, *The English Temperance Movement: A Study in Objectives* (1933), pp. 218–20; Shiman, *Crusade Against Drink*, pp. 218–19.

[70] *Brewers' Journal*, 15 Nov. 1890.

[71] Harrison, 'Rhetoric of Reform', p. 436; *Evid. Lords Comt. Intemp.*, 1877, 11 (418), pp. 98, 107, 117; Sir Wilfrid Lawson, 'Prohibition in England', *N. Amer. Rev.* 157 (1893), 156–7.

More aware of electoral realities than the Alliance, Liberals regarded the problem as insoluble. Their chief whip, Herbert Gladstone, grimly predicted that 'without an adequate amount of grease we shall not be able to overcome the friction of the trade at . . . almost any election'. But equitable compensation, he stressed, would 'enable us to detach from the public house influence the mass of reasonable customers who in a rough & ready way want the publicans to be treated generously'.[72] He and other Liberals perceived that after the 1886 realignment they needed working-class voters for forming an independent government to surmount the Lords' veto. This made the 1895 Election defeat decisive. It prompted Herbert Gladstone and Liberal imperialists to attack both prohibition and the Gladstonian home rule approach for Ireland as reasons for Liberal unpopularity. So influential in fact was this setback on Liberal thinking that within five years new, less ambitious policies had been formulated, withdrawing from home rule as a question of practical politics, de-emphasizing local option and endorsing restricted compensation. These concessions aimed at altering the party's image as irreconcilably committed only to the home rule bills and hostile to drink retailers. Gladstonian home rulers disputed the revised strategy, whereas prohibitionists became bitterly divided.[73]

In recognizing licences as property, the Conservative 1904 Licensing Act apparently ended the drink controversy. Owners of licences abolished by magistrates received as compensation the monopoly value plus goodwill (i.e. custom). As the scheme could progress only as rapidly as limited funds in each licensing district permitted, the total number of licences decreased slowly.

---

72 Gladstone to Campbell-Bannerman, 19 Nov. 1899, Campbell-Bannerman Papers, Brit. Lib., Add. Ms. 41,215, fos. 144 – 6.
73 For the home rule debate, see H.W. McCready, 'Home Rule and the Liberal Party, 1899 – 1906', *Irish Hist. Stud.*, 13 (1962 – 3), 316 – 48; H. C. G. Matthew, *The Liberal Imperialists: The Ideas and Politics of a Post-Gladstonian Elite* (1973), ch. 8; David W. Gutzke, 'Rosebery and Ireland, 1898 – 1903: A Reappraisal', *Bull. Instit. Hist. Res.*, 53 (1980), 88 – 98. The reaction of temperance reformers to this reassessment is explored in David M. Fahey's 'Temperance and the Liberal Party — Lord Peel's Report, 1899', *Jour. Brit. Stud.*, 10 (1971), 149 – 59; Shiman, *Crusade Against Drink*, pp. 229 – 43. For the UKA's increasing difficulty with Liberal candidates over local option after 1895, see D. A. Hamer, *The Politics of Electoral Pressure: A Study in the History of Victorian Reform Agitations* (Hassocks, 1977), pp. 285 – 99.

To expedite reduction, Liberals revived Bruce's proposal, incorporating a 'time limit' in their 1908 Licensing bill which limited compensation for lapsed licences to a stipulated period, originally fourteen but later twenty-one years. Brewers and retailers felt justly alarmed for two reasons. First, the revised scale, designed to eliminate about one-third (over 30,000) of existing licences, would provide full compensation for merely a small proportion. Second, the denial of any compensation whatsoever for licences revoked after the grace period would confiscate brewery companies' biggest assets, their huge investments (reaching upwards of £150 million) in licensed property.[74] Enraged at the bishops' support for the bill, one Cambridge brewer rebuked his local vicar: ' "Thou shall not steal!" There is *no time limit* to this!' The *Brewing Trade Review* likewise observed that 'robbery is not less robbery because it is postponed a little longer'. With monopoly value abolished, brewery company profits during an indeterminate period — one informed brewer forecast fifty years — would have gone, not to shareholders but to replenishing devalued assets. Mindful of this possibility in September 1906, Liberal brewer Edward N. Buxton in a letter to Herbert Gladstone, expressed apprehension about his firm's £3 million of licensed property, despite its annual net profits of £50,000. 'It would be impossible for owners of licences whether Brewers or others to make any serious reduction in their liabilities in any time likely to be granted to them'.[75]

---

[74] E. N. Buxton to Gladstone, 12 Sept. 1906, Herbert Gladstone Papers, Add. Ms. 46,064, fos. 78 – 83. One director of Burton's largest brewery, Bass, Ratcliff & Gretton, thought that licensed houses were worth £170 million (John Gretton, 'The Licensing Bill', *Fort. Rev.*, 89 (1908), 733). For temperance estimates of licensed property market value, see David M. Fahey, 'Brewers, Publicans, and Working-Class Drinkers: Pressure Group Politics in Late Victorian and Edwardian England', *Histoire sociale/Soc. Hist.*, 13 (1980), 88. During World War 1, a government committee placed the value of licensed houses at £250 million (Ian Donnachie, 'World War I and the Drink Question: State Control of the Drink Trade', *Jour. Scot. Lab. Hist. Society*, 17 (1982), 21).

[75] H. Winter to Rev. J. H. Martin (copy), 21 March 1908, Lambeth Palace Lib., Davidson Papers, Licensing and Temp. Box 2. Winter's italics. *Brewing Trade Review*, 1 Apr. 1908; Buxton to Gladstone, 12 Sept. 1906, Herbert Gladstone Papers, Add. Ms. 46,064, fos. 78 – 83; Gretton, 'Licensing Bill', pp. 737 – 8; see also *Brewers' Gazette*, 12 March 1908. On 7 March 1908, the *Statist*, influential newspaper of the financial community, queried the potential severity of the bill, emphasizing that an expanding population would prevent the Liberals' projected reductions.

By the 1870s the primary characteristics of the drink debate had been established: the key issues, monopoly value, compensation and time limit, were identified; the chief remedy, licensing reduction, was proposed; the principal antagonists, the brewing industry and temperance organizations, confronted each other in Parliament; and drink opponents displayed two inherent weaknesses, sectarian programmes and preoccupation with drink as the cause of all social evils.[76] None of these, however, provoked brewers into forming or strengthening organizations to counteract their rivals' efforts. This would only come with renewed parliamentary pressure for prohibition early in the 1880s.

[76]   Harrison, *Drink and Victorians*, p. 355.

3

The Pub Defended

For the brewing industry, as for other late-Victorian pressure groups, political influence demanded national organization, money and unity. Historians describe the trade as nationally organized, well funded and united by the 1870s, but this was not so until much later.

In his wide-ranging study, *Drink and the Victorians*, Brian Harrison undertakes a major reappraisal of R. K. Ensor's view of the 1871–2 licensing crisis. Harrison argues that publicans embraced Conservatism less because of hostile legislation than because Liberals had more closely aligned with temperance, and that Ensor both exaggerated the speed with which the trade transferred its political loyalties and underestimated its persisting disunity.[1]

Although this is quite true, Harrison himself makes some unwarranted assumptions about the brewing industry. He points to the Country Brewers' Society's larger membership after 1871 and collection of a £21,000 fund as evidence of its growing political influence. He further credits retail societies with solidarity and impressive organizational machinery. These circumstances lead him to the tentative conclusion that the trade's political power might have been stronger later in the 1870s.[2]

Certainly the Country Brewers' Society could raise impressive sums during a crisis, but because the £21,000 was an emergency

---

[1] Harrison, *Drink and Victorians*, pp. 279–85; Ensor, *England*, pp. 21–2; see also H.J. Hanham, *Elections and Party Management: Politics in the Time of Disraeli and Gladstone* (1959), pp. 222–5.

[2] Harrison, *Drink and Victorians*, pp. 226, 266, 342–3, 347, 373; see also Dingle, *Campaign for Prohibition*, pp. 31–2; Mathias, 'Brewing and Politics', p. 113; Lambert, *Drink and Sobriety*, pp. 166, 208. David Fahey ('Brewers and Drinkers', pp. 86–7, 89–90) has disputed part of Harrison's interpretation.

fund, little of it went to defence. Repeated deficits and a net income counted in hundreds, not thousands, of pounds, more accurately reflected the CBS's real worth. Retail societies had more money, but relished acrimonious feuding far too much to be distracted by the mundane problems of sustaining agitation against temperance attacks at the national level. Insolvency and insurgency together with weak organization simply prevented the trade from effectively intervening throughout the 1870s.

Scholars portray the trade-temperance battle as one between equals, matched in power, resources and commitment in an escalating political controversy. Those in the drink industry deliberately fostered this myth, boastfully emphasizing their supposed unity by calling themselves 'the trade'. In fact, the half dozen or more societies representing the industry seldom discussed, much less coordinated, tactics and strategy. The trade, far from strenuously opposing its most tenacious enemy, the United Kingdom Alliance, succumbed to petty conflicts engendered by long-standing rivalries. Poorly organized and inexplicably apathetic, brewers relied for defence on licensed victuallers, whose ill-funded societies more often preached the importance of retaining sovereignty than of developing solidarity. The distrust dividing the two principal retail associations caused bitter but inconclusive quarrels, which country brewers suppressed only in 1883 by gaining effective control over provincial organization. Deprived of primacy and much money from brewers, provincial publicans then engaged in a rancorous dispute with the CBS, ending in their own defeat. By 1885, the trade, better organized and politically energetic, had virtually consolidated into two geographic groups, one in London, the other in the provinces, but real power still eluded them.

What hampered the trade's development of more systematic defence in the 1870s and throughout much of the 1880s was the inability of brewer MPs to form an effective parliamentary lobby. No temperance measure was more persistently debated or more repeatedly rejected in the 1874 Parliament than local veto. Four times the Commons resoundingly defeated the UKA sponsored bill before 1878, with majorities ranging from 194 to 285. Among the two major parties altogether 118 MPs (all but twenty Liberals) favoured local veto, whereas 447 MPs (all but ninety-eight Conservatives) opposed it (see table 1). In 1879 Sir Wilfrid Lawson, the Alliance's president and chief parliamentary spokesman, sought wider support with a resolution offering fewer licences as a third choice, but, though almost

Table 1
Party attitudes towards UKA permissive bills, 1874 – 8

	Conservative		Liberal	
For	4.9%	(20)	34.4%	(98)
Against	85.6%	(349)	34.4%	(98)
No Vote	9.5%	(39)	31.2%	(89)
Total	100.0%	(408)	100.0%	(285)

Sources: UKA Annual Reports: 1873 – 4, p. 126; 1874 – 5, p. 119; 1875 – 6, pp. 148 – 50; 1877 – 8, pp. 134 – 6; *Hansard*, 3rd. ser.: 220 (17 June 1874), cols. 58 – 61; 225 (16 June 1875), cols. 74 – 8. The totals exceed total membership of the House because these figures include all MPs elected at by-elections and pairs, except those paired against in the 1874 – 5 divisions. Party labels are based on *McCalmont's Parliamentary Poll Book*.

two-thirds of all Liberal MPs gave approval, a huge Conservative majority blocked it. Stalwart Liberal local vetoists accepted this tactical withdrawal, but clearly disliked the revised strategy's ambiguity which Liberal brewer James Stansfeld underlined in voting with the minority for what he called 'some practical measure of licensing reform'.[3]

With sizeable numbers of Liberals and their front bench hostile to local veto, brewer MPs smugly disregarded prohibitionist attacks. In 1879, on a fairly typical division, only sixteen of the twenty-two brewer MPs voted against local option. Indeed, Liberal Samuel Whitbread, frequent defender of his own interests and those of other large London brewers, was himself absent. Even Conservative brewer MPs, more often present than Liberal ones, ignored the Alliance's perennial ritual. Representing the leading provincial brewers' organization, Thomas O. Wethered, was absent and unpaired, for instance, on a similar debate the year before. In casting only three-quarters of their potential dissenting votes on five prohibitionists divisions, brewer MPs displayed the apathy and

[3] UKA Annual Report, Univ. Wisconsin, Guy Hayler Collection, 1878 – 9, pp. 132 – 5; *Hansard*, 3rd ser., 244 (11 March 1879), col. 730.

complacency that rendered the trade's lobby so disorganized in the 1870s.[4]

The trade's weaknesses inside Parliament betrayed a bigger obstacle to ensuring immunity from legislative attack, the regional or even local basis on which brewers organized themselves. Divided into five chief societies in the 1870s, brewers had not yet acquired the collective identity which promoted unity and national organization. One, the Brewers' Company of London, had long existed, while those in the provinces developed only in the nineteenth century, usually when legislation denied brewers cherished rights. Admittedly, friction between London and the provinces afflicted most Victorian pressure groups,[5] but for the brewing industry this was merely one of several sources of conflict, with beer brands, size, numbers of tied houses and markets equally causing dissent.

The Brewers' Company was undoubtedly the most prestigious. As a London medieval livery society it dispensed philanthropy, but also possessed much political influence. On its governing council, eleven of the city's largest breweries set policy: Barclay & Perkins; Charrington; City of London; Combe; Courage; Hoare; Mann, Crossman & Paulin; Reid; Truman, Hanbury & Buxton; Watney; and Whitbread. Three members, Alexander Barclay (L), Samuel Whitbread (L) and James Watney (C), served in Parliament during the 1870s, enhancing its reputation.[6] Like other brewers' societies, the Brewers' Company preferred confidential discussion to electoral pressure when negotiating with the government.

---

4   Table 1; UKA Annual Reports: 1877 – 8, pp. 134 – 6; 1878 – 9, pp. 132 – 5. For brewer MPs in the 1874 Parliament, see David W. Gutzke, 'Rhetoric and Reality: The Political Influence of British Brewers, 1832 – 1914', *Parl. Hist.* (forthcoming), app. 1.

5   See, for example, David Thompson, 'The Liberation Society, 1844 – 68', Patricia Hollis (ed.), *Pressure from Without in Early Victorian England* (1974), pp. 230 – 1; Paul McHugh, *Prostitution and Victorian Social Reform* (1980), p. 241.

6   Two other brewer MPs with London breweries, Sir Dudley Marjoribanks and James Stansfeld, were not members. For a cursory survey, see Mia Ball, *The Worshipful Company of Brewers: A Short History* (1977). The Brewers' Company's charitable activities were examined in the *Evid. Royal Com. Livery Companies City of London*, 1884, 39 (Cmnd. 4073-II), 3: 121 – 96 and (Cmnd. 4073-IV), 5: 33 – 66. No correspondence or annual reports apparently exist for the Brewers' Company.

Formed in 1822 and thus the oldest brewers' association in the provinces, the Country Brewers' Society (CBS) consisted primarily of brewers in the home counties and East Anglia. Over sixty per cent of those who served many years on its general committee came from these regions between 1863 and 1883, whereas brewers in the six northernmost English counties accounted for only five per cent. Of the 2,073 brewers producing over 1,000 barrels annually in 1883, only 316 (fifteen per cent) belonged to the CBS, a fact which still made it the country's most representative brewers' organization. This need never have been a serious liability had its members not also failed to make up in subscriptions what they lacked in numbers. Compared with UKA expenses of £15,200 in 1883, for example, the CBS could not even find £400 for operating costs. Instead members subsidized licensed victuallers' societies, the only trade agencies then organized widely at the local level. But the CBS was not altogether an impoverished, somewhat inactive body. Some executive members usually sat in Parliament, invariably as Conservatives, and four did so after the 1874 Election.[7] Neither then nor later, however, did the CBS enrol most country brewer MPs; nine, excluding Burton brewers, held parliamentary seats but remained outside its sporadic deliberations.[8]

Liberal licensing legislation of the early 1870s had prompted brewers to form county societies, but most disappeared as quickly as the crisis, except for three in northern England which actively defended trade practices. Those in Yorkshire and Liverpool challenged overly zealous local officials, but neither was as assiduous as the Manchester Brewers' Central Association. Throughout the 1870s it lobbied the Conservative Government for changes in the 1872 Licensing Act, brewers' licence

[7] John P. Cobbold, Sir Edmund Lacon, Pickering Phipps and Thomas Wethered were the four brewer MPs. On John Cobbold's death in 1874, his brother, Thomas, replaced him on the general committee and in Parliament. The statistics for the CBS general committee and membership were compiled from CBS Min. Bks. 2 and 3, B.S., and Parl. Pap., 1883, 64 (27), p. 8. CBS Min. Bk. 3, Oct. 1883; CBS 1883 Annual Report; Dingle, *Campaign for Prohibition*, p. 192. Records of the CBS are quite good, except for the absence of correspondence.

[8] James Agg-Gardner (C), Octavius Edward Coope (C), James Deakin (C), Thomas Earp (L), Gilbert Greenall (C), Edward Greene (C), Alexander Hall (C), and Edward Wells (C). Another brewer, Daniel Thwaites (C), secured election in 1875.

duties and magistrates' discretionary power.[9] Yorkshire brewers, who had more than their fair share of breweries, typified the restricted scope of virtually every brewers' society in donating to theirs just over £100 annually. Wealthier Burton brewers economized even further, with an 'informal association' made up largely of four trade MPs who acted as spokesmen for local brewers in Parliament. In the mid-1870s family politics predominated in Burton, where two Conservative Allsopps, Henry and Samuel Charles, were matched by two Liberal Basses, Michael Arthur and Michael Thomas.[10]

In the 1870s refuting temperance arguments and arousing support for favourable candidates concerned retailers more than brewers. Two organizations defended the 70,000 publicans whose public houses sold beer, wine and spirits for consumption either on or off the premises. The Licensed Victuallers' Protection Society of London, founded in 1833, collected dues of about £700 each year from 3,000 members, well under half of all metropolitan publicans. Brewers, particularly those in London, supplemented the Society's income, but it seldom spent more than £4,000 – £5,000 annually, unless a crisis drew a two- or three-fold increase.[11] The other publicans' society, the Licensed Victuallers' National Defence League, was created in 1872, and by the end of the decade had perhaps 7,200 members federated in over 100 local associations, making it the country's largest retail society. Yet the League never attained power commensurate with its size: twice as large as the Society, it received annually less money from members (£700) and brewers (£200) which kept yearly expenses around £800.[12] The 45,000 retailers with beer or wine licences joined the Beer and Wine Trade National Defence League (1873) or the Northern District League of Beer and Wine Trade Protection Society (1869). By the late

9 Herts. Br. Assoc. 1884 Annual Report, B.S, pp. 4 – 5; *Licensing Struggles of a Generation: A History of the Brewers' Central Association (Manchester) from its Foundation in 1869 to the Present Day* (Manchester, 1897), pp. 37 – 9, 45 – 6, 68 – 71, 77 – 9. I want to thank Mr C. Kilshaw, sec. of the Northwest Br. Assoc., for allowing me to see this rare book.

10 *Brewers' Guardian*, 16 June 1885; Yorks. Br. Assoc. Annual Reports, Yorks. Br. Assoc., 1873 – 9.

11 *Evid. Lords Comt. Intemp.*, 1877, 11 (418), p. 259; LVPSL Annual Reports, Nat. Union Lic. Victs., 1882 – 8; Wilson, *Alcohol and Nation*, p. 396. The Society had extensive correspondence files which were destroyed recently.

12 Membership figures are derived from subscriptions in the 1870s (LVNDL Annual Reports, Nat. Union Lic. Victs., 1874 – 88). The League's correspondence files have also been destroyed.

1890s, the former had rapidly grown to over 4,000 members, while the much smaller Northern District League, twenty federated branches based in Lancashire, was united solely by distrust of the Beer and Wine League. Licensed grocers, however, were not so much distrusted as hated for their Liberal sentiments. Entering the liquor trade only in the 1860s, these Liberals saw no need for a national society until 1886. The brewing industry treated licensed grocers as political outcasts, excluding them from existing organizations.[13]

Three issues, the 1872 Licensing Act, provincial organization and the best way to decide policy, divided the League and the Society, but prejudice and questions of power and prestige also provoked controversy. Liberal legislation in 1872 giving London pubs 121 licensing hours weekly, far more than the ninety-five-115 hours allowed elsewhere, led the two provincial licensed victuallers' societies, the United Towns Association (Birmingham) and the Provincial Defence League (Manchester) to form one league. Provincial publicans felt one comprehensive body would be more effective when lobbying Parliament for uniform hours.[14]

This raised the second divisive topic, provincial organization. Historically provincial retailers were not political activists, so merging two moribund organizations would scarcely command politicians' respect. Of the fifty-two English and Welsh counties, nineteen had only one retail society, while another thirteen none at all. Pleas for amended licensing hours would fail, League officials recognized, unless the League became fully representative. At a 1875 conference, provincial leaders addressed this defect, and submitted a scheme whereby England and Wales would be divided into fourteen districts, each with a centre responsible for forming local retail societies. London publicans thought this a counterproductive proposal, maintaining that the revival of the contentious licensing question would alienate politicians and the public alike. It hardly surprised distrustful provincial publicans that the Society

---

[13] *Evid. Royal Com. Liq. Licensing Laws*, 1898, 36 (Cmnd. 8693), p. 427; Wilson, *Alcohol and Nation*, p. 396. No records of these organizations have survived, except for isolated annual reports. The records of the Beer and Wine League were destroyed by bombing in World War 2.

[14] *Evid. Sunday Bill Comt.*, 1867–8, 14 (402), pp. 371, 393; *Licensed Victuallers' Guardian*, 3 June 1876.

viewed 'with coldness a project which could make no addition to its privileges'. Angered at such transparent obstruction, the conference promptly ratified the plan. Within a year, the dramatic result was a probable doubling in membership, with 146 societies in thirty-three counties.[15]

Licensed victuallers also strongly disagreed on the third question, the composition of a combined committee for formulating common policy and strategy. The Society demanded equal representation, whereas the League insisted that provincial publicans were 'more than ten times as numerous, their electoral power more than twenty times greater, and the varied conditions under which they carried on their business demanding so much more attention'. Both societies, the League countered, should amalgamate in one national organization, with provincial publicans nominating three-quarters of the governing council. The Society, of course, declined.[16]

London publicans had no intention of accepting an inferior position to League members for whose aggressive tactics and ineptness they had nothing but contempt. Petty disputes concealed a fierce struggle for supremacy. In 1875 the Liverpool Licensed Victuallers' Society withdrew from the League, and joined the London and Home Counties Licensed Victuallers' League. Ostensibly created as an autonomous body early in the 1870s, the latter was in fact not only sponsored and run by officials of the Society, who served as chairman, treasurer and secretary and formed the parliamentary committee, but apparently dedicated to undermining League support.[17]

So at least League officials suspected. They pointed to the 1875 conference where Liverpool and London retailers had opposed League reorganization plans as compelling proof of a subversive campaign conducted under the guise of this other so-called 'League'. Four years later the Liverpool society's symbolic defection to a rival front organization for London retailers still rankled. In September 1879 League president

---

15 *Ibid.*, 30 Jan. 1875 and 22 Jan. 1876; LVNDL Annual Reports, 1875–8. In 1880 the League had 240 affiliated societies (LPLVDL Min. Bk., Nat. Union Lic. Victs., 13 Dec. 1880, p. 38).

16 LVPSL Parl. Reports Min. Bk., 14 Nov. 1879, 9 Jan. 1880 and 31 May 1883, pp. 12–13, 30–1, 347–53; *Efforts of the League to bring about a Closer Union with the London Society* (n.p., n.d.), pp. 6–7.

17 LVPSL 1873 Annual Report, pp. 5, 7 and Parl. Reports Min. Bk., 3 Oct. 1879 and 31 May 1880, pp. 6–9, 101; *Licensed Victuallers' Guardian*, 30 Aug. 1879; LPLVDL Min. Bk., 13 Dec. 1880, p. 39.

Joseph Wadhams, in a letter published in the *Licensed Victuallers'
Guardian*, disparaged the Liverpool society's 'cheap alliance
with London'.[18] The Society, eager to block reconsideration of
licensing hours, then mocked League officials' claim to
represent all provincial retailers by renaming its affiliated body
the London and Provincial Licensed Victuallers' League. 'Your
insistence on the presence of Liverpool at meetings of the Joint
Committee in defiance of our known determination convinces
. . . us that . . . combined action is impossible', the League
informed the Society in February 1880. Three years later the
Guardian could be still found denouncing the Society's sinister
misnaming of the other 'League' for fomenting provincial
unrest.[19] For eleven years enmity between provincial and
London licensed victuallers seriously diminished their power,
preventing both a coherent electoral policy and a unified
parliamentary lobby against increased licensed duties.

The 1880 General Election demonstrated the brewing industry's weakness as a pressure group. National societies neither
collaborated nor publicized where staunch opponents stood as
candidates, and brewers themselves remained remarkably
aloof.

Three developments influenced brewers' attitudes. First,
though Liberal licensing legislation had galvanized them into
vigorous intervention at the 1874 Election, the Disraeli Government's amendment of the 1872 Act largely satisfied them, and
they consequently lost interest in politics.

Second, temperance reformers too were less provocative
during the 1880 Election partly because as nonconformists they
concentrated on assailing Disraeli's foreign policy, and partly
because of revised prohibitionist tactics. In 1879, the UKA
substituted a local option parliamentary resolution endorsing
prohibition as a broad principle for the more specific Permissive
bill. This imprecise programme meant that Liberal candidates
could readily accept the general concept, while privately
doubting the practicality, of prohibition.[20] The direct consequence, less temperance pressure, persuaded brewers that
intervention was unnecessary.

---

18 *Licensed Victuallers' Guardian*, 30 Jan. 1875 and Wadhams to editor, *ibid.*, 20
    Sept. 1879.
19 *Efforts of the League*, pp. 15 – 16; *Licensed Victuallers' Guardian*, 26 May 1883;
    LVPSL Parl. Reports Min. Bk., 20 Sept. 1879 and 16 Jan. 1880, pp. 1, 33.
20 Hamer, *Electoral Pressure*, pp. 222 – 5.

Last, brewers felt retailers were abler defenders of the industry. 'Brewers are only too glad to shelter themselves behind the larger and better organised retail trade', the *Brewers' Guardian* recalled some years later. Even so, brewers did play a small but indirect role by giving retail societies record amounts of money. Of the £1,573 which the League spent in 1880, £862 (fifty-five per cent) came from brewers. Other types of assistance were clearly beyond the means of most brewers' associations, which merely circularized prominent brewers for support of pro-trade candidates.[21]

National retail organizations managed the election by having local federated societies submit test questions to candidates. Two questions, supporting compensation for publicans who lost licences and retention of JP authority over licensing drink houses, appeared at every subsequent election. The *Licensed Victuallers' Guardian* published this list, together with statements from the League and Society urging retailers to 'sink political proclivities'. Local branches interpreted this advice as an endorsement of Conservatives. In seventeen of the twenty-two contests in London, for example, the Society and the Beer and Wine Trade National Defence League sponsored Conservative candidates.[22]

In theory, the brewing industry supported Conservatives, but in practice many retailers, violating explicit official instructions, voted Liberal. A confidential League report attacked the 'positive betrayal of trust, rebellion against orders, and treachery to the cause, practised by some leaders, and by very many of the rank and file'. One notorious instance of such disunity was at Carlisle, where the UKA's parliamentary leader, Sir Wilfrid Lawson, retained his seat. Agents of the League and Society had canvassed retailers emphasizing the need to return his opponent, but several nevertheless supported Lawson, including one who even illogically described him as 'the best friend the trade ever had'. This same publican further dismayed

---

[21] *Brewers' Guardian*, 24 Apr. 1883; LVNDL 1881 Annual Report; CBS Min. Bk. 3, 15 March 1880, pp. 140 – 1.

[22] *Licensed Victuallers' Guardian*, 13 and 27 March 1880; *Morning Advertiser*, 30 March 1880. See also Janet Howarth, 'The Liberal Revival in Northamptonshire, 1880 – 95: A Case Study in Late Nineteenth Century Elections', *Hist. Jour.*, 12 (1969), 105, 107, 117.

the agents by promising Lawson his support at future elections.[23]

Elsewhere, cases of defection as well as many close contests led to exaggerated claims that retailers had needlessly sacrificed 100 seats. Liberals captured seventy-two of the 120 seats won by a margin of ten per cent or less.[24] Only in these seventy-two seats, where a little over 4,000 votes determined the outcome, could the League maintain that retail disunity had jeopardized the chances of pro-drink candidates.

Some publicans voted Liberal simply out of personal conviction, much like the nine Liberal brewer MPs in the 1880 Parliament.[25] According to the *Licensed Victuallers' Guardian*, Liberal promises of dealing justly with the brewing industry reassured retailers that upholding their principles would not imperil their livelihoods. One Manchester publican later accused Liberal candidates of restoring trust in their party by less ethical means — from bribery to renting public house committee rooms. 'This', he recollected, 'had the desired effect'.[26]

Still other retailers turned to Liberalism in reaction to attacks from their erstwhile friends, the Anglican clergy. To disrupt the alignment, so powerful at the 1874 Election, of Conservatives, brewers, retailers and Anglican ministers, the UKA focused on transforming the established church into a temperance ally. Within two years, almost 8,000 clergymen had signed a memorial calling for stricter legal control of alcohol, prompting the Archbishop of Canterbury to request an official inquiry. The Conservative Government complied, appointing a House of Lords' committee which recommended a substantial increase in licence duties.[27] The church's public denunciations of the trade

[23] LVPSL Parl. Reports Min Bk., 30 March and 2 Apr. 1880, pp. 84, 88; LVNDL Parl. Rev. 1880, pp. 16 – 19.

[24] Trevor Lloyd, *The General Election of 1880* (1968), pp. 135 – 6, 145; LVNDL Parl. Rev. 1880, pp. 18 – 19.

[25] Basil L. Crapster, 'The London "Morning Advertiser": Two Notes on Its Editorial History', *Vic. Periodicals Newsletter*, 7 (March, 1974), 7; K. Theodore Hoppen, *Elections, Politics, and Society in Ireland, 1832 – 85* (Oxford, 1984), p. 52; see p. 28, n. 38.

[26] J. R. Howe, 'Corruption in British Elections in the Early Twentieth Century: Some Examples from Gloucestershire', *Mid. Hist.*, 5 (1979 – 80), 67; *Licensed Victuallers' Guardian*, 19 March 1881; W. Crawley to editor, *ibid.*, 10 Feb. 1883; Lambert, *Drink and Sobriety*, pp. 209 – 10.

[27] *Rep. Lords Comt. Intemp.*, 1878 – 9, 10 (113), pp. xlix – l; Dingle, *Campaign for Prohibition*, p. 215.

together with probable higher licence fees offended many retailers. Late in 1879, for instance, the Bishop of Manchester advocated fewer public houses and shorter Sunday drinking hours. League president Joseph Wadhams believed the church's new role as a proponent of temperance, discrediting the Conservatives as allies, 'shook the confidence of many and no doubt led to the loss of many thousands of votes'.[28]

Soon after the election, the new Liberal prime minister, W. E. Gladstone, exacerbated differences between provincial and London publicans when he proposed larger fees for spirit licences in his budget.[29] The revised duties, though retaining a sliding scale based on the rateable value of premises, raised the cost of all but the lowest spirit licences between 5s 8¼d and £13 9s 3¼d (see table 2). Publicans condemned these changes, but genuine economic cleavages prevented their putting forward a compromise. Three-quarters of all public houses in the country but virtually none in London's ten metropolitan boroughs were rated at less than £50.[30] With large numbers of valuable premises, London was an awkward anomaly, and thus the source of bitter dissension among retailers.

This disparity in property values shaped League tactics, designed to transfer the heavier taxes largely from poorer provincial to wealthier London publicans. Early in July League representatives, meeting with the inland revenue board, criticized the proposed new scale as onerous at the bottom but indiscriminate at the top. A more equitable scale, they asserted, would continue existing licence fees below the £50 level, and draw clearer gradations above it (see table 2). But the League's secretary unwisely went one step further, complaining that 'the provinces pay . . . much more than their share, while London is unfairly relieved'. He now apparently found himself sanctioning something not calculated to please the Society, a maximum fee higher than £30. To accommodate the League's goal, a scale

28 *Brewers' Journal*, 15 Dec. 1879; LVNDL, The New Parl., Apr. 1880, p. 2.
29 Publicans could obtain 3 types of licences: beer, spirit or wine. Beer licences were held separately, whereas spirit licences also required beer permits. As Gladstone's budget compelled publicans to buy a wine licence, the new spirit licence would include all three. Previously, over half of all publicans whose premises were rated under £50 had beer and spirit but not wine licences (*Licensed Victuallers' Guardian*, 24 July 1880).
30 Increasing property prices and 5 year assessments, begun under the Valuation of the Metropolis Act, led to much higher rates in London during the 1870s (Knox, 'Tied House System', p. 68).

Table 2
Spirit licence scales, 1880

Total U.K. Spirit/Beer Licences	London	Rateable Value (£)	Previous Spirit Licence (£)
		0 – <10	5.10.2½
		10 – <15	7.14.3¾
		15 – <20	
69,848	237	20 – <25	12. 2.6¼
		25 – <30	13. 4.6¾
		30 – <40	14. 6.7½
		40 – <50	15. 8.8
		50 – <60	16.10.8¾
		60 – <70	
		70 – <80	
		80 – <90	
		90 – <100	
		100 – <200	
27,443	5,569	. . .ᵃ	
		200 – <250	
		250 – <300	
		300 – <400	
		400 – <500	
		500 – <600	
		600 – <700	
		700	

Sources: *Licensed Victuallers' Guardian*, 10 and 24 July, and 7 Aug. 1880; *Brewers' Guardian*, 3 Aug. 1880; *Hansard*, 3rd ser., 254 (23 July 1880), col. 1242.
ᵃ For each £10 pounds a 10s increase.

Table 2
Spirit licence scales, 1880

League Proposal (3 July) (£)	Gladstone's Original Proposal (£) (14 June)	Gladstone's Eventual Proposal (£) (23 July)
former duty	5	4.10
	8	6
		8
	11	11
	14	14
	17	17
	20	20
16.10	25	25
17		
17.10		
18		
18.10		
19	30	30
. . .[a]		
24		35
26.10		
29		40
		45
		50
		55
		60

distinguishing categories of expensive premises, Gladstone imposed extra duties of £5 per £100 rateable value on pubs assessed at £200 or more. Without significantly lowering licence fees under £50, the League had unwittingly raised London retailers' duty between £5 and £30.[31]

These startling developments provided ample grounds for misunderstanding. However much League officials decried Gladstone for misusing their even-handed proposal, they could not deny having supported heavier taxes on costly pubs. In response to strident attacks on the League, its newspaper, the *Licensed Victuallers' Guardian*, declared that licence duties should reflect the fact that big, highly rated pubs did more trade than smaller rivals.[32] 'The Trade of London will be great pecuniary sufferers, although the provincial Trade will not obtain any benefit', the Society's secretary angrily replied. H. C. Edwards, League secretary, publicly admitted his complicity in modifying the budget, but rebuked the Society for making its cooperation contingent on preserving the 1,000 additional opening hours which London publicans alone enjoyed. In later stressing the 'suicidal' consequences of continued disunity, the League adopted a more conciliatory stance that did somewhat mollify the Society. Heavier duties still embittered the Society: almost two years later it spitefully contemplated informing each licensed victuallers' society of the League's foolhardy budget tactics.[33]

Differing electoral tactics also fostered bitterness between the League and the Society.[34] A Durham by-election in August 1881 showed why the Society so often denigrated the League's political value. Sir George Elliot, the pro-trade Conservative candidate, stood against Liberal F. Laing, who supported Sunday closing and local option. Once the campaign began FitzRoy Stewart, secretary of the Central Conservative Association, personally urged the Society to arouse retail support for

---

[31] *Hansard*, 3rd ser., 253 (6 July 1880), col. 1787, and 254 (12 July 1880), col. 269; *Licensed Victuallers' Guardian*, 10 and 31 July 1880.

[32] Letters to the editor, *Licensed Victuallers' Guardian*, 31 July, 7 and 14 Aug. 1880.

[33] Edwards to editor, and Ernest Norfolk (sec. of the Society) to editor, *ibid.*, 7 and 21 Aug. 1880; *ibid.*, 16 Oct. 1880; LVPSL Parl. Reports Min. Bk., 3 Apr. 1882, p. 238.

[34] For the Society's criticism of League tactics, see LVPSL Parl. Reports Min. Bk., 14 Oct. 1881 and 14 Dec. 1883, pp. 210–11, 374.

Elliot.[35] Eager to enhance its influence with the Conservative head office, the Society agreed, dispatching its chairman and secretary with strict orders against using noisy methods which might attract publicity. On their arrival in Durham, they were disgruntled but unsurprised to find that the League had neither supervised local retail societies nor revived the Durham Licensed Victuallers' Society, dissolved some three years earlier.[36]

The London delegates quickly executed the pre-arranged campaign. At a meeting convened at their request, Sunderland and Stockton retail leaders emphasized to publicans and beersellers the importance of electing Elliot, of canvassing all drink shops and of discouraging poster or party colour displays. Next the two London officials visited Newcastle. There they eventually dissuaded Blakey, district secretary of the League, from engaging in what they saw as the provincial retailers' chief defect: zeal for strident agitation. Instead he proceeded cautiously, canvassing public houses with the Conservative agent. Travelling to North Shields, the London publicans discovered that the local retail official, Shotton, had despaired of organizing publicans after poor attendance at several meetings. While he agreed to canvass, his reserve excited suspicion and when cross-examined he admitted to his Liberal principles. 'We thought it well', the London retailers reported, 'to urge upon Sir George's Agent to send his brother-in-law over the next morning . . . to ensure that Mr. Shotton *did* canvass as promised'. Despite covert Liberal retailers and League negligence, Elliot won the seat. London publicans naturally regarded his victory as a personal vindication, conclusive evidence of their tactic's superiority over those of provincial retailers.[37]

With retail societies divided by over a decade of quarrels, impetus for solidarity came from leading brewers. At a conference in 1882, they unsuccessfully pressed for the creation of two separate committees, one of retailers for determining general policy, the other of brewers for arbitrating disputes. The

---

[35] Two Conservative candidates contesting by-elections at Plymouth in 1880 and Ipswich in 1883 also requested help from the Society (LVPSL Parl. Reports Min. Bk., 1 July 1880 and 29 Oct. 1883, pp. 129, 371–2).

[36] *Ibid.*, 29 Aug. 1881, pp. 201–5.

[37] *Ibid.* The League also ineffectively opposed the campaign for a Welsh Sunday closing bill (Lambert, *Drink and Sobriety*, p. 220). London retailers' italics.

Brewers' Guardian, exasperated at retailers' seemingly insoluble feuds, caustically noted that the League and the Society 'occupy themselves almost as much with finding fault with each other's plan of action as with the protection of the interests with which they are both equally identified'.[38]

It was not so much the Society as the League, however, that persistently blocked retail unity. During negotiations with London publicans in 1882, the League cited the dubious value of such a committee without brewers as a pretext for retaining its independence. Indeed, its rejection in 1882 of a proposed policy committee with the CBS shows that the League opposed, not the method but the principle of delegating authority. Even a tenuous arrangement in which the League and the CBS cooperated in an advisory capacity came under increasing attack.[39] Impatient at the League's blatant obstinacy, Sir Michael Arthur Bass, MP and Richard Moss (chairman of the CBS), met the Society in May 1883, and unanimously reached two decisions: a retail committee must be set up and brewers would personally guarantee League participation. The CBS quickly fulfilled its pledge, intimating that financial support would be withdrawn unless the League cooperated with the Society. So pointed a threat eliminated League scruples about relinquishing control over policy. In June the protracted eleven-year struggle between the two chief retail societies finally ended when representatives from the Society, League, Scotland and Ireland formed one parliamentary committee.[40]

This had no immediate impact, however, on the problems of the trade at Westminster, where brewers lobbied fitfully and ineffectively. Like most national pressure groups with decentralized authority, the trade contained individuals whose business locality or occupation produced special priorities, uneasily reconciled at national level: London and provincial drink sellers, as the retailers' debate on the 1880 budget illustrated, had varying concerns; brewers and publicans, as Sunday closing and later events revealed, had conflicting

---

[38] LVPSL Parl. Reports Min. Bk., 31 May 1882 and 31 May 1883, pp. 253–4, 256, 347–53; *Brewers' Guardian*, 24 Apr. 1883.

[39] LVNDL 1883 Annual Report, pp. 26–7; LVPSL Parl. Reports Min. Bk., 31 May and 21 June 1883, pp. 338–9, 347–53.

[40] LPLVDL Min. Bk., 21 June 1883; LVPSL Parl. Reports Min. Bk., 31 May 1883, pp. 338–9.

interests. Brewers deemed compensation paramount, whereas retailers, concerned about inconvenienced customers, ranked Sunday closing as equally important. In resort towns, as in popular river bank areas, local publicans and beerhouse keepers, who knew that 'during the season Sunday was generally the best day they had in the week', predicted that Sunday closing would cut their profits in half. But these fears left brewers, owners of many houses, unconcerned. According to the *Brewers' Guardian*, they doubted whether 'any restriction in this direction would seriously affect the consumption of beer'. On 25 June 1880, for example, only six of the fifteen brewers serving as MPs actually attended a debate to oppose a Sunday closing bill.[41]

The trade's political power in Parliament also suffered because brewers and other drink sellers, while represented adequately in the Commons, had no official spokesmen in the Lords before Lords Hindlip (Henry Allsopp) and Burton (Michael Arthur Bass) were ennobled in 1886. Trade MPs, moreover, seldom consulted, and often disregarded the three largest brewers' societies.

Throughout the 1880s brewers mishandled two basic pressure group tactics: parliamentary lobbying and deputations. In fact, the CBS, far from living up to its role as the principal association of country brewers, was insular, short-sighted and blundering, acting more like a recently-established body than one with almost sixty years' experience at Westminster.

Its approach to potentially harmful legislation in 1880 typified these recurrent shortcomings. On 24 May temperance activists introduced a private member's bill, authorizing a mixed body of local ratepayers and JPs to compensate all licence holders, except brewers, for the compulsory purchase of redundant licences. Although regarding such proposals as tantamount to 'confiscation', the CBS executive did not act until 7 June, one day before the scheduled second reading. Its members hastily gathered to consider strategy, but remained totally ignorant of what plans other brewers' associations had formulated or what the government thought. The usual response, the summoning of a general protest meeting of the trade, was now impractical, so the CBS instead telegraphed brewers' societies in Liverpool and Manchester, but not, significantly, in Burton or London.

41   LPLVDL Min. Bk., 17 Apr. 1882, pp. 93, 95; *Brewers' Guardian*, 30 Nov. 1886; *Hansard*, 3rd. ser., 253 (25 June 1880), cols. 916 – 18.

Table 3
Party votes cast on UKA local option resolutions, 1880-3

	Conservative (For/Against)	Liberal (For/Against)	Crossover
1880	7% (12)/93% (158)	85% (203)/15% (37)	12% (49)
1881	8% (11)/92% (126)	91% (177)/9% (18)	9% (29)
1883	8% (11)/92% (128)	97% (209)/3% (6)	5% (17)

Sources: *Hansard*, 3rd ser., 253 (18 June 1880), cols. 386–9; UKA Annual Reports: 1879–80, p. 138; 1880–1, pp. 137–40; 1882–3, pp. 143–6.

The committee also took more definite steps at Westminster, where several members sought support from politicians and brewer MPs and information about the government's attitude. Retail officials, dismayed CBS lobbyists learned soon after arriving, had already arranged for a deputation of MPs, and asked brewers to join them. Ill-prepared, resentful of rival societies and inattentive, brewers themselves contributed virtually nothing to the bill's subsequent withdrawal.[42]

Local option, voted upon three times in the 1880 Parliament, threatened brewers more seriously than radical licensing reform, but the trade again seemed unprepared for concerted opposition. Of the twenty-three trade MPs, thirteen (including four officials of the CBS or Brewers' Company) were absent unpaired in the 1881 or 1883 local option divisions. On neither occasion did any of the eighteen brewer MPs speak, much less offer vehement protest. 'Trade interests have been quite a secondary matter with them, so far as their parliamentary action was concerned', lamented the *Brewers' Journal*. Two, William Findlater and James Stansfeld, actually voted for prohibition.[43]

Protective societies were no better at mobilizing political allies. In 1880 country brewers did receive petitions, endorsing the present licensing powers of JPs and advising the lobbying of MPs to vote against the UKA resolution. So ineffective were

42 CBS Min. Bk. 3, 7 June 1880, 145–7.
43 UKA Annual Reports: 1880–1, pp. 137–41; 1882–3, pp. 143–6; *Brewers' Journal*, 15 Nov. 1885.

these efforts that forty-nine fewer MPs opposed prohibition in 1881 than in 1880, and the majority favouring it rose from twenty-six to forty-two. That majority had more than doubled when MPs voted again in 1883, an indication of the trade's growing political weakness.[44] By 1883, with both parties completely polarized, Liberals supported prohibition as consistently as Conservatives resisted it: twelve per cent of the MPs (excluding Irish Nationalists) had voted against their party majority in 1880, but less than five per cent in 1883 (see table 3).

While the local option majority increased in 1883, more significant was who now voted for it. However cautiously approved, the principle of prohibition had been publicly accepted by two cabinet ministers, W. E. Gladstone and William Harcourt. In declaring that no government should countenance 'any abstract Resolution to which it is not prepared . . . to give effect' and himself supporting local option, Gladstone adopted an unequivocal attitude.[45] Brewers certainly believed prohibition was a distinct possibility. Writing in the *Fortnightly Review* the following year, James Agg-Gardner, Cheltenham brewer and former Conservative MP, felt that the 1883 vote 'points to the conclusion that . . . the present House is in favour of [local option] legislation'.[46]

Hitherto, local option had been a national question, debated only in the Commons and combated through parliamentary lobbying alone. Now local option was part of Liberal plans for local government reform; elected county councils were to be fully empowered to reduce the number of licences. By linking the two, the entire temperance debate would be moved from Westminster to the local level, thereby transforming the trade-temperance conflict. Brewers saw the need to expand local machinery to deal with the proposed county council bodies. But the Country Brewers' Society as a parliamentary lobby had not the means to oppose hostile candidates parish by parish. According to chairman Henry Simonds: 'Under the old system we have known what it is to fight . . . in Parliament, and we can concentrate our efforts on one attack and meet it; but how will it

---

[44] CBS Min. Bk. 3, 25 Oct. 1880, pp. 166–8; table 3.

[45] *Hansard*, 3rd ser., 278 (27 Apr. 1883), col. 1365. Fahey, however, argues that Gladstone's qualifications avoided the principle of local option (David Fahey, 'The Politics of Drink: Pressure Groups and the British Liberal Party, 1883–1908', *Soc. Sci.*, 54 (1979), 77).

[46] *Country Brewers' Gazette*, 24 Oct. 1883; J.T. Agg-Gardner, 'Compulsory Temperance', *Fort. Rev.*, 36 (1884), 211.

be if we have a hundred or two hundred elections of local government boards going on in several parts of the country at the same time?'[47]

The Liberal commitment to local option provoked a two-fold response from the trade: antiquated lobbying techniques were replaced by reliance on the Liberty and Property Defence League; and deficient organizations vastly improved when the CBS established country branches.

The Liberty and Property Defence League (LPDL) from its founding in 1882 was led by Baron Bramwell and Earl Wemyss. These two staunch Conservatives gave the brewing industry what it most lacked at Westminster: energetic and forceful spokesmen without a vested interest in drink who could refute trade critics in the Lords. In the Commons brewers James Agg-Gardner and Octavius Coope along with distiller Frederick Seager Hunt established close long-lasting ties between the trade and the LPDL. The Society, League and CBS all federated, and by the mid-1890s one-fifth of the LPDL's branches were brewers' or licensed victuallers' associations. An annual CBS donation of £26 5s begun in 1885 (comparable to what the Society received), acknowledged the LPDL as a dedicated foe of temperance measures. In cooperating with this body, the trade acquired an ally particularly attractive to Conservatives instinctively distrustful of prohibitionists' collectivist rhetoric.[48]

Conservative leaders in the Lords used the LPDL to defeat a small but steadfast group of temperance sympathizers. It was there that Sunday closing bills, for example, were repeatedly introduced, often by Conservatives, as a method of circumventing procedural constraints on private members' bills in the Commons. Piece-meal legislation rather than one comprehensive act appeared likelier to succeed, so counties with aristocratic supporters such as Conservative Lord Mount Edgcumbe were selected as test cases. With petitions signed by

47 *Country Brewers' Gazette*, 5 Nov. 1885.
48 Edward Bristol, 'The Liberty and Property Defence League and Individual-ism', *Hist. Jour.*, 18 (1975), 780 – 1; N. Soldon, 'Laissez-Faire as Dogma: The Liberty and Property Defence League, 1882 – 1914', Kenneth D. Brown (ed.), *Essays in Anti-Labour History: Responses to the Rise of Labour in Britain* (1974), pp. 213, 227; *Self-Help versus State Help: Being Speeches Delivered at the General Meetings of the LPDL, 1882*, Brit. Lib. Pol. Econ. Sci., pp. 87 – 93; *Self-Help versus State Help: Speeches Delivered at the 3rd Annual Meeting of the LPDL*, *ibid.*, pp. 2 – 5; LPDL 1893 – 4 Annual Rep., *ibid.*, pp. 16 – 17; CBS Min. Bks. 4 – 5 and BS Min. Bk. 2.

over sixty per cent of the county's adult population and Mount
Edgcumbe enlisted as president, the Cornwall Sunday closing
Association was in a formidable position. Edgcumbe himself
warned a former Conservative minister that defying such
overwhelming public sentiment would ruin the party's otherwise encouraging prospects in the St Ives division.[49] On 30 July
1883, with reformers sensing victory, the Cornwall Sunday
closing bill came up for its third reading in the Lords. Wemyss,
however, expressed strenuous opposition, disputing the petition's authenticity, querying the logic of shutting pubs and
beerhouses in a county well known for sobriety, and demanding
compensation commensurate with the loss of one-seventh of
sales. Nothing he said discredited the bill's widespread popularity — mayors, town councils and eleven of Cornwall's thirteen
MPs were among its supporters — or explained the conspicuously few counter-petitions. Nevertheless, in an extremely
close vote, Wemyss prevailed.[50]

Again in 1886 public approval carried a Durham Sunday
closing bill through its preliminary stages in the Lords, and
victory on the final reading seemed assured. Lord Salisbury had
been outwitted in his ruse opposing not the principle or public
opinion but specific details when the Bishop of Durham
introduced a clause with a four-year time limit. To re-establish
Salisbury's position, the CBS arranged protest meetings, and
these, together with a petition presented by Wemyss, enabled
his successful challenge on the grounds that most Durham
residents disliked Sunday closing.[51]

Sometimes even Wemyss could not please all the trade's
heterogeneous groups. After the Commons passed a bill
reducing Scottish licensing hours, Scottish and London retail
representatives wanted an amendment in the Lords permitting
large towns one extra hour of business. Aretas Akers-Douglas,
then Conservative chief whip, pointed out to his prime minister,
Lord Salisbury, the political advantages of this concession: 'We
should thus please the majority of our own party & do more

49 Mount Edgcumbe to Cross, 7 March 1882, Brit. Lib., Cross Papers, Add. Ms.
    51,273, fos. 133 – 4. For the origins and significance of the Sunday closing
    movement, see Shiman, *Crusade Against Drink*, pp. 86 – 90, 222.
50 *Hansard*, 3rd ser., 281 (16 July 1883), cols. 1497 – 8 and 282 (30 July 1883),
    cols. 908, 910, 914, 924 – 5; see also Bristol, 'LPDL', p. 781.
51 *Hansard*, 3rd ser., 305 (11 May 1886), cols. 718 – 19 and 306 (25 May 1886),
    cols. 17 – 21; CBS Min. Bk. 4, 16 June 1886.

good than by any possible — & very problematical — gain from the Temperance party'. If temperance sponsors balked, he recommended that the government withhold support, compelling the bill's withdrawal. Wemyss now put forward his own formula — uniform closing hours extended at magisterial discretion — and won over Scottish delegates. This reversal incensed London retailers who derided it as 'the thin end of the wedge of Local Option'.[52]

Parliamentary support, though extremely important, was only one of many aspects of the LPDL campaign on the trade's behalf. Wemyss and Bramwell disseminated useful literature, giving affiliated societies, MPs and the press critiques of pending legislation and reprinting letters and articles supplied by the CBS in *JUS*, the LPDL's newspaper. Pamphlets on such subjects as drunkenness, Sunday closing and local veto were also distributed.[53] One of these, *Drink*, written by Bramwell and later published in the *Nineteenth Century*, characterized the LPDL's proselytizing work. It contained the classic apologia against prohibition, lauding drink as a splendid beverage, far more beneficial than harmful to the populace. To those sceptics who condemned alcohol as the chief source of social evils curable only by prohibition, he addressed his rejoinder: 'Is it reasonable . . . because some take it [alcohol] to excess, that it is to be denied to millions to whom it is a daily pleasure and enjoyment with no attendant harm?' The CBS was so delighted with this prose that it ordered 50,000 copies. Its explanation for giving them to bookstores affords some insight into one Victorian pressure group's tactics: 'Booksellers . . . would allow them to be sold on their counters, . . . keeping the proceeds for their own pockets, . . . [as] an inducement to . . . push the sale, and also [on the assumption] that those persons who purchased a pamphlet would be more likely to read it than . . . [if sent one] free through the post'.[54]

Some provincial brewers meanwhile, recognizing the defects of their impecunious organization, urged upon the CBS a larger

52 LVPSL Parl. Reports Min. Bk., 11 Aug. 1887, pp. 120 – 1; Akers-Douglas to Salisbury, 4 Aug. 1887, Hatfield House, Salisbury Papers, E/61.
53 CBS Min. Bk. 4, 22 Dec. 1885. See, for example, LPDL 1892 – 3 Annual Rep., pp. 60 – 1, 67 – 8.
54 CBS Min. Bk. 4, 17 Apr. 1885; Lord Bramwell, 'Drink', *Nineteenth Cent.*, 17 (1885), 879, 881.

role in defending the trade. One possible but limited approach, coordinating tactics at joint annual meetings of the two leading provincial trade societies, was advocated by brewers Thomas Wethered and Charles Christie early in 1882, and promptly adopted by the CBS and the League. At a subsequent CBS meeting, members expressed dissatisfaction with this meagre concession. They forced through a resolution commending the recruitment of more country brewers as one approach to acquiring the funds vital for challenging temperance propaganda.[55]

How to achieve this objective and whether it could be attained with the existing twenty-five shilling subscriptions provoked heated debate. Scornful of tight-fisted brewers, one faction recommended giving more money to the League, already better equipped for campaigning but chronically under-funded. No one disputed that temperance reformers spent almost ten times the amount in attacking the trade as the League in defending it. Henry Simonds envisaged collecting twenty-five guineas for provincial publicans in the League: 'Let them do the fighting, as they had the organisation complete and had so used the cudgels hitherto'. Another faction, which wanted the CBS to involve itself directly in trade defence, grumbled about apathetic leaders with unfounded fiscal worries.[56]

Despite these strictures, chairman Henry Blandy had strong misgivings about higher fees. Two brewers suggested creating a voluntary fund of £5,000 to oppose teetotalers as an alternative, but, as so radical a scheme needed the committee's approval, Blandy adjourned the meeting. Reconvening a fortnight later, brewers heard that such a fund exceeded the CBS's scope. Blandy attempted to exonerate himself, arguing that brewers might properly resist legislation, not public opinion. Even so, when the CBS decided to collect funds for the League, brewers subscribed over £700, demonstrating widespread desire for action.[57]

Four major obstacles, two of them originating in the economics of brewing, prevented brewers from protecting themselves more forcefully. Dispersed national markets as well as large industrial cities seemingly safeguarded Burton, London

[55] CBS Min. Bk. 3, 13 Feb. and 1 May 1882, pp. 208 – 9, 216.
[56] *Country Brewers' Gazette*, 10 May 1882; CBS Min. Bk. 3, 1 May 1882, p. 216.
[57] *Country Brewers' Gazette*, 24 May 1882; CBS Min. Bk. 3, 1 and 15 May and 24 July 1882, pp. 216 – 18, 224.

and sizeable country breweries against local option. Paradoxically, areas least needing prohibition — rural agricultural parishes with low drunkenness levels — would have been most likely to enact it. Small country brewers, heavily dependent on local trade and denied the vast funds of bigger competitors, would have been its chief victims. Another closely related economic assumption fostered disunity. Brewers, seldom altruistic, ruthlessly calculated their possible profits from the demise of rivals. Although the *Brewers' Journal* derided such gains as illusory, it conceded that one group of brewers 'continues to disregard repeated warnings'.[58]

Two further problems hindered those who wanted stronger defensive tactics. Despite the lucrative nature of brewing, the CBS was handicapped by recurrent shortages of cash that often caused deficits. In 1883, 316 members, most with thousands and some with hundreds of thousands of pounds invested in brewing, subscribed the magnificent sum of £381.[59] Enrolling more provincial brewers would not solve all the CBS's financial troubles, but might expand local activities, inspiring old and new members alike to make heavier donations. Reformers also faced internal disunity; two factions condemned the lethargic majority, but disagreed over the best means of defending the industry. Simonds led one group; the old guard of conservatives comprised the other.

Three individuals pressed for reform: Thomas Wethered, wealthy Buckinghamshire brewer and former Conservative MP for Marlow, who had long been a general committee member before displaying interest in defence; Andrew Barlow, prosperous Hampshire brewer, as dedicated as Wethered to expanding the CBS; and Charles Denston, not a brewer but editor of the *Country Brewers' Gazette* (the CBS's official newspaper since 1877), who also promoted better organization, both in the press and at brewers' meetings.[60]

These three, committed to reorganizing the CBS, faced stiff opposition, mostly from the old guard whose deep resentment

---

58 *Brewers' Journal*, 15 Dec. 1883; see also *Brewing Trade Review*, 1 Feb. 1891.
59 CBS Min. Bk. 3, 19 Dec. 1881, p. 204; CBS 1884 Annual Report.
60 In 1868 Wethered joined the CBS general committee and entered Parliament for Marlow, the seat which he and T. P. Williams controlled. He left £75,000 at his death, while Barlow's gross estate was almost £400,000. Previously the CBS's newspaper had been the *Brewers' Guardian* (Hanham, *Elections and Management*, p. 410; Davis, *Buckinghamshire*, pp. 218 – 19; probated wills of Thomas Wethered and Andrew Barlow, Somerset House).

of attacks on their authority repeatedly thwarted proposed reforms. From February 1882 Wethered supported schemes which increased the CBS's control over policy, culminating in his most ambitious proposal, the amalgamation of committees with the League. By 1883 Wethered saw local brewers' associations organized under the CBS's auspices as the solution, whereas Simonds' group believed that brewers should merely donate more to retailers. While condemning brewers as parsimonious, this faction had opposed the separate £5,000 fund.[61] Because of the peculiar alignment of forces within the CBS, with the Simonds' factor backing the conservatives, internal reorganization might have been forestalled indefinitely. Some frustrated country brewers took the initiative themselves, and formed societies outside the CBS.

At the beginning of 1883 the old guard felt comfortably secure in its control of the CBS. On 9 April the Society arranged a conference to publicize the growing unrest among brewers and publicans at abusive temperance attacks. Though the *Country Brewers' Gazette* urged brewers to promote unity by attending, the executive did not even bother to send delegates. 'Something must be done', the *Gazette* demanded, 'to prevent the Trade from further spoilation'. At the conference, Andrew Barlow, unofficially representing the CBS, argued that 'if Brewers' Unions were formed in every county similar to that which existed in Yorkshire . . . they could . . . produce a considerable effect on the Legislature'. Favourable comments from the *Gazette* and *Brewers' Guardian* reflected the willingness of some brewers to combine locally as the prelude to affiliating in one national organization.[62] 'Why do the Country Brewers', the dismayed *Gazette* asked, 'concern themselves so little about the question?' In fact, the executive was preoccupied with divisions over reorganizing the CBS. Pressure nevertheless came from Thomas Wethered, who reacted to Liberal leaders' identification with local option by advocating the setting up of county brewers' societies under CBS aegis. Yet the executive procrastinated.[63]

---

61 CBS Min. Bk. 3, 15 May and 16 Oct. 1882, pp. 217–18, 229–30; *Country Brewers' Gazette*, 10 May 1882.
62 *Brewers' Guardian*, 24 Apr. 1883; *Country Brewers' Gazette*, 28 March and 11 Apr. 1883.
63 CBS Min. Bk. 3, 30 Apr. 1883, pp. 247–8; *Country Brewers' Gazette*, 11 Apr. 1883.

Barlow, Wethered and Denston were undeterred, and in the following months forced the CBS to act resolutely, foisting far-reaching changes on the executive, the still complacent old guard. Brewers' associations already existed in Liverpool, Manchester and Yorkshire, and Barlow began a fourth in his own county of Hampshire. Calling a meeting of county brewers, Barlow castigated 'brewers' suicidal apathy' as responsible for the relentless progress of local option. Hampshire brewers agreed, founding a union prepared to work with the CBS. Despite this first example, the CBS executive still did not reconsider Wethered's proposal, even when Denston, embarrassing it further in the *Gazette*, expressed hope that other counties would soon follow.[64] The situation became increasingly awkward, as country brewers, inspired by Denston, Barlow and Wethered, set up such societies. Wethered revived the moribund Buckinghamshire Brewers' Association, while Denston and Barlow gave speeches to meetings of Surrey, Kentish, Dorsetshire and Gloucestershire brewers exhorting the establishment of unions. In September Denston published Barlow's advice on founding county societies. Here and in his speeches Barlow reiterated his central theme, the importance of brewers and publicans demonstrating their superior political power over temperance reformers. 'Organisation and agitation, even if the cause is unsound', he advised Dorset brewers, 'have too much weight with the ministers of the day'.[65]

In late October 1883 CBS members finally considered a new constitution affiliating county societies with the CBS as part of a general reorganization, and rapidly adopted it. By the end of the year twelve such societies had federated with the Country Brewers' Society, six of them as a result of the efforts of Barlow, Denston and Wethered. Thus these three men had compelled the CBS executive to accept a revised constitution, overriding the views of a stubborn and often hostile old guard. Within four years, thirty-six of the forty English counties had affiliated associations, and by 1891 all but Cornish brewers.[66]

---

[64] *Brewers' Journal*, 15 June 1883; *Country Brewers' Gazette*, 6 June 1883.
[65] Glos. Br. Assoc. Min. Bk., 21 Nov. 1883, W. Count. Br. Assoc.; Herts. Br. Assoc. 1884 Annual Report, pp. 5–6; *Country Brewers' Gazette*, 4 July and 26 Sept. 1883.
[66] CBS Min. Bk. 3, 15 and 29 Oct. 1883, pp. 254, 258; *Brewing Trade Review*, 1 Oct. 1887 and 1 Dec. 1890; CBS 1884 Annual Report.

The spread of organization helped unify brewers, but sectionalism still persisted. In 1884, for example, the Gloucestershire Brewers' Association overwhelmingly rejected the CBS secretary's proposal of merging it with the adjoining counties of Herefordshire, Monmouthshire and Worcestershire, where inertia or few brewers had discouraged organizers. Sectionalism also flourished in the north: Bradford and Manchester brewers had the only societies in England which refused to federate. Bradford brewers eventually relented in 1894, but Manchester brewers, who quarrelled almost as frequently with the CBS as with teetotalers, remained independent until 1906.[67]

Now organized locally throughout England, brewers actively intervened at the constituency level. County unions gave brewers more influence, especially with magistrates whose discretionary powers were wide-ranging — from licensing hours and building permits to applications for new licences, renewals or transfers. Through county branches brewers deployed publicans and even customers at temperance meetings to outvote customary motions for local option, Sunday closing or licensing reduction; improved local organization by donating money to retail societies; and realized Barlow's prediction of 'great influence with Members of Parliament'.[68] At a Cambridgeshire by-election in 1884, for instance, the county association questioned both candidates with test questions on such subjects as local option and Sunday closing before endorsing the ultimately successful Conservative. 'Whole columns of statements in favour of the establishment of county unions could not supply arguments more powerful than this', proclaimed the *Country Brewers' Gazette*. Its elation, however, shows just how far brewers were behind the UKA, which had sought pledges from candidates since the late 1850s.[69]

The CBS's general committee, twenty-one brewers elected on a rotating basis at annual meetings, was also quite different after 1884. This change cannot be analyzed simply by examining gross numbers, for the committee expanded and some brewers served much longer than others. If the number of years for each

---

67 Glos. Br. Assoc. Min. Bk., 16 Oct. 1884; Brad. Br. Assoc. Min. Bk., 1 Feb. 1894, Brad. and Dist. Br. Assoc.; see p. 158.

68 *Country Brewers' Gazette*, 26 Sept. 1883; see, for example, Berks. Br. Union Min. Bk., 2 Feb., 5 July and 25 Oct. 1884, and 25 Apr. and 12 Sept. 1885, W. Count. Br. Assoc.

69 *Country Brewers' Gazette*, 12 and 26 March 1884; Harrison, *Drink and Victorians*, pp. 239 – 40.

Table 4
The CBS general committee, 1863-1904:
length of representation as percentage of total years

County	1863-83 (%)	1884-1904 (%)	Rank (Before/After)
Middlesex	19.2	6	1/7
Essex	12.2	8.5	2/2
Hertfordshire	9.3	7.4	3/5
Surrey	7.5	2.5	4/15
Sussex	5.7	2.5	5/16
Berkshire	5.5	8.4	6/3
Oxfordshire	5.5	0.9	7/24
Suffolk	5.5	1.1	8/23
Huntingdonshire	5.5	0	9/26
Hampshire	4.2	8.2	10/4
Buckinghamshire	4.2	9	11/1
Cambridgeshire	4.1	3.8	12/11
Yorkshire	3.6	6.2	13/6
Northamptonshire	1.8	0.9	14/25
Scotland	1.8	0	15/27
Lancashire	1.6	2	16/18
Norfolk	1.6	4.7	17/9
Kent	1.2	4.1	18/10
Dorsetshire	0	4.9	-/8
Gloucestershire	0	3.3	-/12
London	0	2.8	-/13
Wales	0	2.7	-/14
Bedfordshire	0	2.2	-/17
Nottinghamshire	0	2	-/19
Staffordshire	0	1.9	-/20
Northumberland	0	1.6	-/21
Durham	0	1.4	-/22
Other	0	1.0	—

Sources: Compiled from CBS Minute Books; *Country Brewers' Gazette.*

county is expressed in terms of a percentage of the total, two consecutive twenty-one year periods can be compared.[70] Generally, the further brewers lived from London, the less time they spent on the committee. Before 1883 those from East Anglia and the home counties, especially from Middlesex and Essex, predominated, controlling nearly two-thirds of the unreformed committee, whereas two decades later this proportion had declined sharply to about one-third (see table 4).[71] Five other counties (Berkshire, Buckinghamshire, Dorsetshire, Gloucestershire and Hampshire) collectively doubled their percentage, holding over a third of the committee seats.[72] Wales, Scotland and the Midlands, on the other hand, remained largely unrepresented, as did prominent Burton, London, Lancashire and Yorkshire brewers. Thus, the Country Brewers' Society, despite being reorganized, was still very far from establishing itself as the voice of provincial brewers.

Equally important changes occurred in the CBS's finances. According to the 1883 annual report (the sole source of information about finances prior to reorganization), 316 members contributed £381. By 1890, almost twice as many members were subscribing five times as much.[73] Nonetheless, the CBS was not benefitting from the immense wealth of some members. On its general committee were twelve brewers who left average estates of nearly £300,000 before 1900 (see table 5). Inadequate funding, therefore, was due not to few members, but to too few

[70] There were 3 categories of membership on the general committee: representatives of the society elected at the annual meetings; delegates from county brewers' associations; and (after 1884) former chairmen who became vice presidents with seats on the committee (CBS Min. Bk. 4, 26 Oct. 1884). I have benefited from suggestions in Howard LeRoy Malchow's 'Victorian Pressure Groups: Directions for Research', *Albion*, 5 (1973), 108 – 15.

[71] Essex, Kent, Middlesex, Surrey and Sussex are considered home counties, while Cambridgeshire, Bedfordshire, Huntingdonshire, Norfolk and Suffolk are included in East Anglia.

[72] Basil Crapster has contended that 'increased membership did not alter the geographic or economic composition of the [Country Brewers'] Society'. Without membership lists this point can not be proved. But the shift in representation on the general committee suggests that the composition did in fact change (Basil Long Crapster, ' "Our Trade, Our Politics": A Study of the Political Activity of the British Liquor Industry, 1868 – 1914' (Harvard Univ. Ph.D. dissertation, 1949), p. 180).

[73] CBS Annual Reports, 1884 and 1891. The CBS's 614 members represented one-third of all brewers producing 1,000 or more barrels annually in 1890 (Percy Charles Morgan, *Handbook of Statistics and Miscellaneous Information Relating to the Trade in Alcoholic Liquors* (1892), p. 16).

Table 5
Gross estates of CBS general committee members deceased before 1900

Member	Gross Estate (£)
Samuel Blake (d. 1897)	245,800
Col. J. W. Cameron (d. 1897)	336,300
Charles Christie (d. 1898)	457,100
Erza Hammond (d. 1894)	209,500
William Hodgson (d. 1892)	104,700
Sir Edmund K. Lacon (d. 1888)	399,600
Charles Matthews (d. 1891)	163,900
Pickering Phipps (d. 1890)	425,200
Henry Smith (d. 1888)	189,500
Donald Stewart (d. 1898)	107,200
William C. Tamplin (d. 1893)	206,200
William Worthington (d. 1894)	611,700

Sources: Compiled from wills published in the *Country Brewers' Gazette, Brewing Trade Review* and *Brewers' Guardian.*

giving generously. Surviving financial records (the best indicator of what provincial brewers spent locally) suggest that their aggregate annual expenses reached £5,700, probably £3,800 of which came from county brewers' societies. The Hertfordshire and Yorkshire Brewers' Associations each spent annually about £150; some counties fell short of half this figure.[74]

As part of the foremost late Victorian pressure group, the CBS was curiously under-funded. Although Michael Thomas Bass, the first of Burton's brewer millionaires, boasted that 'for every £1 . . . [Alliance supporters] could put down, the Trade could down £100', the CBS's annual expenses between 1884 and 1889 were £1,880 against the UKA's £14,600. Other pressure groups

[74] Glos. Br. Assoc. Min. Bk., 1885–7; Herts. Br. Assoc. Annual Reports, 1884, 1886–8; Yorks. Br. Assoc. Annual Reports, 1880–4.

also easily outspent brewers. In repealing the Contagious Diseases Acts, two major associations expended over £3,000 per year, while the Liberation's Society figure of £9,100 in 1880 – 1 was even more impressive.[75]

London brewers, in contrast, liberally supported efforts to defend the industry, but funnelled their money into the Society rather than the Brewers' Company, donating £2,700 a year in the 1880s, and as much as £7,300 for the 1885 General Election. The Society's 4,100 members themselves contributed only nineteen per cent (less than £700 a year) of its total funds. Compared with other trade societies, London retailers spent prodigiously, three times as much as the CBS. Heavily subsidized by leading London brewers, the Society spent more than £5,700 annually, and was able to find £1,500 for an ambitious petitioning campaign to defeat Sunday closing legislation in 1880. As the most affluent trade organization in the country, the Society was unrivalled in sustaining agitation against the government to protect the brewing industry.[76]

Brewers were less interested in supporting the League, donating only £750 annually, a quarter of what they gave London publicans. Thomas Wethered blamed brewers for the fact that 'the League has often great difficulty in carrying on their work in critical periods'. Unfortunately for the League, twice as many retail members did not subscribe twice as much money: League members paid scarcely more in dues (£870) than those in the Society. For these reasons, the League spent only two-fifths as much as the Society. The League usually still outspent the CBS by about £300 annually.[77]

So long as Gladstone and his cabinet accorded greater priority to Ireland, electoral reform and foreign affairs than to prohibition, the actual amount of money raised by trade societies was less crucial than lobbying skills and national organization. The 1885 Liberal budget therefore provided an ideal means of testing the impact of the CBS's reorganization. CBS leaders thought they had eliminated the most obvious defects: members shrewdly relayed reliable rumours; country, Burton and London brewers consulted; and a network of federated county

[75] CBS Annual Reports, 1884 – 9; Dingle, *Campaign for Prohibition*, p. 192; McHugh, *Prostitution*, p. 279; Hanham, *Elections and Management*, p. 413; quoted in Russell, *Lawson*, p. 74.
[76] LVPSL Annual Reports, 1882 – 8; LPLVDL Min. Bk., 17 Apr. 1882, p. 96.
[77] LVNDL Annual Reports, 1881 – 90; *Country Brewers' Gazette*, 25 Oct. 1882.

branches finally existed to mobilize agitation. Within weeks, however, brewers were acrimoniously divided. Some, like the Brewers' Company and Burton Brewers' Association, were advocating a compromise; others, like the Manchester Brewers' Central Association, were disowning it; and still others, like the CBS, were vacillating between both policies. Little had, in fact, changed.

Although forewarned in mid-January 1885 that the forthcoming budget would probably increase the 6s 3d per barrel tax on beer, only on 3 March did the CBS inconclusively explore possible common strategy with Burton and London brewers.[78] Several weeks later at a CBS meeting, aggressive Liverpool brewers proposed asking the chancellor of the exchequer to lower the current tax as a ruse to forestall increased beer levies. The CBS executive rejected this strategy, and deterred dubious Liverpool brewers from pursuing it independently. Whatever hopes the CBS executive entertained of avoiding confrontation with the Liberal Government ended on 30 April. On that day, Hugh Childers, chancellor of the exchequer, disclosed in his budget extra duties of 1s per barrel on beer and 2s per gallon on spirits.[79]

Brewers initially displayed unaccustomed solidarity. At a meeting on 7 May in London, delegates of the three major societies, Brewers' Company, Burton Brewers' Association and Country Brewers' Society, endorsed a resolution condemning the budget, and sent MPs copies. Support from three Liberal trade MPs, maltster Thomas Earp and brewers Sir Michael A. Bass and Samuel Whitbread, underlined how far economic interests weakened political ties.[80]

Deep divisions soon replaced this new-found solidarity. Because of the budget's seemingly assured passage and the uncertain value of public agitation, the CBS approached Childers privately about a compromise limiting the tax to one year. So badly did CBS leaders misjudge the budget's widespread unpopularity that they forfeited authority to speak collectively for brewers. Manchester brewers, still unaffiliated with the CBS, seized leadership in the debate, repudiating the concession and orchestrating opposition to it both inside and outside the trade. Defying the CBS, they called a protest

[78] CBS Min. Bk. 4, 3 March 1885; CBS Beer Duty Rep. 1885, pp. 3–5.
[79] CBS Min. Bk. 4, 24 March 1885; CBS Beer Duty Rep. 1885, pp. 6–7.
[80] Brewers' Co. Min. Bk., 8 May 1885, Guildhall Lib., Ms. 5468, pp. 97–8.

meeting which fully vindicated their militant stance — implacable hostility to any tax increase. Such Liberal trade MPs as William Findlater and Thomas Earp attended, and more importantly so did representatives of the Society, Liverpool Brewers' Association and eight other CBS federated branches (four of them from northern counties). Their antipathy to the budget was succinctly expressed by one CBS member: 'They felt that they ought not to be . . . harassed out of existence'. Conflict between the CBS and its critics escalated at an interview with Childers some days later. There an embarrassed Henry Simonds, chairman of the CBS, listened while Manchester brewers bluntly contradicted his assurances of a temporary one-year tax placating brewers.[81]

Brewers now began mobilizing public opinion against the budget, not just with public meetings, but with even more combative tactics. Simonds warned Berkshire brewers that 'the Public were all against us, or neutral, and unless we enlisted their sympathy by touching their pockets they would look [on] our wrongs with indifference'. Following his advice, they raised the price of spirits, giving drinkers a foretaste of what to expect if the budget passed. Manchester brewers did likewise with beer prices.[82]

Growing pressure on the cabinet, already split over the renewal of coercive legislation in Ireland, provoked a sharp but unpublicized debate on the budget's drink taxes. Radicals like Charles Dilke and Joseph Chamberlain vehemently opposed them. Dilke was disturbed not at the amount of the tax, but at its unfair burden on the working classes, the primary consumers of beer. Eager to compromise, Childers favoured lowering the proposed spirit tax and removing the beer duty after an unspecified period, but the cabinet instead reaffirmed support for his original drink proposals. Childers did not accept this setback as final. In a letter to Gladstone testifying to the brewing industry's effective campaign, he cited widespread public hostility as proof of the need for some concession.[83]

---

[81] *Morning Advertiser*, 13 May 1885; CBS Beer Duty Rep., pp. 13 – 14; *Licensing Struggles*, pp. 115 – 18.

[82] Berks. Br. Union Min. Bk., 7 May 1885; *Licensing Struggles*, p. 119.

[83] Dilke to Gladstone, 20 Apr. 1885, Brit. Lib., W. E. Gladstone Papers, Add. Ms. 44,119, fo. 336; Childers to Gladstone, 18 May and 18 June 1885, *ibid.*, Add. Ms. 44,132, fos. 146 – 7, 166; J. L. Garvin, *The Life of Joseph Chamberlain* (1932), 1: 608, 615, 619; *Liverpool Daily Post*, 15 June 1885.

Thus Gladstone had to pacify disaffected cabinet colleagues as much as disgruntled brewers. Algernon West, chairman of the inland revenue board, now resurrecting the discarded CBS plan, offered to negotiate a settlement with brewers, rescinding the beer tax after one year. Impressed with his timely advice, Gladstone secured Childers' approval. West then drew up a memorandum, placed it before leading Burton and London brewers — Samuel Allsopp, Sir Michael Bass, Henry Bonsor, John Gretton, James Watney and Samuel Whitbread — and obtained their consent, which both parties saw as the end of the trade's agitation against the budget.[84]

This was a fatal miscalculation. The CBS, originator of this proposal as a basis for compromise, only learned of the secret settlement from press reports of a speech by Sir Michael Bass. Confident that the government could not honourably renege on the pact to repeal the tax in one year, resentful of being excluded, and uncommitted as an onlooker, the CBS promptly renounced the agreement in favour of the Manchester brewers' policy of unconditionally opposing the budget.[85] To sustain the agitation, the CBS established a special guarantee fund of £7,000, and gave the Society £400 for organizing demonstrations. The CBS also sent reports of these to MPs two days before the budget's second reading. Ironically, the cabinet had meanwhile amended the budget on the basis of West's compromise.[86]

By a vote of 264 to 252 the Commons rejected the budget on 8 June 1885. The trade interest (twenty MPs) generally split along party lines with Liberal Burton and London brewers (6) voting for and Conservative country and Burton brewers (7) against it, except for William Findlater (L) who defected. Among other MPs with drink ties, Conservatives (2) and an Irish Nationalist opposed it, while Liberals supported it (1) or abstained (2). Thus with seven votes for and eleven against the drink lobby was as disunited as brewers' organizations. Altogether the CBS spent

[84] Sir Algernon West, *Recollections 1832 to 1886* (n.d. [1908]), pp. 426–7.
[85] CBS Min. Bk. 4, 23 May 1885; *Brewing Trade Gazette*, Dec. 1885. Basil Crapster wrongly states that the CBS ratified the compromise reached by London and Burton brewers (Crapster, 'British Liquor Industry', pp. 315–16).
[86] CBS Min. Bk. 4, 27 May and 29 June 1885; CBS Beer Duty Rep. 1885, pp. 15, 20–1; Dudley W.R. Bahlman (ed.), *The Diary of Sir Edward Walter Hamilton* (Oxford, 1972), 2: 875.

over £1,200 in attacking the budget, all but £325 expended on meetings.[87]

Predictably, recriminations promptly ensued, embittering relations between brewers for many years. The Cambridgeshire Brewers' Association unanimously rebuked Liberals Sir Michael Bass and his brother, Hamar, for betraying promises to vote against what it called the 'monstrously unjust' budget. London brewers also drew harsh criticism. On the day after the budget's defeat, Henry Simonds, speaking as chairman of the CBS before London retailers, accused the Brewers' Company of treachery. In response, the latter pointedly noted that such allegations hardly promoted trade unity. This could be easily ensured, the CBS retorted, provided all brewers' associations ratified agreements with the government. Addressing country brewers at their annual banquet, Thomas Wethered, former CBS chairman and Conservative MP, continued the dispute. Since wealthier London brewers had contributed nothing to the budget's defeat, he asserted, 'country brewers are able to do without them'.[88] As Wethered's comments illustrate, the disparity in income between London and country brewers provoked much discontent. In fact, some provincial brewers thought London and Burton brewers guilty of ulterior economic motives. 'They voted for the advanced duty . . . to crush out the small country brewers', contended the chairman of the Sheffield Brewers' Association in a letter published in the CBS's *Country Brewers' Gazette*. All country brewers, he urged, should boycott those firms of brewer MPs who had approved higher beer taxes. Even in July 1887 the *Brewing Trade Review*, the CBS's recently founded newspaper, was angrily recalling the deceit with which the Brewers' Company 'took upon itself to steal a march upon the others' in the trade as an explanation for London brewers' persisting dictatorial behaviour.[89]

This legacy of mistrust effectively prevented brewers' organizations from cooperating politically, but as the 1885 Election reveals, previous changes meant that the trade had nevertheless

---

87 *Hansard*, 3rd ser., 298 (8 June 1885), cols. 1511 – 15; CBS Beer Duty Rep. 1885, pp. 25 – 40; CBS 1884 – 5 Annual Report.
88 *Country Brewers' Gazette*, 18 June, 24 Sept. and 5 Nov. 1885; CBS Min. Bk. 4, 29 June 1885.
89 *Country Brewers' Gazette*, 18 June 1885; *Brewing Trade Review*, 1 July 1887; see also *ibid.*, 1 Aug. 1888.

taken a decisive step forward in protecting itself. Overcoming the lethargy of the preceding election, the CBS was now in charge with an elaborately planned campaign arranged well over a year in advance, aided by two erstwhile foes, the League and the Society. These three associations, together with the Beer and Wine and the Northern District Leagues, established a central committee which agreed that candidates would gain support only after satisfactorily answering official test questions. To facilitate this selection process, a parliamentary committee of the League and the Society would supply retail societies with two annotated lists of candidates showing past and projected voting attitudes on key issues. Finally, district committees (brewers and retailers from local affiliated societies) would canvass voters on behalf of adopted candidates.[90]

CBS leaders also created a sub-committee devoted primarily to 'counteracting the influence of the teetotalers'. It sought to arouse public opinion and mobilize brewers and retailers against nine staunch Liberal temperance proponents by employing a Mr Hicks as an election agent at a weekly salary of £6 6s. He visited the designated constituencies, armed with propaganda and orders to hold mass meetings.[91]

Two former Liberal cabinet ministers, Sir William Harcourt (advocate of local option since 1883) and Hugh Childers (responsible for the proposed shilling tax on beer in the budget), were also singled out for special treatment. Hicks encountered problems in Derby, where Harcourt disdainfully ignored the test questions and suggested that brewers instead read his Derby declaration. The CBS retaliated, exposing his inconsistency with placards of two speeches: one, given recently, supported local option; the other, made in 1872, denounced it. Copies were sent to his constituency, but he still won.[92] Hicks, however, was more successful against Childers, who, in an extremely close contest decided by just thirty-six votes, lost the seat at Pontefract he had held for twenty-five years.

Of the eleven candidates, six lost their seats, including Sir Wilfrid Lawson whose defeat by ten votes the trade especially

90 LVPSL Parl. Reports Min. Bk., 25 June 1884, p. 17; Jt. Parl. Comt. of the Lic. Victs. of the U.K. Min. Bk., 19 Aug. 1884, Nat. Union Lic. Victs.; CBS Min. Bk. 4, 24 July 1884; *Licensed Victuallers' Guardian*, 5 Dec. 1885.
91 CBS Min. Bk. 4, 13 July, 3 Aug. and 1 Oct. 1885.
92 *Ibid.*, 12 Nov. and 10 Dec. 1885.

savoured. 'The results of the late election', the *Brewers' Guardian* rejoiced, 'are . . . satisfactory when we consider the fate that has befallen several members of the last House of Commons who were conspicuous for their manifest hostility to our trade'.[93]

The trade mostly sponsored Conservative candidates, except for the few who approved of local veto. In all but five of thirty-four contests in London, Gloucestershire and Hertfordshire, for example, brewers and retailers endorsed Conservatives. No Liberal contesting seats in Hampshire, Cambridgeshire, Berkshire or Northamptonshire received trade support.[94] Impressed with this marshalling of strength, Conservative candidates sometimes appealed for assistance: Conservative chief whip Akers-Douglas asked London retailers to help Rowland Winn, Childer's opponent; and Sir William Wheelhouse apparently received £100 unofficially from the CBS to contest Herbert Gladstone's seat.[95]

This election demonstrated the usefulness of county organization. Typical was the Northamptonshire Brewers' Association. After ascertaining each candidate's views on the test questions and sponsoring Conservatives, it sent a list of those recommended to the 1,700 county licence holders and secretaries of trade societies in adjacent counties. Some affiliated branches conducted independent campaigns, but the CBS had to step in to assist with the requisite organization in nineteen counties. The CBS spent almost £1,000 on the election: over half went to county unions and agents, £97 towards printing costs and £129 to Hicks (the special agent). He had proved so successful that the CBS re-appointed him as its first full-time electoral agent — thirteen years after the UKA had hired theirs.[96]

After the election, the CBS asserted control over defence of the trade in the provinces. For over a year, CBS leaders attacked the League for misusing brewers' funds, for stealing credit for

---

93 *Brewers' Guardian*, 15 Dec. 1885. But the return of Lawson's opponent, an advocate of local option, scarcely represented a trade victory (Dingle, *Campaign for Prohibition*, pp. 95 – 6).
94 *Country Brewers' Gazette*, 24 Sept. and 5 Nov. 1885; Berks. Br. Union Min. Bk., 12 Sept. 1885; Northants. Br. Assoc. Min. Bk., 19 Nov. 1885, Northants. R.O., SL 298; *Morning Advertiser*, 25 Nov. 1885; Herts. Br. Assoc. 3rd Annual Report, p. 6; Glos. Br. Assoc. Min. Bk., 18 Sept., 10 and 14 Oct. 1885.
95 LVPSL Parl. Reports Min. Bk., 21 Sept. 1885, p. 51; CBS Min. Bk. 4, 12 Nov. 1885.
96 Northants. Br. Assoc. Min. Bk., 19 Nov. 1885, SL 298; CBS Min. Bk. 4, 10 Dec. 1885 and 16 June 1886; CBS 1885 – 6 Annual Report; Hamer, *Electoral Pressure*, pp. 183 – 4.

what London retailers had achieved and for denying its own federated societies financial support. As the criticism became more strident and demands for economy more frequent, the League, while strenuously refuting the charges, endeavoured to appease country brewers, selling its newspaper, the *Licensed Victuallers' Guardian*, early in 1887. When this failed, League officials eventually conceded defeat. Once a CBS advisory committee had investigated League finances, they agreed to reduce travelling expenses and relocate their Birmingham headquarters in London. In 1890 the League went further, amalgamating with the London and Provincial Licensed Victuallers' Defence League as a means of promoting retail unity. It was through this dispute that the CBS became the dominant force in provincial defence.[97]

For the brewing trade, the 1880s were years in which retailers resolved their debilitating differences, and the Country Brewers' Society adopted a new constitution, acquired new members and assumed a new defensive role. County associations greatly extended the industry's political power; they performed a function recognized as important in modern pressure groups. As one political scientist concludes, 'groups which can ensure that their questions are asked by local members or branches secure a better response [from candidates] than other groups'.[98] Yet these advances can be exaggerated; the brewing industry reacted slowly and half-heartedly when threatened by prohibition and higher taxation. In addition, the three major brewers' societies, interested not in collective but in individual goals, relinquished none of their autonomy, weakening both the industry's lobbying of the government and appeals for additional funds. Only a devastating defeat, revealing these shortcomings, would promote greater unity.

[97] Lic. Vic. Jt. Parl. Comt. Min. Bk., 3 June 1890. This quarrel can be followed in the *Brewing Trade Review*: 1 Nov. 1886, 1 Jan. – 1 June 1887, 1 Jan. 1889, and 1 June 1890; *Country Brewers' Gazette*, 28 Jan. 1886.
[98] J. D. Stewart, *British Pressure Groups: Their Role in Relation to the House of Commons* (Oxford, 1958), pp. 231 – 3.

4

The Pub Preserved

By the mid-1880s provincial brewers, federated with the Country Brewers' Society in county associations, more effectively lobbied magistrates, MPs and the government. Yet neither these bodies, nor regional organizations like the Brewers' Company or Country Brewers' Society could formulate policy for the entire industry. National markets and the Liberal views of Bass, Whitbread and Truman, three of the country's largest firms, aggravated economic and political rivalry, dividing Burton, London and provincial brewers as sharply as retailers a decade earlier. Brewers would not acknowledge the serious liability of independent organizations, with their own policies, priorities and prejudices until the Conservative Government withdrew a compensation plan in 1888. Moving cautiously towards centralized authority, disgruntled brewers as well as distillers established the National Trade Defence Fund. Two subsequent developments, the UKA's successful wooing of Liberal Unionist voters and the failed 1890 compensation scheme, convinced brewers that Conservatives regarded temperance reformers as politically more influential than the brewing industry. In response, brewers emulated their antagonists, enlarging the Fund with a far-reaching and costly electoral scheme which welded brewers and retailers into 'the trade'. From this change would come political power so formidable that the campaign for prohibition was not just defeated, but wholly discredited.

Denied an overall parliamentary majority after the 1886 Election, Lord Salisbury's Conservative party needed support from the seventy-eight Liberal Unionists, former Liberal politicians who rejected Gladstonian home rule. A Conservative government opposed to home rule served as the basis of unity. Conservative pro-trade licensing proposals, however, might endanger this tenuous alliance because many Liberal Unionists, though vocal opponents of a subordinate Irish Parliament, were still committed to temperance. In 1888 a Sunday closing bill, for example, attracted ninety-three per cent of the Liberal Unionists, almost equalling the proportion of favourable Liberals, but only sixteen per cent of the Conservatives.[1] Whether the pro-temperance MPs — thirty-forty Liberal Unionists and about thirty Conservatives — would vote with the Liberal opposition or abstain when the government sought to end the licensing controversy was unclear, but their decision would ultimately decide the outcome.

Liberal Unionists with prohibitionist convictions thus had enormous strategic importance, but posed immense tactical difficulties for the UKA. Former Liberal W. S. Caine typified their priorities in supporting Conservatives as anti-home rule candidates regardless of their temperance views at the 1886 Election. By remaining closely identified with Liberals, the UKA could never win over independent Liberal Unionist temperance voters, who feared being used as dupes in the larger struggle over home rule. To allay this suspicion, early in 1887 the UKA replaced its Liberal alliance with a policy of neutrality, forming district veto societies in each constituency, and then two years later forbidding its agents to hold political offices. Since the trade made no comparable effort, this approach alarmed Conservative candidates who soon became as ardent as Liberal rivals in espousing temperance.[2]

Amid the struggle for Liberal Unionist votes, C. T. Ritchie, president of the local government board, in March 1888 proposed a bill in which newly created county councils would administer and have authority to eliminate superfluous licences. Those so dispossessed would get compensation (the disparity in value between the house when licensed and unlicensed) from a fund of £300,000 supplied not by government general revenue, but by a twenty per cent increase in licence duties. Localities could accelerate the rate of reduction with ratepayers' money. Magistrates would lose their traditional control over licences, but still hear licensing offences, impose penalties and revoke licences for misconduct.[3]

---

[1] *Hansard*, 3rd ser., 332 (14 Dec. 1888), cols. 336 – 8.

[2] Hamer, *Electoral Pressure*, pp. 243 – 5, 256 – 60; Dingle, *Campaign for Prohibition*, pp. 99 – 103.

[3] J. R. Greenway, 'The Local Option Question and British Politics, 1864 – 1914' (Univ. Leeds Ph.D. dissertation, 1974), pp. 241 – 2; Dingle, *Campaign for Prohibition*, pp. 108 – 9.

These moderate provisions, far less sweeping than Bruce's abortive bill of 1872, deeply divided the trade. Manchester brewers denounced the measure as 'unjust and dangerous', and received support from two independent trade newspapers, the *Country Brewers' Gazette* (bitter at being discarded as the CBS's official paper) as well as the *Brewers' Guardian*. The CBS and the Brewers' Company, in contrast, though wanting amendments, expressed approval.[4] Retail societies likewise cautiously endorsed the measure, but this was overshadowed by unrealistic demands. The League and the Society strenuously opposed both the possible closing of pubs on Sundays by councils and higher licence fees, whereas off-licence holders wanted exemptions from council control but compensation for forfeiting their licences. In rebuking off-licence holders, the *Gazette* betrayed both the pervasive bias against them and the trade's disunity. Indecisive brewers and retailers, implacable temperance hostility and the threatened defection of Liberal Unionists, crucial for Salisbury's parliamentary majority, all weakened the cabinet's resolve, leading to the abrupt withdrawal of the clauses before being put to a vote.[5]

Brewers saw this unexpected setback as an indictment of their methods of defence. The *Brewers' Guardian* thought the industry 'sadly deficient in organisation'. Another independent newspaper, the *Brewers' Journal*, instead attributed defeat to the fact that 'the brewing trade . . . has no organization which fully and completely represents it', and as a remedy urged the establishment of one encompassing association. Some brewers, despairing of any concerted action, registered protest with the dramatic step of resigning from their societies. Mounting pressure for reform prompted a defensive editorial in the *Brewing Trade Review*, the CBS's newspaper, showing that most brewers had come to accept the need for stronger organization.[6] Once this consensus had formed, the CBS reacted decisively. Its

---

4   CBS Min. Bk. 4, 22 March and 10 Apr. 1888; Br. Co. Min. Bk., 10 Apr. 1888, Ms. 5468, pp. 182 – 3; *Country Brewers' Gazette*, 4 Nov. 1886 and 3 May 1888; *Brewers' Guardian*, 29 May 1888 and 19 Feb. 1889; *Brewing Trade Review*, 1 Apr. 1888.
5   Lic. Victs. Jt. Parl. Comt. Min. Bk., 4 and 9 Apr. 1888; *Country Brewers' Gazette*, 3 May 1888; Greenway, 'Local Option', pp. 242 – 9; Dingle, *Campaign for Prohibition*, pp. 110 – 24; Shiman, *Crusade Against Drink*, pp. 215 – 16.
6   *Brewers' Journal*, 15 July 1888; *Brewers' Guardian*, 24 July 1888; *Brewing Trade Review*, 1 July 1888.

secretary, John Danvers Power, took the initiative in seeking the support of all brewers for a truly comprehensive committee aimed at vigorously protecting the trade.[7]

Early in August 1888, twenty-two influential trade representatives, all but two of them Liberals, held talks on trade defence, and appointed a committee, composed largely of London and country brewers, to consider Power's proposal. Not surprisingly, their report found trade defence inadequate. Retailers, it stated, through their joint parliamentary committee organized impressive campaigns, but only intermittently opposed temperance agitation. Brewers lacked not organization, but money, unity and solidarity. London and provincial brewers on the committee insisted that neither the Brewers' Company nor the Country Brewers' Society could alone underwrite the cost of protecting the industry. Money was certainly an issue, but for reasons quite different from those given in the report. The trade required a separate, representative association, not because major societies were impoverished, but because organizational problems prevented their fully mobilizing the industry's financial resources. As the recent debacle over the County Councils bill painfully revealed, moreover, the trade had more serious shortcomings than limited resources. Manchester brewers, credited with having 'a well organized Society', were not specifically blamed, but the report pointedly noted that they were 'unfortunately seldom in agreement with other sections of the Brewing Trade'. Burton brewers displayed the third fault, sectionalism. They did not even warrant comment, a tacit endorsement of what the *Brewers' Guardian* had scathingly said some weeks earlier: 'They have a kind of informal organisation, but they rarely move, and then only in defence of their particular branch of the trade'.[8]

---

7   Br. Co. Min. Bk., 12 July 1888, Ms. 5468, p. 206; see also *Brewing Trade Review*, 1 Feb. 1896 and 1 Dec. 1913. Power's role in initiating this plan is clear, but that of Henry Bonsor, wealthy London brewer and distinguished member of the Brewers' Company is not. Years later Bonsor himself disavowed any responsibility, and instead credited Power with the original plan. Yet on several occasions, Powell and others acknowledged his contribution, indicating that he also deserves recognition (*Brewing Trade Review*, 1 Dec. 1895; Bonsor's obituary, NTDA 1929 Report, p. 16). Despite one historian's claim, there is no evidence that Lord Burton helped establish the Fund (Bristol, 'LPDL', p. 782).

8   NTDA Min. Bk. 1, 1 and 7 Aug. 1888, B.S, pp. 2, 6; *Brewers' Guardian*, 24 July 1888.

This cleverly orchestrated presentation duly induced brewers to reach the proper conclusion, the urgency of founding a new organization — the National Trade Defence Fund. Its name aptly denoted the Fund's unprecedented scope, purpose and financial nature. A general committee of ten brewers and two distillers,[9] appointed for at least three years, managed finances and set policy, but not in a democratic fashion. With the brewers drawn from only the Brewers' Company, Country Brewers' Society and Burton Brewers' Association, three organizations which collectively represented roughly one-third of all big firms (over 1,000 barrels annually), it scarcely embodied a cross-section of the industry.[10] In fact, as the *Brewers' Guardian* remarked, the committee was the '*elite* of our trade'. By 1900, nine of the huge breweries initially dominating the Fund had become public companies, with shareholdings over £42 million! Its constitution also ensured control by a coterie of firms. Minimum subscriptions of £20 and the rule linking a firm's number of votes at general meetings with the amount subscribed gave wealthy brewers undue influence. This transparent attempt to stack the committee and manipulate its procedures disturbed independent trade papers. The *Brewers' Guardian* foresaw that excessive subscription rates and exclusion of both Manchester and northern brewers meant that the Fund 'will not be supported by the rank and file of the trade who . . . are its real backbone'.[11] Despite the 2,000 and more substantial brewers in the United Kingdom, just sixty-eight donated £3,900 in 1888 – 9, with twenty breweries (most from London) contributing over two-thirds. Deprived of seats on the general committee, northern brewers in Lancashire, Yorkshire, Durham and

[9] The 12 members were: Baron Burton (Bass, Ratcliff & Gretton); Baron Hindlip (Samuel Allsopp & Sons); Edward Helme (Ind Coope & Co.); Henry Bonsor (Combe & Co.), MP; Edward Courage (Courage & Co.); Robert Barclay (Barclay, Perkins & Co.); George Croft (Charrington & Co.); James Agg-Gardner (Cheltenham Original Brewery Co.), MP; Henry Simonds (H. & G. Simonds); James Wigan (Hawkes & Co.); Frederick Hunt (Seager, Evans & Co.), MP; and William Nicholson (J. & W. Nicholson & Co.). Hunt and Nicholson were distillers (*Brewers' Guardian*, 11 Dec. 1888).
[10] Of the 2,014 brewers who brewed 1,000 or more barrels in 1890, 614 belonged to the CBS, 16 to the Burton Brewers' Association and 12 to the Brewers' Company (CBS 1890 Annual Report; B.S. Candidates for Elections, B.S.; Br. Co. Min. Bk., Br. Co.; Wilson, *Alcohol and Nation*, p. 49).
[11] Compiled from T. Skinner, *The Stock Exchange Year-Book and Diary for 1900*; *Brewers' Guardian*, 11 Dec. 1888; NTDA Min. Bk. 1, 7 Aug. 1888, pp. 7 – 9.

Northumberland denied the Fund money, giving only £180 or five per cent.[12]

The Fund's purpose was to arouse public opinion, not to promote unity in Parliament. Brewers, beset with uncontested temperance attacks in newspapers and at public meetings, felt the public had turned against them. To preserve an open-minded attitude, the trade's case had to be put to the public with the same unremitting zeal as its opponents'. Accordingly, the Fund employed speakers for addressing temperance meetings, and writers for refuting hostile letters in the press. The creators of the Fund anticipated hiring a staff comparable to the fifteen or more full- and part-time lecturers engaged by the UKA from the 1870s. Yet, in excluding all divisive subjects from its agenda, brewers paradoxically formed an organization incapable of eliminating the disunity which had originally inspired demands for change. 'The moment they [brewers] cease to agree . . . operations in respect of the particular question cease', the CBS noted.[13]

It was the outcome of another scheme of licensing reduction, also sponsored by Conservatives, that extended the Fund's scope. Unlike the first compensation proposal, however, this one in 1890 seemed assured of success: brewers gave solid support, an experienced parliamentarian lent guidance and its provisions were uncomplicated. Avoiding the contentious division of magistrates' authority, the scheme simply empowered county councils to compensate brewers and retailers for forfeited licences. George Goschen, chancellor of the exchequer and supervisor of the bill, also raised compensation funds somewhat differently, using the 3d per barrel duty levied on beer in 1889 together with a new 6d per gallon tax on spirits. Of

12 No balance sheets for the Fund exist, but gross expenditure and revenue can be calculated for the years 1888 – 95 from the Cash Book at the B.S. These figures exclude money donated by county brewers' organizations, which accounted for an additional £532. Northern brewers' associations subscribed £150 (28%). Of the Fund's total receipts (£4,432), northern brewers thus accounted for just 7.4% (£330). The impact of alienated brewers on the trade's parliamentary lobby is discussed in David W. Gutzke's 'Rhetoric and Reality: The Political Influence of British Brewers, 1832 – 1914', *Parl. Hist.* (forthcoming).

13 *Brewing Trade Review*, 1 Aug. and 1 Sept. 1888; CBS Min. Bk. 4, 22 Oct. 1888; Anthony Edward Dingle, 'The Agitation for Prohibition in England, 1871 – 95' (Monash Univ. Ph.D. dissertation, 1974), p. 474.

the projected £1,304,000 receipts, only £350,000 was set aside for buying licences. As in Ritchie's proposal, councils might accelerate reduction, but could borrow no more than three times the stipulated grant annually. But the 1890 measure did include the novel idea of virtually banning new licences.[14]

Salisbury's cabinet was still rather apprehensive of defeat. W. H. Smith, then Conservative Commons leader, whose relative (John Danvers Power) probably relayed the antipathy of the CBS and publicans generally to compensation drawn from drink taxes, claimed that 'the Trade desire at all risks to be let alone'. He expressed concern about antagonizing it, but Salisbury disagreed: 'Past experience lends no support to this fear'. Both the prime minister and Goschen felt one aspect of the scheme would effectively neutralize trade opposition. However much brewers and retailers wanted the drink duties repealed and disliked the source of compensation, the prohibition of new licences, both argued, would 'detach a considerable portion of the trade', particularly publicans whose licences would rise in value.[15]

Smith's misgivings soon proved unfounded. After Goschen disclosed the bill's contents, the CBS and Brewers' Company endorsed it, and the Fund, fulfilling Bonsor's pledge to the chancellor that it 'would spare neither energy nor expense in assisting the government', quickly voted £2,000 for enlisting public approval. Even trade newspapers like the *Brewers' Journal* regarded the bill as unobjectionable.[16] Notwithstanding this support, intense temperance pressure, especially on pivotal Liberal Unionist MPs, forced the measure to be abandoned. The trade became irate several weeks later when the government, forbidden by the Speaker to create an interim compensation

---

[14] Greenway, 'Local Option', pp. 252 – 4; Dingle, *Campaign for Prohibition*, p. 124.

[15] The following are in the Salisbury Papers: Salisbury to Goschen (cypher), 12 Apr. 1890, E/77/200; Goschen to Smith (enclosure), 9 Apr. 1890, E/77/199; Goschen's Budget Memorandum, 10 Apr. 1890, E/77/202; Smith to Goschen (enclosure), 9 Apr. 1890, E/77/198; see also Greenway, 'Local Option', p. 255.

[16] CBS Min. Bk. 5, 9 May 1890; Br. Co. Min. Bk., 20 May 1890, Ms. 5468, p. 259; NTDA Min. Bk. 1, B.S, 19 May 1890, p. 35; *Brewers' Journal*, 15 May and 15 June 1890.

fund, instead used the earmarked taxes (popularly called the whisky money) for technical education.[17]

Brewers construed this second defeat as proof of a general Conservative belief that they had less political influence than temperance reformers. Many Unionists, avowed the CBS's *Brewing Trade Review*, had decided 'it is better to bid boldly for the teetotallers' support and to throw over the Trade'. Privately, brewers were even more critical. One Northamptonshire brewer recommended that brewers 'look after Conservative Members & candidates, as . . . they were dallying with the teetotalers'. Attacks on Conservatives naturally fostered pressure for greater organization, the most practical means of safeguarding trade interests against another betrayal if temperance activists orchestrated public hostility. Better funded and more organized brewers, asserted the Northamptonshire brewer, could ' "keep their friends straight" '.[18] Although the *Brewers' Journal* and other trade newspapers agreed, some brewers still procrastinated until rebuked sternly. John Danvers Power accused some Midland brewers of making 'very clever and very earnest after-dinner speeches, when the stereotyped expressions were that they must stand "shoulder to shoulder" and must be "up & doing", but they did not seem to trouble to put their words into action'.[19]

'Let us copy the enemy, and we won't go far wrong', advised the *Brewer and Publican*, aptly describing how brewers proposed to counter their foes. Late in 1890 the trade commenced a policy of neutrality, withholding support from unreliable Liberal Unionist and Conservative candidates as a means of demonstrating its decisive votes. In January 1891 at the Hartlepool by-election, where the Liberal Unionist candidate, Sir William Gray, accepted the anti-drink programme — local option, Sunday closing, shorter licensing hours and no compensation — and his Liberal rival did likewise, temperance organizers

---

[17] The trade wanted the entire amount, not just the compensation levy, refunded (*Brewing Trade Review*, 1 Aug. 1890; LVNDL Min. Bk., 17 March 1891, Nat. Union Lic. Victs.). For temperance activities, see Greenway, 'Local Option', pp. 256–9; Dingle, *Campaign for Prohibition*, pp. 126–7; Shiman, *Crusade Against Drink*, pp. 216–17.

[18] Northants. Br. Assoc. Min. Bk., 29 Jan. and 21 Apr. 1891, SL 298; *Brewing Trade Review*, 1 Feb. and 1 March 1891.

[19] Northants. Br. Assoc. Min. Bk., 29 Jan. 1891, SL 298; *Brewers' Journal*, 15 Aug. 1890.

declared neutrality. Retaliating against Gray's bid for temperance voters, trade societies refused him support, costing him victory in a closely fought contest decided by 300 votes.[20] Similarly, in the adjacent county of Lancashire, brewers threatened F. Bridgeman (C), one of the notorious seventeen Unionists who opposed the 1890 compensation scheme, with trade abstention unless he altered his stance. Impressed with the assertion that Bolton's 600 retailers could deliver 2,000 voters at the next election, he capitulated and approved compensation. Four further Unionist MPs, F. S. Cornwallis (LU), Baron De Rothschild (LU), J. R. Kelley (C) and W. H. Hornby (C), also succumbed to local pressure, recanting their anti-compensation views and pledging resistance to what one called 'any measure of spoliation or confiscation'.[21] Eleven other MPs could not be so influenced, as they retired, became Liberals, succeeded to the peerage, or stood unopposed or for seats outside the Fund's control in Ireland or Scotland.

Whether the trade should, like the UKA, go beyond these preliminary steps and become entirely neutral, was more controversial. At the June meeting of the CBS, Henry Riley-Smith moved a resolution, already sanctioned by Yorkshire brewers and reminiscent of UKA tactics, urging brewers to resign from all political societies as an indication of impartiality. The *Brewing Trade Review* backed him, enjoining brewers to stop being 'slaves . . . of any one party'. Despite these sentiments, the committee rejected the motion and resisted a proposed compromise that brewers only withdraw from political organizations in which candidates supported unfavourable legislation. Clearly brewers were ambivalent, fearing the UKA's increased political power, but unwilling to antagonize their Unionist allies.[22]

Debate on this motion emphasized that brewers strongly disagreed, not on the need for reform but on its extent. Since the

20 *Brewing Trade Review*, 1 Feb. 1891; Hamer, *Electoral Pressure*, p. 260; *Brewer and Publican*, 21 Nov. 1890.
21 *Brewers' Journal*, 15 May 1891; *Bolton Chronicle*, 25 June 1892; *Kent County Standard*, 24 June 1892; *Bucks Herald*, 9 July 1892; *Morning Advertiser*, 18 June 1892.
22 CBS Min. Bk. 5, 1 June 1891; *Brewing Trade Review*, 1 May and 1 June 1891. Brewers like Thomas Wethered pledged to abstain if Conservative candidates did not promise adequate compensation (Wethered to Bright (sec. of the Middlesex Conservative Assoc.), *Northern Brewers' and Victuallers' Journal*, 30 May 1891).

Fund's inception, an influential but unrepresentative clique, situated in Staffordshire and the southeast, had monopolized control: big London breweries which dominated the Brewers' Company, leading provincial ones which directed the CBS, and huge Burton firms organized on an *ad hoc* basis. They sought to extend the Fund by imitating UKA organization. In advancing a conservative, limited and temporary plan, they preserved the Fund's structure and so perpetuated their position as an oligarchy. There were two chief features to their proposal: professional electoral agents and a guarantee fund. English and Welsh counties were divided into ten districts, each with its own agent, his salary and expenses paid jointly by the London office and local brewers. With the expenses of each district estimated at £500, the total outlay involved would be £5,000. The plan's second feature, a £25,000 general election fund, was collected voluntarily from brewers on the basis of 10s per tied house. Even for large breweries this was not financially onerous; of the seventy-six firms owning 100 or more tied houses, each would on average donate £83.[23]

This plan immediately provoked vehement opposition. A fierce but largely unpublicized struggle ensued between the traditional leaders and a coalition of northern and midland brewers, particularly in Lancashire, Warwickshire and Northamptonshire, because the reforms required cooperation from groups previously denied weight on the committees of the Fund and CBS. Vigorously contesting the official scheme, these well-organized but neglected outsiders now challenged the elite's power and authority. They espoused a more ambitious, comprehensive and egalitarian approach, committing the Fund to a permanent scheme far more imaginative and expensive than envisaged by the Fund's oligarchy or implemented by prohibitionists.

Four key issues caused discord. First was the sensitive question of money. 'Those who had assisted in providing these funds [for the Fund]', the *Brewers' Journal* recollected, 'were somewhat jealous as to who should administer them'. Officials of the Fund demanded that brewers have sole control, whereas their critics insisted on a meaningful role for retailers. Second was the Fund's elitist constitution. Midland brewers especially

23 NTDA Min. Bk. 1, 31 Oct. 1890, pp. 36–7; Fund Circular, *Northern Brewers' and Victuallers' Journal*, 10 Jan. 1891; *Brewing Trade Review*, 1 Dec. 1890 and 1 Jan. 1891; Baxter, 'Brewing Industry', pp. 219–20.

championed a Fund with a more democratic general committee, representing not just local brewers, but retailers, hop merchants, maltsters, allied traders and investors. Leading Fund spokesmen abhorred this concept, the *Brewing Trade Review* and Power pointedly denigrating it as 'extreme' and 'ill-considered'.[24] Two other questions dealt with enlarging the electoral scheme's scope. Dissidents advocated an elaborate plan, with divisional committees formed in each parliamentary constituency by local brewers and retailers. Fund leaders deemed this impractical and premature. Finally, midland and northern brewers wanted permanent agents, though the Fund's underwriters had promised subsidies only until the election. The Fund's chief contributors argued that district agencies would find their agents indispensable, and so defray the entire cost of £500 themselves. Addressing brewers in the southwestern district, Power tactlessly clarified this point: 'If they chose to keep the agent on after that [next election], that was their affair'.[25]

Midland and northern brewers incorporated their ideas in a new separate society, the General Association of the Licensed Trade. CBS leaders expected it to follow the customary practice of linking a new body with the CBS and Fund by appointing the same secretary, but delegates instead selected an unknown outsider, George Croxden Powell. The General Association was also seen as subversive in adopting a democratic committee, forty delegates drawn from all districts who easily outvoted the four Fund representatives. Dismayed CBS leaders reiterated the transitory and restricted purpose of the General Association, which they privately resolved would be short-lived. As the *Brewers' Guardian* recalled: 'Certain people, whose personal ambitions were interfered with by the establishment of the General Association, . . . determined at the outset to wreck [it] . . . at all hazards. They first directed their intrigues against the

24 *Brewers' Journal*, 15 Nov. 1891 and 15 Feb. 1892; *Brewing Trade Review*, 1 Dec. 1891; Power's speech on 13 March 1891, Northumberland and Durham Br. Assoc. 1891 Annual Report, B.S., p. 11.
25 Power's speech, *Brewing Trade Review*, 1 March 1891; *ibid.*, 1 Dec. 1891; Northumberland and Durham Br. Assoc. 1891 Annual Report, p. 12; Glos. Br. Assoc. 1891 Annual Report, p. 6; *The General Association of the Licensed Trade: Object, Constitution, and Work* (n.d. [1891?]), pp. 5–6.

secretary [Powell], and then against the whole fabric of the Association, and ultimately succeeded in getting rid of both'.[26]

The General Association was thus destroyed within five months of its founding: the Fund would not supplement the depleted £3,000 grant for expenses. When the General Association's deficit reached £615 in November, defenders of the original scheme reasserted authority over their more enterprising but now insolvent colleagues.[27] 'This association was before its time', the CBS's *Brewing Trade Review* promptly gloated. On 6 November Reginald Mortimer, Power's successor as CBS secretary and Fund manager, formally resumed control of the electoral scheme; the Fund disbanded divisional committees. While its general committee still excluded trades ancillary to the brewing industry, the Fund did as a result of this dispute concede several principles upheld by midland and northern brewers. It guaranteed support for agents beyond the election, made the scheme permanent and reorganized its committee, which now consisted of ten Fund subscribers and forty-four district delegates, including as many as eleven retailers.[28]

The Fund's subsequent power derived primarily from one change, the handful of full-time, salaried agents appointed in 1891. What little is known about some of the forty or more men who served the Fund before 1914 suggests knowledge of the trade was only one of several factors in their recruitment. Publicans like W. R. Foord and J. S. Brown or secretaries of local retail societies like Arthur James Harris were obvious candidates. Legal training was also a definite asset, given the highly technical rules of electioneering, so solicitors like Archibald S. Bennett and John J. Dunne probably represented a much larger group. Individuals with writing skills were attractive because they could do double duty as newspapermen for trade periodicals. E. Lawrence Levy, former editor of the *Birmingham Daily Times*, thus gathered material on one day as an agent and published it another as editor in the *Licensed Trade News*. Others, for example, John Massey, with a background in manufacturing boots and shoes and in lay preaching, were hired for their

26 *Brewing Trade Review*, 1 June, 1 July and 1 Dec. 1891; *General Association*, p. 4; *Brewers' Guardian*, 1 March 1892.
27 NTDA Min. Bk. 1, 25 June, 16 Oct. and 6 Nov. 1891 and 29 Jan. 1892, pp. 52, 58, 60, 72.
28 *Ibid.*, 6 Nov. 1891, pp. 59 – 61; *Brewing Trade Review*, 1 Dec. 1891. The extra delegates came from London, which had been added as the eleventh district.

robust constitution, not their background.[29] Harris underlined this trait's importance in describing his strenuous duties during the 1907 Licensing bill crisis.

> After being busily engaged here [at the office] all day, I have frequently to go to evening meetings, dinners of Associations, teetotal meetings etc. in all parts of the District and the strain, at times, is very great. Last week for instance I did not reach home on any night until 11 o'clock, and on one morning it was 1 o'clock.

His work took him throughout the four counties of Gloucestershire, Somersetshire, Wiltshire and Berkshire.[30] In exchange for this dedicated service, agents received good salaries of £250 – £300, substantially higher than the average earnings of £80 in the Edwardian period, even outranking such groups as foremen, clerks and skilled manual labourers. Agents were better paid than their counterparts in the UKA, and at least as well-off as the travelling agents hired by the National Association for Repeal of the Contagious Diseases Acts in the 1870s. Outstanding efforts, furthermore, merited special bonuses. Following the 1900 General Election, for instance, local brewers and retail societies gave Harris £150.[31]

Agents performed widely ranging functions. Beside those already noted by Harris, they organized petitions, distributed literature, refuted allegations in the press, registered qualified brewers and retailers as voters, arranged transport to the polls,

---

[29] (Brown) NTDA Mid. Dist. Min. Bk., 18 Dec. 1891, Staffs. R.O., D 3163/2/1/1, pp. 47 – 8; (Foord) *Evid. Royal Com. Liq. Licensing Laws*, 1897, 34 (Cmnd. 8523), p. 412. Obituaries: *Licensed Trade News*, (Massey) 22 June 1906; (Bennett) 1 Aug. 1931; (Dunne) 30 Dec. 1899; (Levy) 21 May 1932; (Harris) Glos. Br. Assoc. 1957 Annual Report.

[30] Dist. Agent's Report, NTDA W. Dist. Min. Bk., 6 Feb. 1907, W. Count. Br. Assoc., p. 37a; see also NTDF N. Dist. Min. Bk., 28 Aug. 1895, N.E. Br. Assoc.

[31] Jt. Wholesale and Retail Parl. Comt. Min. Bk., 30 July 1894, Nat. Union Lic. Victs., p. 41; Northumberland and Durham Br. Assoc. Min. Bk., 19 Jan. 1891 and 29 July 1898, N.E. Br. Assoc.; Paul Thompson, *The Edwardians: The Remaking of British Society* (St Albans, 1977), pp. 23 – 4; Dingle, *Campaign for Prohibition*, p. 186; McHugh, *Prostitution*, p. 73; NTDA W. Dist. Min. Bk., 5 March 1891, 24 Nov. 1892 and 29 Nov. 1900.

pressed constituency associations to adopt acceptable candidates and canvassed for them.[32] No task was more crucial than strengthening retail societies, the brewing industry's chief source of influence, and each agent devoted much time to expanding their size and number. This was particularly important early in the 1890s, when most societies had enrolled only a small percentage of retailers. In the forty seat eastern district, John J. Dunne discovered just eleven licensed victuallers' societies, with 700 members, one-fifth of all retailers. Such large towns as Bedford, Bury St Edmunds, Cambridge, Chelmsford, Huntingdon, King's Lynn, Newmarket, Stowmarket and Woodbridge were still unorganized. Within months, he had founded three more societies. Agent Henry Jackson accomplished more spectacular results in the northern district. There seventeen of the thirty divisions lacked societies, but within a year he had organized all but four. In this and other work district agents were frequently assisted by sub-agents, usually local retail officials hired annually for between £4 and £30.[33]

In sharp contrast was the complex scheme in the midlands, the only remnant of the abortive 'General Association'. Intending to raise substantial funds but disliking interference, midland brewers retained absolute control, rejecting the central agency's £250 subsidy and financing the entire district themselves. The Midland Counties Federated Brewers' Association (three Birmingham brewers, one representative each from the county brewers' societies and one Fund delegate) managed Leicestershire, Northamptonshire, Rutland, Staffordshire, Warwickshire and Worcestershire, and appointed an agent for each county, not one for the entire district. Every parliamentary seat contained one divisional committee, which subdivided the constituency into ward and finally polling committees. The scheme was extremely elaborate but immediately successful; within four months thirty-five of the fifty-one constituencies

---

[32] Gen. Assoc., pp. 3–4, 11; NTDA Mid. Dist. Agents' Min. Bk., 16 Nov. and 17 Dec. 1891, D 3162/2/1/10, pp. 13–14; Yorks. Br. Assoc. circular, *Country Brewers' Gazette*, 30 Apr. 1891.

[33] NTDF E. Dist. Report, 26 Oct. 1891, N. Home Count. Br. Assoc., p. 4; NTDF N. Dist. Min. Bk., 20 Nov. 1891 and 1892 Annual Report; NTDF 1893 Report, pp. 7, 9; see also Herts. Br. Assoc. 1895 Annual Report, p. 2; NTDA W. Dist. Min. Bk., 8 Dec. 1908, p. 84 and Reports: 1893, p. 7; 1894, p. 6; 1895, p. 14.

had divisional committees and over £9,000 had been guaranteed. Such commitment and resources explain why midland brewers published the Fund's only newspaper, the *Licensed Trade News*, in Birmingham.[34]

They not merely established the best machinery in the Fund, but attained solidarity unrivalled before the war. Indeed, only Northamptonshire successfully merged all trade societies in the comprehensive trade organization extolled by the General Association. Formed late in 1893, the Northamptonshire Licensed Trade Association eventually embraced brewers, retailers, brewery shareholders, public house brokers, hop and sugar merchants, mineral water manufacturers, wholesale and retail tobacconists, wine and spirit merchants, and brewers' managers and clerks.[35]

Expanding the Fund, of course, immensely increased brewers' expenditure on defence, far more than the anticipated total costs of £5,000. The ten districts were mainly responsible for soaring costs because they exceeded the £250 subsidy by at least £2,500 – 3,500 cumulatively, raising the Fund's total annual expenses to around £14,000 (see table 6).[36] District agencies did send funds through CBS affiliate branches to headquarters, but never became a major source of money (see table 7).

It was influential London brewers who predominantly financed the Fund; of the £37,000 collected between 1888 and 1895, £14,000 (almost forty per cent) was subscribed by ten firms, either directly or through the Brewers' Company. The bulk of the other contributions came from a few breweries rather than from numerous small firms: thirty-eight companies donated over £11,000.[37] One-third of the contributors (forty-eight firms) therefore accounted for two-thirds of the Fund's central office money. Politically, these firms were mostly Conservative, though Liberal companies donated about £3,000: Truman, Hanbury, Buxton & Co. and Hoare & Co., both

---

[34] NTDA Mid. Dist. Min. Bk., 9 Apr. 1891 and 25 Aug. 1892, D 3163/2/1/1, pp. 9, 30; Northants. Br. Assoc. Min. Bk., 21 Apr. 1891, SL 298; *Brewing Trade Review*, 1 June 1891.

[35] Northants. Br. Assoc. Min. Bk., 6 Dec. 1892 and 26 Sept. 1893; *Licensed Trade News*, 14 July 1894 and 9 March 1907.

[36] London, the eleventh district, was financed separately by the Society.

[37] Compiled from the NTDF Cash Book, Aug. 1888 – Sept. 1895; see app. 1 for the Fund's largest contributors.

Table 6

The Fund's expenses, 1888-95

Year	Central Office Expenses[a]	District Expenses[b]	Total
1888	524	–	524
1889	1,029	–	1,029
1890	2,949	–	2,949
1891	3,748	2,500 – 3,500	6,200 – 7,200
1892	6,219	2,500 – 3,500	8,700 – 9,700
1893	7,354	2,500 – 3,500	9,800 – 10,800
1894	6,606	2,900	9,500
1895	9,316	4,800	14,100
Total	37,745	15,200 – 18,200	52,800 – 55,800

Sources: Compiled from the NTDF Cash Book, Aug. 1888 – Sept. 1895; NTDF W. Dist. Annual Reports, 1893 – 5; NTDF N. Dist. Min. Bk., 1891 – 6.
[a] Includes district grants, salaries and office expenses, but not the amount spent by each district agency.
[b] Estimates based on expenses in the northern and western districts.

Table 7

Sources of the Fund's money, 1888-95

Type of Contributor	Amount (£)	% of Total
Brewery Firms	23,684	63.6
Brewers' Company	5,260	14.1
CBS Affiliated Societies	4,415	11.9
Country Brewers' Society	2,050	5.5
Distillery Companies	1,471	3.9
Other	377	1.0
Total	37,257	100.0

Sources: Compiled from the NTDF Cash Book, Aug. 1888 – Sept. 1895.

members of the Brewers' Company (£650 each), Meux's Brewery Co. (£515) and the largest Liberal subscriber, Bass, Ratcliff & Gretton (£1,050).[38]

Distillery companies and Celtic brewers, in contrast, gave the Fund little money. In England, as in Scotland, distillers had strong economic disincentives. They seldom owned tied houses and possessed outlets other than pubs for selling alcohol, so temperance demands for fewer licences did not concern them. Some distillers further felt that eliminating tied houses would stop 'the discounts brewers demanded for the right of supply'. For all these reasons, distillers made nominal donations of £1,500. Scottish and Irish brewers' modest numbers and much smaller markets than those in England also explain contributions of just £1,250.[39]

The UKA relied heavily on northern and, to a smaller extent, Welsh manufacturers for financial support, whereas the Fund's central office received almost two-fifths of its money from London brewers and another quarter from London distillers and midland, home county, Yorkshire and Lancashire brewers.[40] Despite the appreciably higher expenditure of the Fund's central office, the UKA spent over three times more on propaganda. Even if the Fund's district agencies raised the total to £10,000 annually after 1891, this still meant the UKA seemingly spent twice as much as the Fund.[41] There was, in fact, little disparity because the trade always diverted considerable sums to retail societies.

When reorganized in 1891, the Society extended its political activities with money supplied by London brewers, often through the Brewers' Company. Donations more than doubled to almost £6,000 annually for two reasons: they ceased feuding

---

[38] The other two Liberal breweries which donated money were Cobbold & Co. (£80) and Thomas Salt & Co. (£113). Baron Burton also contributed generously to the Liberal party (Arnold Morley to W. E. Gladstone, 21 Sept. 1891, W. E. Gladstone Papers, Add. Ms. 44,254, fo. 138).

[39] Ronald B. Weir, 'The Distilling Industry in Scotland in the Nineteenth and Early Twentieth Centuries' (Univ. of Edinburgh Ph.D. dissertation, 1974), pp. 563–4; NTDF Cash Book.

[40] Dingle, *Campaign for Prohibition*, p. 194; Lambert, *Drink and Sobriety*, p. 181; NTDF Cash Book; see also Harrison, 'British Prohibitionists', pp. 379–82.

[41] Dingle, *Campaign for Prohibition*, p. 192.

with retailers over diluting and adulterating beer,[42] and realized
only the Society could effectively organize London's seventy
parliamentary constituencies. Unlike district agencies which
supervised trade defence elsewhere, the Society, under the
Fund's guidance, kept control over London, and appointed an
electoral agent in 1894. The Brewers' Company shrewdly made
donations contingent on this alliance as a way of deterring the
Society from acting independently.[43] Because the Society's
membership fees reached only £600, one-tenth of what brewers
contributed, it was not in a position to refuse. Wealthy brewers,
less often distillers, invited to preside over the Society's annual
dinner, also helped raise funds. At three of these functions in
the 1890s, prestigious London brewers — W. T. Paulin (Mann,
Crossman & Paulin), Arthur Ridley (Cannon Brewery Co.) and
Spencer Charrington, MP (Charrington & Co.) — donated
altogether over £4,000 apart from the £100 each paid as members
of the Brewers' Company. So lavishly did brewers finance the
Society that it spent £8,800 annually (1891–5), more than the
Fund spent on the other ten districts. Like the expenses of the
district branches, those of the Society, originally projected at
£2,500, rose sharply, increasing sixty per cent over the previous
decade.[44]

Brewers regarded the League quite differently. In 1882 they
had been generous with £1,300, enabling the League to attain its
pinnacle of power. But brewers' enthusiasm for the League
thereafter waned, as the CBS formed county branches and as
the Fund assumed electoral duties. Between 1883 and 1891,
brewers' subscriptions to the League fell by over two-thirds
from £760 to £240. Renewed CBS attacks on the League reduced
them further. In 1892, the *Brewing Trade Review* blamed what it
saw as wasteful expenses on transportation, salaries and

---

42 To offset increased taxation in the mid-1880s, London retailers diluted and
   adulterated beer. Adulteration, mixing beers of unequal strengths, particularly annoyed London brewers. Publicans wanted the retail price of beer
   reduced, but these practices antagonized the Brewers' Company which
   eventually ceased donating to the Society in 1887. Financial support was
   resumed in 1893 (Br. Co. Min. Bk., 8 June 1893, p. 40, Br. Co.; Girouard,
   Pubs, p. 78; LVPSL Parl. Reports Min. Bk: 14 Dec. 1886, 9, 21 and 28 Feb. and
   7 March 1887, pp. 102, 104, 107–10, 115–16; LPLVDL Min. Bk., 10 June and
   18 Nov. 1887, pp. 194, 205).
43 NTDA Min. Bk. 1, 4 March 1892, pp. 78–9; Wholesale and Retail Min. Bk.,
   28 March 1892 and 30 July 1894, pp. 4, 41; Br. Co. Min. Bk., 14 June 1894, pp.
   84–5.
44 LVPSL Annual Reports, 1890–9.

meetings for bloating the League's budget over £1,900, and recommended that brewers discontinue subsidies. Samuel Burghope, secretary of the League, rejected these assertions, attributing them to 'private pique and prejudice'.[45] The League's reputation, however, was seen as so irredeemable that the CBS had already begun privately discouraging donations. In response to the League's appeal for money, the Birmingham Brewers' Association in January had asked the CBS whether the League deserved support with the Fund now enlarged. The CBS, noting the £26 5s grant sent the League yearly, dissuaded Birmingham brewers from assisting. Similarly, the Yorkshire Brewers' Association, contributors of over £100 to the League between 1883 and 1890, also adopted the CBS's new policy. Brewers gave the League progressively less each year, with just £73 donated in 1900. It was solely membership dues that allowed the League to spend roughly £1,400 on defence in the 1890s.[46] Still one of the largest retail organization with 11,000 members, it could not rival the Society, which received nearly fifty times as much money from brewers and spent seven-and-a-half times more on defence.[47]

To provincial retailers, the Fund seemed determined 'to undermine the League & to ignore the work in which they were engaged'. Some saw brewers' domination or financial control of all leading trade societies except the League as part of a broader conspiracy. 'It was intended both by the Country Brewers [Society] & the National Trade Defence Fund', one League member maintained, 'to cripple the League if not break it up'.[48] The Fund, in a conciliatory gesture in 1892, amended its constitution, granting retailers twenty-one of the forty delegate seats on its general committee, and making officials from the

45 LVNDL Annual Reports, 1883 – 92; *Brewing Trade Review*, 1 June 1892; Burghope to editor, *ibid.*, 1 Aug. 1892.
46 LVNDL Annual Reports, 1890 – 1901; Birm. and Mid. Count. Wholesale Br. Assoc. Min. Bk., 28 Jan. and 22 Feb. 1892, Staffs. R.O., D 3163/1/1/1, pp. 57, 59 – 60; Yorks. Br. Assoc. Annual Reports, 1883, 1889 – 1906.
47 In the 1890s Brewers donated £58,306 to the Society and £1,177 to the League. The Society spent £84,828 and the League £11,115. (Annual Reports: LVNDL, 1892 – 1900; LVPSL, 1890 – 9; *Brewing Trade Review*, 1 June 1892).
48 LVNDL Minute Book, 22 Apr. and 3 May 1892; see also NTDA Mid. Dist. Min. Bk., 23 June and 25 Aug. 1891, D 3163/2/1/1, pp. 20 – 1, 30; NTDA Min. Bk. 1, 12 Feb. 1892, p. 73.

Society, League and other major retail trade societies ex-officio members.[49]

Brewers disliked squandering money as much on government taxes as on provincial retailers. In 1889 the government had put 3d per barrel more on beer, and the following year likewise raised spirit taxes by 6d per gallon. Wanting these imposts rescinded, a joint deputation of brewers, distillers and publicans in 1891 met George Goschen, chancellor of the exchequer, but failed dismally to demonstrate the unified trade's 'enormous power' and 'strength'. John Danvers Power, former secretary of the CBS, cited the three-fold increase of rum over beer consumption as justification for repealing the beer duty. Goschen naturally pointed out that this argument hurt the distillers' case for reduced duties, but Power remained unrepentant: 'That is not our affair'. Such opportunism demoralized distiller and retail representatives, and soon, as the *Country Brewers' Gazette* disgustedly observed, 'each section was fighting for its own hand'. Although Goschen retained the taxes, brewers criticized not themselves but the government for this setback. Clearly, the Fund had promoted neither solidarity within the trade nor a more effective parliamentary lobby.[50]

With the Liberal party committed to local veto in its Newcastle programme, political neutrality became irrelevant at the 1892 Election. In London, where the Society superintended the campaign with a £500 subsidy from the Fund, all but one of the sixty-four Unionist candidates received various forms of trade support. Brewers, distillers, mineral water producers and related trades were circularized, and electioneering continued on polling days when 'members . . . in addition to bringing up voters to the poll, provided carriages themselves and obtained others from their private friends'. In no constituency in England or Wales was the standing Liberal preferred to his Unionist opponent.[51]

Liberal brewers found campaigning extraordinarily difficult. Even those who favoured compensation and sometimes faced independent candidates sponsored by temperance activists, could not placate local brewers and retailers. Henry Fenwick illustrated the limited importance of the drink issue, winning his

49 *Brewing Trade Review*, 1 Dec. 1892.
50 *Country Brewers' Gazette*, 16 Apr. 1891.
51 *Morning Advertiser*, 2 July 1892; LVPSL 1892 Annual Report, p. 34; Wholesale and Retail Min. Bk., 9 May 1892, p. 8.

contest despite trade opposition and an unofficial Liberal temperance candidate. More often Liberal brewers sought temperance backing with promises of support for local veto without compensation. This accommodating attitude appeased temperance reformers at Halifax and Luton, two seats contested by brewers James Stansfeld and Samuel H. Whitbread. Accepting both the Liberal programme and the Fund's test question, which wanted a pledge against local veto, forfeited trade neutrality, as George Fuller discovered at Westbury.[52] Altogether the Fund spent almost £5,000 on the election, five times as much as in 1885.[53]

Following the contest, the Fund did achieve a more cohesive parliamentary lobby. On an amendment granting compensation for surrendered licences to the 1893 Welsh Local Veto bill, twelve brewer MPs, including two Liberals and two Liberal Unionists, supported it, while only three Liberals dissented.[54] Five other Liberal brewer MPs reconciled party policy and private interest by abstaining. Brewers had therefore mobilized almost two-thirds of their potential voting strength on this crucial issue. But Liberal brewers willingly sacrificed both profit and trade unity on such lesser questions as increased taxation. When the Liberal Government imposed a 6d per barrel tax on beer in 1894, most Liberal brewers voted with their party, while Unionist ones opposed it. Unlike their predecessors in the 1880s, Conservative trade MPs took their duties seriously, and Liberal ones generally gave support on vital subjects, either openly with votes or tacitly with abstention.[55]

Twice in the years 1893 – 5 the Liberal cabinet sponsored local veto legislation. In the first bill, local ratepayers in a parish, ward or borough could with a two-thirds majority in a referendum prohibit most liquor licences after three years. Brewers and retailers detested these measures, rejecting outright the three-year warning period as inequitable compensation. Both bills became easy targets for attack owing to their impracticality and blatant class bias. Designed to ban drink

---

52 *Brewing Trade Review*, 1 June 1892; Hamer, *Electoral Pressure*, pp. 261 – 5; NTDF 1892 Report, p. 5; *Luton Reporter*, 3, 10 and 17 Sept. 1892; *Halifax Mercury*, 2 July 1892.
53 *Brewing Trade Review*, 1 Sept. 1895; see p. 97.
54 For a list of brewer MPs in the 1892 Parliament, see p. 28, n. 38.
55 *Brewers' Almanack and Wine and Spirit Trade Annual for 1894 – 5.*

sales in poor working-class urban neighbourhoods where intemperance was rampant, neither would have converted enough unregenerates.[56] Sympathetic sober labouring men, moreover, would not give up drinking unless the propertied classes sacrificed it too, but Liberals specifically excluded English inns, hotels, restaurants and railway refreshment rooms. Only the working classes needed reforming, Liberals insultingly implied. There were other class implications. Such legislation 'could be used as a class weapon in districts where the middle class predominated — as a means of forcing the working men to live elsewhere'.[57] Had either bill actually passed, the Lords would have cited the analogous case against home rule as convincing reasons for their veto. In both instances, Liberals would have used not merely Irish votes to impose an unpopular remedy on England where Unionist MPs predominated, but dubious foreign precedents like the Swedish Gothenburg system. No constitutional crisis would have ensued, for both Liberal leaders opposed conducting an election as a referendum on local veto: Gladstone's absorption in his second home rule bill was as strong as Rosebery's personal animus against prohibition. 'Our liquor Veto bill is popular with nobody', Rosebery complained privately late in 1894, soon after becoming prime minister.[58]

Once Liberals introduced their first Local Veto bill in February 1893, the trade campaign began in earnest with standard pressure group tactics: mass meetings, demonstrations and petitions. Exploiting one of the bill's chief defects, the inability of ratepayers to reduce the number of licences, brewers and retailers easily outdid their adversaries, collecting 1,163,259

[56] This was certainly what happened in 1920 when Scottish electors first voted on prohibition or stricter licensing control under legislation enacted in 1913. Those areas which became dry were generally small towns or inhabited by the middle class, not the working class (T. C. Smout, *A Century of the Scottish People, 1830 – 1950* (1986), pp. 146 – 7; Elspeth King, *Scotland Sober and Free: The Temperance Movement, 1829 – 1979* (Glasgow, 1979), p. 24).

[57] Dingle, *Campaign for Prohibition*, pp. 144 – 5; Shiman, *Crusade Against Drink*, p. 222 – 3; see also Fahey, 'Politics of Drink', p. 78 and 'Drink and Reform', p. 51. The 1893 Welsh Local Option bill, however, made no exemptions (Lambert, *Drink and Sobriety*, p. 235).

[58] Rosebery wrote his comments on the letter he received from Sir George Murray (16 Nov. 1894, Nat. Lib. Scot., Rosebery Papers, Ms. 10,049, fo. 76); see also H. C. G. Matthew, *The Liberal Imperialists: The Ideas of a Post-Gladstonian Elite* (1973), p. 238. For the use of foreign analogies in the home rule debate, see Gutzke's 'Rosebery and Ireland', pp. 92 – 3.

signatures compared with temperance totals of 610,769. Not since the 1840s had a popular issue generated as many signatures.[59] It was not just beer drinkers who responded so fervently to the trade's appeal. At a huge meeting arranged by the Brewers' Company, 217 firms representing seventy-two ancillary trades — from boiler makers, coal merchants and coach builders to hop merchants, brewers' engineers and grain contractors — passed a resolution reviling the bill as 'highly prejudicial to the interests of themselves and their employees'. Circulation of petitions among the latter undoubtedly helped swell the trade's aggregate figures. The trade also took its case to the public, hiring sandwich men who strolled about such cities as Bristol.[60]

In compelling the government to abandon the bill before the second reading later that year, the Fund expended large amounts of money, but cash was far less important than historians assume. Anthony Dingle portrays the struggle as one between trade organizations with 'vast financial resources', on one hand, and the Alliance, 'crippled by a lack of finance', on the other. Yet, as the Fund and its district branches probably spent about £10,000 and the Society and the League together another £11,000, the trade's total costs reached no more than £21,000, a larger but indecisive advantage over the Alliance with its £16,900. Since the Society concentrated its £9,600 on London and the League could only devote £1,400 to the entire provincial campaign, the Alliance most certainly outspent the trade except in the capital. The result therefore reflected not so much brewers' legendary wealth as popular sentiment.[61]

In 1895 the Liberals again put forward a prohibition bill which this time would allow ratepayers to reduce as well as forbid liquor licences. Trade and temperance organizers aroused public concern with the usual methods, but each attached greater weight to persuading uncommitted MPs. Fund agents mounted

---

59 Dingle, *Campaign for Prohibition*, pp. 147 – 9; Colin Leys, 'Petitioning in the Nineteenth and Twentieth Centuries', *Pol. Stud.*, 3 (1955), 54, 60.

60 Br. Co. Trade Meeting Min. Bk., 14 March 1893, Br. Co., pp. 15 – 6; NTDF W. Dist. Min. Bk., 13 Apr. 1893.

61 Dingle, *Campaign for Prohibition*, pp. 147, 149, 192 and 'Agitation for Prohibition', p. 533; NTDF Cash Book, 1893; NTDF W. Dist. 1893 Annual Report; LVPSL 1893 Annual Report; LVNDL 1894 Annual Report. The Brewers' Co. gave the Society a special grant of £1,500 (Br. Co. Min. Bk., 8 June 1893, p. 40).

a massive letter campaign, sharing most of the work with local trade officials. 'This continual pelting of Members of Parliament with letters is one of the efficacious methods of rousing their attention and making them feel the voting power which is behind an agitation', observed the Fund's northern agent. When the government collapsed before the second reading, trade and temperance societies had spent about as much as in 1893, though the subsequent election obscures precise figures. The trade's total pre-election expenses did not exceed £22,800, while the UKA's *annual* expenses for 1895 were £15,900.[62]

Since many prominent Liberals like W. V. Harcourt saw the 1895 Election as a referendum on local veto, the trade again gave Unionist candidates unwavering support. Indeed, of the nearly 500 English and Welsh seats, the trade was neutral in only five, three of them involving Liberals with drink interests.[63] Liberal brewer Hugh Hoare's forthright letter denouncing local veto in the *Morning Advertiser*, the retailers' daily newspaper, disarmed Chesterton's brewers and publicans, but ensured an aggressive temperance campaign against him with motions of no confidence enlivening the contest in many rural villages. Despite intense temperance hostility at Kennington, Mark Beaufoy, a wine merchant who had supported the 1893 amendment for compensation, was renominated. Even with trade neutrality he, like Hoare, was defeated. Nor did the trade's restraint seem useful at Lichfield, where Liberal brewer H. C. Fulford satisfied brewers and retailers with his attitudes on compensation and local veto, but as the clear second choice seemed unlikely to win votes. When local members of the trade met to adopt their candidate, one, expressing a widespread sentiment, moved that the Conservative be endorsed. The chairman unofficially agreed: 'although the amendment was in their hearts, they, as a trade organization, ought not to put it on paper'. Without trade

---

62 Dingle, *Campaign for Prohibition*, pp. 165–9, 192; NTDF N. Dist. Min. Bk., 1895 Annual Report. During 1895 the Society spent £12,100 and the League £1,200 (LVPSL 1895 Annual Report; LVNDL 1896 Annual Report). Of the Fund's total expenses of £9,316 in 1895, £4,740 was spent defeating the Local Veto bill (NTDF Cash Book, 1895; NTDA Min. Bk. 2, 5 Dec. 1905, p. 166).

63 Dingle, *Campaign for Prohibition*, pp. 168–70; *Licensed Trade News*, 10, 17 and 31 Aug. 1895; LVPSL 1895 Annual Report, pp. 92–4; *Licensing World and Licensed Trade Review*, 12 July–16 Aug. 1895.

enthusiasm or temperance votes Fulford still won the seat, only to be unseated on petition.[64]

None of these problems arose in two other seats contested by Liberal brewers. Samuel H. Whitbread's abstention on the 1893 compensation vote provoked the trade's opposition, costing him the election. The return of another London brewer, George Fuller, seemed jeopardized because of propaganda distributed by the Fund's agent on two six-week tours through Westbury in a Fair Play van in 1893 – 4. 'We flooded every little hamlet and stray house with excellent literature', the Fund agent proudly reported. Fuller sought to offset this adverse publicity with personal appeals at several retail meetings, handing out leaflets discounting the impact of prohibition and demanding that residents should control licensing. The van countered with a new leaflet, 'Fuller's Fables', which, together with lavish expenditure by the Fund, contributed to his defeat. Such literature bombarded electors throughout England and Wales, and accounted for much of the £4,600 spent by the Fund in defeating local veto.[65]

Four factors made the 1895 Liberal defeat particularly significant. First, the overwhelming rejection of Liberal candidates, eighty-seven lost English or Welsh seats, including such staunch prohibitionists as Caine, Whittaker and John Morley, helped discredit local veto as a question of practical politics, and persuaded many ex-cabinet members of the futility of antagonizing the brewing industry with its formidable political power. Arnold Morley, former Liberal chief whip, in his analysis of the rout, testified to brewers' success in organizing the trade. 'It is . . . difficult to understand the causes which have so disastrously operated against us', he reflected, but one fact was unmistakably clear: 'The Liquor Trade has undoubtedly been the most potent'. Many Liberal candidates had themselves become completely disenchanted with local veto. Following the

---

[64] NTDF 1895 Report, pp. 23 – 4; Hamer, *Electoral Pressure*, pp. 278 – 9, 289; *Brewing Trade Review*, 1 Apr. 1895; *Licensing World and Licensed Trade Review*, 12, 19 and 26 July 1895; Wholesale and Retail Min. Bk., 24 June and 2 July 1895, pp. 113 – 14, 122; *Worcestershire Chronicle*, 13 July 1895; *Burton Guardian*, 13 July 1895.

[65] *Licensed Trade News*, 10 Aug. and 12 Oct. 1895; *Wiltshire Times*, 13 July 1895; *Licensing World and Licensed Trade Review*, 19 July 23 Aug. 1895; *Brewing Trade Review*, 1 Sept. 1895; NTDF 1895 Annual Report, p. 21. The Brewers' Co. donated £4,000 and the CBS £1,000 towards the Fund's election expenses (NTDA Min. Bk. 2, 5 Dec. 1905), p. 166).

election, one prestigious Liberal newspaper, the *Westminster Gazette*, asked Liberal candidates for their explanation of the party's defeat, and 188 of the 231 replies (over eighty per cent) blamed local veto as a contributory factor. According to this survey, just six per cent of these 231 Liberals believed prohibition had attracted votes. Second, crusaders against drink, deprived of their pre-eminent remedy, acquired renewed interest in restricting the sale of alcohol, with licensing reduction seen as the best policy.[66] Third, in consolidating the Conservative/Liberal Unionist alliance, the debacle diminished bipartisan voting on temperance bills, as Liberal Unionists shifted towards Conservatives. On three Sunday closing divisions, for example, ninety-three per cent of the Liberal Unionists voted in favour in 1888, but only forty-one per cent in 1897 and twenty-six per cent in 1899. Conservative MPs consistently opposed each bill, with the proportion well over four-fifths, whereas Liberal MPs voted overwhelmingly for the 1888 bill and unanimously on the last two divisions. Liberal Unionists even staunchly opposed Scottish local veto, with eighty-four per cent voting against a 1899 bill, while Conservative MPs voted as much against as Liberal MPs for it.[67] Finally, the number of MPs who were cross pressured by being Liberals as well as brewers declined, their number falling from nine to two. Dissent no longer embarrassed the trade lobby, for on none of the five recorded divisions in the 1895 Parliament did Liberal brewers vote against their economic interests. Altogether, brewers cast almost sixty per cent of their potential votes against these temperance bills. Such was not the case with those MPs allied with the trade, distillers, company directors, wine merchants among others, who frequently abstained, costing the trade nearly two-fifths of its parliamentary strength.[68]

---

66 Arnold Morley to W. E. Gladstone, 19 July 1895, W. E. Gladstone Papers, Add. Ms. 44,254, fo. 272; Fahey, 'Politics of Drink', pp. 78–9; Shiman, *Crusade Against Drink*, pp. 227–9, 238–9. For the growing hostility to Liberal programmes, see D. A. Hamer, *Liberal Politics in the Age of Gladstone and Rosebery: A Study in Leadership and Policy* (1972), ch. 10.

67 *Hansard*, 3rd ser., 332 (14 Dec. 1888), cols. 336–8, and 4th ser., 46 (10 Feb. 1897), cols. 119–22, 72 (7 June 1899), cols. 565–8, and 70 (3 May 1899), cols. 1271–4.

68 See n. 67. The other 2 divisions were on a 1897 Irish Sunday closing bill and a 1899 bill extending JP authority (*Hansard*, 4th ser., 49 (12 May 1897), cols. 305–10 and 72 (7 June 1899), cols. 587–90).

London, Burton and country brewers created the National Trade Defence Fund in 1888 to combat the disunity and temperance propaganda responsible for defeating Ritchie's compensation proposal. Its unrepresentative structure and limited objectives soon had to be amended. During the next four years the Fund revised its constitution, admitting more provincial brewers and later retailers as equals with subscribers, while retaining the original principle of drawing money primarily from big brewers. The Fund also expanded its activities, appointing agents and underwriting costs of £5,000. Better defence did cost brewers far more than anticipated, but it also allowed the trade to spend about as much as the UKA in contesting prohibition. Yet the Fund, though improving the trade's overall defensive position, alienated provincial retailers by sharply reducing subsidies. Late in the 1890s the League's participation in the Fund had become tenuous, a development immensely important at the 1900 General Election.

5

The Limits of Loyalty

The 1900 Election revealed that the National Trade Defence
Association[1] had given the trade enormous but transitory
political power. For the brewing industry, the failure to
implement a bipartisan electoral policy was as significant a
turning point as the defeat of local veto. In fact, the election in
which Unionists won another impressive victory was a defeat
for the trade, which sacrificed flexibility, power and long-term
security. In repudiating official policy, some brewers and most
retailers ensured that the trade would accept the consequences
of the closer alliance with Unionists forged during the local veto
crisis, the impossibility of holding Liberal sentiments or of
adopting any policy towards Liberalism except implacable
opposition. As outright Unionist allies, the trade lost any
influence with Liberals and so invited retaliation. The election
was also detrimental to the Association. Its efforts to centralize
authority, far from promoting unity, actually intensified
grievances, ultimately reducing the trade's power. Brewers and
retailers had only themselves to blame, for instead of finding a
way of permanently settling the contentious problem of
compensation, they obstinately continued the attack on local
veto, a twice-rejected and now thoroughly discredited solution
to intemperance.

Defeat at the 1895 Election had persuaded many Liberals that
local veto was an electoral liability, and from 1897 onwards
growing numbers began repudiating it. Much of the impetus
appropriately came from Herbert Gladstone, whose father had
made it party policy. Local veto, he concluded, had sacrificed

---

[1] In June 1900 brewers, displeased with the Fund's somewhat sinister name,
rechristened it the Association.

the votes of many working-class drinkers, whose hostility reflected the awesome influence of trade propaganda dispensed daily with pints of beer at thousands of pubs and beerhouses. By late 1897 Gladstone had ceased being a prohibitionist, admitting publicly that fewer pubs, administrative reforms, compulsory medical treatment and harsher penalties would more effectively reduce insobriety than local veto.[2] On becoming chief whip in 1899, he candidly informed Sir Henry Campbell-Bannerman, Liberal leader in the Commons, that his constituents' opposition to his views might compel him to resign. Gladstone, though the most prominent, was not the only Liberal to disown prohibition. At the West Staffordshire and North Norfolk by-elections, Liberals displayed such hostility that the trade offered no opposition. Sitting MPs also began disavowing prohibition, even choosing the most offensive occasions. T. F. Shaw defiantly renounced local option and Sunday closing, for example, before the Staffordshire Licensed Victuallers' Association.[3] Further north at Osgoldcross the Alliance suffered its most damaging defeat. Sir John Austin, Liberal MP and maltster, had acrimoniously divided his constituency association by violating campaign pledges in opposing Scottish local veto and Irish Sunday closing bills. Several members, including the president, had resigned in protest, but the rest adopted a mollifying posture, resisted a no-confidence motion and passed instead a resolution merely regretting Austin's local veto vote. He then unexpectedly resigned his seat and sought re-election as an Independent Liberal. Two local retail associations assisted him against Charles Roberts, the official Liberal candidate who endorsed local veto. Trade support literally rolled in: a beer barrel falling off a brewers' dray stopped in front of Austin's committee room, prompting the comment that 'another of Sir John's supporters' had turned out to vote. Although prominent

---

2   *Leeds Mercury*, 25 Nov. 1897. Gladstone's speech is more fully discussed in David Edwin Wright, 'The British Liberal Party and the Liquor Licensing Question, 1895 – 1905' (McMaster Univ. Ph.D. dissertation, 1972), pp. 185 – 200.

3   Hamer, *Electoral Pressure*, pp. 292 – 7; NTDF Mid. Dist. 1899 Report, D 3163/ 2/1/1, p. 289; Gladstone to Campbell-Bannerman, 12 Apr. 1899, Campbell-Bannerman Papers, Add. Ms. 41,215, fo. 66.

Alliance leaders spoke on Roberts' behalf, Austin won convincingly.[4]

Before the Liberal party could formally drop local veto, the Royal Commission on Liquor Licensing Laws issued two reports. They materially altered the trade/temperance debate, so long deadlocked on whether owners losing their drink licences deserved compensation. Appointed in 1896, the Royal Commission (popularly known as the Peel Commission) contained twenty-four members, sixteen drawn equally from liquor and temperance organizations as well as eight others with unbiased opinions. It ended three years and thousands of questions later in complete disarray largely because of Lord Peel, selected as chairman for his well-known moderate views. He was so appalled at the human misery caused by excessive drinking and so impatient with retail representatives for relentlessly challenging unfavourable testimony that he became a temperance convert. Discarding the guise of the neutral leader who promoted consensus with compromises, he instead submitted his own radical anti-drink proposals as the basis for discussion. Amid bitter contention the Commission drafted two separate sets of recommendations, the Majority Report (produced by trade and disinterested members) and the Minority Report (founded on Peel's ideas and supported by temperance members). Both wanted fewer licences and compensation funded by surviving retailers. Lord Peel, however, advocated an extensive reduction scheme in which about 40,000 retailers would forfeit their licences, and receive progressively less compensation as a time limit of seven years contracted. Thereafter no licence, whether old or new, would get compensation if unrenewed. Carefully distinguishing between the state's legal obligations and charity to preclude demands later for better terms, Peel's temperance faction insisted it was compensating, not for surrendered licences but in lieu of adequate warning. The pro-trade Majority Report, in contrast, suggested eliminating fewer licences with full compensation — payment of market value — unrestricted by any time limit. Both Reports thus rejected prohibition as an antidote to insobriety, though the Minority Report thought local veto might be eventually tried in Scotland

---

4 *Licensed Trade News*, 3 and 17 June 1899; *Pontefract Telegraph*, 17 June and 8 July 1899; *Wakefield Express*, 24 June and 1 July 1899; *Hansard*, 4th ser., 49 (12 May 1897), col. 307 and 70 (3 May 1899), col. 1271; Hamer, *Electoral Pressure*, pp. 297 – 8.

and Wales. No agreement, in contrast, prevailed on grocers' licences. Peel, backed by the temperance faction, urged their abolition, whereas the Majority Report called for the far less drastic remedy of giving magistrates control over them.[5]

Both trade and temperance members could adopt these Reports only by modifying previous demands. While the Royal Commission collected evidence, the chairman of the Association, John Gretton, and the CBS reiterated the trade's position of allowing licensing reduction only on Chamberlain's 1894 compensation terms, market value plus ten per cent for disturbance. The Majority Report rejected these inflated amounts, but retailers remained dissatisfied with the trade representatives' concessions. Both Walker (chairman of the Society) and Samuel Hyslop (chairman of the League) qualified their approval with appended objections. The Society's newspaper, moreover, pointedly noted that the Report's 'recommendations fall far short of honest compensation'. But most brewers and retailers still accepted its formula on compensation.[6] With the Minority Report, temperance reformers would also realize long-cherished goals, closing many drink shops and refusing to recognize licences as a form of property, but not without certain concessions — granting compensation, however restricted, and indefinitely postponing local veto in England. But in accepting the Minority Report, anti-drink critics did not so much compromise on the UKA's prohibitionist programme as tacitly admit its growing unpopularity.

David Fahey, in his analysis of the effect of the Peel Report on the Liberal leadership, portrays Sir Henry Campbell-Bannerman as sincere but politically inept in attempting to define party policy. Some months after replacing Sir William Harcourt as Liberal Commons leader, C.-B. astonished his new chief whip,

---

[5] *Report Royal Com. Liq. Licensing Laws*, 1899, 35 (Cmnd. 9379); Thomas P. Whittaker, 'The "Temperance" Reply to Sir Algernon West', *Nineteenth Cent.*, 47 (1900), 518 – 20; Fahey, 'Peel's Report', pp. 134 – 7.

[6] Late in 1899 Walker reiterated his demand for compensation drawn in part from public revenue. Another trade representative on the Commission, Henry Riley-Smith, a Yorkshire brewer, though favouring a liquor tax as the source for compensation, still signed the Majority Report (*Licensing World and Licensed Trade Review*, 18 Nov. 1899; *Report Royal Com. Liq. Licensing Laws*, 1899, 35 (Cmnd. 9379), pp. 68 – 9). CBS Min. Bk. 6, 4 July 1898; NTDA Min. Bk. 1, 29 June 1898, pp. 299 – 301; *Licensing World and Licensed Trade Review*, 22 July 1899.

Herbert Gladstone, with a provocative temperance declaration, apparently committing the party to the Minority Report. Criticism came not only from Gladstone, but from the Liberal liquor contingent, which threatened to defect, and Lord Kimberley, C.-B.'s counterpart in the Lords.[7]

Gladstone felt C.-B. overestimated the trade's gratitude for the right to insure itself against abolished licences. Despite the reluctance of trade representatives in signing the Majority Report, C.-B. still believed that the temperance movement's acceptance of limited compensation would 'help us to soften the stubborn opposition of the trade in England'. Gladstone disagreed. Unopposed to restricted compensation drawn from the trade itself, he advised that Liberals amply compensate dispossessed licence holders for several important reasons. First, prohibitionists such as Thomas Whittaker, W. S. Caine and even Sir Wilfrid Lawson now recanted their opposition to any compensation, and insisted only on two conditions: the trade finding the money and excluding all new licences. Second, as the time limit lengthened, so did chances of legislative success. Gladstone, displeased with the Minority Report's scanty compensation provisions, glumly foresaw that the Lords would veto C.B.'s temperance bill, possibly force an election and then 'the trade will make a record effort against us & will probably prove once more that [they] (plus the Ch. of England & the whole Tory Party) . . . are too strong for us'. Third, public house patrons could vote for the Liberal party only if assured it would deal fairly with retailers. It was to these voters that Liberals must direct their appeal: 'A skimp & grudging measure of compensation . . . would not enable us to detach from the public house influence the mass of reasonable customers who in a rough & ready way want the publicans to be treated generously'. As a pragmatist, Gladstone would neither court nor countenance political defeat. The trade's electoral power convinced him that 'without an adequate amount of grease we shall not be able to overcome the friction of the trade at the next or almost any election'.[8]

---

7 Fahey, 'Peel's Report', pp. 140 – 9.
8 Gladstone to Campbell-Bannerman, 19 Nov. 1899, Campbell-Bannerman Papers, Add. Ms. 41,215, fos. 144 – 7; Campbell-Bannerman to Spencer, 12 Dec. 1899 (copy), Nat. Lib. Scot., Kimberley Papers, Ms. 10,244, fos. 13 – 18; Shiman, *Crusade Against Drink*, pp. 237 – 8.

Herbert Gladstone as chief whip fully appreciated the way in which the Minority Report antagonized one significant group of Liberal supporters. Some twenty with drink connections, including fourteen current or past brewer MPs, three distillers and four wine merchants, were valued as 'essential friends' for their contributions, parliamentary experience or local influence.[9] Their political devotion had been strained by C.-B.'s seeming adoption of the Minority Report as party policy. Percy Barlow contemplated contesting Bedford, but only if aided by its former MP, Samuel Whitbread, who made his support contingent on a pledge for full compensation and no commitment to any part of the Minority Report. Barlow willingly complied with these terms.[10] Gladstone's plans in Norfolk and Derby ended less satisfactorily. Both the North-West and the East Norfolk Liberal Associations were vetting Buxton as a possible candidate, but he withdrew his name, citing inability to stand on the Minority Report. Haig similarly abandoned South Derbyshire, where he had already been adopted as the Liberal candidate.[11]

Licensed grocers, another key Liberal group, naturally detested the Minority Report for seeking their elimination. Soon after the Commission polarized and began drafting separate reports, Walter Gilbey, partner in the large wine merchant firm bearing his name, sent Gladstone an indignant letter in which he assailed Lord Peel's one-sided attitude and requested help in negotiating a compromise on grocers' licences with temperance representatives. C.-B.'s subsequent sympathy for the Minority Report estranged the Gilbey firm from the Liberal party. Gladstone, worried about the Minority Report's controversial ban on grocers' licences, cautioned C.-B. that 'we cannot afford to lose the Gilbeys & all their grocer clients'.[12]

9   Herbert Gladstone to Campbell-Bannerman, 12 Dec. 1899, Campbell-Bannerman Papers, Add. Ms. 41,215, fos. 169–70. For Liberals with drink connections, see p. 28, n. 38.

10 Appointment Diary, 8 and 19 Dec. 1899, 23 Feb. 1900, Herbert Gladstone Papers, Add. Ms. 46,483, fos. 53, 55, 118.

11 Ibid., 19 July 1899, ibid., Add. Ms. 46,483, fo. 33; Kimberley to Sydney Buxton (copy), 3 Sept. 1899, Kimberley Papers, Ms. 10,249, fos. 72–3; E. N. Buxton to Kimberley, 19 Nov. 1899, ibid., fos. 119–20; Gladstone to Campbell-Bannerman, 12 Dec. 1899, Campbell-Bannerman Papers, Add. Ms. 41,215, fos. 169–70.

12 Gilbey to Gladstone, 19 Apr. 1899, Herbert Gladstone Papers, Add. Ms. 46,057, fos. 154–7; Gladstone to Campbell-Bannerman, 8 and 12 Dec. 1899, Campbell-Bannerman Papers, Add. Ms. 41,215, fos. 159, 169–70. Gladstone's italics.

Discord at Saffron Walden, where the prospective candidate was Armine Wodehouse, Lord Kimberley's son, apparently justified these fears. Charles Gold (W. & A. Gilbey), the sitting Liberal MP, and his partners were furious with C.-B. for endorsing the Minority Report which not only betrayed their steadfast allegiance and lavish party donations, but jeopardized Gilbey profits. When Gold announced that he had 'ceased to support the Liberal Party . . . [and] will take no further part in politics on the Liberal side', Wodehouse despaired of his candidature. For other reasons it disturbed Gladstone, faced with losing a safe seat, political and financial support from the Gilbey nexus, licensed grocers' votes and the goodwill of Lord Kimberley. Gladstone acted promptly. He persuaded Buxton, ostensibly uninterested in grocers' licences, to intercede with Gold. While C.-B. regarded such licences as 'the worst cause of evil', Gladstone eventually deterred him from following his Scottish instincts to urge suppressing them as the Minority Report strongly advised.[13]

Under growing pressure, C.-B. 'clarified' his statement, asserting that the Liberal party viewed the Minority Report as simply a general basis for legislation.[14] According to Fahey, Liberal drink members, who prevented their party's identification with drastic temperance proposals, achieved a modest but important victory. For the temperance movement, however, C.-B.'s revised policy was extremely divisive, as moderates and radicals became polarized just before the election.[15]

Certainly the Minority Report fostered disunity among temperance organizations, as Fahey argues, but there is little evidence that it ever seriously interested Liberals with drink ties. The trade, whether Liberal or Unionist members, never saw the Minority Report as a viable framework for legislation not because of broader licensing reduction but because of the time limit, which would appropriate the large sums invested in licensed property. C.-B. himself may not have grasped this fundamental point, but Edward N. Buxton, the Liberal brewer on the Peel Commission, scarcely concealed his contempt for

13 Wodehouse to Gladstone, 16 Dec. 1899, Herbert Gladstone Papers, Add. Ms. 46,057, fos. 232 – 4; Appointment Diary, 18 and 19 Dec. 1899, ibid., Ms. 46,483, fo. 55; Campbell-Bannerman to Gladstone, 9 Dec. 1899, ibid., Add. Ms. 45,987, fos. 53 – 4; Gladstone to Campbell-Bannerman, 18 Dec. 1899, Campbell-Bannerman Papers, Add. Ms. 41,215, fo. 185.
14 Dundee Advertiser, 20 Dec. 1899.
15 Fahey, 'Peel's Report', pp. 149 – 57.

the Minority Report's compensation scheme. He thought it unworkable, harsh and expropriative. 'I fail to see any difference in principle between a complete denial of any compensation whatever and a fractional compensation such as this', he observed of an analogous plan, exemplifying pervasive attitudes in the brewing industry. The trade and temperance reformers, disagreeing on so much else, fully concurred on this one crucial matter: no measure with a time limit was really compensatory. Prohibitionists like Thomas Whittaker, another Peel Commissioner, called the Majority Report — without a time limit — 'infinitely worse than nothing'. Buxton thus felt C.-B.'s speech upholding the Minority Report embodied 'extreme' temperance remedies, and so withdrew his name from consideration as a possible Liberal candidate for East Norfolk.[16] Since he had 'screwed up the other representatives of beer on the Commission to accept the Majority scheme of compensation', Buxton would compromise no further, lest 'the benefit of having nailed them to that should be lost'. Compromise was unthinkable because temperance advocates insisted on retaining a time limit, which compensated for short notice, not for abolished licensed property as the trade demanded. It was this vital distinction that made the Reports wholly irreconcilable.[17] However loosely pledged, the Liberal party had still accepted the Minority Report, making the position of Liberal drink members ultimately untenable.

Ideally qualified to stop this conflict from escalating into a schism between Liberals with drink ties and their party was Edward N. Buxton. As director of one of the largest London breweries, leading member of the Brewers' Company and of the Association, and the main Liberal trade member on the Peel Commission, Buxton was a vital linch-pin. With his wide understanding of diverse viewpoints, and Unionist backing for the Majority Report already assured, he could mediate between the brewing industry and his political party at the next election.

Buxton devised an imaginative electoral strategy, sanctioned by Herbert Gladstone, in which the Association would offer

---

[16] Buxton quoted in Whittaker, 'Temperance Reply', pp. 520, 524; Herbert Gladstone to Campbell-Bannerman, 19 Nov. 1899, Campbell-Bannerman Papers, Add. Ms. 41,215, fo. 147; E. N. Buxton to Kimberley, 19 Nov. 1899, Kimberly Papers, Ms. 10,249, fos. 119–20.

[17] Buxton quoted in Bryce to Campbell-Bannerman, 16 Dec. 1899, Campbell-Bannerman Papers, Add. Ms. 41,211, fos. 75–6; Whittaker, 'Temperance Reply', pp. 518–20.

Liberal candidates trade neutrality in exchange for acceptance of its two test questions. Whether he succeeded, Buxton assumed, depended less on sheer numbers of MPs than on influence within a future Liberal cabinet. With Gladstone committed to safeguarding what the trade wanted most and destined as a chief whip for a cabinet post, Buxton felt that only 'a little band of Liberals' in the next Parliament was necessary for lending support. As advocates of full compensation, their threatened defection would effectively block an adverse Liberal temperance bill, particularly one with a time limit.[18] Buxton shared with many other Liberals like Gladstone the strong conviction that the 1886 realignment, so damaging to their party's electoral appeal, would prevent their reacquiring the overall parliamentary majorities of 1868 and 1880.[19] Another minority government, as in 1886 and 1892, could not enact a sweeping temperance bill with a disaffected cabinet minister, backed by a small but uncompromising group of Liberal MPs.

Buxton first revealed his plan, discreetly concealing Gladstone's past role and future significance, when informally addressing representatives of the Society in February 1900. Substantial numbers of Liberal MPs, he predicted, would reject the Minority Report's most radical parts, already adopted by C.-B., and for this fully deserved trade support:

Where the Liberals show their willingness to listen to us, . . . we shall . . . promote the election of candidates of that kind. It is even more important to us to have representatives in the Liberal Party who take our views than it is . . . on the other side, because if there were a sufficient number of them it would be impossible for this excessively drastic legislation to be introduced.[20]

---

[18] LVNDL Min. Bk., 25 Sept. 1900, Meetings of the United Parl. Council of the Retail Liquor Trade, Verbatim Shorthand Notes.

[19] Gutzke, 'Rosebery and Ireland', p. 89.

[20] *Licensed Trade News*, 10 Feb. 1900. David Fahey interprets this speech differently, arguing that Buxton referred to the election of Liberals with drink interests (Fahey, 'Peel's Report', p. 149). Buxton would disclose in Sept. his 'frequent communication with many [Liberal] candidates, some of them very influential', notably Gladstone who had given a 'pledge' to support the trade test questions (LVNDL Min. Bk., 25 Sept. 1900).

Campbell-Bannerman's failure to endorse the Minority Report thus guaranteed that Liberals who approved trade test questions did not violate party policy.

There was another dimension to Buxton's plan, the arrangement of a rapprochement between two, politically opposed groups, the Unionist trade and Liberal grocers. Gladstone saw C.-B.'s later speech retreating from the Minority Report as responsible for placating them. Wodehouse himself was doubtful, unable to see how it modified earlier statements. In fact, grocers were appeased, not by C.-B.'s rhetoric, but by Buxton who had made off-licence holders trade allies. This explains both Buxton's ease in subsequently assuaging Gold's wrath, and Gilbey's renewed support for Wodehouse.[21] Speaking at the Society's annual dinner early in May 1900, Buxton disclosed this crucial and newly established accord: 'Since this time last year I think we [the Association] . . . have brought into our forces a most important branch of the trade in the off-license holders, commonly called grocers licenses. . . . That adds very much to our strength, no doubt owing to the fact that they are attacked in the recent Minority report'.[22]

This rapprochement was indeed remarkable given the trade's traditional animosity against licensed grocers. Retailers especially resented them as economic rivals. Off-licence shopkeepers not only operated on smaller profit margins, but invested less when setting up in business than publicans, and so had lower overheads. As these advantages would be offset if off-licences were to be placed under magistrates' control, aggrieved publicans sought this restriction in test questions at the 1880 and 1885 Elections.[23] Grocers also used aggressive commercial practices, advertising drink prices and illegally canvassing homes for liquor sales while apparently collecting orders for groceries, that outraged publicans. From his iron works in

---

21 Herbert Gladstone to Campbell-Bannerman, 18 and 22 Dec. 1899, Campbell-Bannerman Papers, Add. Ms. 41,215, fos. 185, 188; Appointment Diary, 18 Dec. 1899, Herbert Gladstone Papers, Add. Ms. 46,483, fo. 55; Wodehouse to Gladstone, 22 Dec. 1899, ibid., Add. Ms. 46,057, fos. 244 – 5.

22 Licensed Trade News, 5 May 1900. Charles Walker, chairman of the Society, also spoke of a 'band of union' between grocers and the trade (Licensing World and Licensed Trade Review, 18 Nov. 1899).

23 Licensed Victuallers' Guardian, 13 March 1880 and 5 Dec. 1885; Lic. Vic. Jt. Parl. Comt. Min. Bk., 23 June 1885; see also pp. 27 – 8. Irish publicans and grocers also had an acrimonious relationship (Malcolm, Drink and Temperance in Ireland, pp. 210 – 11).

Durham during the 1870s, Joseph Pease often witnessed rows of grocers' wagons, laden with bottles of alcohol and accompanied by several men who solicited orders in mining villages. Whatever the alleged reason, animus against the grocer derived primarily from the fact that he 'takes away . . . the most profitable part, of the trade of the licensed victualler'.[24]

Frustrated publicans condemned the grocer on moral grounds as the promoter of insobriety, especially among females. He was censured for conspiring with wives in concealing purchases of alcohol from their husbands, listing them on receipts under general goods. Some publicans like Alfred Cole, testifying as chairman of the Society before the Lords Committee on Intemperance late in the 1870s, claimed that grocers went further, pressing alcohol on unsuspecting customers.[25] One of its members, Lord Kimberley, however, exonerated grocers, demanding detractors either prove or withdraw their allegations. 'Not a shred of evidence', he recalled in a letter to Campbell-Bannerman in 1899, 'was produced . . . to show that they [grocers' licences] were objectionable, altho' there was a great deal of confident assertion that they did great harm'. Kimberley was obviously more easily satisfied than other members of the Lord Committee, for they recommended that grocers guilty of omitting alcohol sales from bills forfeit their licences.[26]

Retailers felt that these scandals discredited all drink sellers. As the *Country Brewers' Gazette* contended in 1886, 'no class of licence has so lowered and depreciated public houses and beer retail houses as this [grocer's licence]'. Years later brewer

---

24 *Licensing World and Licensed Trade Review*, 1 Dec. 1892; *Evid. Lords Comt. Intemp.*, 1877, 11 (418) ⸳ 51, 268 and (271), p. 368; Michael J. Winstanley, *The Shopkeeper's World, 1830–1914* (Manchester, 1983), p. 136.

25 *Evid. Lords Comt. Intemp.*, 1877, 11 (418), p. 268; *Brewing Trade Review*, 1 Apr. 1890; *Brewers' Guardian*, 4 Dec. 1883; *Licensing World and Licensed Trade Review*, 1 Dec. 1892. Temperance reformers made similar accusations (*Evid. Lords Comt. Intemp.*, 1877, 11 (271), pp. 199, 214–15 and (418), p. 266; Buxton and Hoare, 'Temperance Reform', p. 193; Gerald Wayne Olsen, 'Pub and Parish — The Beginnings of Temperance Reform in the Church of England, 1835–75' (Univ. W. Ontario Ph.D. dissertation, 1972), pp. 365–6). In 1899 Rowntree's survey of York did supply evidence of more women patronizing 1 off-licence shop than men (Rowntree, *Poverty*, p. 332).

26 Kimberley to Campbell-Bannerman, 17 Dec. 1899, Campbell-Bannerman Papers, Add. Ms. 41,221, fos. 174–81; *Report Lords Comt. Intemp.*, 1879, 10 (113), p. lxi.

Sydney Nevile could still remember how licensed victuallers had regarded licensed grocers as ' "vermin" '.[27]

Grocers or their employers retaliated. W. & A. Gilbey, owner of many off-licences, accused publicans and brewers of causing drunkenness, of charging exorbitant prices and of defrauding consumers. It was not wholesome wine or spirits, but beer, the firm claimed, that fostered intemperance. Nor did grocers resign themselves to losing custom when confronted with reprisals from publicans who began founding co-operative stores late in the 1870s. Retribution took the form of lobbying candidates at the 1880 Election for legislation outlawing such tactics. 'Strife between opposing trades will reach a great height', the *Brewers' Guardian* gloomily predicted before the campaign began.[28]

Religious convictions strengthened political and economic cleavages. One Association agent ridiculed many Portsmouth, Brighton and Southampton licensed grocers as 'Nonconformist radical teetotalers, who make all they can out of one licence on *six* days of the week and denounce *all* licences in their chapels on the *seventh*'.[29]

Grocers also formed separate protective societies to emphasize their distinctive identity. During the 1870s off-licence holders had organized locally in such cities as Sheffield, Nottingham, London and Leeds, but only in 1886 established one national organization, the National Federation of Off-Licence Holders' Association. By 1900, its seventy-eighty affiliated societies had around 12,000 members, whose Liberalism naturally prevented their federating with the predominantly Unionist National Trade Defence Association.[30]

Brewers, retailers and licensed grocers eventually cooperated, despite rivalry, simply out of self-interest. Trade officials realized that Parliament, prompted by continued criticism of grocers' licences, might abolish them without compensation, a

---

[27] *Country Brewers' Gazette*, 14 Jan. 1886; Sydney O. Nevile, *Seventy Rolling Years* (1958), p. 35.
[28] W. & A. Gilbey to Northcote, March, 1878, *Evid. Lords Comt. Intemp.*, 1878, 14 (338), pp. 512 – 15; *Brewers' Guardian*, 17 Feb. 1880; see also Winstanley, *Shopkeeper's World*, pp. 36 – 9.
[29] NTDF S. Count. Dist. Report, *Licensed Trade News*, 26 Jan. 1895. Agent's italics.
[30] *Evid. Sel. Comt. House of Lords on Early Closing of Shops*, 1901, 6 (369), p. 99. Charles Gold became the Federation's first president. Henry Gilbey helped found the Wine and Spirit Trade Benevolent Society (Waugh, *Merchants of Wine*, p. 97).

dangerous precedent for on-licences. To secure recognition of compensation, the brewing industry's primary defence against radical temperance legislation, publicans must stop feuding with the grocer and risking their own livelihood. 'Dispossess a grocer because the publican thinks his trade injurious and the turn of the publican himself will certainly come next', the *Brewing Trade Review* warned in 1894. Now it even denied that grocers' licences led to furtive drinking at home. In addition, off-licence holders as allies gave the trade several benefits: it gained 12,000 supporters in the Federation, more political leverage with the Liberal party and electoral flexibility. Licensed grocers saw alliance with the trade as not just useful but essential. Walter Gilbey's letter to Gladstone early in 1899 indicated their alarm at Peel's move towards a full assault on off-licences. The Minority Report fulfilled their worst expectation, with three-quarters of them potentially endangered.[31] They could more readily reconcile themselves to the Majority Report, which merely suggested placing off-licences under magistrates' supervision. Forced to sacrifice either their politics or trade, licensed grocers had cogent reasons for becoming Association members.

Mindful of the urgent need to eliminate internal dissent, trade leaders had already inaugurated a new policy in the 1890s, the conciliation of licensed grocers. After the Fund studiously excluded off-licence holders from test questions at the 1892 Election and promised it would oppose legislation refusing them compensation for revoked licences, one of their protective organizations, the Wine and Spirit Association, agreed to become federated in 1893.[32] The Fund, far from making a nominal commitment, tenaciously defended its new allies against all attacks, including those from within the trade itself. Intense local hostility to grocers inspired S. A. Brain (chairman of the South Wales Brewers' Association) and J. M. Gerhold (chairman of the Cardiff Licensed Victuallers' Association) to challenge official policy. On 23 January 1895, in a letter to *The Times*, they demanded that publicans monopolize beer and

---

[31] *Brewing Trade Review*, 1 Oct. 1894; Gilbey to Gladstone, 19 Apr. 1899, Gladstone Papers, Add. Ms. 46,057, fos. 154 – 7; Wilson, *Alcohol and Nation*, p. 397. W. & A. Gilbey initially funded and later controlled the first chain of licensed grocer establishments (Waugh, *Merchants of Wine*, pp. 23 – 4).

[32] Jt. Wholesale and Retail Min. Bk., 9 May 1892, pp. 9 – 10; LVNDL Min. Bk., 4 March 1892; NTDA Min. Bk. 1, 4 March 1892 and 10 Jan. 1893, pp. 78, 102. No records of the Wine and Spirit Association evidently survive.

spirit sales, hinted that grocers were unscrupulous and backed a pending bill banning grocers' licences. Gerhold's position as a member of the Fund's general committee pointedly tested its resolve. Within a week, the committee, citing the danger to the trade's case for compensation and the agreement to safeguard all licences, implicitly censured Gerhold by resolving unanimously that every trade society should oppose the bill. Other regional branches, such as the Fund's northern district, finally accepted defeat, giving seats on their committees to officials of local off-licence societies. Life-long critics of licensed grocers like C. G. Long, vice-president of the League, disliked but reluctantly upheld the avowed policy. In evidence before the Peel Commission, Long, though conceding he wanted 'no grocers' licenses at all', hastily denied any personal knowledge of their part in female drunkenness.[33] During debates on the Peel Commission Report, trade representatives, supported by neutral members, demonstrated further solidarity, resisting Lord Peel's attempt to abolish 'mixed trader' licences.[34]

Some sceptical provincial retailers still vilified their economic competitor, but, chastened by Gerhold's reprimand, only at private gatherings. To a group of Lancashire and Cheshire retailers, George Ball complained of grocers 'securing the best of the trade, employing several assistants to do nothing but serve bottles of wine and spirits . . . [and] by selling an inferior article, to cut prices down'. He was particularly incensed because 'all the harm that these licences did in promoting drunkenness the licensed victuallers got the blame for'. For Ball, as for many publicans, the only recourse against these swindling, irresponsible undersellers was to put off-licences under magistrates' control. The League consequently resolved in September 1899 to promote such legislation.[35]

The League raised its resolution at the November meeting of the only body entitled to speak for all retailers, the United Parliamentary Council. Formed in 1896 to co-ordinate electoral

---

33 NTDA Min. Bk. 1, 30 Jan. 1895, pp. 196–8; *The Times*, 23 Jan. 1895; NTDF N. Dist. Min. Bk., 2 Feb. 1895; *Evid. Royal Com. Liq. Licensing Laws*, 1898, 36 (Cmnd. 8693), pp. 422, 437.

34 Sir Algernon West, 'The Two Reports of the Licensing Commission', *Nineteenth Cent.*, 47 (1900), 262; Gilbey to Gladstone, 19 Apr. 1899, Gladstone Papers, Add. Ms. 46,057, fos. 154–7. For another interpretation, see Fahey, 'Peel Report', p. 145, n. 31.

35 *Licensed Trade News*, 22 Apr. 1899; *Licensing World and Licensed Trade Review*, 30 Sept. 1899.

activities among retailers, it was dominated by the Society and the League, the two most powerful retail associations which appointed two-thirds of the members and elected the chairman and vice-chairman.[36] Opposition to the League's goal, the mobilization of on-licence retailers against grocers' privileges, unexpectedly came from Charles Walker, chairman of both the Council and the Society. Walker, a previous critic of off-licences, now disputed whether either their total numbers or rights would diminish if regulated by magistrates. In endorsing the League's anti-grocer stance, he further argued, the Council would repudiate 'the band of union for the commonweal of our trade'. This he characterized as 'a grave responsibility'. The Council, ignoring his plea for restraint on a deeply emotive issue, went ahead and ratified the League's resolution. Thus, even before the Association officially selected its general election test questions, publicans and beerhouse keepers had pledged themselves to introducing anti-grocer legislation.[37]

On 2 February 1900 the Association, with the chairmen of the Society and the League present, formally sanctioned Buxton's strategy, adopting two test questions: one supported the Majority Report's compensation proposals; the second opposed the Minority Report's recommendation on grocers' licences. Two optional questions dealt with licensing hours and liquor sales by private clubs. Several days earlier Buxton had given the proposed questions to Gladstone, who had thought them 'reasonable'.[38]

Growing tensions between off-licence holders and other retailers immediately threatened this unity. The Federation saw its understanding with the Association scorned by publicans' insulting speeches and the Council's combative resolution. Equally provocative was the peculiar coalition of publicans and temperance reformers who opposed the renewal of off-

---

[36] The 5 other organizations were the Beer and Wine Trade National Defence Association, the Northern District League of Beer and Wine Trades' Association, the Scottish Licensed Trade Association, the Central Committee of the Liquor Trade of Ireland, and the Dublin Licensed Grocers' and Vintners' Protection Association.

[37] *Licensing World and Licensed Trade Review*, 18 Nov. 1899; see also *ibid.*, 5 May 1900. For Walker's prior dislike of licensed grocers, see his interview with the *Pall Mall Gazette*, published on 23 Jan. 1893.

[38] NTDA Min. Bk. 1, 2 Feb. 1900, pp. 324–6; Appointment Diary, 31 Jan. 1900, Herbert Gladstone Papers, Add. Ms. 46,483, fo. 58.

licences.[39] Outraged grocers promptly took retaliatory action. In April the Federation approved the Association's second test question (opposing the abolition of off-licences), but not, significantly, the first one on compensation.[40]

In an effort to avoid a retail schism, Buxton himself addressed the Society in May 1900. Prohibition, he stressed, was no longer a threat: 'the Local Veto Bill has been dropped — let us hope finally — out of the programme of . . . [the Liberal] party'. Grocers' licences, not local veto, ranked as one of two key issues for the trade. Brewers and retailers, he argued, had vastly increased electoral power as a result of the grocers' alliance with the trade in exchange for being protected in an Association test question. Compensation was the other chief issue. Publicans had broader concerns, he acknowledged, but must seek legislative redress cautiously. Public comfort, he urged, should determine licensing hours and limitations on child messengers, whereas retailers could demand that Parliament intervene in such a purely administrative subject as the spread of private clubs. Beyond persuasive rhetoric, he had one powerful weapon, the vast sums of money brewers gave the Society: his firm and the Brewers' Company alone donated £1,800. All but ten per cent of its funds came from them.[41] This subtle rebuke evidently persuaded the Federation to adopt the Association's question on compensation.

But when Lord Salisbury called an election in September, both the Society and the League disregarded Buxton's advice, following independent policies with test questions on compensation, Sunday closing and local veto but not on grocers' licences. Their disavowal of Buxton's electoral strategy created immense difficulties for Liberal candidates, particularly as C.-B. endorsed Scottish and Welsh local veto in his electoral manifesto.[42]

---

39 *Licensing World and Licensed Trade Review*, 28 Apr. 1900; *Licensed Trade News*, 10 March 1900. Late in the 1890s Swansea's local temperance and publican societies had campaigned together against grocers' licences, one retailer told dismayed trade representatives on the Peel Commission (*Evid. Royal Com. Liq. Licensing Laws*, 1898, 36 (Cmnd. 8693), p. 445, 447, 450).

40 *Licensing World and Licensed Trade Review*, 28 Apr. 1900.

41 *Licensed Trade News*, 5 May 1900; LVPSL 1900 Annual Report. Other brewers donated an additional £4,200 in 1900.

42 *Morning Advertiser*, 24 Sept. 1900; LVNDL Min. Bk., 24 and 28 Sept. 1900; UPC Retail Min. Bk., Nat. Union Lic. Victs., 25 Sept. 1900.

In his campaign for re-election in East Leeds, Herbert Gladstone attempted to gain trade neutrality by omitting any reference to local veto. To disarm suspicious retailers, he carefully defined the Minority Report as less an agenda for future Liberal policy than as a list of possible topics for legislation. On this very general basis, he adopted the Report, except on the crucial issues of grocers' licences and compensation. The former, he contended, should be placed under magistrates' authority, not abolished on flimsy evidence. Gladstone also saw no obstacle to allowing full compensation as recommended in the Majority Report, provided the trade supplied the funds. Reacting angrily to his speech, a prominent local temperance group advised its members to deny him their votes. Although Gladstone fulfilled his agreement with Buxton, incurring hostility from temperance activists, like the Good Templars, the local trade society still contemplated adopting his Conservative opponent.[43]

Buxton, distraught at the sabotaging of his strategy, personally attended a meeting of the Council, making a desperate appeal for unity.[44] Unionists, he stated, would doubtless stay in office, but the trade must anticipate the inevitable 'swing of the pendulum' which would put Liberals in power. 'It is not the part of prudent men to put all their goods into one ship and to rely exclusively on the support of one political party'. A Liberal Government would accept market value for compensation only if the trade cultivated Liberal allies. Buxton repeatedly emphasized the overriding importance of honouring 'pledges' from leading Liberals on the Association's test questions.

Retailers were now jeopardizing his work by approving additional unofficial test questions. When Charles Walker and other members had helped draft the original questions, Buxton reminded the Council, 'it was especially recommended that those [Liberal] candidates who were able to conform to those [Association] questions should be supported'. The questions, though widely publicized, were not criticized by the Council. How could he not but conclude that they had accepted the

---

43 *Leeds Mercury*, 19 and 24 Sept. 1900; *Licensing World and Licensed Trade Review*, 29 Sept. 1900. Some temperance groups, such as the Good Templars, opposed the Minority Report (Fahey, 'Peel's Report', p. 151; Shiman, *Crusade Against Drink*, p. 238).

44 Unattributed quotations in the following 3 paragraphs are drawn from LVNDL Min. Bk., 25 Sept. 1900, UPC Meeting, Verbatim Shorthand Notes; UPC Retail Min. Bk., 25 Sept. 1900.

Association's policy? Could it blame him for feeling tricked at the belatedly adopted supplementary questions on child messengers, Sunday closing and local veto? Such independent action betrayed bad judgment, and would seriously damage the trade. Of these issues, none so angered him as the pointless revival of local veto, not even recommended by the Minority Report for England and acutely embarrassing to Liberals otherwise sympathetic to the trade's policies. Even as he spoke, Buxton, drawn aside by George Croft, learned of one Liberal candidate who had just abandoned his agreement owing to retailers' prevarication. Buxton immediately reported this, and then discussed retail qualms about one of the 'most influential' Liberals, Herbert Gladstone. The chief whip had accepted the Minority Report, Buxton admitted, but merely as a necessary formality to placate C.-B. More importantly, Gladstone had with his rejection of its proposals on grocers' licences and compensation alienated his own temperance supporters. In advancing other subsidiary questions as an acid test for adoption, retailers were jeopardizing his re-election. 'The Trade will show an extraordinary want of foresight if they throw out such a candidate', Buxton declared, and then asked: Would disregarding the pledge of a future cabinet minister enhance the trade's position?

Buxton also disputed the Council's rejection of the 'effective weapon', the alliance with licensed grocers whose test questions had greatly enhanced the Association's political power. Treating off-licence holders with such disloyalty, he warned, would discredit the retailers' voice in framing future trade policies. Now thoroughly exasperated, Buxton threatened to boycott all subsequent negotiations unless the Council capitulated. 'Your charter', he remonstrated, 'is in the first question and if you spoil my own work . . . in securing a little band of Liberals who won't vote for the suppression of licensed houses without [full] compensation, all I can say is I will never take any trouble again'.

Buxton's estrangement from retailers partly derived from differing perceptions of the Association's authority. Brewers viewed it as the sole trade society representing the entire industry, whether in formulating policy, in resolving political disputes or in negotiating with the government. After Buxton left, the Council contested this interpretation, strenuously denying it surrendered any power. 'Here is foreshadowed a difficulty you will have to deal with sooner or later', Charles

Walker observed. 'I do not go to the [National] Trade Defence Fund meeting simply because they are my masters . . . [but] because I am an ex-officio member'. In this capacity, all Council members spoke for themselves, not for their organizations. The League, though not the Society, could genuinely claim that it had also adopted test questions before the Association.[45] Nor did Buxton rightly believe himself duped; Society and League officials had stated their priorities by dissenting from the Majority Report's proposals on child messengers, shorter licensing hours and Sunday closing.[46] Retailers, in fact, sought pledges on these issues to avoid misunderstandings if the government later introduced legislation. This, too, explains why licensed victuallers interrogated candidates in uncontested seats.[47]

Buxton's impassioned plea did convert some retailers who moved that the Council employ only the Association's two test questions. But on an extremely close division, they lost by two votes, unable to counter opponents who pointed out that candidates had already received retail questions. Retailers were not altogether inflexible; the Society at least modified its attitude to compensation, which produced an ambiguous electoral policy reflecting internal trade divisions. The Council's election manifesto advocated compensation from public revenue, whereas the Society's test questions conceded such funds would come from the trade itself.[48]

The Association's midland district also staunchly resisted changing trade policies. When the Association approved the two test questions, it newspaper, the *Licensed Trade News*, expressed confidence that 'the retrocession of Local Veto from the range of practical licensing reform and temperance legislation is *un fait accompli*'. But late in February 1900 Midland

---

[45] The League approved test questions in Sept. 1899, the Association on 2 Feb. 1900 and the UPC on 20 Feb. 1900 (*Licensing World and Licensed Trade Review*, 30 Sept. 1899 and 24 Feb. 1900; see n. 38).

[46] The Majority Report urged prohibiting alcohol to persons under 16, 4 licensing hours on Sunday rather than the current 6–7 and closing Monmouthshire licensed houses on Sundays. Walker and Hyslop opposed them all (*Report Royal Com. Liq. Licensing Laws*, 1899, 35 (Cmnd. 9379), pp. 67–9).

[47] The trade, for example, submitted questions to the unopposed Conservative candidates at Bury St Edmunds and Faversham, though no consistent policy was followed (NTDA E. and S. Count. Dist., General Election 1900, B.S).

[48] *Licensing World and Licensed Trade Review*, 29 Sept. 1900; LVNDL Min. Bk., 25 Sept. 1900, UPC Meeting.

brewers disagreed. Long-standing rivals of bigger London and Burton firms which controlled the Association, they approved the general committee's first question on compensation, but made the second on off-licences optional. It was not simply that Midland brewers had become accustomed to fighting local veto, the licensed grocer and Liberalism, but that they disliked centralizing power in one agency. Distrustful of outsiders, they still refused subsidies from the central office as a means of ensuring their autonomy, which included determining strategy. The general committee tactfully requested giving the official questions a fair trail.[49] Privately, George Croft, large London brewer and the Association's treasurer, reassured Midland brewers that the questions would be reviewed before the general election. Charles Showell, chairman of the midland district, deemed this an inadequate solution, and resigned in March. Pressure then came from John Gretton, another influential member of the Association representing the huge Burton brewery, Bass, Ratcliff & Gretton, who reaffirmed Croft's guarantee. Showell finally yielded, withdrawing his resignation but not abandoning his opposition. Following his lead, Midland brewers defiantly passed several resolutions: one reiterated the need for revising the test questions; another authorized employing meanwhile at by-elections the 1895 General Election questions (opposing local veto and supporting full compensation). This impasse persisted into the election, with the 1895 questions used almost universally throughout the midlands. Like the Council, Midland brewers had re-introduced the divisive issue of local veto and refused to assist licensed grocers, tactics which not only subverted the policy but directly challenged the primacy of the Association.[50]

Despite dissent from retailers and Midland brewers, Buxton's strategy did achieve some success at the 1900 Election. The trade regarded Unionists, upholders of the Majority Report, as natural allies, and supported them in all but twenty-nine English and Welsh constituencies. In some of these twenty-nine

[49] *Licensed Trade News*, 10 Feb. 1900; NTDA Mid. Dist. Min. Bk., 22 Feb. 1900, D 3163/2/1/1, pp. 292 – 3; NTDA Min. Bk. 1, 6 March 1900, p. 328.
[50] NTDA Mid. Dist. Min. Bk., 22 March and 24 Sept. 1900, D 3163/2/1/1, pp. 296 – 8, 300 – 1; NTDA Min. Bk. 1, 25 July 1894, pp. 178 – 9; NTDA Mid. Dist. Election Material, Questions and Answers from Candidates at the 1900 General Election, D 3163/2/3/3; *Licensed Trade News*, 19 Jan. 1901.

cases, the hostility of both candidates prevented the trade from intervening. But in most of them Liberals, pledged to full compensation and to blocking the abolition of grocers' licences, secured trade neutrality. Collectively there were at least twenty-four such Liberals in 1900, sixteen of whom were elected. This minimum figure of twenty-four, while not large given the total number of English and Welsh seats (495), still represented nearly a five – fold increase over those Liberals receiving trade neutrality in 1895.[51]

Buxton's electoral arrangements came closest to reaching fruition in the south-east, which contained half of the twenty-four seats in which the trade stayed neutral. Two involved Liberal brewers: Felix Cobbold at Woodbridge, and Hugh Hoare at Chesterton, who opposed a Unionist brewer, Walter Raymond Greene. The trade also declared neutrality at Charles Gold's former seat of Saffron Walden, where Lord Kimberley's son stood.[52]

With three cases of avowed neutrality, including Herbert Gladstone's West Leeds seat, the Yorkshire/Lancashire region ranked second.[53] What ultimately proved decisive in Gladstone's obtaining trade neutrality was the UKA's fierce campaign against him. Gladstone won re-election as much because he was unopposed by the local trade as because not all temperance voters abandoned him. At two meetings of local temperance advocates, Gladstone received unanimous votes of confidence. Another eleven temperance-minded ministers, also disregarding the UKA's strictures, commended him to drink reformers.[54] In fact, it was not Gladstone but the UKA agent who met with a humiliating rebuff. On appealing to customary donors for money, he discovered that 'pious Wesleyans want to

---

[51] See p. 122. Writing soon after the election, Noel Buxton and Walter Hoare, two temperance advocates whose families engaged in brewing, noted that at least 30 Liberal candidates had accepted the Majority Report's compensation proposals, thereby avoiding trade electoral opposition (Buxton and Hoare, 'Temperance Reform', pp. 169, 209).

[52] The other 9 constituencies were Colchester, Ipswich (both seats), Mid-, N., E. and S. Norfolk, S. Huntingdon and Grantham (NTDA E. Dist. 1899 – 1900 Report, pp. 1 – 11).

[53] The trade also declared neutrality at Hallamshire and Rotherham (NTDA 1900 Report, p. 12).

[54] Gladstone was denied support from the W. Leeds Temperance Council (Leeds Mercury, 5 Oct. 1900). NTDA 1900 Report, pp. 10 – 12; Leeds Mercury, 2 and 3 Oct. 1900; Alliance News, 27 Sept. and 4 Oct. 1900.

drown me, others prefer shooting me, and the parsons have deserted me'.[55]

In London, the Society classified candidates as favourable (Unionist) or unfavourable (Liberal), except for five Liberals and one Unionist.[56] Even this limited attempt to implement Buxton's scheme was repudiated in West Southwark, where the local publicans' association supported the Unionist candidate.[57]

Most of these twenty-four seats were either safe Liberal constituencies (11) or marginal (11), with just two being traditionally Unionist.[58] Since Liberals did much better in marginal seats (+ one per cent) than in their own safe seats (− four per cent),[59] the trade's neutrality helped win doubtful constituencies, perhaps at the expense of alienating Liberal supporters of temperance.[60]

At least another nineteen Liberals had entered into Buxton's compact, but later withdrew, often because they answered the supplementary retail questions unsatisfactorily. At West Lindsay, E. Bainbridge declined to oppose Sunday closing, local veto and restraints on child messengers, while at Westbury and Christchurch, John Fuller and T. A. Brassey unwisely endorsed local veto.[61] Sometimes trade societies demanded more exacting

---

55 Quoted in Fahey, 'Politics of Drink', p. 80.
56 *Licensing World and Licensed Trade Review*, 29 Sept. 1900. The 5 Liberal candidates were at N. Camberwell, S. Hackney, Poplar, Peckham and W. Southwark. Every Unionist candidate, except Diggle (N. Camberwell), was classified favourably (*ibid.*, 6 Oct. 1900).
57 Chairman of the S. London Lic. Vict. Assoc. to editor, *Morning Advertiser*, 4 Oct. 1900.
58 The trade also adopted neutrality at Hastings, Maidstone, Northwich, E. Birmingham and E. Bristol. In E. Birmingham, the Labour candidate gave a pledge against local veto (NTDA 1900 Report, pp. 1 – 13; *Licensed Trade News*, 27 Oct. and 1 and 8 Dec. 1900).
59 These seats were: (safe Liberal) Rotherham, E. Bristol, Poplar, Osgoldcross, Saffron Walden, W. Leeds, N. Norfolk, Hallamshire, Northwick, Mid-Norfolk and S. Hackney; (marginals) Woodbridge, E. Norfolk, Grantham, S. Huntingdon, Ipswich (2 seats), Colchester, S. Norfolk, Chesterton, Hastings and Peckham; (safe Unionist) E. Birmingham (no Liberal candidate), and Maidstone (petition nullified Liberal victory).
60 The trade's influence can be exaggerated in an election dominated by imperial issues, a point underlined by the Liberals' overall rise of 2.1% in the poll. Sir William Gurdon (N. Norfolk) was the only pro-Boer Liberal who had no trade opposition (John W. Auld, 'The Liberal Pro-Boers', *Jour. Brit. Stud.*, 14 (1975), 100).
61 *Retford, Worksop, Isle of Axholme and Gainsborough News*, 5 Oct. 1900; *Licensed Trade News*, 13 Oct. and 8 Dec. 1900; NTDA W. Dist. 1900 Annual Report, pp. 8 – 9; NTDA E. and S. Count. Dist., General Election, 1900.

terms unacceptable to Liberals. Stowmarket brewers and retailers sought publicly funded compensation, and supported the Conservative, despite the Liberal's disclaimer of local veto in his election address.[62]

Agreements between Liberal candidates and the Association also collapsed owing to the trade's entrenched prejudice against Liberalism. Lionel Holland, denied trade neutrality at Romford despite favourable replies to trade test questions, recalled that 'no assurance of fair dealing can persuade a brewer or publican that every Liberal does not aim at the destruction of his livelihood'. Local trade societies mistrusted Liberal candidates who even talked to the enemy. G. W. Palmer's willingness to answer temperance test questions convinced Reading retailers 'how dangerous it was to rely upon a man who received teetotal support'. Revoking their unappreciated neutrality, they then adopted his Conservative opponent.[63]

Altogether another eleven Liberals committed to Buxton's programme could have been returned; six in seats where Liberals won notwithstanding the trade's rejection of their pledges, and five in seats where the trade probably guaranteed a Unionist victory.[64] Certainly the election of only sixteen Liberals, with avowed sympathies for full compensation and grocers' licences, fell markedly short of Buxton's expectations, but neither he nor the Association had foreseen the extent of trade disunity and apathy.

This lack of commitment was equally reflected in lower campaign expenditure. With £1,200 from the Brewers' Company and £500 from the Country Brewers' Society, the Association laid out £2,000 for the election, less than half of

---

[62] NTDA E. Count. Dist., General Election 1900.

[63] Lionel Holland, 'Liberal or Whig', *New Liberal Rev.*, 1 (1901), 181; NTDA E. Dist. 1899 – 1900 Report; NTDA W. Dist. 1900 Annual Report, pp. 5, 13; *Reading Observer*, 27 Oct. 1900; NTDA 1900 Report, pp. 15 – 16.

[64] Liberals considered adopting the Association test questions at N. and S. Somersetshire, Mid-Northants., W. Southwark, S.W. and N.W. Norfolk, Peterborough, S. Dorsetshire, Bedford, Eastbourne, E. Grinstead, Maldon and Ramsey (*Sussex Daily News*, 6 Oct. 1900; *Licensed Trade News*, 8 and 15 Dec. 1900; NTDA W. Dist. 1900 Annual Report, pp. 7 – 8; NTDA E. Dist. 1899 – 1900 Report, p. 3; NTDA E. and S. Dist. General Election, 1900; NTDA E. Dist., General Election, 1900; NTDA Min. Bk. 1, 23 Nov. 1900, pp. 339 – 40; see n. 57).

what it spent in 1892 or 1895.[65] Based on the activities undertaken in the western district (Gloucestershire, Wiltshire, Somersetshire and Berkshire), where brewers and retailers spent twice the £200 allocated by the London office, total district expenses probably added another £1,000 – £1,500.[66]

Following the election, brewers and retailers alike reconsidered the Council's anomalous position. At a Council meeting in November 1900, Charles Walker, though reasserting its role as the arbiter of retail policies, admitted retail leaders' ex-officio status in the Association caused discord, and proposed joint conferences as a solution. While Council members ratified this scheme, the Association instead suggested that ten of them — five each from the Society and the League — sit on its general committee. Brewers ostensibly wanted retailers officially represented to suppress dissent on both the test questions and licensed grocers as allies, but the real issue was power. More interested in centralizing than in sharing it, brewers saw binding all members to decisions of the majority as an important step towards strengthening the Association's authority. London publicans, sensing refusal would imperil future donations from the Brewers' Company, duly consented.[67] Impervious to this sort of pressure, the League delayed action until its annual conference in May 1901. There many hostile League officials, largely from the midlands and north, led the opposition to surrendering any independence. They accused brewers of being narrow-minded, of subscribing paltry sums of money and of damaging League recruitment by enlisting publicans into the Association. Some publicans even saw a conspiracy against the League. The League, John Cumberland asserted, had not 'a tenth part of the Associations in the West and East of England affiliated with [it] . . . because the agents employed by the National [Trade] Defence persuaded societies that there was no necessity to belong to it'. There was certainly a large disparity in membership in the southern counties, where the Association

---

65 NTDA Min. Bk. 2, 5 Dec. 1905, p. 166; CBS Min. Bk. 6, 5 Oct. 1900; Brewers' Co. Min. Bk., 11 Oct. 1900, pp. 321 – 2; see pp. 119, 123. The Society spent the lowest amount since 1897 (LVPSL 1897 – 1900 Annual Reports).

66 Western district brewers spent £466 on the election. Printing and stationary (£117), parliamentary registers (£59) and agent/sub-agent gratuities (£116) represented the largest costs (NTDA W. Dist. 1900 Annual Report).

67 UPC Min. Bk., 20 Nov. 1900 and 14 March 1901; Brewers' Co. Min. Bk., 11 Apr. 1901, p. 368.

enrolled five times as many publicans as the League. These arguments so disturbed the executive that it vetoed the plan. Only the timely intervention of the Council's leaders, Edward Morrall (president of the League) and Charles Walker (chairman of the Society), with forceful speeches on behalf of cooperation between trade societies, convinced the conference to override the executive and appoint the five delegates.[68]

Had brewers not been so committed to incorporating licensed grocers into the trade, this attempt to establish the Association's pre-eminence over retail societies might have succeeded. The League had, in fact, already emphasized that prejudice against licensed grocers would supersede dictates of the Association by insisting on passing at the May conference the familiar resolution urging legislation which placed them under magistrates' control. A month later the Association re-adopted its 1900 test questions, despite protests from League representatives who vainly urged that their grocer resolution be included. When the Association's newspaper, *Licensed Trade News*, stated that representatives approved the questions unanimously, League officials predictably contradicted this and likewise reconfirmed their own 1900 test questions. Renewed controversy over licensed grocers therefore led to a deeper, more acrimonious schism.[69]

Similarly, grocers' licences fostered friction between the League and the Society. The League, in its 1901 Annual Report, quoted one former president's dictum that the licensed grocer 'has done more public mischief and created more drunkenness among women than all the public-houses ever did'. At the Association's June meeting, defiant London publicans had helped brewers outvote the League's grocer resolution. In publicly maintaining that the Association test questions had been reaffirmed unanimously, the Society further exacerbated the dispute. Betrayed and then misrepresented, the League

---

[68] LVNDL Min. Bk., 16 May 1901; LVNDL 1901 Annual Report, pp. 91–3; NTDA S. Dist. Report, 1900. League affiliated societies seceding to join the Association also caused acrimony (LVNDL Min. Bk., 17 Sept. 1902).

[69] LVNDL 1901 Annual Report, pp. 102–3; NTDA Min. Bk. 1, 28 June 1901, pp. 360–1; *Licensed Trade News*, 6 July 1901; E. Morrall and J. Turner (president and vice president of the League) to the editor, *ibid.*, 13 July 1901; LVNDL Min. Bk., 17 Sept. 1901.

retaliated, withdrawing from the Council.[70] Debate on grocers' licences continued relentlessly. The unrepentant Society printed editorials in its own newspaper refuting claims that grocers were responsible for female intemperance. Two grievances, grocers and money, now became linked. The League implied that the Society, which brewers subsidized heavily, had been bought off by their money: 'Charles Walker has for a number of years been a paid agent of the wholesale trade'. By 1902 the League was blaming grocers for isolating it from other trade societies. As one of its officials complained, 'anything we might take up in the interests of the League would find strenuous opposition from that [National Trade Defence] Association, which is decidedly under the influence of the grocer element'. Henceforth, League members would 'fight their own battles' unfettered by rival societies. For retailers, the proposed alliance with grocers thus had far-reaching but fatal consequences, embittering the League against the Society and Association, aggravating provincial unrest arising from brewers' nominal subsidies and finally destroying the Council.[71]

According to David Fahey 'before the general election [of 1900] what support the Majority Report had was only as an alternative to the Minority Report. The liquor trade either clung to the *status quo* as the best of all attainable worlds or in the case of some publicans agitated for legislation to protect them from local temperance reformers'.[72] Yet this verdict should be revised given the significant contribution made by Buxton and the Association in mobilizing support for the unpopular Majority Report within the trade. Brewers, displaying much flexibility in 1900, were pragmatic, not obstinate, opponents of temperance reform. Obstinacy was a characteristic of publicans and some Alliance members, two groups which persistently put forward untenable policies. Similarly, Campbell-Bannerman's ineptitude nearly disrupted his party, whereas his chief whip, Herbert Gladstone, realistically concluded that local veto must be dropped and the trade appeased before Liberals could regain working-class votes. In arranging an understanding with over

---

70 LVNDL Min. Bk., 17 and 18 Sept. 1901 and 12 Feb. 1902 and 1901 Annual Report, p. 5; *Licensing World and Licensed Trade Review*, 6 July 1901; E. Morrall and J. Turner (president and vice president of the League) to editor, *ibid.*, 20 July 1901.

71 LVNDL Min. Bk., 18 Sept. 1901 and 12 Feb. 1902; *Licensing World and Licensed Trade Review*, 19 Oct. 1901.

72 Fahey, 'Peel's Report', p. 139.

forty Liberal candidates, Buxton had transformed licensed grocers into trade supporters and revised the Association's electoral policy, though by 1901 this strategy had alienated the League, one of Britain's largest retail organizations, and annihilated the Council. In a broader context, the election was the culmination of persisting provincial discontent over brewers' meagre donations to the League and their suspected covert efforts to undermine it. However much licensed grocers were detested by the League as competitors and allies, they precipitated, not provoked, this crisis. Totally devoid of long-term perspective, the self-absorbed, insular and myopic publicans could never surmount their petty feuds and pursue the wider objective of permanent security. Money and authority would continue to beset the League's troubled relations with the Association in the Edwardian era.

6

Crisis of Faith

Three developments seemed to strengthen the trade in the Edwardian period. First, London, Burton and country brewers amalgamated into the Brewers' Society, gaining greater prestige and influence. Second, ancillary industries were mobilized in the Allied Brewery Traders' Association, which enlarged the trade's electoral power and supplied an 'independent agency' for disseminating propaganda. Finally, Balfour's cabinet with the 1904 Licensing bill enacted a gradual scheme of licensing reduction fully compensating brewers and retailers for lost property. To protect compensation, trade leaders abandoned any pretence of neutrality, and openly supported Unionists. Yet despite these advances, the rank and file became increasingly dissatisfied and apathetic. Deteriorating markets, heavier taxes imposed by both parties, shortages of funds and three consecutive defeats at general elections demoralized many in the trade, prompting demands for a policy of political neutrality.

By late 1902 magistrates, thoroughly irritated by the government failure to implement the Peel Reports and reduce excessive licences, had come to recognize the need for an initiative on licensing reduction. Their authority to do so, on grounds other than misconduct and without compensation, had been clearly established in the *Sharp v. Wakefield* case early in the 1890s.[1] Justices throughout the country were also inspired by the repeated failure of the trade's appeals to higher courts, the last concluding in 1902, against the action of one local Surrey bench, which had cited Farnham's redundant number of licences as

---

[1] Fahey, 'Brewers and Drinkers', p. 91; Shiman, *Crusade Against Drink*, p. 214; Henry Carter, *The English Temperance Movement: A Study in Objectives* (1933), pp. 210 – 12.

adequate justification for withdrawing many without compensation.[2] As the *Country Brewers' Gazette* observed, 'the Farnham judgment . . . imports an additional element of precariousness into the tenure of licensed property'.[3]

These two factors prompted magistrates to revoke unprecedented numbers of drink licences. 'There has never before been a movement so widespread, so serious, and so likely to bring staggering losses upon those who are interested in licensed property', the *Brewers' Journal* contended. More licences, in fact, were denied renewal in 1903 than in the previous six years combined.[4] Frantic brewers and publicans implored Balfour's cabinet for legislation restraining these attacks on their 'property'. But the prime minister, though aware of publicans being 'again on the war path', procrastinated.[5]

What chiefly blocked legislation was the aversion of numerous brewers and retailers to accepting the compensation proposed in the Peel Commission's Majority Report. One solution, the imposition of levies on the trade itself for compensation, was incorporated into a private member's bill in 1903, and approved by the Association.[6] This did not prevent dissent. A sizeable group within the trade still regarded heavier liquor taxes by drinkers as the best means of generating revenue for compensation. Edward Johnson (chairman of the Society) supported this as the Council's policy. In a widely publicized speech before the Society, Johnson rejected 'the idea that one licensed victualler should pay for the other', since it was untrue 'that he would benefit by the destruction of his brother'. Another member of

2   In 1901 the Farnham bench, convinced the ratio of 1 licence per 118 inhabitants exceeded local requirements, had submitted a voluntary scheme of licensing reduction to local brewers and retailers. Their reluctance to negotiate antagonized the justices, who refused to renew all 45 licences in March, 1902. Eventually, 9 retailers lost their licences. Appeals to higher courts led to only 2 licences being reinstated (*Country Brewers' Gazette*, 27 March, 3 July and 9 Oct. 1902).
3   *Ibid.*, 3 July 1902.
4   *Brewers' Journal*, 15 Feb. 1903. Magistrates refused to renew 1,043 on-licences between 1897 and 1902, but 1,105 in 1903 (*Statistics as to the Operation and Administration of the Laws Relating to the Sale of Intoxicating Liquor in England and Wales*, 1914–16, 54 (Cmnd. 7981), p. 4).
5   Douglas to Sandars, 3 June 1903, Bodleian Lib., Sandars Papers, Ms. 739, fo. 46.
6   NTDA Min. Bk. 2, 4 March 1903, p. 63; *Hansard*, 4th ser., 121 (24 Apr. 1903), cols. 427–32. Brewer MPs unanimously supported the bill.

the Association, the League, disliked further taxes, so instead suggested that the government simply use the revenue, 3d per barrel on beer and 6d per gallon on spirits, appropriated for the aborted 1890 compensation scheme. Brewers like Howard Tripp, whose partner represented Ind, Coope & Co. on the Association's committee, fully agreed. Although disaffected brewers and retailers reached no consensus, they all opposed the principle of providing compensation themselves.[7]

In April 1904 Balfour's Government defied these demands, introducing a Licensing bill based on the Majority Report. This established the central principle, so vehemently contested by prohibitionists and most Liberals, of compensating all owners of on-licences denied renewal other than for misconduct. Brewers and other licensed property owners would contribute annually between £1 and £100 for each licence depending on its value to a special fund, creating £1.2 million each year for compensation, far larger than the £300,000 – £350,000 stipulated in the 1888 and 1890 schemes. Even if inexpensive pubs and beerhouses were selected, no one expected 8,000 redundancies annually, the level needed to reach the ratio of one on-licence for every 750 inhabitants advocated in the Minority Report. This was so for two reasons. First, licensing reduction could proceed only as quickly as local funds in the levy permitted. Second, licence owners received full compensation, the difference in value between the premises licensed and unlicensed. Using the Majority Report's gradualist approach, the bill might eliminate 2,500 of the 100,000 existing licences annually, ultimately lowering the licence density considerably without causing brewers and retailers undue economic hardship. Magistrates lost as well as gained some authority. Henceforth, they must specify reasons for withdrawing a licence, but could abolish pre-1869 beerhouses, previously safeguarded by parliamentary statute. Finally, the bill contained one novel feature to appease temperance critics, the monopoly value would be charged as the fee for new licences.[8]

All major trade organizations, while dissatisfied with the source of compensation, gave the bill grudging assent. Many retailers, the *Brewers' Guardian* stressed, 'have all their work cut out to keep their heads above water'. They wryly dubbed the

[7] *Brewers' Journal*, 15 March 1903; LVNDL Min. Bk., 10 March 1903; *Brewers' Guardian*, 10 Dec. 1903.
[8] Wilson, *Alcohol and Nation*, pp. 110 – 11.

bill the 'Mutual Burial Fund'. The CBS objected to the licensing reduction scheme as inferior to the simple suspension of JP powers to revoke licences, while the Association derided compensation entirely from the trade as 'unreasonable'.[9]

Brewers and retailers protested vehemently against paying compensation not so much because of heavy levies as because of the brewing industry's depressed markets. Falling beer consumption, earlier purchases of tied houses at inflated prices and large-scale investments in rebuilding and renovating them, all led to sharply declining profits. The average dividends of breweries with £1 million of ordinary shares had reached eleven per cent (1900), but fell to 8.5 per cent (1904) and finally stabilized at five per cent (1910) before slowly recovering. Watney, Combe Reid & Co., one of the country's largest breweries, missed dividends in 1901, and other firms likewise experienced problems.[10] This depression, far worse in London than elsewhere, hit hardest those firms which most heavily subsidized trade defence, thus exaggerating the trade's hostility towards increased financial burdens and prompting test questions demanding lower taxation.[11]

The Act had considerably less impact than expected chiefly because one court case set the precedent for generous compensation.[12] Brewers themselves estimated annual reductions of 1,500 and some unrealistic government spokesmen predicted 2,500, but even with the poorest premises chosen, only 1,000 licences (almost two-thirds of them beerhouses) were eliminated

---

9 *Brewing Trade Review*, 1 May 1904; CBS Min. Bk. 7, 21 Apr. 1904, p. 50; *Licensed Trade News*, 23 Apr. and 23 July 1904; LVNDL Min. Bk., 26 Apr. 1904; *Brewers' Guardian*, 10 May 1904; NTDA Min. Bk. 2, 28 Apr. 1904, pp. 106 – 7; *Brewers' Journal*, 21 Apr. 1904 (special supplement); Nevile, *Seventy Years*, p. 56.

10 Baxter, 'Brewing Industry', pp. 242, 244 – 5; Vaizey, 'Brewing Industry', p. 408; Alan Crawford, Michael Dunn and Robert Thorne, *Birmingham Pubs, 1880 – 1939* (Oxford, 1986), pp. 9 – 10; Girouard, *Victorian Pubs*, ch. 4.

11 NTDA Min. Bk. 2, 16 Dec. 1904, p. 145; *Morning Advertiser*, 22 Dec. 1905; *Country Brewers' Gazette*, 13 Oct. 1904; Knox, 'Tied House System', pp. 82 – 3; Crawford, Dunn and Thorne, *Birmingham Pubs*, p. 10. For another interpretation, see Gourvish and Wilson, 'Profitability in Brewing'.

12 In 1906 the Kennedy judgement based compensation on the house's market value when closed, barrelage and part of its property income. This definition substantially increased brewers' compensation, in some cases tripling the amount (Wilson, *Alcohol and Nation*, pp. 111 – 12; St Aldwyn to Balfour, Aug. 1908, Brit. Lib., Balfour Papers, Add. Ms. 49,695, fos. 167 – 8; Home Office Memorandum, 28 Apr. 1908, Brit. Lib., Gladstone Papers, Add. Ms. 45,994, fos. 93 – 6).

annually in the years 1905 – 9. Closing dearer pubs and beerhouses meant higher compensation, and so the figure thereafter fell to 900 annually (1910 – 14). By 1915, almost 9,900 on-licences had been extinguished, representing about ten per cent of the total, while another 3,500 (three per cent) had lapsed without compensation. Altogether £9 million was granted in compensation, but little of it, eleven per cent, went to retailers.[13]

Brewers sacrificed much less than they publicly claimed. Between 1905 and 1914 Greene, King & Co., for example, paid £1,500 annually into the compensation levy on nearly 400 tied houses, a sum equivalent to about three per cent of its profits. In fact, brewers did quite well out of surrendering licences. '*I know* that the brewers have got more [than] the houses were worth', asserted one prominent Conservative peer. Having paid exorbitant sums for unprofitable drink shops, brewers exploited licensing reduction as a means of unloading bad investments. Richard Wilson's recent study of Greene, King & Co. strongly suggests that brewers actually profited from the Act. In the years 1905 – 11, this Suffolk brewery contributed £9,300 to the compensation fund, received £11,100 in compensation and sold the former drink shop sites for another £6,000, giving a net balance of £7,800. Another East Anglian brewery, Steward & Patteson, also had no financial grounds for complaint, netting a profit on closed licensed premises. Nor were brewers necessarily worse off with fewer licences. St Aldwyn told Balfour in 1908 that 'brewers . . . in some cases have largely benefited by their [licences'] abolition, most of the trade being merely transferred to other houses belonging to the same firm'. Magistrates disregarded this factor in determining the compensation fee.[14]

Meanwhile, the prospect of legislation finally resolving the protracted compensation issue had induced the three major brewers' organizations, the Country Brewers' Society, Brewers' Company and Burton Brewers' Association, to amalgamate into one comprehensive national organization, the Brewers' Society. One of the most compelling reasons for this merger was to

13 Bruce K. Murray, *The People's Budget 1909/10: Lloyd George and Liberal Politics* (Oxford, 1980), p. 140; Wilson, *Greene King*, p. 142; *Brewing Trade Review*, 1 June and 1 July 1904; Wilson, *Alcohol and Nation*, p. 381; *Statistics as to the Operation and Administration of the Laws Relating to the Sale of Intoxicating Liquor in Eng. and Wales*, 1914 – 16, 54 (Cmnd. 7981), pp. 4 – 5.

14 Wilson, *Greene King*, pp. 142 – 4, 270, 274 – 5; St Aldwyn to Balfour, Aug. 1908, Balfour Papers, Add. Ms. 49,695, fos. 167 – 8; Gourvish and Wilson, 'Profitability in Brewing', p. 155. St Aldwyn's italics.

promote unity with aloof Lancashire and Yorkshire brewers, who customarily opposed official policy. The new chairman, James G. Groves, underlined this strategy in expressing the hope that the Manchester Brewers' Central Association would be 'one of the first to place itself in close touch with the Brewers' Society'. Yet not until late 1906 did Manchester brewers become federated. At the same time the Brewers' Society so successfully recruited members from Yorkshire and Lancashire that the general committee grew from thirty-six to forty-two. Integrating northern and southern brewers decidedly enhanced the Brewers' Society's authority as the official brewers' organ.[15]

The influx of London, Burton, Lancashire and Yorkshire brewers fundamentally changed the Brewers' Society's general committee (see table 8). Previously, almost half the CBS's elected members came from Hampshire, Berkshire, Buckinghamshire, Hertfordshire, Essex and Middlesex. London brewers now dominated, ousting the 'old guard' on the CBS general committee. More Lancashire, Staffordshire and, to a lesser extent, Yorkshire brewers also served on the general committee. In the 1905 – 25 period, they and London brewers together comprised nearly half the representation.

Following the 1904 Licensing Act, trade leaders, indebted to the Unionist party and fearful of Liberal hostility to compensation, somewhat altered their rhetoric and political stance. 'The Trade cannot . . . cast off its allegiance to a party which has been just, fair and equitable in its attitude', the *Licensed Trade News* asserted in December 1905. 'Identity with the Unionist cause just now is compulsory', the paper concluded. Others echoed these views. 'They must support the Unionist party', Edward Johnson advised Finsbury licensed victuallers and beersellers, 'to preserve the integrity of the trade'.[16] Another way in which trade officials discarded the guise of neutrality, and more overtly identified with Unionists was by adopting a new electoral policy, the endorsement of candidates on the basis of party affiliation instead of answers to test questions. Midland brewers, for instance, submitted test questions only where both candidates' opinions were unknown.[17]

15 *Brewing Trade Review*, 1 July 1904, 1 Aug. and 1 Dec. 1906.
16 *Licensed Trade News*, 24 June and 16 Dec. 1905; see also *ibid.*, 26 Nov. 1904, 9 Dec. 1905 and 6 Jan. 1906.
17 Birm. and Aston Trade Comt. Min. Bk., 2 March and 12 Dec. 1905, Staffs. R.O., D 3163/2/1/6, pp. 79 – 80, 84 – 5.

Table 8
The CBS/BS general committee, 1884 – 1925: length of representation as percentage of total years

County	1884 – 1904 (%)	1905 – 1925 (%)	Rank (Before/After)
Buckinghamshire	9.0	2.4	1/13
Essex	8.5	4.9	2/6
Berkshire	8.4	2.1	3/19
Hampshire	8.2	5.8	4/5
Hertfordshire	7.4	3.8	5/9
Yorkshire	6.2	6.7	6/3
Middlesex	6.0	2.2	7/14
Dorsetshire	4.9	2.2	8/15
Norfolk	4.7	2.9	9/11
Kent	4.1	4.9	10/7
Cambridgeshire	3.8	4.2	11/8
Gloucestershire	3.3	2.2	12/16
London	2.8	19.8	13/1
Wales	2.7	2.9	14/12
Surrey	2.5	2.2	15/17
Sussex	2.5	0.1	16/24
Bedfordshire	2.2	1.5	17/21
Lancashire	2.0	12.3	18/2
Nottinghamshire	2.0	0	19/25
Staffordshire	1.9	6.2	20/4
Northumberland	1.6	1.7	21/20
Durham	1.4	0.6	22/23
Suffolk	1.1	0	23/26
Warwickshire	0	3.3	-/10
Scotland	0	2.2	-/18
Derby	0	1.4	-/22
Other	2.8	1.5	–

Sources: Compiled from CBS Min. Bks., *Country Brewers' Gazette*, and *Brewing Trade Review*.

Many ordinary brewers and publicans, however, resisted this transparent alignment with Unionists at the 1906 Election, where Liberals with their anti-compensation policy achieved a stunning victory. According to the Midland Counties Report, internal divisions made the trade 'comparatively powerless to influence the electorate'. Displeased with Unionists' continued wartime taxation,[18] meddlesome restrictions on child messengers,[19] and compensation scheme, many members of the trade abandoned customary electoral activities, even in some cases defecting. 'A goodly number of those engaged in the Trade felt . . . hardly treated by the [1904] Act, and did not . . . support the party who introduced and passed it', the *Licensing World and Licensed Trade Review* reported after the election. Liberal activists like Dunstan Fraser Cobham also noted trade disunity: 'the trade has hitherto gone Tory, but last election . . . there was some hesitation & in some cases a turn over'.[20]

The declining commitment of many brewers and retailers threatened the trade as seriously as an unfriendly Liberal government. Both prompted reforms within the brewing industry. Late in 1906 the Association hired a special full-time agent, R. Mitchell Banks, with a salary of £600 to improve protective machinery. Removing defects in organization and maintaining its efficiency, the Association calculated, would require an increased income of £6,000.[21]

Brewers naturally felt that founding one national body, the Brewers' Society, would help to centralize the collection of funds for the Association, especially since temperance organizations like the UKA were spending over £13,000 each year.[22] Yet

---

[18] In 1900 Salisbury's Government put a temporary 1s tax per barrel on beer, raising the overall duty to 7s 9d. *Morning Advertiser*, 13 Jan. 1906.

[19] Late Victorian and Edwardian children often fetched beer for their fathers' meals. Under the 1901 Child Messenger Act, children 14 years or younger could purchase alcohol for off-consumption, provided it was sealed and corked in vessels of at least 1 pint. Publicans disliked the inconvenience of fixing labels with glue or wax as much as the insinuation that they fostered child drunkenness (NTDA Mid. Count. 1906 Jt. Comt. Report, D 3163/2/2, pp. 4–5).

[20] *Licensing World and Licensed Trade Review*, 20 Jan. 1906; Cobham to Brodie, 22 Aug. 1907, Campbell-Bannerman Papers, Add. Ms. 41,240, fos. 69–71; see also *Morning Advertiser*, 5 Jan. 1910; *Licensed Trade News*, 19 March 1904, 3 Feb. 1906, 16 Nov. 1907 and 9 May 1908.

[21] NTDA Min. Bk. 2, 29 Nov. 1906, p. 196.

[22] In the years 1903–7, the UKA spent £16,800, £17,400, £14,000, £13,500 and £14,200 (UKA Reports, 1903–7).

the Brewers' Society executive concluded that 'the time was not opportune' for enlarging ordinary receipts, despite that fact that the Association could barely find £3,000, much less the £6,000 demanded, and had spent only £4,000 on electioneering in 1906, twelve per cent less than in 1895.[23] This was scarcely a resolute attitude for restoring trade morale. Shortages of money, scarcely a recent problem, had troubled the Association since the defeat of local veto; its normal income had almost halved to less than £3,000. With district agencies included, the Association's total expenditure rose to about £6,500, less than half what the UKA spent.[24]

Inadequate funding hindered the special agent's efforts for the next six years. Banks extended retail membership, particularly in the southeast, reconstructing the eastern and southern districts into a home and southern counties region. In the midlands, he concentrated on Nottingham, where the county brewers' association had withdrawn from the Fund in 1894 and dissolved some years later. After forming the Lincolnshire and Nottinghamshire Brewers' Association, he combined it with Rutland and Peterborough in a new district branch, which soon federated with the Association.[25]

Meanwhile the trade was attempting to bring into its system of defence neglected but important allies, the vast network of ancillary industries which depended largely on beer sales. It was Reginald Mortimer who provided the main impetus. Trained as a barrister, he served the Fund in various capacities: as manager (1891 – 3), as an elected member (1899 – 1913) and as one of its executives (from 1913). His connection with allied trades justified his influence. For a time, White, Tompkins & Courage, a malt factors firm, employed him as managing director, but in 1903 he assumed new duties with Garton, Hill & Co., distributors of brewing sugar. Brewers so valued his influence

23 BS Min. Bk. 2, 18 and 26 Oct. 1906, B.S., pp. 4, 8; NTDA Min. Bk. 2, 11 Jan. and 29 Nov. 1906, pp. 172, 196; see p. 123. The Brewers' Company donated £1,800 and the BS £2,500 towards election expenses (BS 1907 Annual Report, B.S.; Br. Co. Min. Bk., 10 and 11 Jan. 1906, pp. 127 – 8).
24 See table 6, p. 114. The Yorkshire Brewers' Association annually spent over £480 in the years 1900 – 6, while the NTDA's Western District over £290 (Yorks. Br. Assoc. Annual Reports, 1900 – 6; NTDA W. Dist. Annual Reports, 1901 – 6).
25 NTDA Home and S. Count. Min. Bk. 1, 18 Nov. 1907, N. Home Count. Br. Assoc., p. 18; Lincs. and Notts. Br. Assoc. Min. Bk., 19 Feb. 1908 and 23 Feb. 1909, E. Mid. Br. Assoc.; NTDA Notts., Lincs., Rutland and Peterborough Min. Bk., 1 March 1909, ibid.

that they made him an honourary general committee member of the CBS and Brewers' Society, the only non-brewer accorded such status after 1905.[26] With his first-hand knowledge of trade organizations and his own business background, Mortimer was well-suited to act as the promoter of unity among allied traders. For their part, brewers undoubtedly encouraged him in this enterprise.[27]

Maltsters, hop and malt factors and brewing material manufacturers, men who had been nominal contributors to the Fund in the 1890s,[28] in February 1907 formed their own protective society, the Allied Brewery Traders' Association (ABTA). Mortimer deserved much of the credit, and was appropriately appointed secretary. The malt, hop and barley trades dominated the executive committee, electing twelve of its twenty members. Other members included coopers, distillers, engineers, analysts and sugar manufacturers. Within two months, the ABTA attracted 194 members whose token subscription rates totalled £500. By June 1909, membership had reached 1,700, with an annual income of £2,000 – £3,000.[29] Like the brewing industry, the ABTA did establish affiliated district associations, but differed in one significant respect. The CBS required sixty-one years and the Association twenty-nine months to do so, whereas the ABTA, with another Licensing bill imminent, took only twelve months. Five federated branches were eventually created, covering nineteen English and Welsh counties and Scotland.[30]

[26] Mortimer's obituary, *Brewing Trade Review*, Apr. 1940; *Brewers' Journal*, 15 Feb. 1903; CBS, BS and NTDA Annual Reports. William Garton acquired several breweries late in the nineteenth century. In 1902, his son, Richard, became a director of Watney, Combe and Reid, the large London brewery (Janes, *Red Barrel*, pp. 148 – 9, 153). For additional information on Garton, Hill & Co., see Richard Garton's testimony before the *Royal Com. Arsenical Poisoning*, 1904, 1 (Cmnd. 1845), p. 225.

[27] Allied traders denied strenuously that their organization was promoted by brewers (*Brewing Trade Review*, 1 July 1907).

[28] Allied traders accounted for just 1% of the Fund's receipts in the early 1890s (NTDF Cash Book, 1888 – 95).

[29] ABTA Min. Bk. 1, 15 Feb., 17 Apr. and 4 June 1907, ABTA, pp. 1, 8, 14 – 15; Brad. Br. Assoc. Min. Bk., 24 June 1909.

[30] ABTA Min. Bk. 1, 22 Jan. 1908, p. 32; *Trade Paper*, March 1909; *Brewing Trade Review*, 1 June 1907 and 1 March 1908. Federated unions were formed for the midlands, Yorkshire/Lancashire, the western counties, Scotland and South Wales.

Founders of the ABTA anticipated solving several problems which had long impaired the trade's power. First, the trade had conspicuously lacked influence with Liberal ministers, especially since its closer alignment with Unionists after 1904. An independent but sympathetic organization might more credibly present the case for fair treatment. Second, the trade had an adverse press image. Control over most pubs and beerhouses purchased unwisely at exorbitant prices earned brewers a reputation for uncompetitive practices and financial irresponsibility. The ABTA, dedicated to countering antagonistic newspaper editorials, would publicize the severe economic hardship temperance legislation would cause both investors and employers in the diverse industries with an auxiliary role in beer production. ABTA members would also augment the trade's political power with more traditional methods, as petitioners, public demonstrators and voters.[31]

Initially the ABTA decided that it 'should act independently of brewers', and went so far as to answer all their inquiries confidentially. Because it was particularly sensitive about being seen merely as a front organization for the trade, the ABTA declined brewers' well-intentioned but heavy-handed assistance. Recruiting members became such a problem, however, that some affiliated unions had no choice but to accept brewers' help. Of the eighty-five firms canvassed in Bradford, only eleven had joined. Brewers suggested the ABTA's agent try again, and 'afterwards report to the secretary . . . those who refused to join . . ., [so that] the names could be placed before the Bradford Brewers with a view to influence being brought to bear upon them to do so'. Similarly, an ABTA midland branch was founded only when Manchester brewers intervened and made their suppliers subscribe.[32] If persuasive methods failed, the ABTA was clearly ready to overcome apathy with stronger tactics. With the avowed policy of autonomy abandoned, the ABTA and brewers worked increasingly closely. Early in 1910, for example, the Association interviewed allied firms as part of a

31 *Brewing Trade Review*, 1 March 1907; *Licensed Trade News*, 23 Feb. and 1 June 1907; Hawkins and Pass, *Brewing Industry*, p. 25. For criticism of tied houses, see, for example, the *Economist*, 12 Apr. 1890.
32 ABTA Min. Bk. 1, 17 Apr. 1907 and 12 Feb. 1908, pp. 10 – 11, 33; Brad. Br. Assoc. Min. Bk., 24 June 1909.

survey estimating how much unemployment would result from Liberal anti-drink measures, and underwrote half the costs of publishing the findings in a pamphlet, sent to both the House of Lords and press.[33]

Conflicting economic interests which embittered relations between some allied traders and brewers limited the ABTA's appeal just as much as apathy. Hop growers exemplify both the difficulties of mobilizing groups uninvolved in brewing or selling beer and the origins of brewers' public unpopularity.

Despite cheaper brewing materials during the late nineteenth century, beer prices remained remarkably stable, ultimately sapping the loyalty of some inveterate beer drinkers. 'The consumer has to pay just as much for his beer as before . . ., although most other articles of food . . . have been greatly reduced', the Economist charged in 1895.[34] At 2½d per pint, beer competed with few consumer goods throughout the 1870s, and working-men earning higher wages paid the price, fostering rising beer consumption. Then, from the early 1880s, decreasing prices meant higher real wages just when the 'mass market' developed with cheaper food, a wider range of inexpensive consumer goods (including non-alcoholic beverages) and other forms of entertainment such as organized football. As alternative leisure activities and consumer goods became affordable, per capita beer consumption plummeted. Beer had become relatively dearer, visibly less attractive and undeniably less popular, at least for respectable better paid workingmen. Burgeoning *total* beer consumption temporarily insulated brewers against these altered drinking patterns.[35]

Brewers changed their marketing strategy because of pressure from the government as well as from the beer drinker. They resorted to cheaper materials and hop and malt substitutes to offset heavier beer taxes. They also brewed weaker beers which paid less duty after Gladstone's 1880 budget transferred the tax

---

33 ABTA Min. Bk. 1, 26 Jan. 1910, p. 93.
34 *Economist*, 13 Apr. 1895.
35 A. E. Dingle, 'Drink and Working-Class Living Standards in Britain, 1870–1914', *Econ. Hist. Rev.*, 25 (1972), 618–19; Peter Mathias, 'The British Tea Trade in the Nineteenth Century', Oddy and Miller (eds.), *Modern British Diet*, pp. 91, 98–9; see also Lowerson and Myerscough, *Time to Spare*, p. 70.

from malt to the gravity of the wort.[36] In 1894 Liberals put 6d per barrel more on beer, prompting Sir William Harcourt's boast that brewers, not consumers, would pay. Irritated London brewers outwitted him, decreasing the strength (i.e., gravity) of their beers.[37] In the struggle between the Liberal Government and the Conservative trade, brewers successfully shifted the duty, but provoked a fierce public outcry which portrayed them as greedy businessmen. 'If the process of thinning down goes on indefinitely', the *Statist* complained, 'the consumer of beer will reach the stage of paying for little better than coloured water the same price that he used to pay for good ale'. When the Unionist Government added a war tax of a shilling per barrel in 1900, the *Statist* maintained that with lower gravities brewers could 'recoup most of the extra charge, and cheaper materials can do the rest'.[38]

Government statistics soon confirmed these allegations. During the 1890s they had not distinguished between standard barrels, the amount of beer theoretically produced at standard gravity (now 1,055 degrees), and bulk barrels, the actual quantity of beer brewed. More bulk than standard barrels indicated reduced gravities. According to an inland revenue report in 1900, there was a discrepancy of 202,000 extra bulk barrels. Brewers were obviously selling consumers weaker beers at old prices. The following year Sir Michael Hicks-Beach, chancellor of the exchequer, explained the even bigger gap of 739,000 more bulk barrels: 'Dealers in beer imposed the additional duty [of 1900] on their customers, not by raising the price, but by what is euphemistically called "lowering the gravity" '.[39] Investors saw this as a shortsighted policy undermining consumer confidence; the government said that brewers

---

[36] Standard gravity was the amount of beer, estimated at 4 barrels, which would be brewed from a quarter of malt. For taxation purposes, gravity (basically alcoholic strength) was arbitrarily set at 1,057 degrees in 1880. By reducing it, brewers paid the same tax but produced more beer (*Hansard*, 3rd ser., 252 (10 June 1880), col. 1648 and 254 (20 July 1880), col. 963; Wilson, *Alcohol and Nation*, p. 58).

[37] As one financial paper commented, 'the chief incentive to reduce gravity is to evade payment of beer duty' (*Statist*, 19 Apr. 1902). Br. Co. Trade Meeting Min. Bk., 12 Apr. 1894, pp. 28–9.

[38] *Statist*, 30 Jan. 1897 and 10 March 1900.

[39] *Hansard*, 4th ser., 92 (18 Apr. 1901), cols., 618–19; *Brewing Trade Review*, 1 Sept. 1905. By 1913 the average gravity had fallen to less than 1,053 degrees (*Reports from Commissioners: Customs and Excise*, 1914, 17 (7), p. 33).

could only blame themselves for declining consumption, as the public disliked the 'diluted article'.[40]

Brewers replied that lower gravities resulted not from higher taxation, but from public taste for more lightly hopped beer. They summarized their case in a Brewers' Society memorandum in 1909:

Mild ale . . . probably constitutes two-thirds of the beer produced. The requirements of this beer are fullness and sweetness of flavour, . . . attributes . . . inconsistent with a high hop rate. If more than a certain proportion of hops were used the flavour would be rendered more dry and bitter, and this alteration would be resented by the regular mild ale drinker.[41]

Whatever brewers' motives, hop growers certainly suffered from the switch to less hopped beer, but this aggravated rather than caused the depressed hop trade. Foreign hops, increased yields and falling beer consumption had been primarily responsible for eliminating half the hop acres under cultivation between 1878 and 1914.[42] Some dubious hop growers still cited the brewer's use of hop substitutes in brewing as a prime reason for their plight, and for their steadfast refusal to emulate hop factors and hop merchants in joining the ABTA.[43]

---

[40] *Hansard*, 4th ser., 106 (14 Apr. 1902), cols. 167 – 8; see also *Statist*, 19 Apr. 1902.

[41] BS Memorandum, 'Reasons Against the Hops Bill', *Brewing Trade Review*, 1 Apr. 1909; see also *ibid.*, 1 Apr. 1906; *Evid. Royal Com. Liq. Licensing Laws*, 1897, 34 (Cmnd. 8356), p. 327. This lighter beer was consumed immediately, so brewers used fewer hops. Formerly, beer had been stored for long periods, preserved with extensive hops which produced a distinctly bitter taste (*Evid. Sel. Comt. Hop Industry*, 1908, 8 (213), pp. 192 – 3, 243, 393; Julian L. Baker, *The Brewing Industry* (1905), p. 60; Hubert H. Parker, *The Hop Industry* (1934), pp. 93 – 4; H. S. Corran, *A History of Brewing* (1975), pp. 223 – 5).

[42] Parker, *Hop Industry*, pp. 97 – 8, 143 – 4, 310. Technological advances in refrigeration also hurt hop growers. With cold storage, hops could be kept for longer periods, preventing prices from rising in years of poor harvests (*ibid.*, p. 149; Corran, *Brewing*, pp. 196 – 7, 200; Baker, *Brewing Industry*, p. 58). The number of cultivated acres reached a pinnacle of 71,800 (1878), and thereafter steadily contracted to 32,500 (1909) (Parker, *Hop Industry*, pp. 307 – 9).

[43] Both growers and brewers worked through intermediaries. Growers sold their hops to factors, who stored them for examination by brewers' agents, the hop merchants (Parker, *Hop Industry*, pp. 157 – 9). ABTA Min. Bk. 1, 17 Sept. 1907, pp. 23 – 4.

Amid these problems of membership and organization, the Liberals introduced the 1908 Licensing bill. Intended to modify the 1904 Licensing Act, this measure restricted compensation, accelerated and expanded licensing reduction, raised licensing fees and permitted referenda on local option. The bill had two chief features: the elimination of 30,000 – 32,000 licences (about one-third of the total), and less generous compensation which diminished progressively over a fourteen-year period. Once this time limit expired, retailers, already paying substantially higher licence fees, would be charged the monopoly value as the basis for selling drink, and receive considerably smaller profits. Localities might exact still more stringent terms. Ratepayers could pass two different local option referenda: one immediately prohibiting all new licences; another later (after the time limit lapsed) shutting down all on-licences. Liberals, of course, deliberately excluded off-licence holders from the bill. However stridently brewers and retailers attacked these proposals, it was much less severe than the Minority Report, which had recommended considerably fewer licences, a time limit of seven instead of fourteen years and somewhat less compensation.[44]

To these demands, the trade vowed vigorous and uncompromising opposition. The *Brewing Trade Review* condemned the licensing reduction scheme as iniquitous, pointing to surveys showing the loss of almost two-thirds of the licences in some areas of Manchester.[45] Such editorials galvanized indignant brewers and retailers, but for the public the trade focused on portraying the bill as a blatant assault on property, the first step in a much broader Liberal campaign. Quite characteristic was the LPDL's manifesto calling the measure 'a precedent for the nationalization of every trade and industry in the land'. Even some Liberal brewers thought their party demanded unreasonable financial sacrifices in subjecting all licences to both local option and payment of monopoly value. Writing to the prime

---

[44] For towns and cities, the 1908 bill sought a ratio of licences per inhabitants of 1/500, whereas the Minority Report had urged 1/750 (*Report Royal Com. Liq. Licensing Laws*, 1899, 35 (Cmnd. 9397), p. 267). *Hansard*, 4th ser., 185 (27 Feb. 1908), cols. 79 – 81; Wilson, *Alcohol and Nation*, p. 397.

[45] *Brewing Trade Review*, 1 Aug. 1908; BS Min. Bk. 2, 20 May 1908, p. 101; NTDA Min. Bk. 2, 10 March 1908, pp. 247 – 8.

minister, John Fuller warned that the bill would 'upset the Liberal party, & all for which it stands'.[46]

The trade mobilized public opinion with well-tried tactics: mass meetings, petitions and deputations. In organizing a large protest meeting at Albert Hall with Arthur Balfour (leader of the Opposition) as chief speaker, the trade garnered enormous publicity for its cause but allowed the Unionist party to take the entire credit. Another huge mass meeting at Hyde Park again demonstrated not so much public sympathy as brewers' efforts in packing it with retailers given free round-trip railway tickets. Above the vast crowds were banners proclaiming the names of the allied industries: barley, malt, hops, engineers, copper-smiths, bottle and cork makers, coopers, wheelwrights, glass manufacturers, builders, plumbers, printers and shippers. Leaving no potential source of support untapped, the trade sought Liberals as petitioners against the bill.[47]

The trade publicized its views through an array of techniques. Paid music hall entertainers recited poems satirizing the bill as 'Asquith pap'. Their impact was short-lived. Angry temperance reformers, entering the dens of iniquity to occupy strategic seats, created turmoil with catcalls, hisses and much shouting of ' "what are the brewers paying you for this?" ', forcing the artists to retreat in despair. Propaganda for the working classes also included posters raising the spectre of higher beer prices, and a travelling publicity cart, 'The Liberty Van', which toured rural areas dispensing leaflets, collecting petitions and plastering the countryside with posters. Altogether the Association handed out or pasted up forty tons of material, 409,000 posters, 790,000 cartoons and over 10 million leaflets.[48]

Brewers were not above coercive methods when faced with huge financial losses. At private meetings, brewers threatened brewery workers with either lost jobs or lower wages if the Licensing bill passed. Brewers likewise alarmed firms selling

---

46 NTDA Min. Bk. 2, 28 Feb. 1908, p. 242; Gretton, 'Licensing Bill', p. 740; *The Times*, 7 March 1908; Greenway, 'Liquor Question', p. 72; Fuller to Asquith (copy), 26 March 1908, Wilts. R.O., Fuller Papers, Ms. 1196/9.

47 Sandars to Balfour, 1 May 1908, Balfour Papers, Add. Ms. 49,765, fo. 134; Northumberland and Durham Br. Assoc. Min. Bk., 23 July 1908; ABTA Min. Bk. 1, 27 Aug. 1908, pp. 51–2; NTDA W. Dist. 1908 Annual Report, p. 6.

48 Wilfrid Winterton, *Harvest of the Years* (Birmingham, 1969), pp. 66–7; Glos. Br. Assoc. Min. Bk., 2 March 1908; NTDA W. Dist. Min. Bk., 13 Aug. 1908, p. 82 and 1908 Annual Report, p. 8; NTDA N. Dist. Min. Bk., 29 Apr. and 13 May 1908; NTDA Min. Bk. 2, 26 Nov. 1908, p. 274.

ancillary products with ominous forewarnings that the passage
of the 'Licensing bill means the ultimate extermination of our
trade when orders from brewers must cease'. Innocent parties
such as charities also had a foretaste of their own sacrifices to
temperance reform. One Watford brewery symbolically dis-
continued its largess, the half-guinea subscribed for thirty years
to give ragged school children a holiday.[49] A Cambridge brewer
who refused his vicar's request for charitable donations instead
suggested directing such appeals more aptly to the Archbishop
of Canterbury, well-known temperance activist and leader of
the CETS. The Archbishop, though himself deluged with letters
orchestrated in many instances by the trade, still recognized the
sincerity of the trusts and women who pleaded for protection as
shareholders in brewery companies. This dilemma, in fact,
neutralized the CETS as a powerful supporter of the Liberal
measure, emphasizing the success of the trade's appeals to
shareholders.[50] In a more direct attack on antagonists, retailers
followed brewers' orders, disrupting temperance meetings with
awkward questions, votes against anti-drink resolutions or
counter amendments. Some brewers did query these tactics. But
the Association defended its behaviour, arguing that 'when the
chairman at public meetings gave the opponents of the Bill a fair
hearing they [brewers and retailers] could be relied upon to give
the supporters of the Bill the same fair treatment'.[51]

The ABTA equally undertook diverse activities. Whether
distributing handbills and posters, collecting petitions, assisting
at elections, arranging public meetings, passing resolutions or
marching in demonstrations, it emphasized the thousands of
wage-earners and millions of pounds that depended on the sale
of beer. Allied traders had access to groups denied to the trade.
Armed with posters and handbills, they approached farmers'
and agricultural societies, asking for sympathetic resolutions.[52]

[49] Norman Longmate, *The Waterdrinkers: A History of Temperance* (1968), p. 250;
Soms. Br. Assoc. Min. Bk., 31 Jan. 1908, W. Count. Br. Assoc. Brewers as
directors of public companies contended that 'they had no right to give away
money which did not belong to them' (Nevile, *Seventy Years*, p. 58).
[50] H. Winter to Rev. J. H. Martin (copy), 21 March 1908, Davidson Papers,
Licensing and Temp. Box 2; Greenway, 'Liquor Question', pp. 72–4.
[51] Soms. Br. Assoc. Min. Bk., 31 Jan. 1908; Bristol and Thornbury Lic. Trade
Electoral and Parl. Comt. Min. Bk., 12 June 1908, W. Count. Br. Assoc.;
NTDA Min. Bk. 2, 10 March 1908, p. 248.
[52] ABTA Min. Bk. 1, 2 March, 8 Apr. and 11 May 1908, pp. 35, 39, 44.

But even the Licensing bill could not make hop growers staunch allies of the trade. Representing Kentish farmers in 1908 before a Select Committee exploring the troubled hop industry, Thomas May avowed that falling hop prices were the result of brewers using hop substitutes and engaging in a price-fixing conspiracy. In Kent, as in many other counties with large hop crops, hop growers' societies had already approved resolutions demanding bans on all chemical preservatives and flavouring. Liberals successfully exploited these divisions by announcing proposed legislation outlawing hop substitutes. Hop growers were delighted. A. J. Thompson, president of the Herefordshire and Worcestershire Hop Growers' Association, delivered an impassioned speech to members praising it as a likely promoter of hop production. Enraged at brewers for depressing the hop market, he not only refused to campaign against but actually welcomed the Liberal Licensing bill for undermining one practice which harmed hop growers, the brewers' monopoly of tied houses.[53] When the ABTA sought help in opposing the Licensing bill and appealed to the thirty-two farmers' clubs and agricultural associations, in which hop growers predominated, the response was revealing: fifteen showed indifference, three were 'apolitical', seven got as far as considering the request or expressing sympathy, and seven actually managed meetings and resolutions. In contrast, hop factors and merchants organized a mass meeting and passed a resolution attacking the bill. By periodically introducing pro-hop bills, Liberals effectively prevented hop growers from assisting the trade in the pre-war era.[54]

The Licensing bill, treated strictly as a party measure, received huge Liberal majorities in the Commons but few votes in the Unionist controlled Lords. On the second reading in May, it passed by 394 to 148: all but eight Liberals and eight Unionists voted on party lines. Of the brewer MPs, all eight Unionists and one Liberal opposed the bill, while the other two Liberals supported it. Both Guinness brothers (U) abstained in November on the third reading, approved by 350 – 113. Those

---

53 *Evid. Sel. Comt. Hop Industry*, 1908, 8 (213), pp. 40, 56, 148 – 9, 200; *Brewing Trade Review*, 1 Oct. 1908.
54 Parker, *Hop Industry*, pp. 48 – 9, 84, 153; ABTA Min. Bk. 1, 8 Apr. 1908, p. 39. Although the BS did not oppose bills disallowing hop substitutes, it protested vigorously when hop measures, as in 1909, attacked the use of alternative preservatives (*Brewing Trade Review*, 1 Jan., 1 Apr., 1 June, 1 Aug. and 1 Sept. 1909 and 1 May 1913).

connected with the drink lobby also demonstrated solidarity: Unionists voted with their party while all Liberals abstained, except for Richard Causton who supported only the second reading. Clearly the trade lobby was more united than in the 1880s and 1890s. In the Lords, the decisive second reading came late in November, when unanticipated numbers of peers attended to give it 'a first-class funeral', rejecting the bill by 272 to 96.[55]

Little credit for the bill's defeat belonged to the League, hampered by declining membership and limited funds. Cabinet ministers who complained of the trade's 'terrible apathy' must have had the League specifically in mind. It cancelled a London meeting on 4 November because nearly two-thirds of the affiliated branches, unwilling to underwrite travelling expenses for delegates, ignored the summons. Chronic shortages of funds undoubtedly caused this apathy. The League depended solely on members' annual subscriptions of £1,400, almost twice as much as brewers donated during the *entire* Edwardian era. Impeded by brewers' paltry financial support as well as by low membership fees, the League struggled to find money for its activities, spending only £1,600 annually.[56]

Securing ample funds was no problem for the Society. Brewers betrayed their obvious bias towards London publicans in donating more to the Society each year than to the League altogether between 1900 and 1913. Still lavishly funded and allowed complete control over London organization, the Society remained England's most sophisticated and best-equipped trade association with £5,600 a year. With fewer but wealthier members, it devoted £9,700 per year to defence, and thus outspent both the League and the Association's central office together.[57]

London brewers, although less generous to the Association, continued to be the largest source of its meagre funds. This reflected the dismal failure to integrate important northern brewers: the Association enrolled only five of Lancashire's 135

55 *Hansard*, 4th ser., 187 (4 May 1908), cols. 1791 – 8 and 196 (20 Nov. 1908), cols. 1653 – 60; Lord Fitzmaurice quoted in Roy Jenkins, *Mr. Balfour's Poodle: Peers v. People* (New York, 1954), p. 63.
56 NTDA Home and S. Count. Min. Bk. 1, 18 Nov. 1907, pp. 24 – 5; LVNDL 1908 Half-Yearly Meeting, pp. 18 – 20 and Annual Reports, 1901 – 14.
57 LVPSL Annual Reports, 1900 – 13.

brewers and just four of Yorkshire's 104 brewers. Between them these nine could only find £172. Not much more but with far less justification was subscribed in Staffordshire, where the country's biggest breweries produced three members from sixty-two firms and a mere £355. Such sacrifices hardly made smaller breweries altruistic, so the 101 in Devon, Worcestershire, Bedfordshire, Cambridgeshire and Huntingdonshire donated nothing at the national level. As in the 1890s, slightly over one-third of the Association's contributors accounted for two-thirds of its receipts. In 1908, for example, London brewers donated forty-five per cent of its total revenue of £3,000, whereas brewers in Staffordshire gave twelve per cent, in Kent 4.8 per cent and in Ireland 3.3 per cent. In an industry in which 1,300 English and Welsh brewers had boasted of licensed property worth £150 – £200 million, less than 100 became subscribers to the Association in 1908, giving an average of £30.[58] Yet, within the previous twenty-five years, twelve brewers, over half of them officials of trade societies, had died as millionaires.[59] Another fourteen brewers who served on the CBS or Brewers' Society general committee during the same period amassed smaller but still respectable fortunes averaging £283,000.[60] It was this sharp contrast between well-publicized vast corporate riches, on one hand, and the unpublicized shoe-string budgets of virtually all trade societies, on the other, that misled so many contemporaries into exaggerating the trade's political influence.

---

[58] In 1908 93 firms and 8 associations donated £2,728, while non-brewing companies subscribed £256, giving the Association a total income of £2,984 (BS 1908 Annual Report; Berks. Br. Union Min. Bk., 1 May 1909). In 1906, the Association had received £3,000 (NTDA Min. Bk. 2, 29 Nov. 1906, p. 196).

[59] Sir Henry Meux (£1.3 million), Sir Andrew Walker (£2.9 million), Sir Gilbert Greenall (£1 million), Thomas V. Smith (£1.9 million), Vyell E. Walker (£1.6 million); Burton Brewers' Assoc.: Michael T. Bass (£1.8 million), John Gretton (£2.9 million); Richard Ratcliff (£1.1 million); Brewers' Co.: James Watney (d. 1884, £1.3 million), James Watney (d. 1886, £1.3 million), Spencer Charrington (£1.3 million); Brewers' Soc.: 1st Baron Burton, Michael A. Bass (£1 million) (Rubinstein, 'British Millionaires', pp. 209 – 12; Br. Co. Min. Bk., Ms. 5468; BS Min. Bk. 2).

[60] In addition to the twelve listed in table 5 (p. 90), were Andrew Barlow (d. 1904, £385,000) and John Bonham Carter (d. 1905, £267,500). Compiled from wills published in the *Country Brewers' Gazette*, *Brewing Trade Review* and *Brewers' Guardian*.

Early in 1909 the Brewers' Society revived its plans for assuming the cost of running both the Association and its county branches. Now the goal was almost £20,000, substantially more than the £6,000 advocated in 1906, though with 750 members not even large firms would need to subscribe more than £100 or £200. With approval uncertain, leaders of the Brewers' Society conducted a survey and were daunted by its findings: fourteen per cent actively opposed the scheme and fifty-six per cent chose not to respond. London brewers apparently disliked diverting funds from the Society as strongly as most provincial brewers hated heavier dues.[61] By late July pledges totalled £5,500, just over one-quarter of the desired amount. Reluctantly the Brewers' Society postponed further action, raising money on an *ad hoc* basis until 1911.[62]

The Brewers' Society was less successful in extracting money from brewers than the Liberal Government. In April Lloyd George had astutely pursued the Liberals' goal, the sweeping reduction of licences, by the novel method of imposing heavier licence duties. The manufacturers' licence, formerly £1 a year, was now calculated at 12 shillings for each fifty barrels brewed beyond the first 100. Guinness was hardest hit with £25,600, but overall brewers would be paying £800,000 rather than £11,000 in

---

61 Under the proposed scheme, London would have received only £1,500, compared with the Society's annual expenses of almost £9,700 (Berks. Br. Union Minute Bk., 1 May 1909; LVPSL Annual Reports, 1901–9). BS Min. Bk. 2, 20 Jan., 20 Apr., 21 June, 20 July and 20 Sept. 1909, pp. 136–7, 160, 176, 184, 193–4).

62 To meet the heavier expenditure anticipated in 1908, brewers resorted to a special 'guarantee fund' as a means of averting shortages of money. Such funds were a common procedure, being established for the 1885, 1892 and 1895 Elections, and the 1885 budget, but had never exceeded £25,000. On none of these occasions was the guarantee fully exhausted. In 1908, the Brewers' Society created an unprecedented fund of £100,000, to combat the Licensing bill and then the 1909 budget. It again raised a fund for the Dec. 1910 Election. Probably most of this money went towards newspaper advertisement during the campaigns, but how much was in fact spent remains unclear, since no financial records survive (CBS 1884–6 Annual Reports; *Brewing Trade Review*, 1 Sept. 1895; BS Min. Bk. 2, 24 Feb. 1908, pp. 86–7 and 3, 18 Nov. 1910; Neal Blewett, *The Peers, the Parties and the People: The British General Elections of 1910* (Toronto, 1972), pp. 332–3, 335). The inability of the Association not only to circularize shareholders on a national basis at the 1910 Elections owing to inadequate funds but to match the amount of district grants during the local veto crisis, strongly suggest the guarantee fund was used only to a very limited extent (see p. 227, and pp. 232–3).

licence fees.[63] The budget would, therefore, sharply reduce shareholders' dividends, and for many breweries meant paying more taxes than dividends. To the forty-four per cent of its profits already contributed to the government, Hodgson's Kingston Brewery Co. would add another twelve – sixteen per cent. Retail licences, too, would cost appreciably more, with publicans assessed at a half and beer sellers a third of their licenced premises' annual value. Taxes on London's most sumptuous establishments started at £300 and could reach over £700, compared to the £50 – £60 charged previously. Instead of almost £2 million, retail licences now cost nearly £5.9 million. From taxes on liquor licences, Liberals would extract £6.8 million altogether, over a three-fold increase.[64]

In response, the Association inaugurated a new policy, supporting Unionist MPs who had opposed the 1908 Licensing bill and the budget's licensing clauses, while standing neutral in those few seats where Liberal MPs had done so as well. Test questions were submitted in contests without any incumbent candidate. Emulating the advice of one leading trade newspaper, which declared that the 'Licensed Trade is pledged to the hilt . . . to ensure the defeat of the Liberals and the triumph of the Unionists at the next General Election', some local societies did endorse unsatisfactory Unionist candidates.[65] Likewise the ABTA supported Unionist candidates, and lent them speakers, canvassers and vehicles. It inundated voters with literature, 120,000 leaflets, 100,000 pamphlets on unemployment, 25,000 general posters and 7,000 cartoons; farmers received 35,000 pamphlets and maltsters 8,000 circulars.[66]

This outpouring of propaganda fostered the contemporary view of the trade as a corrupt political force which devoted

---

[63] Cabinet Memorandum, 20 May 1909, Bodleian Lib., Asquith Papers, Ms. 100, fo. 100; Wilson, *Alcohol and Nation*, p. 419.

[64] *Brewers' Gazette*, 6 Nov. 1913; Marks to Montgomery, 8 May 1909, BS, Correspondence/1909: Budget Licensing, 1, fos. 54 – 6; Knox, 'Tied House System', p. 83; *Brewing Trade Review*, 1 Jan. 1910. Murray (*People's Budget*, pp. 154 – 7, 163, 167 – 8, 177) examines how the liquor taxes were formulated in the cabinet.

[65] NTDA Min. Bk. 2, 8 Oct. 1909, pp. 304 – 5; *Licensed Trade News*, 13 Nov. 1909. Birmingham brewers continued their 1906 electoral policy of using test questions only where both candidates' views were unknown (Birm. and Aston Trade Min. Bk., 21 Dec. 1909 and 28 Nov. 1910, D 3163/2/1/6, pp. 217 – 18, 222; NTDA Mid. Dist. Min. Bk., 25 Nov. 1910, D 3163/2/1/2, p. 130). Test questions were not submitted in Yorkshire (*Trade Paper*, 20 Jan. 1910).

[66] ABTA Min. Bk. 1, 16 Dec. 1909 and 26 Jan. 1910, pp. 88, 92 – 3.

unlimited sums to forwarding selfish interests. Writing to Lord Rosebery early in January 1910, one former Liberal agent asserted that 'the Trade is fighting with fury & with £40,000 provided by the Brewers, Spirit Merchants & the Trade at large'.[67] Based on district outlays, however, the Association probably expended less than £4,000 on both elections, and so failed to equal, much less surpass, the amount spent on the 1906 Election.[68] Nor did retail societies make larger commitments. Since the Society spent on average thirty-five per cent more in the three previous election years than in 1910, the expenses of £2,600 on the 1910 Elections and parliamentary activities doubtless represented a steep decline.[69] Whatever the financially crippled League spent fell short of this, even with all its annual expenses of £1,600 included, while the ABTA laid out less than £500.[70]

The fact that the leading protective organizations, apart from the Society, were hard pressed for cash explains why the trade generally spent these relatively modest sums, but not the resigned attitude of brewers towards a Liberal victory. During the campaigning for the January 1910 Election, the Northumberland and Durham Brewers' Association, for instance, dismayed at only six members attending a meeting, vehemently criticized brewers' indifference 'at a time when the very existence of the Trade is threatened'. These sentiments resembled those following the December Election: 'It was . . . regrettable . . . that the wholesale trade, whose interests were so vitally concerned, showed such apathy in these times of crisis'.[71] Brewers failed to offer strenuous opposition because they had become wholly demoralized at their economic plight —

---

[67] Allard to Rosebery, 4 Jan. 1910, Rosebery Papers, Ms. 10,172, fo. 171; see also W. J. Fisher, 'Electoral Abuses', *Independent Rev.*, 9 (1906), 36 – 7, 40 – 1.

[68] The northern district spent £173 on the 1910 Elections, whereas the western district spent £512 on the Jan. 1910 contest (NTDA N. Dist. 1910 – 11 Annual Reports, p. 12; NTDA W. Dist. Min. Bk., 4 Feb. 1910, pp. 104 – 7).

[69] In previous election years the Society's total expenses were £12,100 (1895), £10,700 (1900) and £13,600 (1906), but reached only £8,000 in 1910 (LVPSL Annual Reports: 1895, 1900 and 1910). *Trade Paper*, 16 Feb. 1911.

[70] ABTA Min. Bk. 1, 26 Jan. and 16 Dec. 1910, pp. 92 – 3, 129; LVNDL 1911 Annual Report.

[71] Northumberland and Durham Br. Assoc. Min. Bk., 23 Dec. 1909 and 25 Nov. 1910.

slumping beer consumption which had fallen twelve per cent since 1899, finances strained by over-commitment to purchases of costly licensed premises, and finally onerous taxes already imposed by friends and soon by foes, too.[72]

Both the issues and their context promoted this defeatist attitude. In the debate on the budget's licensing proposals, unlike the local veto struggle, the trade was fighting complicated tax reforms, more detrimental to the dividends of middle- and upper-class shareholders than to working-class drinkers. Labouring men saw no immediate threat to their local, nor were their class sensibilities offended. By assuring the survival of most pubs and avoiding attacks on drink outlets solely in labouring communities, Liberals adroitly averted the disastrous mistakes of the early 1890s. There was another reason why brewers and retailers faced an impossible task in trying to win traditional working-class support. Both political parties advocated divergent policies for funding social reform, the central issue in the elections which easily overshadowed arguments over drink taxes. Working-class voters quickly demonstrated a preference for retaining free trade, even with the likelihood of fewer pubs and beerhouses, rather than the radical alternative of protection.[73] The retailer discovered that as a political activist with loyalties anathema to his patrons, he lost much business. Agents thus complained of publicans 'afraid to exhibit bills in or on their premises owing to the aggressive attitude of customers'. Even in London, where the Society received huge subsidies from brewers, retailers displayed political reticence. 'The licensed victualler has been shy', the *Morning Advertiser* grumbled. 'He has not cared to run the risk of perhaps offending the political susceptibilities of some of his customers on the chance of winning the votes of others'. Fear sometimes made sound economic sense. At Westbury avowed Conservative publicans, thoroughly intimidated by previous consumer hostility which had escalated into boycotts, would not 'come out boldly' at the 1910 Elections. For many retailers, questions of economics now outweighed those of politics,

---

[72] Wilson, *Alcohol and Nation*, p. 333; see pp. 155–6, 160, n. 18.
[73] Blewett, *Elections of 1910*, p. 407; P.F. Clarke, *Lancashire and the New Liberalism* (Cambridge, 1971), pp. 398–9.

especially since both parties had levied burdensome taxes in a deteriorating market.[74]

Following the two Liberal victories, the Brewers' Society tried yet again to reorganize its finances. In May 1911, it proposed an amended plan in which heavier compulsory levies, based on beer output, would be substituted for voluntary fees. One important concession was made: districts would control locally subscribed money. The Brewers' Society then sent 745 members a circular, citing the Association's annual receipts of £3,000 – £4,000 which came from only 116 firms as the chief rationale for raising additional funds. 'It is unfair', the circular contended, 'that less than one-seventh of the [Brewers' Society's] members should bear a burden which should fall with even incidence on all'. This time members approved. Within two years, the Brewers' Society collected over £24,000, almost £14,000 of which eventually went to doubling the Association's annual income. Such success was nevertheless achieved at considerable cost. Completely disenchanted with politics and the trade's ineffectual protection, nearly one-fifth of the Brewers' Society membership (128 firms) resigned in protest.[75]

Apathy persisted. Scarcely four years after federating with the Brewers' Society, the revived Lincolnshire and Nottinghamshire Brewers' Association disbanded. In April 1913 several Nottingham brewers called a meeting to discuss amalgamating all sections of the trade in one association. Of the thirteen brewers invited, only three attended. F. P. Whitbread, chairman of the Association, was himself rebuffed on personally canvassing seeking six Nottingham brewers for membership of the Brewers' Society and Association.[76] Retailers seemed as dispirited as brewers. Higher licence duties and declining business now prompted some publicans and beerhouse keepers to begin withdrawing from local retail societies. According to the *Licensed Trade News* in 1910, roughly half all licence holders belonged to

[74] NTDA W. Dist. 1911 Annual Report, pp. 6–7; *Morning Advertiser*, 10 Jan. 1910; see also Bristol and Thornbury Trade Min. Bk., 8 Jan. 1910; *Licensing World and Licensed Trade Review*, 15 Jan. 1910. For previous examples of customers exerting economic pressure, see Vincent, *Liberal Party*, pp. 135–8; Nossiter, 'Shopkeeper Radicalism', p. 428; Lambert, *Drink and Sobriety*, pp. 210–11.

[75] BS Min. Bk. 3, 8 and 19 May 1911 and Annual Reports, 1912–13; *Brewing Trade Review*, 1 June 1911.

[76] Lincs. and Notts. Br. Assoc. Min. Bk., 22 Apr. 1912, 11 Apr. and 10 July 1913.

no trade organization. In the western counties and midlands the proportion was still higher, but the situation was worse in the home and southern counties, where two-thirds of the 15,400 retailers were unorganized.[77]

Apathy was not the only symptom of declining trade morale. Three consecutive losses at general elections convinced many brewers and retailers of the political shortcomings of relying on one party. Demands for a revised trade electoral policy grew. The conduct of Unionist MPs as much as their electoral defeat provoked discontent. Considering the trade's unpopularity fatal to their political chances, they had omitted the licensing question in denunciations of the budget.[78] The *Trade Paper*, an independent newspaper reflecting rank-and-file sentiments, ridiculed a strategy which gave unreciprocated support to Unionists and pointlessly antagonized Liberals. Whenever possible, it concluded, the trade should cultivate bipartisan support. Retailers wholeheartedly agreed. At the Beer, Spirit and Wine Trade National Defence League annual meeting in May 1913, one publican expressed the widespread but long-standing disquiet of retailers with Unionists who 'kicked' licence holders when in office but 'neglected them' while in opposition. Retailers overwhelmingly approved his resolution suggesting a trade policy of political neutrality. Brewers joined retailers in questioning Unionist loyalty to the trade. As chairman of the trade's leading organization, F. P. Whitbread carried enormous weight, and, though obviously reluctant to reproach Unionists, rising dissent induced him to disavow previous political alignment. Brewers must 'never be considered as tied to either political party', he stressed in a speech to members of the Brewers' Society late in 1913. Unionists, Whitbread warned, would get no assistance whatsoever at the next election if they spurned trade support because ' "you are

---

[77] NTDA W. Dist. 1912 Annual Report, p. 10; *Licensed Trade News*, 21 May and 8 Oct. 1910; NTDA Home and S. Count. Min. Bk. 1, 18 Nov. 1907, p. 18; Birm. Br. Assoc. 1911 Annual Report, D 3163/1/2/12, Corr. File, pp. 12 – 13; *Licensing World and Licensed Trade Review*, 1 Jan. 1910.

[78] Of the Unionist candidates' election addresses, only 29% in Jan. and 10% in Dec. mentioned the licensing question, ranking it eleventh and fifteenth respectively. By the second election, licensing as an issue ranked last, even falling behind electoral reform and payment of MPs (Blewett, *Elections of 1910*, pp. 317, 326).

so unpopular and so discredited that you do us more harm than good" '.[79]

Unionist uncertainty about repealing the 1909 licence duties likewise caused trade unrest. Arthur Balfour pointed to the unpredictable interval before he resumed office as one crucial impediment to his making a public commitment. Within several years, he maintained, Liberal taxation would force many retailers either out of business or to sell their houses at devalued prices, rendering subsequent remedial Unionist legislation quite useless. 'They had been suffering for a long period, and . . . were not content to know that they were only required at election times', one retailer retorted, typifying trade dissatisfaction with Balfour. By 1914 a frustrated member of the Brewers' Society proposed obtaining a pledge from Unionist leaders to reduce drink taxes, but trade MPs forced the withdrawal of the motion.[80]

One historian characterizes the trade in 1914 as quite undisturbed by heavier Liberal taxes because of its unshakable faith in a future Unionist Government's sympathy.[81] Many brewers and retailers had in fact become acutely distrustful of the Unionist party, which they regarded as disloyal, opportunistic and extremely unlikely to win the next election. Hence the escalating pressure to dissociate themselves from an unappreciated and politically debilitating alliance. Even before the last electoral defeat, many of them had resented Unionists for retaining a 'temporary' war-time beer tax, for curbing child messengers and for conceding a scheme of insurance, not the long sought compensation paid out of public revenue. In declining to voice their criticism of the People's budget and in losing the Elections of 1910, the Unionist party further undermined trade solidarity and encouraged demands for political neutrality.

Brewers and retailers in part were using the Unionist party as a scapegoat, for neither the issues nor the context allowed them to mobilize their traditional supporters, working-class drinkers. Two forces destroying trade unity, frustration and apathy, derived as much from economic as from political circumstances.

---

[79] *Trade Paper*, 17 Feb. 1910; *Brewing Trade Review*, 1 Dec. 1913; *Licensed Trade News*, 31 May 1913; see also *Licensee*, 13 June 1914.
[80] Balfour to Maunder (copy), 29 May 1911, Balfour Papers, Add. Ms. 49,861, fos. 206–7; *Licensed Trade News*, 31 May 1913; BS Min. Bk. 4, 11 Feb. 1914.
[81] Turner, 'Liquor Trade', pp. 592–3.

Falling beer consumption, together with excessive investments in licensed property, created a depression in the brewing industry, aggravating the tax burdens of 1904 and 1909. For the industry, these problems were to some extent self-inflicted. Brewers resolutely refused to fund the League and Association adequately, thus preventing vital reforms in organization, hindering agitation against Liberal legislation and demoralizing provincial retailers. Whether apathetic or restive, many brewers and retailers were apprehensive about the future.

7

Divided We Stand

In evaluating the trade's role as a pressure group, historians have consistently overlooked the crucial economic relationship between brewers and retailers. Their economic solidarity was the fundamental source of the trade's political power. Yet by the late 1890s, economic rivalry had provoked discord, which supplanted the long-standing paternalistic attitudes of brewers towards retailers.[1]

As breweries became large-scale and corporate management replaced private control, retailers found their brewer-landlords increasingly impersonal and inflexible, even ruthless in maximizing profits. What so strained the loyalty of both publicans and beerhouse keepers to trade defence was the encroachment on their monopoly as distributors of beer by brewers who themselves entered the business of retailing. Brewers adopted this strategy because of changing market conditions. First, restrictive licensing policies of many magistrates, together with the spread of the tied house system, gave some breweries virtual monopolies in various localities, provoking retaliation from excluded competitors. Second, falling beer consumption after 1899 and the collapse of licensed property values reduced profits of many brewing companies, fostering heightened commercial rivalry. Finally, new drinking patterns freed consumers from relying on pubs or beerhouses for purchases.

With the dramatic expansion of the tied house system in the nineteenth century, brewers acquired greater power over retailing practices, and more opportunities for both exploiting and abusing the landlord-tenant relationship. By 1914 one former publican could write a nostalgic article, lamenting the demise of the shrewd, self-reliant mid-Victorian retailers. No longer, he reflected, could they profit from fluctuating wine and

---

[1] Clark, *English Alehouse*, p. 290.

spirit prices, opportunely buying hundreds of gallons priced twenty-five to thirty per cent below the open market, or select their own stock.[2] Many, though not all, publicans had lost these privileges. Tenancy contracts varied widely throughout the country, even within small geographic areas. This was stressed in testimony to the Peel Commission late in the 1890s by John White, long-term tenant of Bristol's Georges & Co. Relying on information gained as secretary of the Bristol Licensed Victuallers' Association, he distinguished between two broad groups, full and partly tied tenants. The former, usually connected with small breweries, were obliged to sell some specific beers, wines, spirits, tobacco and cigars, but in some cases the tie was more comprehensive, specifying all beers as well as relatively minor items such as matches, sawdust and newspapers.[3] Some fully tied tenants did not buy spirits through the brewer, but for this privilege he collected a surcharge of 6d per gallon. Partly tied tenants, in contrast, were tied just for beer, and could freely order several other select brands from a non-local brewer. This greater latitude afforded publicans like White 'a chance of making a profit to pay our way', whereas the more fettered fully tied ones invariably went bankrupt. 'I have never known one [tenant] succeed in a fully tied house', White stated unequivocally.[4]

The tie itself was thus onerous enough without another recurring and widespread problem, the poor quality of the landlord's beers. According to White, the worst offenders, small breweries, also insisted on the most rigorous ties. Their beers, he said, were 'so weak with water that you can hardly tell what they are'. Critics elsewhere, such as the chairman of one Devonshire licensed victuallers' society, thought the size of the brewery irrelevant: 'The "tied" man had to take almost anything sent [to] him'. One Norfolk publican expressed the

2   [A Retired Licensed Victualler], 'Through Practical Spectacles: Things as Seen by a Licensed Victualler', *Brit. Rev.*, 5 (1914), 387; see also *Licensed Trade News*, 4 Nov. 1905. Knox mistakenly asserts 'that there is usually no requirement as to brands of wines or spirits sold in these [tied] houses' (Knox, 'Tied House System', p. 66).

3   *Evid. Royal Com. Liq. Licensing Laws*, 1897, 35 (Cmnd. 8523), p. 418. J. W. Green, a Luton brewer, also supplied his tenants with soda water, seltzer, potash, lithia and lemonade as well as temperance drinks like ginger beer which contained less than 3% alcohol (J. W. Green's 1910 Price List, reproduced in H. A. Monckton, *A History of the English Public House* (1969), pp. 116 – 18).

4   *Evid. Royal Com. Liq. Licensing Laws*, 1897, 35 (Cmnd. 8523), pp. 415, 418, 420.

general retail discontent in condemning the tied house system generally as the chief obstacle to better beer.[5]

Tied tenants also disparaged the whisky they sold, often purchased wholesale from landlord-brewers. Angry distillers retorted that they were not at fault, and accused brewers of diluting or adulterating whisky. Privately, distillers had another strong reason for disliking the brewer, the heavy discounts he demanded as middleman. At a meeting of the Malt Distillers' Association in 1901, distillers considered a pending bill prohibiting tied houses. Chairman Cowie denounced brewers as 'our greatest enemies' for serving 'vile' whisky in pubs. He gave the measure wholehearted support, personally recalling a brewer who confessed to the fear that quality whisky would compete with beer. Other distillers were ambivalent, sympathizing with Cowie but drawn to brewers as mutual sellers of alcoholic beverages. The Association's decision to follow a policy of neutrality, underlining the tacit hostility between distillers and brewers, gave weight to retail claims of being supplied with inferior whisky.[6]

However much retailers disliked the tied house system, they seldom complained publicly lest their protective societies forfeit brewers' subsidies. County associations, formed throughout the country in the mid-1880s, further strengthened brewers' control over retail societies. To ensure that the Northamptonshire Brewers' Association 'would have some hold over the Retail Associations', it replaced individual brewing companies as the sole source of donations. Here, as in other counties, brewers acting through their association deducted from subsidies any money which a firm contributed privately to retail societies. In often paying tenants' membership dues in retail societies, CBS affiliated branches also wielded enormous financial influence.[7]

5 *Ibid.*, p. 418; *Licensed Trade News*, 4 Apr. 1896 and 9 May 1903; see also *Evid. Lords Comt. Intemp.*, 1877, 11 (271), p. 102. Brewers themselves attributed defective beer at least in part to retailers, whose gross ignorance of cellar conditions and other careless practices damaged it (Nevile, *Seventy Years*, p. 158; Barclay, 'Public-House', p. 1000).
6 Ronald B. Weir, *The History of the Malt Distillers' Association of Scotland* (Elgin, n.d. [1975]), pp. 36–7. Some publicans adulterated whisky to increase profits (Patrick McGeown, *Heat the Furnace Seven Times More* (1967), pp. 46–7, 53).
7 Northants. Br. Assoc. Min. Bk., 26 Jan. and 12 Apr. 1892, SL 298; Birm. Br. Assoc. Min. Bk., 22 June 1891 and 2 Nov. 1894, D 3163/1/1/1, pp. 30, 157; Birm. Br. Assoc. Corr. File, 8 Dec. 1897, D 3163/1/2/2; *Brewers' Guardian*, 10 May 1892.

The Federation's conference in Birmingham in 1897 showed how readily brewers resorted to financial pressure to stifle dissent. One Nottingham representative charged brewers with demanding that pubs and beerhouses open on Sundays and with denying tenants refunds for spoilt beer. He said he would reveal to the Peel Commission, then taking evidence, the plight of the tenant who must 'give away his profits to increase the profits of the brewers'. Several members questioned these tactics, including one Birmingham retailer who warned that brewers would take financial reprisals, but nevertheless the motion passed. Birmingham brewers promptly withheld their usual annual grant until the city's off-licence society issued a disclaimer. At the next meeting its chairman duly complied, pointing to local brewers' well-known integrity as a convincing reason for dismissing recent criticism of tenancy conditions. Whatever prevailed elsewhere, 'relations between the brewers and off-license holders of the city were singularly cordial'. Appeased Birmingham brewers forwarded the £26 5s grant.[8]

Friction between brewers and their tenants originated in differing views about the role of retail societies. Retailers naturally regarded their society as an agency for redressing economic injustices, whereas brewers saw it as a strictly social and political institution, wholly unauthorized to discuss confidential landlord-tenant relationships. Retail societies daring to challenge brewers by interceding for a member with tenancy problems lost subsidies.[9] Brewers often successfully forestalled such conflict with a policy of suspicious paternalism, using their salaried servants, managers, to manipulate the internal affairs of retail associations. When retailers chose officers, managers nominated and supported candidates vetted by brewers. Intent on pre-empting these underhanded manoeuvres, many local retail societies joined with the League in excluding managers as members. The League safeguarded its independence, but was penalized severely, for brewers' donations fell nearly eighty per

[8] *Birmingham Daily Post*, 1 Apr. 1897; *Licensed Trade News*, 3 Apr. 1897; Birm. Br. Assoc. Min. Bk., 13 Apr. and 11 June 1897, D 3163/1/1/1, pp. 248–9, 252–3; *Birmingham Daily Gazette*, 13 May 1897.
[9] Birm. Br. Assoc. Min. Bk., 9 Nov. and 1 Dec. 1893 and 27 Nov. 1896, D 3163/1/1/1, pp. 124–5, 128, 222.

cent in a decade, declining from a peak of £1,300 (1882) to under £250 (1891).[10]

By the early 1890s, when brewers owned the vast bulk of pubs and beerhouses, temperance-minded Liberals promoted retail discontent to neutralize the trade's political power. This strategy began in 1894 with the founding of a new organization, the Tied House Tenants' League. Though publicly pledged to freeing tenants from harsh, restrictive contracts with brewers, it was privately staffed by prohibitionists.[11] Its secretary, moreover, was none other than George Croxden Powell, formerly secretary of the short-lived but widely mistrusted General Association of the Licensed Trade. He was thereafter disqualified from acting as the trade's primary organizer, but not from serving as a fomenter of retail agitation.[12] Brewers soon had good reason to regret his departure. His new allies introduced parliamentary bills abolishing tied contracts, while he helped disseminate election propaganda at pubs and beerhouses, emphasizing 'the extraordinary, and in some cases scandalous, conditions which are despotically imposed upon tied houses by wealthy brewers'. Typical exploitative agreements appeared in Liberal newspapers like the *Star*. Where they controlled the local bench, Liberals also encouraged retail unrest. In 1893 – 4 Liberal JPs at Crewe, for instance, balked at renewing licences until they could scrutinize tenancy contracts, and awarded tenants of Peter Walker & Co. higher retail profits on beer sales as well as other concessions.[13]

Throughout 1894 and 1895 the Tenants' League divided the trade in some areas. Dissatisfied Ipswich publicans approached the Tenants' League for information, while Leeds retailers

---

10 *Licensed Trade News*, 27 May and 2 Aug. 1899 and 19 Sept. 1903; Birm. Br. Assoc. Min. Bk., 1 June 1891 and 22 Feb. 1892, D 3163/1/1/1, pp. 27, 61; LVNDL Annual Reports, 1883 – 92.

11 See p. 24. The MPs were W. Allen, A. Billson, Sir J. Brunner, T. Courtenay Warner, H. S. Leon, J. W. Logan, J. Fletcher Moulton and Sir W. Pearson. J. T. Hincks, Liberal candidate for Worcester, and F. Tomalin were the other members (*Worcestershire Chronicle*, 13 July 1895; BS 1908 Parl., Bk. H., B.S., pp. 2 – 5).

12 Powell, in controversial testimony to the Peel Commission, repeatedly refused to divulge information about his League's activities, composition or membership (*Evid. Royal Com. Liq. Licensing Laws*, 1897, 35 (Cmnd. 8523), pp. 373 – 98).

13 *Star*, 17 Apr. 1895; *Oxford Chronicle and Berks and Bucks Gazette*, 20 Apr. 1895; BS 1908 Parl., Bk. H., pp. 2 – 5; W. H. Chaloner, *The Social and Economic Development of Crewe, 1780 – 1923* (Clifton, New Jersey, 1973), pp. 174 – 6; NTDF 1895 Report, p. 8.

resolved that the tied house 'acted injuriously to the public interest, prejudicially to numerous license-holders, and is contrary to the spirit and intention of the Licensing Laws'. Prohibition was the chief issue for the trade at the 1895 Election, but some Coventry publicans still submitted the Tenants' League test questions to W. H. W. Ballantine, Liberal advocate of local veto and Sunday closing. Retail protest against tied houses sometimes escalated into a trade schism. In the mid-Norfolk constituency, the Liberal candidate's denunciation of them appealed to some retailers who actually signed his nomination form with still more pledging votes.[14]

Tied house practices were simply one of many contentious issues polarizing Leicestershire brewers and retailers. When the Fund began organizing the county in 1891, publicans had obstinately refused to cooperate with local brewers, whose business tactics angered them. Retailers repeatedly declined to put official trade test questions to candidates, and exasperated brewers then fired James Brown (secretary of the Leicestershire Licensed Victuallers' Society) as Fund agent for the county.[15] The dispute also took place on another front. At the 1892 Election, the Conservative standing for re-election at Loughborough was the notorious Edwin De Lisle, whose opposition to the 1890 licensing scheme automatically disqualified him from trade support. Local publicans, far from following the official policy of neutrality, endorsed him. 'De Lisle is set upon a pinnacle by the Licensed Victuallers, asked to preside over them, and cheered when he addresses them', the *Brewing Trade Review* grimly observed. De Lisle portrayed himself as the trade's 'best friend'; retailers saw him as the brewers' avowed enemy.[16]

In 1894 the Leicester Licensed Victuallers' Association resumed its quarrel with brewers over tied houses. One of its members, enraged at his landlord's 'harsh and unfair' conduct, sought protection by asking the Association to contest his licence's renewal. 'By a small extra subscription', another member argued, 'they could make up the donations received from the brewers and turn round on them and say they desired

---

14 *Star*, 18 Apr. 1895; NTDF 1895 Report, pp. 24 – 5; *Licensed Trade News*, 6 and 20 July 1895.
15 NTDF Mid. Dist. Min. Bk., D 3163/2/1/1, 25 Aug., 13 Oct., 17 Nov. and 18 Dec. 1891 and 18 Feb. 1892, pp. 30 – 1, 37, 43, 47 – 8, 67.
16 *Brewing Trade Review*, 1 Nov. 1891 and 1 July 1892.

none of their money, but only fair and square treatment'. This speech galvanized the Leicester Association, which agreed unanimously that it would no longer seek or accept subsidies from tied house owners who treated tenants unjustly. Some members demanded even stronger defiance; the lobbying of MPs for protective legislation or the complete severance of ties with brewers. These same dissidents elatedly endorsed a bill the following year, introduced by Henry Broadhurst of the Tenants' League, allowing tenants to buy alcohol anywhere. Other Leicestershire retailers, off-licence holders, also expressed approval. Their society, in fact, retained James Hincks, executive member of the Tenants' League, as solicitor. Opposed to local veto but not to compensating retailers who lost their licences, he was the drafter of a bill outlawing tied houses.[17]

For several years more the Tenants' League periodically appeared at by-elections throughout the country, though relations between brewers and retailers never escalated into an open schism. This was so not because, as brewers so often claimed, the Tenants' League merely fabricated grievances, but because retailers distrusted prohibitionist sympathy. C. G. Long, vice president of the Licensed Victuallers' National Defence League, clearly revealed retail thinking in a speech in 1896. Tenants, while regarding legislation regulating tied house conditions as a 'burning question', wanted it introduced rather 'by their [Unionist] friends than their [Liberal] enemies', he stated.[18]

In ignoring demands for remedial legislation in 1904 and sponsoring instead a Licensing bill primarily benefitting the brewer-landlord, the Unionist party alienated many retailers. Typical of their acute sense of betrayal was the bitter feud at the Oswestry by-election, shortly after Parliament began considering the compensation scheme for reducing the number of licences. It was approval of this plan which members of the Salop Licensed Victuallers' Association made a litmus test for their support at a meeting on 27 June. Both candidates, W. C. Bridgeman (C) and A. H. Bright (L), would get the test question,

17 *Licensed Trade News*, 17 Nov. 1894, 23 Feb. and 24 Aug. 1895; *Worcestershire Chronicle*, 6 and 13 July 1895.
18 *Licensed Trade News*, 23 Feb. 1895 and 15 Feb. 1896.

but one official conceded that the Association expected to endorse only the Conservative.[19]

R. A. Downes, vice president of the Salop Association, promptly contested this assumption, resigning in protest as district secretary of the League and becoming the secret instigator of a new renegade body, the Shropshire Free Licence Holders' Association. Assisted by roughly 100 tenants, nearly one-quarter of local retailers, he led what soon became a vigorous campaign against the division of compensation awards in the Licensing bill. Unionist 'blessings', Downes asserted, 'have been showered on the wealthy owners and brewers, and the poor tenants and publicans have been sent empty away'. As a 'brewers' bill pure and simple', it deserved strenuous opposition. Since tenants who lost licenses after 1904 received on average eleven per cent of the compensation, they were not so harshly treated as he alleged. But his point, though exaggerated, was still valid: brewer-landlords as the largest investors in licensed property reaped most of the rewards from a business built up by hard-working but often impoverished tenants. Fully realizing the strong possibility of reprisals for challenging both official policy and brewer-landlords, tenants nevertheless rejected acquiescence: 'Better [to] be turned out than robbed by the brewers'.

Paltry compensation was not the only source of retail discontent, nor brewers the only foe. Tenants stressed that traditionally Unionist, not Liberal, governments increased beer taxes. Unionists, in fact, had been responsible for almost three-quarters of the 21d/barrel imposts levied on beer since 1889.[20] Some of this revenue had been further squandered, tenants believed, when Unionists had retained a special tax on beer intended for an aborted scheme of licensing reduction. Now Balfour's Government with its Licensing bill proposed extra heavy fees for compensation. For all these reasons, retailers had become disenchanted with Unionists as trade allies. 'If they

---

[19] The following 7 paragraphs are based on *Oswestry and Border Counties Advertiser, and Montgomeryshire Mercury*: 13 July and 7 Dec. 1904; 'One of the Trade' to editor, 20 July 1904; Craston to editor, 23 Nov. and 7 Dec. 1904; Byrne to editor, 30 Nov. 1904; Downes to editor, 7 Dec. 1904 and 4 Jan. 1905; Downes to Byrne, 7 Dec. 1904; Byrne to Downes, 7 Dec. 1904; *Newport and Drayton Advertiser*, 23 July 1904; *Shrewsbury Chronicle*, 15 July and 5 Aug. 1904; *Licensed Trade News*, 31 Dec. 1904.

[20] Beer taxes were raised by Unionist governments in 1889 – 90 (3d) and in 1900 (1s), and by the Liberal Government in 1894 (6d).

looked at their account with that [Unionist] party for the last
fifteen years they could preach a good sermon from the text
"Whom the Government loveth it chasteneth" ', Downes
maintained.

Tenants also saw their own trade protective society, the
League, as thoroughly discredited for cooperating with brewers
and Unionists. In 'coquetting with . . . the Brewers' N[ational]
T[rade] Fund', Downes asserted, the League, its independence
compromised, had ceased to represent the true interests of
provincial retailers. Another leading disaffected retail official,
J.A. Byrne (secretary of the Salop Association), agreed, denigrating the League for debasing retailers into mere 'Puppets of
the Brewers'. These retailers felt their overriding problem
derived not from unrepresentative protective societies, much
less from unfaithful Unionists, but from something more
fundamental, the trade's deliberate policy of becoming a 'Tory
electioneering machine'.

Members of the Shropshire Free Licence Holders' Association, who viewed the Oswestry by-election as a referendum on
the detested Licensing bill, repudiated official trade policy by
adopting two test questions seeking the abolition of tied houses
and more compensation for tenants. These were submitted to
both candidates, despite Bright's approval of the UKA test
questions on local option and Sunday closing. He had,
however, also pledged his opposition to the Licensing bill as the
UKA demanded, and it was this that appealed to disgruntled
tenants. Their stance was even secretly supported by some
prominent leaders of the Salop Association. In reply to a letter
from Downes, Byrne felt that the Free Licence Association was
addressing 'the only sensible questions . . . on our behalf for a
long time'.

This internal disunity guaranteed an extremely acrimonious
meeting when the Salop Association selected the official trade
candidate on 11 July 1904. Bridgeman seemed so likely a choice
but so little regarded that only twenty of the town's 400 retailers
attended. Downes predictably denounced both the Unionist
Licensing bill and Bridgeman, but had no hope of getting the
Liberal candidate endorsed. Trade officials had seen to this by
suppressing a letter from Bright, in which he cited the Salop
Association's virtual adoption of Bridgeman on 27 June as his
reason for refusing to answer the test question. Bridgeman, the
only candidate publicly committed to the official trade test
question, thus won by default.

Such deceitful tactics ensured not only that Bridgeman became the Salop Association's official candidate, but that large numbers of disaffected tenants would adopt Bright, already backed by the Alliance. 'The trade vote in Shropshire is split from top to bottom', one of them remarked. Bright, he predicted, 'will get half of it'. This certainly explains why Bridgeman lost an otherwise safe Unionist seat by less than 400 votes. Some tenants therefore allowed economic to outweigh political issues, helping elect a Liberal whose prohibitionist sentiments mattered less than his hostility to Balfour's Licensing bill.

The Salop Association, making Downes the scapegoat for this humiliating defeat, immediately expelled him. He appealed against the decision, and forcefully defended himself at the next meeting. In an unrepentant speech to members, he declared that defects in the Licensing bill and the trade's fruitless electoral policy justified his conduct. Downes' impassioned plea prompted calls for his reinstatement. One supporter advanced the practical argument that purging every member who had recently voted Liberal would markedly deplete the Association's membership. Downes' expulsion was nevertheless upheld, though almost one-third of those present dissented. The *Licensed Trade News*, gloating over his defeat, applauded this verdict as apt punishment for such apostasy.[21] Retail animus against tenancy conditions, as the by-election clearly illustrated, could thus aggravate economic dissension between landlords and tenants, dividing retailers, provoking attacks on brewers as well as Unionist allies and disproving the brewing industry's boasted electoral influence.

When in 1904 and 1909 legislation raised drink taxes, brewers responded with opportunistic policies which further strained trade loyalty.[22] Technically, they were obliged to pay the 1904 compensation levy, but many used devious ploys — manipulating rents, wholesale beer prices or discounts — to shift it onto helpless tenants. Some Manchester and Salford brewers, for instance, not only recovered their compensation fees through higher wholesale prices, but actually netted a profit. Others resorted to managers, cheaper salaried employees who gave brewers bigger profits. Two hundred local beersellers publicized

21 *Licensed Trade News*, 10 and 31 Dec. 1904.
22 Crapster contends, however, that retail discontent with the tied house system gradually diminished after 1900 (Crapster, 'British Liquor Industry', p. 165).

these grievances at a meeting in February 1906, where one expressed their conviction of the impossibility of reform 'until the tied house system was swept away'. According to a bitter London tenant, the Act explicitly forbade 'contracting out, but the methods adopted by some brewers did not come within the scope of that clause'.[23] Tenants found offloading higher prices on consumers attractive but impractical since local competitors might not follow suit. Putting the smallest coin, the farthing, moreover, on a 3d pint would raise prices by almost ten per cent, and might simply reduce beer consumption, which had slumped since 1899.[24] As economic conditions worsened, League officials warned brewers of the hopelessness of sustaining 'that unity of action . . . essential for the protection and defence of the Trade'. Similarly, it was often tenants, not brewers, who largely paid huge new licence fees instituted in the People's budget, which failed to specify the proportion owed by landlord and tenant. Brewers again increased prices and rents, tactics which retailers stridently condemned as exploitative. At the League's 1911 conference, delegates decided to request an amendment repealing licence taxes for those tenants swindled into paying their landlord-brewers' budget duties. Three years later, the conference was once more deriding brewers for evading taxes at the expense of defenceless tenants. One East Anglian retailer described a 'system of coercion, which meant that unless they [tenants] did as they were ordered they had to leave their houses'.[25]

Economic strife between brewers and retailers directly contributed to trade divisions at the 1910 Elections. Off-licence holders took the most drastic action, pushing through the Federation a test question demanding changes in tied house

---

23   *Licensed Trade News*, 17 Feb. and 24 March 1906; see also *ibid.*, 21 Oct. 1905; LVNDL 1910 Annual Report, pp. 52 – 4.

24   Publicans would receive at least 6s more per barrel from a ¼d per pint increase, which meant that their weekly total would probably exceed higher rent or wholesale price changes (Diana M. Knox, 'The Development of the London Brewing Industry, 1830 – 1914, with Special Reference to Messrs. Whitbread and Co.' (Oxford Univ. B. Litt. thesis, 1956), pp. 53 – 4).

25   LVNDL Min. Bk., 20 Feb. 1906; LVNDL Annual Reports: 1911, pp. 50 – 5; 1914, pp. 65 – 6; LVNDL 1912 Half-Yearly Meeting, pp. 30 – 1. Free licence holders suffered more because they paid the entire licence duty. Lloyd George partly alleviated this burden in 1912, introducing an amendment making owners of houses occupied by free licence holders responsible for part of increased licence fees. For complaints, see LVNDL Annual Reports: 1909, pp. 73, 75; 1910, pp. 54 – 6; 'Through Practical Spectacles', p. 384.

practices. Publicans and beerhouse keepers, likewise disgusted with unprincipled brewers who transferred tax burdens, instead spurned appeals for solidarity: some would not work with local officials, others withheld votes from Unionists, while yet others believed Liberal promises that the budget would help tenants. Numerous confused Burslem retailers, for instance, 'were supporting the Liberal party because in this particular case they were doing something to help the tied tenant'. It was in fact not so much persuasive propaganda as outrage at unscrupulous brewers who had victimized tenants that made retailers Liberal voters. By 1911 retail charges of brewers' 'autocratic' behaviour had become the theme of editorials in leading trade newspapers, with one gloomily convinced of an imminent schism.[26]

Relations between brewers and retailers were also damaged by the rapid expansion of clubs in many late Victorian cities.[27] Much of the impetus came from brewers who supplied financial assistance by exploiting ambiguous licensing laws. These establishments, catering predominantly to a working-class clientele, antagonized retailers whose pubs and beerhouses lost business. Clubs had an anomalous status as unlicensed dispensers of alcoholic beverages, usually beer. Outside the licensing system and its two chief agencies for enforcing morality, policemen and magistrates, clubs had virtually unrestricted hours, musical entertainment, gambling and drunkenness.[28] Three enormous economic advantages, no licence duties,

[26] LVNDL Annual Reports: 1910, pp. 52–4; 1914, pp. 65–6; LVNDL Half-Yearly Meetings: 1911, p. 20; 1912, pp. 30–1; *Licensing World and Licensed Trade Review*, 3 Dec. 1910; *Licensed Trade News*, 25 Nov. 1911; NTDA Mid. Dist. Agent's 1911 Report, D 3163/2/2, p. 13.

[27] The mid-Victorian development of clubs is examined in Peter Bailey, *Leisure and Class in Victorian England: Rational Recreation and the Contest for Control, 1830–1885* (1987), ch. 5; Richard N. Price, 'The Working Men's Club Movement and Victorian Social Reform Ideology', *Vic. Stud.*, 15 (1971), 117–47; John Taylor, *From Self-Help to Glamour: The Working Men's Club, 1860–1972* (Oxford, 1972); B.T. Hall, *Our Sixty Years: The Story of the Working Men's Club and Institute Union* (1922).

[28] Ross McKibbin does not discuss gambling in the club context, but Booth noted of East London bogus clubs that 'betting and various forms of gambling, but chiefly betting, are their main objects' (Ross McKibbin, 'Working-Class Gambling in Britain, 1880–1939', *Past and Present*, 82 (1979), pp. 170–1; Booth, *East London*, p. 94; see also Arthur Shadwell, *Drink, Temperance and Legislation* (1902), p. 222; Pettit to Davidson, 16 March 1908, Davidson Papers, Licensing and Temp. Box 3; Sherwell, *West London*, p. 139).

membership dues subsidizing rents and brewers' generous discounts on beer, meant clubs charged lower beer prices, customarily one-third less than at pubs or beerhouses. Disgruntled retailers had long sought a remedy, uniform wholesale prices. Brewers dismissed this as unacceptable, contending that their costly tied house repairs offset any supposed discrepancy in wholesale prices. Retailers underrated their problems. Cheaper beer obviously generated custom, but so did the club's more congenial environment and longer opening hours.[29]

Retailers objected less to *bona fide* working-men's clubs which encouraged social intercourse than to bogus ones devoted solely to drinking, often to excess. Distinguishing between them was difficult. Both served alcohol, and licensing laws offered no basis for separating them. Legal authorities and informed critics gradually developed a criteria for prosecution. Genuine clubs usually had a constitution with certain common provisions: all members periodically paid subscriptions, divided profits equally as communal owners of the property, and elected a governing committee which controlled finances; new applicants, after a reasonable interval elapsed, were regularly admitted as members; and guests could attend but never order alcohol themselves. Bogus clubs, in contrast, seldom bothered with these elaborate regulations in pursuing their goal, the sale of vast quantities of beer to enrich promoters. Such drinking dens, one Cardiff JP avowed, all displayed similar shortcomings: 'One man at its head . . . works the whole concern with sham committees, sham secretary, sham treasurer, and a manager who takes all the profit'.[30]

Respectable *bona fide* clubs generally affiliated with the Working Men's Club and Institute Union, which counted 600 of them as members late in the 1890s. It fostered and regulated working-men's clubs, providing legal and administrative advice and a circulating library. Enrolling only authentic groups, the Union rigidly insisted only members manage the club, and

---

[29] *Licensing World and Licensed Trade Review*, 30 Apr. 1910; Northants. Br. Assoc. Min. Bk., 5 and 6 March 1888, SL 298; Wilts. Br. Assoc. Min. Bk., 11 March 1909, W. Count. Br. Assoc; *Statist*, 29 Sept. 1894; Rowntree, *Poverty*, p. 330; *Evid. Sel. Comt. Clubs Registration Bill*, 1893 – 4, 10 (314), p. 133; *Brewers' Gazette*, 22 Oct. 1908.

[30] *Evid. Royal Com. Sunday Closing (Wales) Act, 1881*, 1890, 40 (Cmnd. 5994-I), pp. 5, 18, 22, 25 – 6; *Evid. Sel. Comt. Clubs*, 1893 – 4, 10 (314), pp. 79, 81 – 2, 155; *Evid. Royal Com. Liq. Licensing Laws*, 1897, 34 (Cmnd. 8356), p. 29; see also Wilson, *Alcohol and Nation*, pp. 134 – 5.

banned gambling, insobriety and any financial interest in dispensing alcohol. Rejected outright were clubs 'under the thumb of a brewer', notorious for two disreputable features: bad management and bad beer. Refusing brewers' loans imposed no hardship on legitimate establishments seeking federation. Under the Industrial and Provident Societies' Act (1876), registered clubs could themselves raise capital for purchasing and building premises.[31]

Two legal obstacles prevented Parliament from simply outlawing spurious clubs. Most proprietary clubs, run strictly as a commercial venture by several members in working-class neighbourhoods, were bogus, whereas many in London's respectable West End, frequented solely by the upper-classes, were unquestionably *bona fide*. Rich, influential and exclusive, West End Clubs like the Athenaeum and Brooks' 'will seriously resent any interference with their internal control and management', cautioned William Minet, one informed barrister. Legislation drawing class distinctions between proprietary clubs was legally possible, but politically and socially inadvisable. 'You must not have one law for the rich and one for the poor', Minet told the Select Committee exploring this subject in 1893.[32] Difficulties in acquiring proof of illicit activities also blocked legislation. Clubs were like private homes; authorities could enter only with a search warrant. Magistrates would grant it, but not without sworn testimony to the unlicensed sales of alcohol. Though Somerset House had no scruples about using a roving officer with his own staff who visited clubs incognito, most local police officials feared private detectives would arouse intense public indignation. Robert Peacock, chief constable of Oldham, knew that 'it is considered very un-English for a police officer to break the law for the purpose of detecting it'. Other alternatives threatened the sanctity of the home. In 1890 the committee investigating Welsh Sunday closing would not recommend authorizing a policeman, accompanied by a superior officer, to search places suspected of illegally selling alcohol

---

[31] *Evid. Sel. Comt. Clubs*, 1893–4, 10 (314), pp. 151–3, 155; *Report Royal Com. Liq. Licensing Laws*, 1899, 35 (Cmnd. 9379), p. 259.

[32] *Evid. Sel. Comt. Clubs*, 1893–4, 10 (314), pp. 82, 84, 89, 91. Minet, member of the Working Men's Club and Institute Union's Council, had written several pamphlets, including *Clubs and How to Start and Manage Them* (George Tremlett, *Clubmen: History of the Working Men's Club and Institute Union* (1987), pp. 59, 78).

because they feared 'so extensive a power of interfering with domestic privacy'.[33]

Frustrated local authorities and informed witnesses blamed bogus clubs for many social evils. Captain Lindsay Burnett, chief constable of Wolverhampton, contrasted his city in the early 1890s, its quiet pubs and beerhouses observing licensing laws and sober patrons returning home after an evening's drinking, with what it became four years later after ten spurious clubs had opened. Inhabitants now drank into the early morning hours, and would 'remain hanging about the vicinity of the club buildings to the disturbance of others, and to the prejudice of good order in the borough'. Few experts doubted the club's responsibility for increased drunkenness. Wives furnished solid evidence, complaining of husbands and sons squandering their money. The Reverend F. Ernest Spencer, a vicar in London's East End, had first-hand experience of the harmful effects of clubs on family life. Technically they closed at midnight in his parish, but drinking usually continued for several hours. With parents off carousing, 'children are left . . . to roam the street', he lamented.[34]

Early in the 1880s retailers were only concerned about clubs in Wales. There the Welsh Sunday closing Act of 1881 stimulated the spread of clubs, notably in large southern cities such as Cardiff, where within one year club membership grew by 900 per cent. But in England pubs stayed opened on Sundays, and bogus clubs posed no serious problem.[35]

But from the mid-1880s clubs proliferated in England and Wales. By 1885, both the League and the Society were urging stricter control of spurious ones.[36] Between 1887 and 1896 those serving alcohol rose from 1,982 to 3,655, and thereafter the level escalated, reaching some 8,700 in 1914. Meanwhile the number

---

33 *Evid. Sel. Comt. Clubs*, 1893 – 4, 10 (314), pp. 20 – 1, 162; *Report Com. Sunday Closing*, 1890, 40 (Cmnd. 5994), p. xxxvii; *Evid. Lords Comt. Intemp.*, 1877, 11 (171), p. 204; *Evid. Royal Com. Liq. Licensing Laws*, 1897, 34 (Cmnd. 8356), pp. 29 – 31, 58, 134.

34 *Evid. Sel. Comt. Clubs*, 1893 – 4, 10 (314), pp. 145 – 7; *Evid. Royal Com. Liq. Licensing Laws*, 1897, 35 (Cmnd. 8523), pp. 130 – 3; see also Sherwell, *West London*, p. 139.

35 W. R. Lambert, 'The Welsh Sunday Closing Act, 1881', *Welsh Hist. Rev.*, 6 (1972), 177 – 8; *Country Brewers' Gazette*, 2 March and 6 July 1881.

36 The League approved an anti-club resolution in 1881, but annual motions only became standard in 1884 (LVNDL Annual Reports: 1881, p. 57; 1884, p. 70; 1885, pp. 37 – 8; 1886, p. 42; 1887, p. 40). Retailers used an anti-club test question at the 1885 Election (Jt. Com. Lic. Vict. Min. Bk., 23 June 1885).

of licensed premises diminished steadily, especially after the
1904 Act accelerated reduction, prompting the *Brewers' Gazette*
complaint in 1910 that 'the club is replacing the public-house'.
In 1887 there was one club for every fifty on-licensed premises;
in 1914 the ratio was one to ten.[37] Yet clubs, though largely
nullifying the alleged advantages of fewer licences, diverted
little trade from surviving drink shops. By 1914, clubs annually
accounted for just 1.5 per cent of the gross expenditure on
alcohol, or 2.4 per cent on beer.[38] These meagre takings strongly
suggest that retail animus against clubs stemmed not from
serious economic rivalry but from the action of brewers in
encouraging competitors.

Brewers established or assisted clubs for diverse reasons. In
1894 the *Statist*, a prominent business newspaper, pointed to
minimal legal restraints, smaller investments and fewer
financial risks as giving brewers stronger incentives for invest-
ing in clubs rather than in public houses. No doubt brewers
appreciated these benefits, but profits seemed to have been
decisive. Club promoters seeking capital naturally approached
brewers, who provided it in exchange for extra outlets. In
London, Charles Booth noted how easily clubs secured brewers'
loans to buy accessories. 'Repayment is not pressed, nor is the
security scrutinized; for the lender is repaid by profit on the beer
supplied'.[39] Some brewers took a more active role, as at
Llandudno where the Northampton Brewery Co. found larger
quarters for the Blatchley Club, apparently paid £800 for them

[37] *Brewers' Gazette*, 18 Aug. 1910; Wilson, *Alcohol and Nation*, pp. 140, 145, 396.
In the years 1905 – 14, nearly 9,900 on-licences were referred for compensation (see p. 157).

[38] These figures are derived from the duty, first imposed in the Edwardian era,
paid by clubs on the sale of intoxicating liquor (George B. Wilson's 'Drink
Bill', *The Times*, 13 Apr. 1915; *Return Showing the Rates of Duty, Taxes, or
Imposts, Collected by Imperial Officers*, 1914, 50 (434), p. 7).

[39] *Statist*, 29 Sept. 1894; *Evid. Sel. Comt. Clubs*, 1893 – 4, 10 (314), pp. 144, 160;
Booth, *East London*, p. 96; T. G. Ashplant, 'London Working Men's Clubs,
1875 – 1914', Eileen and Stephen Yeo (eds.), *Popular Culture and Class
Conflict, 1590 – 1914: Explorations in the History of Labour and Leisure* (Brighton,
1981), p. 245, 251 – 3; Brad. Br. Assoc. Min. Bk., 10 June 1909. For retail
allegations of brewers financing clubs, see *Licensed Trade News*, 11 June 1898,
18 Nov. 1899, 15 Feb. 1902 and 30 July 1910; LVNDL Annual Reports: 1897,
p. 156; 1898, pp. 97 – 8, 101; 1901, p. 100; 1910, pp. 57 – 9. Brewers were also
financing music halls in London and probably elsewhere (Penelope
Summerfield, 'The Effingham Arms and the Empire: Deliberate Selection in
the Evolution of Music Hall in London', in Yeo (eds.), *Popular Culture*, p.
221).

and lent £200 for redecoration. The club, with beer sales of nearly £200 during the past six months, had become a thriving business, and the source of considerable controversy. Both the local brewer, Andrew Tanqueray, and his tenant resented what they saw as unfair outside competition. 'This Club is run in direct opposition to . . . [our] Licensed House a few yards away, and has seriously affected its Trade', Tanqueray grumbled in 1909. Brewers frequently converted public houses which had forfeited licences into clubs as a protection against sizable financial losses. So did dispossessed retailers. When magistrates closed one Welsh publican's free house, the 'George and the Dragon', he quickly reopened it as the 'Bangor Social Club'. Brewers also created clubs themselves. In Wolverhampton, for instance, two nearby Warwickshire breweries, Showell's Brewery Co. and Flowers & Sons, established nine clubs for boozing, despite owning numerous local tied houses. Determined to expose these frauds but denied legal access, Captain Burnett used undercover detectives who concluded that these firms 'started, furnished, and financed' the clubs. There was ample evidence of bogus operations: nominal membership dues, simulated pub interiors, drinking facilities only, tied covenants with breweries and brewer-appointed managers. These so-called clubs, he avowed, were 'simply unlicensed public-houses — drinking saloons' set up to make more money. Sham clubs yielded 'such profit that sometimes the payment of fines is not . . . any difficulty', related one government official.[40]

Some brewers backed clubs, but not primarily for greater profits. Following the 1892 Election, the *Wolverhampton Chronicle* commented that over 200 pub drinkers, irked with publicans' aggressive support for Conservative candidates, had formed the North Wolverhampton Working Men's Club. These long loyal pub patrons had expected publicans to oppose the Conservative party for sponsoring countless clubs which hurt retailers' business. Hence the club punished retailers for misplaced loyalty. 'Similar clubs', the *Chronicle* reported, 'will be established in other parts of the town where the publicans have become active politicians'. Local railway labourers, however,

---

40 Tanqueray to Causton, 9 Sept. 1909, House Lords R.O., Bonar Law Papers, 18/5/101; *Licensed Trade News*, 7 May 1898; *Evid. Sel. Comt. Clubs*, 1893 – 4, 10 (314), pp. 55, 57, 76, 79; *Hansard*, 4th ser., 105 (7 Apr. 1902), col. 1173; *Report and Evid. Royal Com. Liq. Licensing Laws*, 1897, 34 (Cmnd. 8356), pp. 27, 30; 35 (Cmnd. 8523), pp. 130 – 3, 252; 1898, 36 (Cmnd. 8693), pp. 151 – 2; 35 (Cmnd. 9379), p. 257.

gave the Wolverhampton Licensed Victuallers' Society an entirely different account, which disputed the origin but not the purpose of the clubs. Showell's Brewery Co., not drinkers, had in fact promoted the clubs as a reprisal against the recent political activities of two retailers. Wolverhampton retailers verified this evidence before warning Showell's Brewery Co. of the adverse impact on trade organization. Asked by retailers to intervene, the Fund's midland district discovered only one convenient discrepancy, the money came not from the brewery's directors but from their agent who had acted on his own initiative. Nevertheless, no one contested the club's punitive aim, except the brewery, which persisted in supplying beer despite publicans' protests.[41]

Some brewers' associations did recognize the validity of retail complaints against clubs. Bradford brewers, owners of clubs in the 1890s, disarmed retail criticism in the Edwardian era by uniformly withdrawing all investments in such enterprises. The same accord also existed in Poole and throughout Northamptonshire, though brewers continued supplying clubs with beer.[42] Clubs could still become a contentious issue when firms in nearby towns, like Bournemouth, just miles from Poole, disobeyed the rule. Non-local brewers equally caused problems late in the 1890s. One publican felt 'it a great shame that the leading company in the country should come in and do what the Northamptonshire brewers . . . thought should not be done'. The Birmingham Brewers' Association formulated particularly rigorous standards, penalizing brewers who invested in clubs with heavy fines and seizures of profits. Elsewhere local brewers sometimes informally agreed to boycott clubs altogether, or support more stringent club legislation.[43]

Brewers and retailers differed sharply over the best legal remedy for bogus clubs in the 1890s. Publicans advocated a policy of club registration, with much stricter supervision. Two million club members with vast political power precluded more drastic changes, the Society's *Licensing World and Licensed Trade Review* admitted. Privately publicans defended registration as a

[41] *Wolverhampton Chronicle*, 21 Dec. 1892; NTDA Mid. Dist. Min. Bk., 22 Dec. 1892 and 26 Jan. 1893, D 3163/2/1/1, pp. 134–6, 139–40.
[42] Brad. Br. Assoc. Min. Bk., 6 Feb. 1911; *Evid. Sel. Comt. Clubs*, 1893–4, 10 (314), p. 80; *Licensed Trade News*, 18 Nov. 1899.
[43] LVNDL Min. Bk., 7 May 1907, p. 20; *Evid. Sel. Comt. Clubs*, 1893–4, 10 (314), p. 82; *Licensed Trade News*, 18 Nov. 1899, 16 Nov. 1901 and 1 Apr. 1911; *Evid. Royal Com. Liq. Licensing Laws*, 1897, 35 (Cmnd. 8523), p. 151.

compromise between their dislike of commercial rivals, on the one hand, and overwhelming desire for retaining the legal distinction between themselves and clubs, on the other.[44] Brewers disagreed. Registration had one chief drawback, clubs would still sell alcohol without paying licence fees, so the only sensible option was licensing them like other distributors of drink. Licensing clubs, of course, would give brewers large numbers of cheap outlets, including many former pubs and beerhouses previously written off as a total loss.[45]

These conflicting approaches provoked friction during the Peel Commission's investigation of licensing laws late in the 1890s. When the Fund appointed an advisory body to gather material on clubs for this body, retailers saw a conflict of interest if any brewer served as chairman. Instead a publican was appointed, but such suspicion ominously foreshadowed deeper dissension. In November 1896, the United Parliamentary Council (UPC), composed of London and provincial retailers, arranged a meeting with B. T. Hall, secretary of the Working Men's Club and Institute Union. Drawn together through common hatred of spurious clubs, their alliance threatened brewers' investments. Somehow the Fund learned of this meeting, and privately dissuaded Hall from attending. As the sole representative trade society, the Fund felt its actions fully justified. But angry UPC members, whose authority had been subverted, attacked this underhanded manoeuvre, and insisted on seeing Hall.[46] The UPC, now convinced of the importance of providing the Peel Commission with damaging testimony against clubs, inaugurated an independent policy. Two eager but inept detectives were hired to investigate six suspect London clubs. This covert activity ended disastrously, as police caught them on a raid and arrested them.[47] Neither evidently

44 *Licensing World and Licensed Trade Review*, 26 Sept. 1896. Although Crapster states that 'publicans would have preferred clubs be licensed in the same way as public-houses', the UPC, representing the League and the Society, resolved in 1896 that it 'strongly objects to the licensing of Clubs in any form whatever' (Crapster, 'British Liquor Industry', pp. 169 – 70; LVPSL Min. Bk., Meetings of the Royal Commission Comt., 8 June 1896, Nat. Union. Lic. Victs.; see also *Licensing World and Licensed Trade Review*, 5 Sept. 1896; League resolutions: *Northern Brewers' and Victuallers' Journal*, 25 Apr. 1891; LVNDL Annual Reports: 1893, p. 92; 1894, p. 99).
45 *Licensed Trade News*, 22 Feb. 1902.
46 UPC Trade Min. Bk., 5 Nov. 1896; LVPSL Royal Com. Min. Bk., 17 Nov. 1896.
47 LVPSL Royal Commission Min. Bk., 30 Nov. 1896 and 15 Feb. 1897.

chose to recount this experience publicly, so retailers exposed only their own bumbling conduct, not bogus clubs.

The Peel Commission's findings, published in 1899, not only stressed the inadequate laws regulating clubs, but suggested reforms which served as the basis for subsequent legislation. Both Reports recommended registering clubs, examining their rules and forbidding off-consumption. Only signers of the Minority Report attacked brewer-clubs. No club should be registered, it urged, unless members were free of tied contracts with liquor sellers, owned the property themselves and had occupied premises unconnected with drink sales during the previous five years. Retailers had become so impatient with brewers that assistance even from long-standing adversaries was welcomed. W. S. Caine, prohibitionist and Liberal MP, swiftly put pressure on the Unionist Government to act, introducing his own Club Registration bill in 1901. In his letter to Chamberlain, he noted the many licensed victuallers' societies which had 'passed resolutions thanking me personally . . . and pledging themselves to support it in Parliament'. These resolutions gained further credibility when the more representative League formally expressed support for Caine's bill. The following year the government enacted a Club bill allowing magistrates greater freedom in issuing search warrants, banning non-members from purchasing drink for off-consumption and making registration compulsory. Clubs with few members arrested for drunkenness, a representative committee supervising liquor supplies and limited numbers of guests could easily qualify, provided none had been pubs or beerhouses within the previous year. Retailers meanwhile suspended pressure, awaiting the Club bill's impact.[48]

By resuming agitation for stricter club legislation after 1904, the League ensured that Liberals would address the problem if only to divide the trade. Unlike the Society and the Association, the League submitted a test question to candidates at the 1906 Election seeking tighter control of clubs. In an unprecedented move at the League's annual conference in 1905, delegates had endorsed the executive's recently drafted bill requiring that clubs obtain excise certificates as a prerequisite for operation. Specifically disqualified were clubs violating licensing hours,

---

[48] *Report Royal Com. Liq. Licensing Laws*, 1899, 35 (Cmnd. 9397), pp. 48, 262–3; LVNDL 1901 Annual Report, p. 100; Wilson, *Alcohol and Nation*, p. 139; Caine to Chamberlain, 31 Oct. 1901, quoted in John Newton, *W. S. Caine, MP: A Biography* (1907), pp. 295–7.

operating under tied covenants and owned or leased by breweries. Certificate fees ranged between £2 5s and £17 10s, much less than most provincial retailers paid for licences. The League then took the extraordinary step of lobbying Sir Henry Campbell-Bannerman, Liberal prime minister. In requesting Liberal support for its bill, the League stressed the glaring defects in the 1902 Club Act: unregulated conditions, unlimited opening hours and unrestricted off-consumption.[49] Despite opposition from the Association which deemed the League's bill unwise and wanted it deferred, League officials still pressed for stronger club laws.[50] Politicians of both major parties, however, feared offending working-class voters, though some like Herbert Gladstone (Liberal home secretary) privately favoured suppressing bogus establishments. Writing to an official of a legitimate club in Leeds, he argued that those 'under some covenant are bound perhaps to a Brewery Company similar to the "tie" of Public-houses, cannot be looked upon as bona-fide Working-Men's Clubs'. These convictions may explain the somewhat stiffer club rules contained in the Liberal 1908 Licensing bill. Had it passed, clubs would have been unable to supply drink in small quantities for consumption off the premises, subjected to police inspection and possibly abolished if used within the past five years as pubs or beerhouses.[51]

Neither abortive legislation nor unsympathetic brewers dissuaded League members from relentlessly agitating for club reform. By October 1910, the Beer and Wine Trade National Defence League, the country's largest society of beerhouse keepers, had endorsed the League bill. The League itself was seriously considering the re-adoption of an anti-club test question. To avert a spiralling controversy, the Brewers' Society passed a conciliatory resolution, discouraging brewers from both financially aiding or founding clubs. The *Brewers' Journal* cited this as ample proof of the fact that 'the club is the enemy of the brewer no less than of the licensed victualler'. A sceptical League rejected this sympathy, submitting a club reform test

[49] NTDA Min. Bk. 2, 16 Dec. 1904, p. 145; LVNDL 1905 Annual Report, pp. 50 – 2, 88 – 9, 100; *Morning Advertiser*, 22 Dec. 1905 and 9 Nov. 1906.
[50] NTDA Min. Bk. 2, 5 and 13 Feb. and 6 March 1907, pp. 201 – 2, 207, 211 – 12. The Society backed brewers against the League.
[51] Gladstone to Smith, 29 Apr. 1907 (copy), Herbert Gladstone Papers, Add. Ms. 46,064, fos. 185 – 6; *Alliance Temperance Almanack for 1909*, p. 4; Tremlett, *Clubmen*, pp. 101 – 2.

question at the December 1910 Election and re-introducing a modified bill in 1911.[52]

The League had compelling reasons for distrusting brewers. First, they had merely expressed an opinion, not sanctioned a binding policy enforced by financial penalties, and as such could ignore the resolution with impunity. Second, those involved with clubs escaped not just censure but disapproval. Yet a third reason was brewers' sheer hypocrisy. Retailers scarcely concealed their contempt for brewers who often publicly denounced but privately promoted clubs. Finally, brewers overlooked their own role as financial backers in condemning clubs for counteracting licensing reduction.[53] Yet not all brewers were insincere. One prominent Birmingham brewer, W. Waters Butler, himself extremely critical of brewer-financed clubs and supporter of the League bill, pointed out the dangers of categorically attacking all clubs. Brewers and retailers, he stated, 'had no desire to add a powerful clubland opposition to the many enemies they already possessed'.[54]

In becoming backers of clubs, brewers alienated retailers, the chief organizers of voting at elections. After visiting Wiltshire's Cricklade division, the Association agent blamed flourishing numbers of clubs for dissuading retailers from joining trade societies in 1895, and for his difficulty in mobilizing support behind the Conservative candidate at the 1900 Election. The trade candidate barely won the first contest, but resoundingly lost the second. In 1910 they divided the trade in the Westbury division, where retailers were 'seething with discontent' at the bigger discounts clubs received from brewers. Fighting a by-election the following year, the Conservative candidate could not arouse retailers, whose customers had begun frequenting newly set up Conservative clubs supplied by local brewers. He failed to unseat his Liberal opponent, though not more than 100 votes had decided the last election.[55]

---

52 *Licensing World and Licensed Trade Review*, 30 Apr. 1910; *Brewing Trade Review*, 1 Oct. 1910; *Brewers' Journal*, 15 Oct. 1910; LVNDL 1910 Half-Yearly Meeting, p. 41. The League re-adopted the club test question in 1913 (LVNDL 1913 Annual Report, pp. 13–14).

53 Gretton, 'Licensing Bill', p. 739. Hawkins and Pass (*Brewing Industry*, p. 152, n. 62) uncritically accept brewers' stance towards clubs.

54 *Licensed Trade News*, 1 Apr. 1911; see also NTDA Notts., Lincs., Rutland and Peterborough Dist. Min. Bk., 10 July 1913.

55 NTDA W. Dist. Annual Reports: 1895, p. 8; 1900, p.9; 1911, pp. 6–7; Wilts. Br. Assoc. Min. Bk., 29 July 1910; see also the attacks on a Welsh Conservative club (*Licensed Trade News*, 26 Oct. 1912).

Working-class drinkers not only had the club as an alternative to pubs and beerhouses, but could enjoy beer at home, conveniently delivered by breweries. Increased home consumption reflected an improved quality of life for the Edwardian working class: many labourers no longer preferred the pub to their homes.[56] Public demand rather than breweries inspired the spread of direct suppliers, and bottled beer made it possible.

Historians recognize that drinking habits shifted late in the nineteenth century. Large numbers of middle-class beer drinkers abandoned heavy pale ales for those with fewer hops, and a sparkling appearance. These new ales, still quite bitter but lighter in taste, had less alcohol and were often bottled for home consumption. 'The light beers, of which increasing quantities are being brewed every year, are more or less the outcome of the demand of the middle classes for a palatable and easily consumable beverage', explained Julian Baker in his study of the brewing industry in 1905. But temperance strictures as much as opposition to mixing with the working class kept respectable drinkers out of pubs. 'Certain . . . people . . . prefer to have their beer sent to them', acknowledged J. F. Ealand, president of the Beer and Wine Trade Defence League, in 1910.[57]

What has not been appreciated is that working-class drinkers also turned to lightly-hopped carbonated bottled beer, and drank it at home, not at the pub. This trend in working-class drinking, which deprived the pub of some of its traditional clientele, has been ignored because historians wholly discount the rise of bottled beer in Edwardian England. In these years, John Vaizey contends 'bottling was essentially . . . still a small-scale process; its development is important for the growth of the national trade after 1918, when taste swung rapidly towards bottled beer'. More recently two other economic historians, K. H. Hawkins and C. L. Pass, reaffirm this view.[58] National statistics of drink consumption provide no guide, merely

56 James Walvin, *Leisure and Society, 1830 – 1950* (1978), p. 40; Arthur J. Taylor, 'The Economy', Simon Nowell-Smith (ed.), *Edwardian England, 1901 – 14* (1964), pp. 127 – 30; Thompson, *Edwardians*, p. 285 – 6. For another view, see T. R. Gourvish, 'The Standard of Living, 1890 – 1914', Alan O'Day (ed.), *The Edwardian Age: Conflict and Stability, 1900 – 14* (1979), pp. 29 – 31.
57 Sigsworth, 'Science and Brewing', p. 546; Brown, *Malting Industry*, pp. 21 – 2; Julian L. Baker, *The Brewing Industry* (1905), pp. 9, 12; The Sale of Beer and Adjustment of Prices Conference, 13 Apr. 1910, LVPSL 1910 Annual Report, p. 21.
58 Vaizey, *Brewing Industry*, pp. 5, 17 – 18 and 'Brewing Industry', pp. 409 – 10; Hawkins and Pass, *Brewing Industry*, pp. 39, 53.

recording how much, not in what ways or where, beer was drunk. Historians underrate the role of bottled beer before 1914 because they overlook an entirely new form of distribution, the direct delivery by breweries to working-class homes. Publicans offered further proof of burgeoning bottled beer sales: they fiercely opposing home delivery as a serious threat to their role as sole purveyors of beer in working-class communities.

Brewers had previously lacked both the scientific and technological expertise to exploit this market. By the late nineteenth century, however, the two primary scientific obstacles to mass production of bottles, prolonged conditioning and ruptures, were solved by pasteurization, refrigeration and carbonization. These three new processes gave the new beers greater stability and distinctive flavours much sought after by discriminating middle-class drinkers.[59] Growing demand for bottled beer, more suitable than barrels for the middle classes at home, could be met only when another technological advance emerged early in the 1900s, large-scale bottling. Mass production was the result of the Boucher and Forster semi-automatic bottling machines (later supplanted by the fully automated Owens bottling machine), together with the automatic capping of the 'Crown Cork', a metal, cork-lined top.[60] With these innovations, brewers could tap a shift in public taste, the potentially lucrative Edwardian vogue for bottled beer. New technology in manufacturing the beer glass, borrowed from bottling, also helped popularize light bottled beer among beer drinkers. They liked its clear, effervescent appearance which translucent beer glasses accentuated. Booth had detected this trend in the demise of 'potmen' in the mid-1890s: 'Until comparatively recent years the publican's customers were very

---

[59] Corran, *Brewing*, pp. 233–6; Sigsworth, 'Science and Brewing', p. 546; Donnachie, *Brewing in Scotland*, pp. 183–4, 189–90, 214–15; Frank E. Lott, 'Bottled Beers', *Jour. Federated Inst. Brewing*, 7 (1901), 191; Wilson, *Greene King*, pp. 153–4.

[60] The Owens machines were first introduced in Britain in 1903, not in the late 1890s as Sigsworth states, and this new technology was disseminated more slowly than he suggests (Sigsworth, 'Science and Brewing', pp. 546–7; W. E. S. Turner, 'The Early Development of Bottle Making Machines in Europe', *Jour. Society Glass Technology*, 22 (1938), 255, 257–8; R. S. Biram, 'The Introduction of the Owens Machine into Europe', *ibid.*, 42 (1958), 32–4; Edward Meigh, 'The Development of the Automatic Glass Bottle Machine: A Story of Some Pioneers', *Glass Technology*, 1 (1960), 33; R. W. Gleadow, 'Bottled Beers', *Jour. Federated Inst. Brewing*, 7 (1901), p. 252; *Brewing Trade Review*, 1 Nov. 1906 and 1 Nov. 1907).

particular as to their ale being served in a "nice bright pewter pot", and the essential virtue in a potman was that he should be a good pewter cleaner; the pot is, however, being now largely supplanted by the glass'.[61]

By 1910 many brewers, retailers and commentators had noticed 'a change of fashion' towards 'off' consumption. This shift in drinking habits was not universally appreciated. Brewers profited greatly from burgeoning sales of beer directly to the public, whereas retailers remonstrated against the sharp decline or even virtual disappearance of the bottle-and-jug trade. Retailers associated two related changes, the popularity of bottled beer and the desire to drink it at home, with the diminution of the role of pubs and beerhouses in the working-class community.[62] Complaints against home delivery, relatively few in the 1880s and 1890s, became widespread in the Edwardian era, as brewers vigorously vied for what they called the private trade. Trade in bottled beer expanded rapidly. At the London brewery of Whitbread & Co., for example, it accounted for fifty-eight per cent of gross sales in 1914. Similarly, at Burton bottling beer, practically unknown in 1877, was routine at all but two or three of the nineteen breweries in 1901. Nor was this development confined to large breweries. Small provincial firms like Greene, King & Sons in Bury St Edmunds doubled the amount of bottled beer between 1906 and 1913. Contrary to what Vaizey and other historians have argued, the shift to bottled beer was already well established before World War 1.[63]

With the creation of the beer dealers' additional retail licence in 1864, brewers could, like publicans, beerhouse keepers or off-licence holders, sell beer on a retail basis. But those who supplied customers at home with beer for off-consumption were obliged to follow specific legal procedures. Taking orders from

61 Booth, *Population Classified by Trade*, p. 236; John Hatcher and T. C. Barker, *A History of British Pewter* (1974), pp. 300–1; Brian Spiller, *Victorian Public Houses* (Newton Abbot, 1972), pp. 28–9. China mugs persisted as common drinking vessels in rural areas after 1900 (Holdenby, *Furrow*, p. 209).

62 Sale of Beer Conference, pp. 4, 13, 26–8; *Statist*, 9 Feb. 1907; Wilson, *Greene King*, pp. 153–4; W. H. Blake, *The Brewer's Vade Mecum* (1902), p. 129.

63 *Statist*, 9 Feb. 1907; Wilson, *Greene King*, pp. 153–4; Knox, 'Tied House System', p. 79; M. W. Greenslade and J. G. Jenkins (eds.), *Victoria County History of Stafford* (n.p., 1967), 2: 246; Nevile, *Seventy Years*, p. 41; *Evid. Royal Com. Sunday Closing*, 1890, 40 (5994-I), p. 512. Courage & Co., another large London brewery, built a bottling plant before 1914 to meet expanding demand for bottled beer (Pudney, *Story of Courage*, p. 30).

customers at their residences, the brewer's agent acted as a messenger, fetching bottles of beer from the brewery's licensed depot and receiving payment only on delivery. Direct supply was then perfectly legal, provided that the agent formally collected the beer at the outlet adjoining the brewery and that payment followed delivery. Beer hawking, the illegal peripatetic sale of beer, was altogether different. It meant sales entirely transacted off the licensed premises, as in the case of pre-payment, or totally divorced from them, as when the agent filled orders with stock he carried. Magistrates interpreted the laws broadly, allowing direct suppliers much flexibility. Agents who canvassed working-class districts miles away from the brewery found the retrieval of beer particularly troublesome, so they soon inaugurated a new system, the distribution of postcards with a return address and space for a customer's name and order. As the customer paid after delivery, magistrates offered no opposition. One other technically had to be observed. Beer bottles could be sold only with the customer's name clearly on the labels. In 1895 one traveling agent was thus convicted of beer hawking for leaving unnamed jars of beer ordered the previous week, at a residence. He had sold beer without a definite order, thereby consummating both purchase and delivery off the licensed premises.[64]

The retailer detested direct suppliers, misleadingly stigmatized as beer hawkers. He strenuously objected to laws permitting their canvassing, especially when surrogates transported the beer. Economically and legally disadvantaged, he had to pay for both licence duties and good will before engaging in a business which depended largely on customers' wanting drink served in pubs. Magistrates could also suddenly revoke his licence according to community need. None of these disabilities burdened direct suppliers, who saw themselves simply as catering to public taste. 'We are all suffering from . . . the advent of the glass bottle', claimed Charles Babington as vice-chairman of the Brewers' Society in 1910.[65] Once commercial breweries began amalgamating in the 1890s, the relative number of beer dealers' additional retail licences grew enormously (see table 9).

---

[64] William W. MacKenzie, *The Licensing Acts, Being the Acts of 1872 and 1874* (1896), pp. 5–6; Sale of Beer Conference, pp. 3–5, 14; *Evid. Royal Com. Liq. Licensing Laws*, 1898, 36 (Cmnd. 8693), pp. 306–7.
[65] Sale of Beer Conference, pp. 26–7.

Table 9
Growth of domestic drinking

Year	Beer dealers additionsl licences	Commercial breweries[a]	Col 1 as % of Col 2	% Change On-licences
1870	3,282	2,173	151	+ 10.5[b]
1880	5,445	2,270	240	− 5.6
1890	3,910	2,014	194	− 6.4
1900	4,447	1,531	290	− 2.4
1910	4,251	1,257	338	− 1.8

Sources: Wilson, *Alcohol and Nation*, pp. 49, 395 – 7.
[a] Minimum production of 1,000 barrels.
[b] Increase since 1860.

It was not so much the law as the ways in which brewers exploited it at the expense of pubs and beerhouses that so embittered retailers. Most breweries, located in working-class areas, had accessible markets for home sales, and so brewers could as wholesalers offer the public delivery of cheaper beer. Lower prices alone did not antagonize retailers. 'It is time now for us to speak', one Middlesex publican exclaimed, 'when . . . we are tied to a firm of brewers who come and canvass next door to us and charge a less price than we supply at'. Reckless brewers who sought residential trade where they held tied houses thus threatened to ruin their own tenants. Publicans generally bought beer from brewers at a shilling a gallon and sold it at 1s 4d, making only 4d per gallon towards their costs, wages and profit. But in Southend some brewers charged almost ten per cent less than what their own tenants paid. At 11d per gallon these brewers were undercutting by over thirty per cent retail prices at their tied houses. Nor was this atypical. One London brewery advertised a gallon at the unbelievably low price of 9d — 7d off the usual public house rate, or a forty-four per cent discount. All these cut-throat practices provoked one publican's outraged protest:

We are face to face with two classes of robbers, and the term I use advisedly. One . . . is the wholesale trade, which has robbed us of half of our means of livelihood. The other is the enemy who would rob us of the whole of it. That puts us in an awkward position, because if we split up our forces it is probable that we shall both meet with disaster.[66]

In aggressively competing for home custom, brewers extended concessions denied to retailers. Brewers exempted customers from paying deposits on bottles and crates but not tenants, whose profits plummeted as a result. Losses, too, mounted for the brewer whose agents likewise failed to retrieve empty bottles and crates, but fierce rivalry led him to see this as an unavoidable marketing cost. Estimates of uncollected bottles and crates costing small breweries hundreds and large ones thousands of pounds annually deterred giant firms like Newcastle Breweries and Whitbread & Co. from becoming direct suppliers.[67] Brewers, unlike retailers, also gave home customers cash rebates between ten and twenty per cent, discounts which were deducted from prices already below tenants' wholesale costs. With beer fetching 4d per quart at local pubs, poor working-class families undoubtedly preferred buying it from travelling vans. It was not only cheaper at 2¼d or 2¾d if paid in cash, but more convenient.[68]

Customers were also enticed with free beer, the third means of cutting prices. One Bristol brewery liberally distributed quart flagons in working-class neighbourhoods as a promotional tactic, then dispatched its vans, justifiably expecting a flood of orders to match the flood of beer. As a further attraction, it charged the standard price of 3d per quart, or 2¾d with cash in hand. Some years later, one disgruntled retailer stated, Nottingham brewers became still more generous, turning the flood of free beer into a torrent: 'One firm . . . send out gratuitously four quart bottles of beer, and after the lapse of a few days they send their representative to inquire how the people like the quality of the beer. If it is all agreeable . . . the representative

---

66 *Ibid.*, 7, 9 – 12; Harrison, 'Pubs', pp. 169, 176 – 7; see also *Licensed Trade News*, 26 March and 27 Aug. 1904; NTDA Home and S. Count. Min. Bk. 1, 8 Dec. 1909, pp. 138 – 44; NTDA W. Dist. Min. Bk., 11 Nov. 1909, p. 98; LVNDL 1905 Annual Report, pp. 87 – 8; *Brewing Trade Review*, 1 Aug. 1903.
67 *Brewing Trade Review*, 1 Aug. 1903; NTDA Home and S. Count. Min. Bk. 1, 7 Dec. 1908, pp. 96 – 8; Sale of Beer Conference, pp. 9, 20, 28.
68 *Evid. Royal Com. Liq. Licensing Laws*, 1897, 35 (Cmnd. 8523), p. 414; Sale of Beer Conference, p. 12.

asks for an order. That practice has been indulged in to a very large extent'. Sympathetic trade newspapers like the *Brewers' Guardian*, publicizing several similar incidents in 1905, backed retail attacks on brewers who hurt tenants by distributing free beer.[69]

Incensed at all these brewer-sponsored schemes aimed at diverting working-class custom away from pubs and beerhouses, retailers assumed the unaccustomed guise of temperance reformers, stridently assailing the direct supply system. Its pernicious impact on public morality, they argued, required legislation imposing stricter control. Retailers condemned brewers' agents for soliciting orders on Saturday afternoon, soon after labourers returned home from work with their pay, and even for demanding payment on Sunday mornings for beer delivered the previous week. Direct suppliers were also accused of fostering drunkenness. Public pressure, which discouraged intemperance in pubs, was absent when wives or husbands drank at home, the retailer contended. He further indicted home delivery as a promoter of female insobriety, encouraging housewives' secret tippling. John White himself gave as evidence numerous court cases in Bristol in which wives had hidden flagons at home.[70]

Retailers not only devised a critique to discredit the direct supplier, but took aggressive action against him. In 1895, Bristol publicans, angry with a local brewery for distributing free beer, recited before magistrates a lengthy list of objections before requesting the withdrawal of the firm's retail licence. While censured for promoting drunkenness, the brewery still retained its licence. Retailers wanted firms convicted of the more serious charge, beer hawking, but seldom obtained adequate proof. There was no doubt, however, as the *Morning Advertiser* forcefully stated, that some breweries 'constantly . . . evaded, or only colourably complied with' cumbersome legal restrictions. Retailers successfully prosecuted Lovibond & Sons for beer hawking at Southampton, though the token fine of £5 scarcely justified the effort. The *Licensed Trade News* did concede the validity of retail grievances, but stressed that the logical first

---

[69]   *Brewers' Guardian*, 10 May 1905; *Evid. Royal Com. Liq. Licensing Laws*, 1897, 35 (Cmnd. 8523), p. 414; Sale of Beer Conference, p. 12.

[70]   *Brewers' Guardian*, 10 May 1905; LVPSL 1910 Annual Report, p. 12; *Evid. Royal Com. Liq. Licensing Laws*, 1897, 35 (Cmnd. 8523), pp. 415, 422; *Morning Advertiser*, 9 Nov. 1906.

step, consultation with trade officials, could produce a workable compromise.[71]

This was unrealistic advice. Influential brewers certainly had much of the power but none of the resolve for imposing a settlement impairing their own economic interests. Nor was the Association seen as a valid forum for eliminating internal disputes. From the beginning, brewers and salaried agents had reiterated its limited electoral function, and as recently as 1909 R. Mitchell Banks had reaffirmed this policy when Nottinghamshire, Lincolnshire and Rutland brewers formed a new branch affiliated with the Association. The CBS, the only other possible agency with regional members, was likewise opposed to acting as an arbitrator between brewers and retailers. In discussions with the Federation on direct suppliers in 1903, CBS officials based their refusal to help on the argument that offending breweries were not members. Yet George Robinson, secretary of the League, several years later contested this explanation, asserting that the brewery directly supplying beer at Southend 'is not only identified with the Brewers' Society, but is also one of the principal firms'.[72]

Local or regional brewer societies, in contrast, fully appreciated the economic hardships inflicted on retailers by direct suppliers, even proposing remedies which belied the Association's avowed policy of separating economics from politics. Some London brewers furnished tenants with carts for delivering bottled beer to customers. Bristol retailers expected much more from two large local breweries, which eventually capitulated, suspended canvassing and established 4½ gallons of bottled beer as the minimum sale. Hertfordshire brewers, though accepting smaller orders, agreed on a standard retail price, 16d per gallon, fining violators £5.[73] Birmingham brewers instead implemented a strict ban, officially resolving to turn all orders for bottled beer over to publicans. Continued complaints from the city's off-licence society prompted a still stronger

---

71   *Evid. Royal Com. Liq. Licensing Laws*, 1897, 35 (Cmnd. 8523), pp. 414, 416; *Morning Advertiser*, 23 Dec. 1905; *Licensed Trade News*, 24 Aug. and 7 Sept. 1895; see also LVNDL Min. Bk., 11 Oct. 1905 and 19 Feb. 1909, p. 70.

72   NTDA Notts., Lincs., Rutland and Peterborough Dist. Min. Bk., 1 March 1909; *Brewing Trade Review*, 1 Aug. 1903; Sale of Beer Conference, p. 18.

73   NTDA W. Dist. Min. Bk., 11 Nov. 1909, p. 98; Berks. Br. Union Min. Bk., 1 May 1909; Beer and Wine Trade Nat. Defence League 1905 Annual Report, Birm. Br. Assoc. Corr. File, D 3163/1/2/10, pp. 20 – 1. In some counties like Wiltshire brewers never canvassed for home sales (Wilts. Br. Assoc. Min. Bk., 3 May 1909).

resolution denouncing sales of less than twenty-four quart beer bottles. This, too, failed.[74]

Had home sales not been so lucrative or brewers as a group not so heterogeneous, the Birmingham Brewers' Association and others elsewhere might have suppressed direct delivery. It took just one firm, for example, to undermine a scheme at Southend-on-Sea in which brewers approved 16d per gallon as the going rate. Agreements among local brewers setting minimum beer prices also collapsed when those nearby came in with cheaper beer. This rivalry usually came from two, dissimilar, sources. Some brewers, formerly suppliers of 'free' houses, used direct delivery as a substitute for outlets lost in the 1880s and 1890s to competitors who invested huge sums in pubs and beerhouses to monopolize markets.[75] Another group, dubbed 'pirate brewers' but commonly called 'family brewers', dealt almost exclusively with the private domestic business. Owners of few public houses, they paid correspondingly less in licence duties, local rates and taxes, giving them lower overheads which were passed on to their customers in lower prices. Tied tenants regarded family brewers as the worst direct supply transgressors for supposedly selling beer below cost. Family brewers acknowledged larger sales, but denied this charge, insisting that such a short-sighted policy would bankrupt them.[76]

Legal action seemed the only recourse against obstinate family brewers. In Birmingham the Davenport Brewery Co.'s successful advertising and energetic canvassing had built up a big domestic trade, which had cut deeply into the business of local brewers with tied houses. When its licence came up for renewal in 1910, Birmingham brewers lodged objections. Since this firm was not a member of the city's trade society, they requested the help of the bench in suppressing a system adverse to public interests. Within a week Baron John Davenport, director of the Davenport Brewery Co., had sent magistrates a

---

74   Birm. Br. Assoc. Min.. Bk., 27 March 1903, D 3163/1/1/2, p. 174; *Licensed Trade News*, 26 March, 2 and 16 Apr. and 27 Aug. 1904.
75   NTDA Home and S. Count. Min. Bk. 1, 7 Dec. 1908, pp. 96 – 8; Sale of Beer Conference, p. 11. In central London, some of the impetus for beer hawking probably came from population migration which reduced the business of pubs after 1890. 'In the suburbs', Baxter notes, 'there was no opportunity of getting outlets for trade as local brewers held all the licences' (Baxter, 'Brewing Industry', p. 84).
76   Sale of Beer Conference, pp. 10, 22 – 3, 25 – 6, 29 – 30; NTDA Home and S. Count. Min. Bk. 1, 7 Dec. 1908 and 8 Dec. 1909, pp. 96 – 8, 138 – 44.

letter, boasting of his firm's leading role as 'direct supply brewers'. Home delivery, he urged, far from injuring the public, was beneficial as an alternative to the pub, and moreover circumvented one troublesome issue, the granting of new licences. His persuasive defence convinced justices who approved the licence. Later in the year he triumphantly published a pointed but inaccurately titled pamphlet *Beer Hawking, or the Penalties of Pioneering*.[77]

Meanwhile the League had pursued other, more controversial remedies. In 1905, it passed a resolution decrying the rapid spread of beer hawking. By late September 1906, provincial publicans had become impatient with apathetic brewers, and adopted a more radical policy, committing the League to repealing the beer dealers' additional retail licence. Brewers, with the Society's approval, attempted to thwart the League, denying it the Association's support for lobbying the Liberal Government. League spokesman still met with Campbell-Bannerman the next month. Edward Morrall, League chairman, predictably condemned the recent expansion of the direct supply system as unjust to publicans. Brewers, he reasoned, were 'diverting from us trade that legitimately belongs to the public-house, where the openness of each transaction is a protection against excess'. He then appealed for restrictions in the forthcoming Liberal bill.[78] Since Liberals ignored this request the next year in proposed licensing legislation, the League considered submitting a test question demanding the abolition of brewers' retail licences. Again brewers in the Association tried to block the League's strategy by fostering grocers' fears that Parliament would curb the rights of all off-licence holders. The long-standing distrust between grocers and other retailers, which brewers now adeptly revived, prevented the Federation from aligning with the League. Aware that publicans detested canvassing as much by grocers as by brewers, the Federation cautioned the League that any attack on the privileges of off-licence holders would provoke a retaliatory question. The

---

[77] *Brewing Trade Review*, 1 Apr. and 1 Oct. 1910; see also Crawford, Dunn and Thorne, *Birmingham Pubs*, p. 69.

[78] LVNDL Min. Bk., 26 Sept. 1906; LVPSL Exec. Com. Min. Bk., 4 Oct. 1906, p. 6; BS Min. Bk. 2, 26 Oct. 1906, p. 9; NTDA Min. Bk. 2, 2 Nov. 1906, pp. 185 – 6; *Morning Advertiser*, 9 Nov. 1906. In the home and southern counties escalating inter-trade rivalry 'was becoming unendurable', one Eastbourne retailer asserted (NTDA Home and S. Count. Min. Bk. 1, 18 Nov. 1907, p. 28).

League was outmanoeuvred but undaunted. It defied this threat at the January 1910 Election with the expected test question seeking the banning of brewers' retail licences. Both the Federation and the Association counterattacked with a question asking candidates to oppose any measures limiting the business of off-licence holders. Confused retail societies, federated to the Association and the League, placed both lists of questions before still more bewildered candidates. Following the election, the dispute escalated, as the League's bill was introduced into Parliament. The purpose of this measure was not to eliminate direct suppliers, but to limit drastically their activities: canvassing was confined to the immediate vicinity of retail licences and 4½ gallons or twenty-four quart bottles set as a minimum order.[79]

To forestall a schism in the trade, the Society called a conference on direct supply and price cutting in April. In attending in his capacity as chairman of the Association, Francis P. Whitbread emphasized the internal threat of such economic issues to the trade's political power. Retailers undermined their position by disagreeing on both grievances and the best remedy. London publicans wanted uniform prices; their provincial counterparts saw discounts as only part of a much broader problem which required legislation abolishing canvassing. The Federation and the Beer and Wine Trade National Defence League agreed with the Society on the shortcomings of the League's tactics: its bill encouraged the Liberal Government to impose additional restraints, publicly exposed trade feuds and jeopardized the brewing industry's solidarity. Frederick Millar, secretary and parliamentary agent of the Beer and Wine League, further expressed concern about antagonizing not just politicians. He admonished the League:

The public come in here as well as the publican . . . because . . . a large section of the public to whose wants this section of the Trade caters . . . would regard [a measure] with grave apprehension and indignation, and . . . a large section of the House of Commons, . . . which is not fanatically temperate,

---

79 LVNDL Annual Reports: 1909, pp. 85 – 7; 1910, pp. 17, 63 – 6; NTDA Min. Bk. 2, 1 and 6 Dec. 1909, pp. 311, 313; *Licensed Trade News*, 1 Jan. 1910; NTDA Home and S. Dist. 1910 General Election Report, p. 4; *Brewing Trade Review*, 1 Oct. 1910.

but which believes in moderation and . . . wishes to keep the people out of the public house, would be against you.[80]

Brewers were better at identifying the reasons for the widening direct supply business than at offering practical solutions. Speaking for big London and country brewers, Whitbread advised publicans of the futility of striving to regain custom lost thorough the rise of domestic drinking. The *Brewing Trade Review*, organ of the Brewers' Society, stated the brewers' case more bluntly: 'The [canvassing] system is . . . largely supported by the public, and attempts to put back the clock on the ground that one section of the Trade is hit by extreme competition on the part of another will not successfully prevail'. This intransigent posture stemmed from brewers' refusal to admit that they were even partly responsible for larger home delivery sales. Instead they blamed family brewers; publicans, whose neglect of non-pub drinkers had forced brewers' agents to canvass the streets; or sometimes the Brewers' Society, which had neither the coercive powers nor comprehensive membership for negotiating local agreements. Implacably opposed to far-reaching concessions, brewers did take steps to appease the Society, pledging to discontinue price discounts and follow a standard policy for selling bottled beer.[81] As the wider but more divisive question of canvassing was left unresolved, the League had achieved nothing. Retailers, prominent brewers suggested, could discuss guidelines with the county brewers' branch, but progress seemed unlikely as family and non-local brewers seldom belonged to it.[82]

Brewers' staunch commitment to canvassing embittered the League. Isolated from other retail societies, reproached for causing disunity and ridiculed for resisting new public drinking

---

[80] Sale of Beer Conference, pp. 5 – 6, 13 – 14, 16; *Licensing World and Licensed Trade Review*, 30 Apr. 1910.

[81] Sale of Beer Conference, pp. 8, 19 – 20, 25 – 6, 30 – 1; *Brewing Trade Review*, 1 Oct. 1910; see also *ibid.*, 1 May 1910; NTDA Home and S. Count. Min. Bk. 1, 7 Dec. 1908, pp. 96 – 8.

[82] Brewers in Gloucestershire and in the home and southern counties did make price concessions, but no uniform policy prevailed. In Northumberland and Durham, in contrast, brewers refused to discuss price grievances (Glos. Br. Assoc. Min. Bk., 12 Apr. 1910; NTDA Home and S. Count. Min. Bk. 2, 4 Dec. 1912, pp. 66 – 8; Northumberland and Durham Br. Assoc. Min. Bk., 8 Aug. 1912).

habits, the League was goaded into taking extreme measures. It promptly re-introduced a revised and far more radical anti-canvassing bill, ostensibly designed to discourage the insobriety arising from home delivery. Customers could only place orders at licensed premises; canvassing for less than 4½ gallons or twenty-four quart bottles was prohibited; and violators would incur stiff penalties — licences would be suspended at the first offence and forfeited for a subsequent one. Locally federated societies quickly pressed parliamentary candidates for support. Similarly, the League circularized magistrates, hoping that they would insist on brewers meeting tighter canvassing rules in its proposed bill as the prerequisite for renewing beer dealers' retail licences.[83] Tension further heightened when both the League and the Association re-adopted their test questions with contradictory stances on direct suppliers. The Association now came to see the danger to the trade's political power of a spiralling conflict in which brewers and retailers alike subordinated their overriding goal, the defeat of Liberals, to an acrimonious feud. Brewers therefore made two important concessions. First, trade representatives could obtain copies of League test questions from Association agents. Second, Association leaders extended this neutral attitude to the League's anti-canvassing bill, which they had previously opposed unconditionally. Though both the Brewers' Society and the Federation still regarded such legislation as inimical to their interests, the Association's timely intervention had averted a bitter schism.[84]

The prolonged but inconclusive debate on direct supply demoralized many retailers, who increasingly declined to participate in customary electoral activities. L. Leeder's experience in the midlands, where he earned his living as a retailer, typified the disruptive political results of economic grievances.

> The present system of trading for off consumption is severely shaking the stability of the retail trade. During the . . . [January] election I had under my control the licensees of the

---

83 *Brewing Trade Review*, 1 Oct. 1910 and 1 Apr. 1912; BS Min. Bk. 3, 10 Oct. 1910; LVNDL 1910 Annual Report, p. 63; *A Bill to Amend the Licensing Laws with Regard to 'Off' Sales by Retail*, 1911, 2 (64).

84 NTDA Min. Bk. 2, 28 Oct. and 4 Nov. 1910 and 15 March 1911, pp. 334 – 5, 336 – 7, 349; LVNDL 1910 Annual Report, p. 17; *Brewing Trade Review*, 1 Oct. 1910 and 1 Apr. 1912; *Licensed Trade News*, 29 Apr. 1911; Bristol and Thornbury Trade Min. Bk., 18 Nov. 1910.

whole of Leicester and . . . of Rutland, and we had the greatest difficulty . . . in getting them to interest themselves in the election. They said the brewers were getting everything and they should do the work.

Returning from Westbury in July 1910, the Association sub-agent informed Wiltshire brewers of rebellious retailers who resented the better prices given private customers. Further evidence of disaffected retailers came from the *Licensed Trade News*, edited by the Midland agent. In May 1911, he warned brewers of the risk to the trade's influence, based primarily on intimacy with customers, if 'in our insane desire for business, we ruin the publican and substitute the travelling public-house on wheels, the Beer Hawking spectre, for the . . . License-Holder in his bar'. Strident criticism of direct delivery by Bristol retailers the following month again alarmed the *Licensed Trade News*, which linked such ill-will to declining numbers of publicans and beerhouse keepers in retail societies. Direct delivery, the paper observed, could 'do more to divide us than all the Tied House Tenants' Leagues, all our most implacable foes have ever achieved'.[85]

Economic rivalry between brewers and retailers reflected the recurring problem of sectionalism. It was the tied house system which led retailers as tied tenants to protest fiercely against the club assisted or sponsored by the brewer or his direct delivery of beer. Under the tenancy contract, they became less independent entrepreneurs than dependent servants, easily victimized by the landlord-brewer. Not surprisingly, tenants became outraged at what they saw as unfair competition with brewers for working-class customers. Tenants exaggerated their plight. Neither clubs nor direct delivery materially reduced retailers' income, but the lost business came when beer consumption was falling and taxes rising. For the hard pressed retailer, even a very small loss in trade seemed quite devastating. Not all brewers were as

---

[85] Sale of Beer Conference, p. 25; Wilts. Br. Assoc. Min. Bk., 29 July 1910; *Licensed Trade News*, 25 May, 3 and 10 June 1911. In the following pre-war years, the League abandoned neither its quest for legislation nor test question seeking limits on direct delivery (LVNDL 1913 Annual Report, pp. 13 – 14; *A Bill to Put Certain Restrictions on the Sale by the Holders of Wholesale Licences of Beer or Stout in Retail Quantities to be Consumed Off the Premises*, 1913, 3 (145)).

insensitive to his complaints as retail societies usually portrayed. Many brewers' societies, especially in the midlands, prided themselves on treating him equitably. Brewers rightly argued that consumer taste and new technology were transforming the industry's distribution system. For two major reasons, however, they were wrong to distinguish stubbornly between economic and political issues. First, only the Brewers' Society as the sole national brewers' organization could propose and implement a satisfactory remedy, the establishment of uniform guidelines for tenancy contracts, clubs and direct delivery. Private brewers might violate such an understanding, but, as a numerically small group with limited sales, hardly undermine it. Moreover, a national agreement, unlike a local one, would prevent outsiders from disregarding rules binding only on brewers who were members of the county brewers' society. Second, brewers, displaying their own type of sectionalism, myopically assumed that economic unrest had no serious political consequences. The trade's electoral power required solidarity between brewers and retailers on political and economic questions. In failing to achieve this unity, membership in trade societies slumped as many retailers withdrew from political activism, thus vastly diminishing the trade's political power.

8

Appealing to All Classes

The brewing industry, like most Victorian pressure groups, sought public support by employing both customary and novel tactics to woo working-class drinkers, and middle- and upper-class shareholders. It was this constituency which stood to lose most if pubs were closed down and profits reduced by prohibition, higher taxation or restrictive compensation. Shareholders would lose their dividends, and the working class their traditional meeting place for friendly societies and trade unions. Gaining the support of Liberal voters within these groups further strengthened the trade's power. With these natural and reputable allies, the trade had no need of such coercive electoral strategies as independent candidates, abstention and voters' pledges.[1]

Rivalry between temperance reformers and drink sellers assumed many forms, but none became as violent as the battles in many provincial towns between 1878 and 1891. Conflicts arose then because the Salvation Army aggressively attacked drinking by congregating outside pubs and beerhouses. Unregenerate publicans retaliated, enlisting working-class ruffians in 'Skeleton Armies' which greeted intrusive reformers with stones, mud and occasionally dead cats.[2] Since neither group retreated prudently when besieged by the enemy, numerous clashes escalated into riots. Local publicans sometimes incited these confrontations with paid agitators, but the

---

[1] Hamer, *Electoral Pressure*, pp. 23–8; Norman McCord, *The Anti-Corn Law League, 1838–46* (1975), pp. 83–8, 155–60.

[2] Victor Bailey, 'Salvation Army Riots, the "Skeleton Army" and Legal Authority in the Provincial Town', A. P. Donajgrodzki (ed.), *Social Control in Nineteenth Century Britain* (1977), pp. 231–53; Donald C. Richter, *Riotous Victorians* (1981), ch. 6.

Society and the League strongly disapproved. 'We cannot . . .
see the advantage of the use of violence, in lieu of argument,
against our Teetotal opponents', the *Licensed Victuallers'
Guardian* commented in 1883. 'To encourage drunken rowdies
to attack the sober rowdies of the Salvation and Blue Ribbon
"Armies" is to descend to the level of the leaders of the latter,
and should be utterly repugnant to respectable and moderate
men and women'.[3]

Such violence seldom characterized the trade/temperance
struggle; more often the trade simply outmanoeuvred
teetotalers by copying their tactics. In the 1880s brewers started
giving retail societies money for public speakers to disrupt
temperance meetings with pro-drink resolutions. Once
appointed, district agents normally undertook this work,
assisted by orators specially hired by local brewers' associations.
In both cases, brewers ensured ample support with sizeable
contingents of nearby retailers whose presence could be
distinctly offputting; in one town 'the promoters of a public
meeting abandoned it when they found a large number of
opponents outside the doors waiting for admission'.[4]

However gratifying to harassed retailers and brewers, this
approach had obvious drawbacks in winning converts, so the
trade spent more time, effort and money on arousing the
sympathy of the masses. Most Victorian pressure groups
engaged lecturers to address public meetings and distribute
literature, but the CETS took the show on the road in 1892 by
employing several vans to proselytize the public at racecourses,
fairs and villages.[5] Not to be outdone, the trade sent out its own

---

3   LVPSL Parl. Reports Min. Bk., 7 Feb. 1883, p. 300; *Licensed Victuallers'
     Guardian*, 8 Dec. 1883. For similar conflicts between two earlier pressure
     groups, the Chartists and Anti-Corn Law League, see McCord, *Anti-Corn
     Law League*, pp. 97 – 103.
4   NTDA Min. Bk. 1, 8 Nov. 1889, p. 29; NTDA W. Dist. 1893 Annual Report,
     p. 6; *Licensed Trade News*, 25 May and 8 June 1895; Leics. and Rutland Min.
     Bk., 8 Apr. 1899, E. Mid. Br. Assoc.; Northumberland and Durham Br.
     Assoc. Min. Bk., 27 Oct. 1887.
5   The Good Templars also had a touring van in the 1890s (Fahey, *Forsyth*, p.
     10). McCord, *Anti-Corn Law League*, pp. 56 – 63, 65 – 7, 72 – 4, 80, 121,
     133 – 4, 137 – 8, 175 – 6; William H. Mackintosh, *Disestablishment and
     Liberation: The Movement for the Separation of the Anglican Church from State
     Control* (1972) , pp. 30, 61, 125, 129, 135, 142, 217 – 18, 296 – 7; Howard
     Temperley, *British Antislavery, 1833 – 70* (1972), p. 13; Lilian Lewis Shiman,
     'Crusade Against Drink in Victorian England' (Univ. Wisconsin Ph.D.
     dissertation, 1970), p. 228.

'Fair Play' vans, each carrying a lecturer who castigated the Local Veto bill and collected petitions in rural areas. 'This is just the sort of work that is needed', the *Licensing World and Licensed Trade Review* enthused, 'for it is precisely in outlying villages that the teetotalers are able to indulge without check in their wildest exaggerations and slanders'. Three vans visited remote areas in the summers of 1893 and 1894, costing the Fund almost £1,200.[6]

Unlike temperance reformers, the trade had a natural constituency of males, already handily organized with a vested interest in protecting the pub. Friendly societies and trade unions, two numerically large and important working-class institutions, held meetings in public houses not simply out of choice but out of desperation. Churches and other local agencies had much space, but little desire to share it. Publicans, far more accommodating, enticed labouring men with cheap, warm, well-lit and clean rooms. Beer was another attraction. In Edwardian Salford, Robert Roberts' father attended meetings of the Royal and Ancient Antediluvian Order of the Buffaloes at his local pub. When Robert's sister asked about the organization's purpose, Mrs Roberts sourly replied that 'it was an order dedicated to beer and to assisting those "brothers" who fell ill through supping it!' These and other men in fraternal bodies certainly supplied publicans with much business: well over two-thirds of the seven million members in friendly societies relied on pub facilities in the 1890s. So did nearly all branches of the Amalgamated Society of Engineers.[7]

Prohibition would thus destroy the only accessible venues for these working-class organizations. Brewers calculated on generating lower-class resistance with rhetoric stressing the pub's unrivalled amenities and prohibition's class bias. 'Why should your members who are not voters be subject to the votes of those who are not members?', trade propaganda repeatedly inquired. Elaborating on this theme, brewers portrayed the

---

6 NTDF Reports: 1893, pp. 10, 14; 1894, p. 17; NTDF W. Dist. 1893 Annual Report, p. 6; NTDF Ledger 1, General Election Scheme, pp. 66–8, 71; *Licensing World and Licensed Trade Review*, 6 Oct. 1893.

7 Robert Roberts, *A Ragged Schooling: Growing Up in the Classic Slum* (1978), p. 46; Harrison, 'Pubs', p. 175; *Licensed Trade News*, 16 Feb. 1895; *Licensing World and Licensed Trade Review*, 2 May 1908; Rowntree, *Poverty*, p. 362; P. H. J. H. Gosden, *Self-Help: Voluntary Associations in the 19th Century* (1973), pp. 48, 91, 109, 119 and *The Friendly Societies in England, 1815 – 75* (Manchester, 1961), pp. 117, 123; *Temperance Record*, 4 (1906), p. 495.

trade as 'defending the right of your lodge to meet where it likes free from dictation', and assailed local veto as 'an outrageous specimen of class legislation' for proposing to close poor men's pubs but not rich men's clubs. In the 1890s the Fund organized a successful petitioning campaign in which friendly societies and trade unions protested against the Local Veto bill as a threat to their places of meeting. Over 200 organizations in the north alone returned petitions to Parliament. According to the district agent, such working-class outcries immensely assisted the trade's efforts against prohibition:

A certain number of these [petitions] were dispatched to the House of Commons each week and . . . the continual flow . . . was an important factor in ultimately securing the shelving of the measure. Leading articles appeared in Government organs, urging them to give serious consideration to the position before acting in opposition to the views of so many working men's Societies.[8]

Friendly societies were useful in other ways. At the request of the Brewers' Company in 1893, they publicly demonstrated against the Local Veto bill in London. Similarly, western brewers asked them to pass anti-prohibition resolutions. Prompted by the 1908 Licensing bill, Midland brewers established the League of Friendly and Kindred Societies Meeting on Licensed Premises, which sent delegates to the Hyde Park protest demonstration. When these tactics failed to defeat the 1909 budget, however, some brewers quickly retaliated, cutting donations to friendly societies. Although the role of friendly societies declined, Midland brewers revived their 'League' at a 1913 meeting, where 200 organizations represented 40,000 – 50,000 members. The Association agent, of course, carefully orchestrated this timely outburst of 'public' indignation against local licensing proposals. 'The utmost possible care . . . was taken that the Meeting should not have a suspicion of being engineered by the Trade', he reassured brewers. While no member of the trade was present and only

8   *Licensed Trade News*, 16 Feb. 1895; NTDF W. Dist. 1893 Annual Report, p. 8; Birm. and Aston Trade Min. Bk., 9 June 1893, D 3163/2/1/5, pp. 50 – 1; Birm. Br. Assoc. Min. Bk., 23 Apr. 1895, D 3163/1/1/1, p. 184; NTDF N. Dist. Min. Bk., 2 March 1894.

delegates from friendly societies delivered speeches, it was behind all aspects of the meeting — from the resolutions prepared by the agent to the printing costs underwritten by the Association. Public house patrons lured with free tickets and, doubtless, free beer, guaranteed an impressive audience.[9]

Yet by 1914 several factors had made friendly societies and trade unions less reliable as trade allies. First, after 1875 many friendly societies gave insurance priority over fellowship. Second, those societies with the fastest growth rates, the Co-Operative Society, the Independent Order of Rechabites and the Hearts of Oaks which together enrolled over 1.5 million new members between 1875 and 1900, met either elsewhere than in pubs or not at all, relying instead on correspondence. By the 1890s over 2 million members of friendly societies (almost one-third of the total) avoided licensed premises.[10] Third, in the Edwardian era temperance reformers began exploring better alternatives for trade unions, still large users of pub facilities. In 1902, all but 670 of 2,400 branches of nine important trade unions did so, and estimates suggested that altogether 50,000 men, women and children attended branch meetings in pubs per day. Appalled by the 'temptations of licensed premises', two Labour MPs, Arthur Henderson and David Shackleton, cooperated with the National Temperance League in creating the Trade Union and Labour Officials' Temperance Fellowship in 1906. This new organization, dominated by Labour MPs and limited to trade union officials, attracted 108 men representing about 200,000 trade unionists at its inaugural meeting. Committed to promoting total abstinence and to ending trade union meetings at pubs, they soon discovered formidable problems. In response to public appeals for meeting places unconnected with sales of alcoholic beverages, only one offer had been received from religious organizations. 'The publican . . . was a better business man than e.ner the minister, the schoolroom or the coffee-house keeper', one delegate sadly observed. By 1908, however, the Temperance Fellowship was jeopardizing the

[9] Br. Co. Trade Meeting Min. Bk., 22 March 1893, p. 14; NTDA W. Dist. Min. Bk., 13 Apr. 1893; Soms. Br. Assoc. Min. Bk., 11 June 1910; NTDA Mid. Dist. Min. Bk., 30 Jan. 1913, D 3163/2/1/2, pp. 186–8. The UKA also organized meetings without acknowledging its role (Anthony Edward Dingle, 'The Agitation for Prohibition in England, 1871–95' (Monash Univ. Ph.D. dissertation, 1974), p. 547).

[10] Gosden, *Friendly Societies*, pp. 211, 214–15 and *Self-Help*, pp. 59, 62–3, 91, 103, 106–7, 195, 206.

trade's deployment of trade unions. Two years after its foundation, the number of delegates had more than doubled, and one of its vice presidents, John Burns, Liberal cabinet minister, had authorized 1,200 local authorities to provide premises for the Fellowship.[11]

Those lacking a personal stake in safeguarding the pub, such as the business community, could render vital assistance while escaping charges of self-interest. At the behest of the Brewers' Company in 1893, virtually all London brewers joined the London Chamber of Commerce, which comprised over 3,400 companies and fifty-eight MPs, as a means of gaining support against the Local Veto bill. As a politically influential body with a pro-business outlook, the London Chamber of Commerce could easily reconcile its avowed goal of promoting the common interests of trade, commerce and manufacturing with protection of the brewing industry.[12] Later, in the fight against the 1908 Licensing bill, several members of the Brewers' Society lobbied London stock exchange officials for a public pronouncement indicating how the time limit would harm brewery assets. Bankers and solicitors were sometimes approached for similar reasons.[13]

As a business lobby, the trade had one major resource denied its opponents — shareholders. In the 1870s and 1880s the Railway Association did contact MPs and peers holding railway shares, organize deputations and mass meetings of shareholders, and form a Railway Shareholders' Association, but only on a sporadic basis.[14] Shareholders played a far more decisive role in the trade's propaganda campaign. When

11 *Temperance Record*, 1 (1903), p. 430, 4 (1906), pp. 231 – 2, 491 – 5, 501 – 3 and 5 (1907), pp. 437, 441 – 2, 444; Trade Union and Lab. Officials' Temp. Fellowship, Sept. 1908, Univ. Wisconsin, Guy Hayler Collection, pp. 3, 6.
12 A. R. Ilersic, *Parliament of Commerce: The Story of the Association of British Chambers of Commerce, 1860 – 1960* (1960), pp. 2, 139 – 40; Lee L. Grugel, 'Late Victorian Chambers of Commerce and the Intensification of British Nationalism', *Rocky Mountain Soc. Sci. Jour.*, 10 (1973), 37 – 47; Br. Co. Scrap Book, vol. 30, p. 107 and Trade Meeting Min. Bk., 15 and 22 March 1893, pp. 11 – 12, 14.
13 BS Min. Bk. 2, 20 Feb. 1907, p. 30; NTDA Min. Bk. 2, 10 March 1908, p. 248. Private individuals or financial institutions owning freeholds of licensed property were naturally circularized, and impressed with the need for defending investments by writing to MPs (NTDF 1893 Annual Report, p. 6; Birm. Br. Assoc. Corr. File, 13 Apr. 1895, Local Veto Circular, D 3163/1/2/1).
14 Geoffrey Alderman, *The Railway Interest* (Leicester, 1973), pp. 38 – 9, 74, 86, 93, 112.

breweries became joint stock companies in the 1880s, brewers acquired in shareholders vast numbers of potential supporters whose votes could extend the trade's political power. With local veto officially part of the Liberal programme at the 1892 Election, the Fund sent brewery, railway and shipping shareholders information intended to 'awaken . . . a sense of their responsibilities'.[15] In London 9,000 shareholders received a circular with the names and constituencies of trade endorsed candidates. Warned of imperilled investments during debates on the 1893 Local Veto bill and 1894 budget, shareholders were urged to write their local MPs asking for dissenting votes.[16] Shareholders also learned of trade-supported candidates at by-elections and at the 1895 General Election, but not from the Fund. A central register proved simply too much work, so after 1892, in an informal but less comprehensive arrangement, brewery companies or the Fund's district branches circularized shareholders. Even this taxed the overworked western district agent who communicated with shareholders instead by inserting letters in the local press.[17]

The trade relied less on shareholders after the Unionist victory in 1895 discredited prohibition as a temperance solution, but expressed renewed interest in them when Liberals advocated a time limit to compensation. Energetic midland brewers took the first step towards an anticipated national scheme late in 1902, founding the Brewery Debenture and Shareholders' League. It would not only provide general information, but help collect petitions, forewarn members of pending or possible trade legislation, encourage voter registration and identify trade-sponsored candidates. Despite these attractive features, only thirty-four companies joined, all of them in the midlands,

---

[15] NTDF 1892 Annual Report, p. 14; NTDF Ledger 1, p. 79; see also pp. 25, 113.
[16] Wholesale and Retail Min. Bk. 1, 20 June 1892, p. 16; NTDF 1893 Annual Report, p. 6; Glos. Br. Assoc. Min. Bk., 8 March 1893; Birm. Br. Assoc. Corr. File, 13 Apr. 1895, Local Veto Circular, D 3163/1/2/1; *Licensed Trade News*, 12 May 1894 and 4 May 1895.
[17] NTDA Min. Bk. 1, 22 Jan. 1894, p. 149; *Licensed Trade News*, 2 March 1895; Brad. Br. Assoc. Min. Bk., 10 July 1895; NTDF Mid. Dist. Min. Bk., 31 Jan. 1895, D 3163/2/1/1, p. 225; NTDA W. Dist. Min. Bk., 11 July 1895; NTDA 1895 Report, p. 16.

forcing the plan's withdrawal. Indifferent shareholders, unwilling to put it on a self-financing footing, were chiefly responsible.[18] In the western district, just forty-six of the 2,600 shareholders approved and grudgingly donated £15 7s 6d. 'As the cost of printing, stationary, and postages had considerably exceeded this sum', the agent gloomily reported, 'it was decided not to press the matter further'. Though magistrates cancelled large numbers of licences in 1902–3, apathetic shareholders ignored pleas from brewery companies to contact MPs to demand support for legislation granting compensation. The *Country Brewers' Gazette* reflected the growing disenchantment with stockholders. Unlike its optimistic comments on the Shareholders' League in 1902, the paper the following year seriously doubted whether sizeable public investment would safeguard the brewing industry from attack.[19]

Shareholders lacked enthusiasm largely because many companies, beset with slumping beer consumption after 1899 and overpriced, recently rebuilt or refurbished pubs and beerhouses, missed or reduced dividends. Between 1899 and 1902 the stock quotations of forty-seven breweries fell £9.6 million, about a twenty-five per cent decline. Public houses sold for a fraction of what they commanded in the boom years; one in central London had fetched £28,000 in 1898, but went for as little as £1,150 in 1910. So alarmed were shareholders in Meux & Co. that they instituted voting reforms. In creating public distrust and press hostility, this protracted depression forced brewers to postpone organizing shareholders.[20]

Brewers revived the idea of exploiting shareholder influence in 1907, but, seeing no prospect of forming a separate organization, now opted for a less ambitious register of investors. Proposed Liberal legislation curbing compensation overcame the related problem, brewers' opposition to underwriting the entire expenses. In a letter to the 1,350 brewing firms in the United Kingdom, the Brewers' Society, Brewers' Company and Association derided defective trade organization,

---

18 *Licensed Trade News*, 26 July 1902; *Brewing Trade Review*, 1 Sept. 1902; *Country Brewers' Gazette*, 11 Sept. 1902; NTDA Min. Bk. 2, 15 July 1902, p. 45; NTDA Mid. Count. Jt. Comt. Reports, D 3163/2/2: 1902, p. 8; 1903, pp. 8–9.

19 NTDA W. Dist. 1903 Annual Report, p. 10; *Country Brewers' Gazette*, 11 Sept. 1902 and 10 Sept. 1903; see also *Brewing Trade Review*, 1 Jan. 1906.

20 *Economist*, 23 Aug. 1902; Vaizey, *Brewing Industry*, pp. 12–16; *Statist*, 7 Jan. 1911; Hawkins, 'Development of the Brewing Industry', pp. 192, 206–7, 209, 215–16; see p. 156.

outlined an electoral plan and requested the names of the roughly 250,000 enfranchised shareholders. To defray the register's cost, initially estimated at £600 and thereafter £300 annually for revisions, companies would donate 3d per investor up to a maximum of £50.[21] Even so inexpensive a scheme was rejected by almost two-thirds of all the United Kingdom brewing companies.[22]

Nevertheless, the trade went forward and organized the shareholder register. In January 1908 the Association began its campaign against the Licensing bill with a pamphlet to shareholders which stressed the trade's already onerous financial burdens, the steady progress of licensing reduction under the 1904 Act and the dangers of a time limit. Shareholders also received a circular requesting letters to MPs demanding opposition to the time limit and further taxation.[23] Some brewers, like those in Durham and Northumberland, gave shareholders still stronger incentives for becoming active correspondents. A time limit, emphasized another more pointed circular, would require the appropriation of future dividends for reclaiming debentures issues, thereby resulting in 'the immediate and total loss of your Capital invested in this Company'. Religious leaders, too, came under intense pressure from shareholders. 'I am inundated with letters from those who hold property in Brewery Shares and Debentures, assuring me that unless "the Bishops' oppose a 'time-limit' " they . . . will forthwith cease to subscribe to any religious or charitable objects', protested one vicar. The register also facilitated the calling of public meetings of shareholders who passed resolutions condemning the bill.[24]

It was not as public supporters or angry constituents, but as voters that shareholders displayed their value to the trade. At the 1909 Bermondsey by-election, for example, the Society circularized and canvassed brewery and distillery shareholders,

21 NTDA Min. Bk. 2, 30 Jan. and 7 Feb. 1907, pp. 200, 203; Br. Co. Scrap Book, vol. 30, 22 Feb. 1907, Register of Share and Debenture Holders in Brewing Companies Circular, p. 161.
22 NTDA Min. Bk. 2, 10 Apr. 1907, p. 213; NTDA 1908 – 9 Reports, p. 17.
23 NTDA Min. Bk. 2, 20 Dec. 1907, p. 235; NTDA 1907 – 8 Reports, pp. 19 – 20; Br. Co. Scrap Book, vol. 30, 28 Jan. 1908, Licensing bill Circular, p. 162.
24 Northumberland and Durham Br. Assoc. Min. Bk., 5 March 1908; Cantuar to Littler (copy), 16 March 1908, Davidson Papers, Licensing and Temp. Box 2. For typical examples of brewery company circulars, see Brewers' Gazette, 14 March and 9 May 1907 and 30 July 1908.

enabling the Unionist candidate to recapture a marginal seat held by Liberals with a commanding majority in 1906. London retailers likewise contacted almost 9,000 brewery shareholders for the January 1910 Election. Nothing comparable was undertaken in the provinces owing to the prohibitive costs of notifying 250,000 shareholders. According to Archibald S. Bennett, assembler of the register, even excluding the salaries of sixty full-time clerks working for five days licking, sealing and addressing envelopes, the postage itself would exceed £1,000, one-third of the Association's annual receipts. Hence, the Association sent election material to shareholders only in selected seats — 134 in January and 165 in December — at the 1910 Elections.[25]

The mobilization of shareholders as trade allies clearly influenced political perceptions. Writing to John Fuller, MP in 1908, one ambivalent Liberal supporter applauded the temperance objectives in the recently introduced Liberal bill, but strongly disliked its financial proposals. Many Liberals, he confided, 'think that it hits investors in brewery preference & debenture shares unnecessarily hard — and that an extension of the time limit — even to 40 years — would pull people together and would do no real harm to the cause of temperance'. Unionists like Akers-Douglas, former Conservative chief whip, cited the prospective damage inflicted on shareholders as justification for opposing the fourteen-year time limit in the 1908 bill.[26] Other Unionists had emphasized the strategic advantage of shareholders in 1907 with the founding of a Brewery Debenture Holders' Committee, designed to protect debenture holders from both ruinous taxation and the time limit. In March 1908 the Unionist party went further, and sought access to the register as a means of enrolling shareholders in its own local organization, but the Association refused. The view, so carefully fostered by the trade, of a large group of shareholders with unsettled Liberal loyalties obviously beguiled Unionists. Trade appeals, in fact, probably caused few Liberal shareholders to

25 *Brewing Trade Review*, 1 June 1907; NTDA 1909 – 10 Reports, p. 20; LVPSL Min. Bk., 4 Nov. 1909 and 10 Feb. 1910, pp. 16, 64.
26 Akers-Douglas to Pollard (copy), 13 Jan. 1908, Kent Area Office, Akers-Douglas Papers, U564 CLp 7, fo. 107; Amory to Fuller, 2 Apr. 1908, Fuller Papers, Ms. 1196/9; see also Rowntree and Sherwell, *Temperance Problem*, p. 32.

defect. 'Financial identity with a brewery', the *Licensed Trade News* admitted in 1912, 'does not always weigh strongly enough with a man to induce him to change his political faith'.[27]

Like other pressure groups, the trade disseminated propaganda to the middle and upper classes through the newspapers, but was slow to exploit this medium. Not until the appointment of John Danvers Power as CBS secretary in 1883 did someone regularly refute temperance polemics in the press; the hiring of a full-time correspondent came much later in 1888 and then under the auspices of the newly-created Fund. By 1894 he and an assistant were contributing 150 letters annually to unaffiliated newspapers, and district agents wrote many more. Finally, in 1895 the Fund, emulating a tactic followed by the UKA since 1889, organized a press agency for collating propaganda which deluged the local and national press.[28]

The brewing industry promoted solidarity, resolution and commitment in its trade newspapers, which proliferated late in the nineteenth century: the *Brewers' Guardian* (1871-7),[29] the *Country Brewers' Gazette* (1877–86)[30] and the *Brewing Trade Review* (1886–1972) served as official organs of the Country Brewers' Society and Brewers' Society; the *Licensed Trade News* (1894–1955) spoke for the Fund and the Association; the *Licensed Victuallers' Guardian* (1876–87)[31] was financed by the League as was the *Licensing World and Licensed Trade Review* (1892–1967) which the Society owned; and the *Off-Licence Holder* (1901) received support from the Federation. All these papers supplemented the long-established retail newspaper, the *Morning Advertiser*, the only daily trade paper.[32]

As a late Victorian pressure group, the brewing industry resisted prohibition and other less drastic but harmful Liberal reforms with more traditional than novel methods. Publicity vans and a press agency marked no new departure in seeking

---

[27] *Licensed Trade News*, 13 Apr. 1907 and 10 Aug. 1912; NTDA Min. Bk. 2, 10 March 1908, p. 246.

[28] Dingle, *Campaign for Prohibition*, p. 211; CBS Min. Bk. 4, 26 Oct. 1884, 25 Oct. 1886, 24 Oct. 1887 and 22 Oct. 1888; NTDA Min. Bk. 1, 20 Nov. 1888 and 12 March 1889, pp. 11–12, 16; NTDF Annual Reports: 1894, p. 15; 1895, p. 33; see also Soldon, 'LPDL', p. 218; Mackintosh, *Disestablishment*, pp. 52, 217.

[29] CBS Min. Bk. 3, 16 July 1877, p. 100.

[30] *Country Brewers' Gazette*, 21 Oct. 1886.

[31] *Licensed Victuallers' Guardian*, 1 Jan. 1876; *Brewing Trade Review*, 1 Feb. 1887.

[32] For temperance newspapers, see Brian Harrison, ' "A World of which We had no Conception". Liberalism and the Temperance Press: 1830–72', *Vic. Stud.*, 12 (1969), 125–58.

public support, but both did put the trade's case before a wider audience. Of the two, the press agency was clearly more important. Its creation was not as surprising as the fact that brewers copied prohibitionists so slowly and displayed so little originality in exploring the agency's other possible uses.

This same lack of imagination characterized all the trade's political tactics. Despite their mutual interest in *laissez-faire* economics and the sanctity of private property, the trade never lobbied the business or financial community systematically or continuously. Even with its most innovative tactics, the trade failed to exploit fully two natural groups of allies, working-class organizations meetings at pubs and shareholders. Never organized into a formal organization under trade auspices, friendly societies and trade unions were regarded with complacency, except during a crisis. Shareholders might have formed such a body, but brewers, tight-fisted businessmen with unrealistic expectations, refused to provide funds. Equally money hindered the more restricted shareholders' register, which needed but never received several thousand pounds for operating on a national scale at the 1910 Elections. Brewers were remarkably consistent. With their profits at serious risk if the People's budget passed, they resolutely declined to aid those most capable of offering protection — shareholders, the Association and the League. What mattered most, of course, was less these lost opportunities than the trade's popular image. George Whiteley, Liberal chief whip and former brewery director, was surely but one of many anti-drink critics whose views had been deeply influenced by trade propaganda. 'It was difficult enough when only the big brewer was to be attacked', he reflected early in 1907. 'Now, in the place of each big brewer are hundreds, if not thousands, of shareholders; and this, with all the allied trades revolving around the liquor interest, makes licensing reform peculiarly hard to compass'.[33]

---

[33] Whiteley to Campbell-Bannerman, 1 March 1907, Campbell-Bannerman Papers, Add. Ms. 41,231, fos. 232 – 3. Whiteley had managed and acted as director of Dutton & Co., the Blackburn brewery owned by his wife's family, between 1889 and 1897 (*150 Years of the House of Dutton, 1799 – 1949* (1949), pp. 6 – 13; see also David W. Gutzke, 'Rhetoric and Reality: The Political Influence of British Brewers, 1832 – 1914', *Parl. Hist.* (forthcoming).

9

Myths and Realities of Trade Power

In 1897 Lord Rosebery, expressing a widely shared contemporary belief, declared that 'the power of "the trade" has become an alarming feature in this country. It resembles more the power of the Trusts in the United States than anything else that we have'. Temperance reformers themselves deliberately promoted this fear. How could they otherwise explain why their huge financial resources, sophisticated organization and overwhelming evidence of a pressing social evil had still failed to prevent astonishing defeats on prohibition, the time limit and sweeping licensing reduction? In contrast, David Fahey, Ronald Weir and other historians have recently rejected the omnipotent trade as a myth, stressing its disunity, its subsidiary role by 1900 in a 'mature industrial economy', retail apathy and the larger incomes of temperance societies.[1] This revisionism, however, simply creates a new myth of a continuously beleaguered trade. The reality lies somewhere in between. Certainly many difficulties afflicted the trade between 1875 and 1914, but not throughout the period. At some points the trade's organization, funds and allies ensured dominance over its opponents. The influence of the trade, far from being static, thus fluctuated within the changing political, economic and social context. Too often analysts of pressure groups have concentrated on internal factors, neglecting outside influences. Drink's position in the national economy, the brewing industry's prestige and sympathetic voters would have made the trade a powerful adversary even if brewers and retailers had done nothing in their own defence.

---

[1] Rosebery to Sir W. S. Haldane, 28 Dec. 1897 (copy), Rosebery Papers, Ms. 10,131, fo. 164; Fahey, 'Politics of Drink', p. 80 – 1 and 'Brewers and Drinkers', pp. 94, 97 – 8, 100; Weir, 'Drink Question', p. 98 and *Malt Distillers' Association*, p. 37.

Table 10
Membership in leading brewers' associations

Year	Burton Brewers' Co.	Brewers' Assoc.	CBS	BS	Col 1: total	Col 2: Commercial brewers[a]	Col 1 as % of Col 2
1883	11	16	316	–	343	2,073	16.5
1890	12	16	614	–	643	2,014	31.9
1900	8	14	575	–	597	1,531	39.0
1910	–	–	–	750	750	1,257	59.7
1914	–	–	–	610	610	1,111	54.9

Sources: BS and CBS Annual Reports; BS Candidates for Election, B.S.; Brewers' Co. Trade Min. Bk., Ms. 5468; Brewers' Co. Min. Bk., 1892 – 1903; Wilson, *Alcohol and Nation*, p. 49; *Parl. Pap.*, Accts. and Papers, 1883, 64 (27), p. 8.
[a] Minimum production of 1,000 barrels annually

The trade's popular image as an effective pressure group was belied at Westminster, where brewers and retailers never lobbied with full strength.[2] Too few of them joined protective societies for any one organization to claim it represented a cross-section of the industry. Before 1904 major brewers' associations contained less than half of the substantial commercial brewers (see table 10). Not until the 1908 – 10 crisis could the Brewers' Society legitimately speak for most brewers. Even then, with just three-fifths of them as members, it had to place more emphasis on enrolling 'the large majority of the 521 brewers who brew 90 percent. of the total output'.[3] Membership in regional retail societies was likewise low, but lower still after 1906 (see table 11). The Fund, allowing local retail societies to federate without subscription fees, did register higher numbers of licence holders, though never more than half of them.

Low membership in protective societies seemingly supports those scholars who point to another aspect of the trade's weakness, its finances. Fahey regards the heavier expenditure

[2]   See David W. Gutzke, 'Rhetoric and Reality: The Political Influence of British Brewers, 1832 – 1914', *Parl. Hist.* (forthcoming).
[3]   *Brewing Trade Review*, 1 May 1913.

Table 11
Membership in major retail societies

Year	League	Society[a]	Federation	Beer/Wine League	Total	% of licen
1896	10,914	4,539	12,000	4,000	31,500	2(
1902	10,936	7,055	12,000	4,000(?)	34,000	28
1911	10,961	4,400	9,000	4,000(?)	28,400	2(

Sources: *Evid. Sel. Com. Shops (Early Closing) Bill*, 1895, 12 (273), pp. 142-3; *Evid. Sel. Com. Lords Early Closing Shops*, 1901, 6 (369), p. 99; *Evid. Royal Com. Sel. JPs*, 1910, 37 (Cmnd. 5358), p. 120; *Evid. Royal Com. Liq. Lic. Laws*, 1898, 36 (Cmnd. 8693), p. 427; Wilson, *Alcohol and Nation*, p. 397; LVPSL and LVNDL Annual Reports.

[a] Estimate based on subscription rate
[b] Excludes beer and spirit dealers additional licences as well as those for sweets, passenger boats and restaurant cars.

of temperance organizations as convincing evidence of the exaggerated contemporary view of the brewing industry's political power.[4] But the trade was not as poorly funded as he and other historians have portrayed (see table 12). While the UKA outspent the trade by a third before 1884, both spent comparable sums in the years 1884 – 8. Early in the 1890s, with the Commons controlled by Liberals pledged to local veto, the trade actually outstripped the UKA. When Unionists resumed office, brewers resumed their frugal policy. Compared with the £6,500 typically collected annually during the early 1890s, the Fund's central office received no more than £4,000 and often just £3,000 annually during most of the Edwardian era, despite the threats of harmful legislation.[5] District grants of £2,400 in the 1890s were consequently cut, falling by nearly two-thirds.[6] So hard pressed was the Association during the 1908 – 10 struggle

---

4   Fahey, 'Brewers and Drinkers', pp. 97 – 8.
5   The Association received £3,000 in 1906 and 1908, and £3,000 – £4,000 in 1910 (NTDA Min. Bk. 2, 29 Nov. 1906, p. 196; BS Min. Bk. 2, 18 Oct. 1906, p. 4 and Min. Bk. 3, 19 May 1911; Berks. Br. Union Min. Bk., 1 May 1909).
6   District grants averaged £850 (1902 – 8) (Compiled from NTDA Min. Bk. 2).

that district grants did not reach, much less exceed, levels of the early 1890s.[7] In fact, brewers donated more money to the Fund in the 1890s than at any other time until 1912, long after the political confrontation with Liberals had ended. The trade's expenditure, therefore, followed three contrasting trends: after a period of financial weakness early in the 1880s, spending rose slowly from 1884 and sharply between 1891 and 1895, then fell again until late in the Edwardian era, though the Society's larger expenses after 1899 obscured this decline.

The trade, however, had one huge asset often forgotten by scholars but not by politicians. Few other industries had as much economic importance to the government as the drink trades: taxes on alcohol generated much of the state's total revenue — over two-fifths early in the 1880s and still as much as one-quarter before the war.[8] Prohibition would reduce this source of funds. District taxes, either on personal incomes or landed property, could be substituted, but only at the risk of alienating middle- and upper-class taxpayers, and causing unemployment in specialized industries supplying the trade with hops, malt, beer pumps and so on. This strategic economic role helped offset low membership in protective societies and periodic shortages of funds.

It also enhanced the trade's appeals to sympathetic voters. A receptive constituency awaited trade propaganda. In the middle and upper classes were vast numbers of anxious investors in breweries, including many prominent politicians and aristo-crats, who regarded Liberals' temperance legislation as socialistic attacks on property. At the other end of the social scale, the trade relied on support from trade unionists and members of friendly societies.

Temperance reformers displayed considerable misunder-standing of working-class culture in denouncing retailers for manipulating customers into voting against anti-trade candi-dates. Two drink detractors, in an influential study published in 1899, calculated that each publican and beerhouse keeper swaying one voter helped defeat over 150 Liberal candidates in the 1890s. Other critics, drawing strong parallels with corrupt machine electioneering in the US, accused retailers of debasing

---

[7] District grants rose 40% (£1,200) annually during the crisis over Liberal legislation and the 1910 Elections, though this still fell 50% short of the Fund subsidies to districts in the 1890s (*ibid.*).

[8] Harrison, *Drink and Victorians*, p. 346.

Table 12

Comparative annual expenses of the Trade and UKA
(£)

Period	CBS	CBS Branches	Society	League	Fund (Association)	District Expenses	Total	UKA
1880 – 8	1,900[a]	3,800[b]	5,700[c]	2,200	–	–	13,600	15,000
1889 – 98	–	–	9,100	1,400	5,300[d]	3,000 – 3,600	18,800 – 19,400	15,800
1899 – 1908	–	–	11,000	1,600	3,000[e]	3,700[g]	19,300	15,900
1909 – 13	–	–	7,600	1,600	6,400[f]	3,700[h]	19,300	14,600

Sources: CBS Annual Reports, 1884 – 8; 1912 – 13; LVNDL Annual Reports, 1882 – 1914; Herts. Br. Assoc. Annual Reports, 1883, 1886 – 8; Yorks. Br. Assoc. Annual Reports, 1880 – 4; Glos. Br. Assoc. Assoc. Min. Bk. (1885 – 7); NTDF Cash Book, 1888 – 95; NTDT W. Dist. Annual Reports, 1893 – 9, 1901 – 13; NTDF N. Dist. Min. Bk. (1892, 1894 – 5, 1909 – 14); Berks. Br. Union Min. Bk., 1 May 1909; NTDA Min. Bk. 2, 29 Nov. 1906, p. 196; Dingle, *Campaign for Prohibition*, p. 192; UKA Annual Reports, 1899 – 1913; BS Min. Bk. 2, 18 Oct. 1906, p. 4, Min. Bk. 3, 19 May 1911, and Annual Reports, 1912 – 13.

[a] Average for years 1884 – 8
[b] Average for years 1883 – 8 based on brewers' societies in Herts., Glos. and Yorks.
[c] Average for years 1882 – 8
[d] Average for years 1889 – 95
[e] Based on income of £3,000 in 1906 and 1908
[f] Based on income of £3,000 – £4,000 in 1910 and donations from BS, 1912 – 13
[g] Estimate based on W. Dist. expenses and district grants
[h] Estimate based on N., W. and Notts. district expenses

politics into a 'British Tammany' Hall.[9] In fact, retailers were not
ward bosses dictating to voters, nor were drinkers dupes too
sozzled to cast ballots independently. Such theories not merely
ignored similar unpaid counter-efforts from the pulpit, but
grossly oversimplified the retailer/customer relationship, which
was far more complex and less one-sided than temperance
advocates supposed. Many working-class drinkers needed little
prompting to see local option or the time limit as blatantly unfair
to the drink seller. As Herbert Gladstone realized and reiterated
to his dubious leader, Sir Henry Campbell-Bannerman, they
would vote for no Liberal unless there was a firm guarantee
retailers with revoked licences would receive fair compensation.
It was not just the likelihood of victimized retailers, of course,
that estranged working-class men from Liberalism. Labourers
resented the transparent class bias as acutely as the moralizing
tone of temperance supporters. 'Why don't 'em make a start by
shutting up some rich people's hotels or the wine merchants'
shops where they buys their wine an' spirits by the case?', two
fictitious but typical Devonshire fishermen pointedly asked.
Class distrust also convinced them that drink critics castigated
pubs and beerhouses "cause they'm working-men's houses,
kept by the likes of a fellow's self-men what can't defend
theirselves proper'. Whatever the merits of temperance reform,
the way in which Liberals pursued it had serious electoral
consequences. After visiting working-class homes for three
decades in Middlesbrough, Lady Bell concluded that the trade's
propaganda 'is most potently reinforced by the tendency of
those to whom it addresses itself. The latter are more than ready
to listen to the one side; they cannot listen to the other'.[10]

To exploit investors' anxiety and pub goers' animosity,
brewers and retailers had to mobilize as an effective pressure
group. Historians often credit brewers and retailers with
organizing on a national scale much sooner than was the case.[11]
No comprehensive body capable of formulating trade policy for
both sections, brewer and retail, was founded before brewers

9   Rowntree and Sherwell, *Temperance Problem*, pp. 502 – 16; *Hansard*, 4th ser.,
    89 (19 Feb. 1901), col. 558; see also pp. 51 – 2.
10 Gladstone to Campbell-Bannerman, 19 Nov. 1899, Campbell-Bannerman
    Papers, Add. Ms. 41,215, fos. 144 – 6; Bell, *Manufacturing Town*, p. 249;
    Stephen Reynolds, Bob Woolley and Tom Woolley, *Seems So! A Working-
    Class View of Politics* (1911), pp. 60 – 1; see also George Bourne, *Change in the
    Village* (1912; reprint edition, 1984), pp. 43 – 7.
11 See p. 60, n. 2.

created the Fund in 1888. This preliminary step towards unity proved so difficult and required issues of such urgency because neither brewers nor retailers had consolidated into national organizations. Institutional rivalry, partly caused by the geographic split between London and the provinces, together with long traditions of autonomy and differing legal privileges and markets, provoked petty but disabling feuds among retailers. Without comparable legal grievances or responsibility for electioneering, brewers quarrelled less but did little beyond collecting funds for retailers, the only political activists with anything approaching county or local machinery. By the mid-1880s, provincial brewers had not merely strengthened, reinvigorated and extended the CBS, but seized from retailers control of defence outside London. Unlike the Society, the League never exchanged its autonomy for brewers' subsidies, and so paid dearly by being chronically underfunded and undervalued. Cooperation between brewers and retailers was only one of several problems besetting the trade. Lobbying activities and petitioning campaigns, both vital for an efficient pressure group, were principally undertaken not by brewers or retailers but by the LPDL. Yet other allies, friendly societies, trade unionists, auxiliary industries and off-licence holders, remained unorganized. During the 1880s, brewers and retailers thus possessed little of the organization and less of the power which the public often attributed to them.

It was in the 1890s that the trade deserved its reputation as an awesome political force. In capitalizing on the uncertain post-1886 party alignment and demonstrating superior fund raising and campaigning prowess, prohibitionists had twice blocked compensation schemes. Had the trade instead succeeded, complacent brewers, denied strong incentives for emulating their rivals, would have fought against prohibition with smaller resources, fewer paid organizers and members, poorer machinery and less zeal than opponents. Ironically, the Alliance's victory was primarily responsible for galvanizing brewers into implementing the reforms which later led to its own defeat. The reorganized Fund, with big brewers' money, smaller provincial firms' support, full-time salaried agents and a wider network of local retail societies, established a decisive superiority over prohibitionists. These crucial developments explain why two consecutive governments, committed to enacting legislation advanced by supporters through pressure groups, both unexpectedly abandoned major drink proposals. Between 1888

236

and 1895, Liberal prohibitionists thwarted Conservative compensation bills for the same reason that the Conservative trade successfully stymied Liberal prohibition bills, better organization, comparable or more funds and greater success in arousing public sympathy than their adversaries. Of these factors, the last was especially important in the anti-prohibition agitation. Never before had the trade moved beyond traditional pressure group tactics, enlisting influential groups with a vested interest in the survival of pubs and beerhouses. Across the class spectrum were thousands of outraged voters: middle- and upper-class shareholders would surrender their entire investments, while working-class men in friendly societies and trade unions would lose irreplaceable venues. At the 1895 Election, the trade's vehement attack on prohibition cost many Liberal candidates numerous votes. Campbell-Bannerman, an unrepentant local veto enthusiast, paid brewers and retailers perhaps the best tribute: 'The noisy fussiness of the Teetotalers is as nothing against the steady pressure of the interest they attack'.[12]

Despite impressive campaigns against prohibition, brewers and retailers never developed a collective identity capable of transcending loyalty to their own regional or national societies, which embodied specific economic interests of either wholesalers or retailers. From deep internal divisions among brewers and retailers in the 1870s and 1880s emerged a sectional mentality, distrustful of centralized authority and preoccupied with protecting the economic status of regional groups. For brewers, differences in tied house holdings, beer output and wealth reinforced geographic rivalry, setting big London, Burton and the largest provincial firms against most country brewers. For retailers, varying economic roles, wealth and brewers' subsidies fostered a complicated three-fold schism in which provincial and London retail on-licence holders opposed each other almost as much as off-licence holders. Brewers and retailers, moreover, cooperated warily since their economic relationship, much closer with the spread of the tied house system, often intruded on political issues.

These cleavages meant that the Fund's policies, goals and leadership would cause unrest and acrimony. Sectionalism pervaded the Fund from its inception. Prominent London,

---

[12] Campbell-Bannerman to Rosebery, 20 July 1895, Rosebery Papers, Ms. 10,003, fo. 137.

Burton and some country brewers founded a so-called representative body in which they held disproportionate influence. As
the chief subscribers, they dominated the Fund, forming an
oligarchy which denied all retailers and most provincial brewers
any meaningful role. Affronted powerful Lancashire and
Yorkshire brewers naturally refused to join or donate money.
When the Fund's creators proposed enlarging its scope and
activities without altering their power, leading midland and
northern brewers combined in a bigger, more ambitious and
democratic rival scheme. These outsiders challenged the elite's
control as much as its unrepresentative policy. The result was a
more egalitarian Fund, but not the full integration of dissident
brewers. Midland brewers exemplified the enduring sectionalism, rejecting subsidies from central office and disputing moves
to centralize authority at the 1900 Election. Sectionalism also
prevented retailers from conceding the Fund pre-eminence in
trade defence. In London, as in the provinces, publicans had
historically resented and attacked licensed grocers as competitors and Liberal allies. It was less the incorporation of
grocers into the trade than the Association's claim of sole
responsibility for policy, however, that retailers vigorously
repudiated in 1900.

Sectionalism equally explains another recurring feature of the
trade as a pressure group, the remarkable modest resources of
nearly all protective societies. Wealthy London brewers through
the Brewers' Company comprised the primary source of the
Fund's receipts. But they persistently gave more money to the
Society, which consequently spent two and even three times as
much as the Association, nominally the trade's central body.
Their overriding concern with protecting London, where they
brewed beer and owned licensed property, established a pattern
of self-interest which other brewers copied. Elsewhere brewers
supported only their own local retail societies and county
branches without seeing themselves as part of a national
pressure group. London brewers had another reason for heavily
subsidizing the Society. The Brewers' Company not only gained
enormous influence over London publicans, but effectively
obstructed their alignment with provincial retailers. Not surprisingly, the League and the Society, two of the largest organizations of publicans, could form no united front against brewers
on economic or political issues, except briefly in 1899–1900.
Provincial retailers naturally regarded the Society's independence as seriously compromised, often accusing it of being a

brewers' lackey. In the provinces, on the other hand, the CBS displaced the League as the chief defender of the trade in the mid-1880s, and followed a different financial strategy, withdrawing retail subsidies as a means of gaining supremacy. Two priorities, protecting sectional interests and securing loyalty, determined how the Brewers' Company and CBS dealt with the Society and the League, but neither promoted the most extensive, unified or effective trade organization.

The reputation of brewers and retailers as a formidable political force, acquired in the 1890s, outlasted their actual power. Three factors steadily undermined their solidarity, diminishing the trade's influence in the Edwardian era: the industry's depressed state, new political issues and resurgent sectionalism.

Brewers and retailers faced considerable economic difficulties from 1900 onwards. In that year, total beer consumption, which had risen almost forty per cent in the previous two decades, suddenly slumped, declining twelve per cent in the next decade before somewhat recovering. Historians disagree as to the reasons for this change, some suggesting falling standards of living while others stressing shifts in consumer purchasing patterns.[13] Whatever the cause, those in the brewing industry suffered quite severely: brewing companies had lower profits which resulted in reduced or missed dividends; retailers lost custom and income. Beyond new compensation levies, beer duty rose as did licence fees, so brewers and retailers were paying more taxes with shrunken profits. There was a strong incentive for brewers to recoup losses by utilizing clubs, direct delivery and revised tenancy contracts, on one hand, and to decrease or even discontinue subsidies to trade societies, on the other. Retailers instead sought scapegoats, blaming unfaithful Unionists, unscrupulous brewers and detested licensed grocers for plummeting profits.

New political issues, like economic hardships, demoralized members of the trade. Liberal temperance proposals, restricting compensation and raising licence fees, neither affronted the working-class drinker's sense of class justice nor aroused his fear of losing the local. Denied both outrage and personal involvement, he had less reason to respond to trade propaganda than in the 1890s. The political debate itself, not fundamentally on temperance but on free trade and protectionism, caused

[13] See p. 203, n. 56.

further problems. Though sympathetic to the retailer, many working-class men would not jeopardize free trade by voting Unionist. They forcefully expressed these feelings at the neighbourhood pub or beerhouse, discouraging many retailers from their customary political activities at the 1910 Elections. In the midlands, for instance, the agent identified the growth of what he called 'the mercenary spirit' which caused retailers to place profits before politics. He repeatedly found 'license-holders making their Houses the centres of political sections which are distinctly inimical to the best interests of our Trade, and doing this for business purposes only'. Late in 1910, the *Licensed Trade News* wrote contemptuously of retail officials whose fear of offending customers prevented active support for Unionist candidates.[14]

Likewise, intensified sectionalism destroyed trade solidarity, undermining the commitment and loyalty of brewers and retailers to protective societies. Many of the rank and file heartily disliked their leaders' renewed efforts to centralize authority in the Association at the 1906 Election, when the trade began a new electoral policy of open alliance with Unionists. Unrest partly arose from Unionist legislation: increased taxes, troublesome curbs on child messengers, and insurance, not compensation, for forfeited licences angered many retailers who abstained or defected at the election in protest. Another sign of sectionalism was the League's resumed attacks on licensed grocers, some of whom as a result stopped campaigning against the 1908 Licensing bill.[15]

No other form of sectionalism, however, hurt trade unity more than the bitter economic rivalry between retailers and brewers. Tied house practices, clubs sponsored or assisted by brewers and direct delivery of beer all generated retail rancour because brewers, exploiting their powerful economic position as landlords, competed unfairly with tenants for working-class customers. Tenants could not match offers of lower prices, cash discounts, credit and free beer, but brewers were not always the

---

[14] NTDA Mid. Dist. 1910 Jt. Comt. Report, D 3163/2/2, p. 11; *Licensed Trade News*, 24 Dec. 1910.
[15] LVNDL 1908 Annual Report, pp. 81–2; 'Through Practical Spectacles', p. 391; see the lengthy correspondence between Arthur Giles (president of the Federation) and H. G. Robinson (sec. of the League), LVNDL 1908 Half-Yearly Meeting, pp. 8–15.

greedy capitalists depicted by retailers. However ardently publicans and beerhouse keepers insisted on monopolizing drink sales, legitimate working-men's clubs and direct delivery reflected consumer preference and technological change. Brewers are more justly criticized for rigidly separating economic grievances from political issues, forcing the League to adopt counter-productive policies which risked trade defence. Much of this conflict could have been avoided had the Brewers' Society set national guidelines for tenancy contracts, clubs and direct delivery. The alternative, pronounced sectionalism, promoted the goals of opponents rather than those of the trade.

By 1914 trade organization was deteriorating. Brewers and retailers were not, as one historian contends, confident and optimistic that Unionists would alleviate the budget's onerous duties. Unionists, unwilling to denounce the budget at the 1910 Elections and seemingly incapable of ever ousting the Liberal Government, were discredited as trade allies. Internally divided and externally harassed, all major trade societies betrayed some form of decline. Falling membership was a common problem. The Brewers' Society lost nearly one-fifth and the Society almost two-fifths of their members in the Edwardian era.[16] Though the League's membership remained stable, many previously powerful local affiliated bodies in such leading cities as Birmingham, Leeds, Leicester and Wolverhampton reported severe declines: among the strongest provincial retail societies in 1902, they collectively enrolled thirty-seven per cent fewer members by 1914. In Southampton, the large local retail society disappeared altogether, as did the Lincolnshire and Nottinghamshire Brewers' Association. Trade societies lost financial resources as well as members. By the Edwardian period, the income of the Association's central office was fifty per cent lower than during the prohibition scarce of the 1890s, while the Society's donations from brewers also halved between 1904 and 1911 and subscriptions fell by forty per cent. So impoverished was the League that it scarcely participated in the agitation against the Licensing bill.[17] Frustrated and apathetic, brewers

---

[16] Turner, 'Liquor Trade', pp. 592–3; see tables 10–11, pp. 231–2.
[17] LVNDL Annual Reports, 1903–14; LVPSL Annual Reports, 1904–11; see tables 6 and 12, pp. 114, 234.

and retailers were now disunited, paying the price for their own limited goals and absence of collective identity.

Less tangible than organization but still quite important in determining power was the trade's prestige. In the years 1880 – 1914 the fifty-five brewers who served as MPs clearly enhanced the trade's reputation.[18] They formed not a cross-section of all brewers but an elite. Of those connected with public companies, over two-thirds came from breweries which represented the top third of the industry, with assets of more than £500,000.[19] These men had accumulated enormous wealth, and succeeded, as Dr. Johnson had foretold, in 'growing rich beyond the dreams of avarice'. The mean size of their probated estates approached £500,000. Even in a party of rich landowners and businessmen, Conservative brewers ranked among the wealthiest. Compared with all Conservative MPs in the 1895 and 1906 Parliaments, roughly three times as many Conservative brewer MPs proportionately had gross estates exceeding £200,000. The unprecedented and unequalled number of millionaire brewers in Parliament underlined the new role of wealth as the chief criterion of social approval. Of the thirteen brewers who amassed such fortunes and died between 1868 and 1914, seven sat as MPs.[20]

In society, as in national politics, brewers had their social prestige affirmed through coveted honours. Serving as a county magistrate symbolized gentry status, but the Victorian landed class refused to appoint most upstarts with business ties, except landed brewers.[21] Aristocratic marriages also emphasized assimilation with landed society. The Best, Guinness, Hanbury and Whitbread families soon exchanged well-dowered

18 See n. 2.
19 Compiled from T. Skinner's *The Stock Exchange Year-Book and Diary for 1900*.
20 Michael Arthur Bass (1st Baron Burton), Michael Thomas Bass, Spencer Charrington, Sir Gilbert Greenall, Sir Benjamin Guinness, William McEwan and James Watney (Rubinstein, 'Millionaires', pp. 208 – 14). W. D. Rubinstein, 'Modern Britain', W. D. Rubinstein (ed.), *Wealth and the Wealthy in the Modern World* (1980), p. 73; Johnson quoted in Pudney, *Courage Group*, p. 64; brewers' wills, Somerset House.
21 F. M. L. Thompson, *English Landed Society in the Nineteenth Century* (1963), pp. 110 – 12, 128 – 32, 287 – 8; David W. Gutzke, 'The Social Status of Landed Brewers in Britain Since 1840', *Histoire sociale/Soc. Hist.*, 17 (1984), 93 – 113. At least 39 brewers served as county magistrates between 1828 and 1870.

daughters for aristocratic connections, while such lesser families as the Buxtons, Marjoribanks, Meuxs and Walkers did so after acquiring baronetcies. Of the various forms of new commercial and industrial wealth ennobled from the mid-1880s, brewers' primacy again demonstrated high social status, symbolized in the House of Lords' new nickname, the 'beerage'.[22]

Brewers, however, lost prestige after 1900. In buying most drink shops, they acquired a reputation first for greed, and later, once the licensed property boom collapsed, for recklessness. The trade was apparently besieged by widely publicized problems: investors clamoured for higher dividends; hop growers condemned the quality of English beer; and bogus clubs provided the subject for debate and legislation. It was, in fact, just this unfavourable public image that inspired the founding of the ABTA.

The trade's popularity also suffered from the rhetoric of national efficiency. Large numbers of army recruits rejected as physically unfit during the Boer War focused public attention on physical degeneration, prompting anxiety about sustaining the Empire if high infant mortality rates persisted. Commentators often associated these social problems with increasing female intemperance. Some distinguished doctors expanded this analysis into a new critique of alcohol as a factor in infant mortality and national inefficiency. Endorsing their testimony in 1904, the Report of the Inter-Departmental Committee on Physical Deterioration imputed racial degeneration to alcohol abuse. This conclusion, its medical implications enlarged and disseminated by anti-drink doctors in articles, books and speeches, deeply impressed George Sims. In a series of newspaper articles entitled 'The Cry of the Children' in 1907, he disclosed working-class mothers' custom of going into pubs, where they gave their babies and toddlers alcohol and exposed them to deadly respiratory diseases. His discoveries provoked a national campaign in which a committee of Liberal politicians, leading medical authorities, temperance officials and religious

---

[22] Thompson, *English Landed Society*, pp. 19 – 20, 292 – 7; Ralph E. Pumphrey, 'The Introduction of Industrialists into the British Peerage: A Study in Adaptation of a Social Institution', *Amer. Hist. Rev.*, 65 (1959), 2, 7 – 8; Gutzke, 'Landed Brewers', pp. 106 – 7.

leaders eventually secured legislation excluding children under fourteen from licensed premises.[23]

Anti-drink propaganda based on the 1904 Report deluged the working classes, lowering the trade's already besmirched public image. Between 1905 and 1907 numerous municipal officials, emulating French tactics, issued posters quoting the Report as proof of alcohol's pernicious effects on health, reproduction and longevity. A typical placard admonished working-class men that 'it is a mistake to say that stimulants are necessary for those doing hard work', and advised women that *if the mother as well as the father* is given to drink the future of the race is imperilled'. These warnings repeatedly linked alcoholism with insanity, consumption and infant mortality.[24] Although Warrington's mayor protested that 'the people for whom the placard was intended would be too drunk to see it', his objection was nonetheless overruled. Some local authorities were particularly enterprising: in Glasgow 120,000 households each received a leaflet; in Hull over 12,000 youthful critics wrote essays on the poster for a contest; and in two suburban Manchester schools, classroom walls displayed framed copies.[25]

All these factors explain why the trade's political influence was not constant but fluctuated between 1875 and 1914. Early in the 1880s what few brewers' societies there were received token donations and intervened but fitfully in politics. While better organized and funded, retail societies were disunited, unable to devise policy for the trade. Between 1883 and 1890 the industry acquired greater power but it could still be challenged: provincial brewers reorganized the CBS, prominent London

---

23 Gutzke, 'Edwardian Medical Campaign', pp. 71–84; see also David Wright and Cathy Chorniawry, 'Women and Drink in Edwardian England', *Hist. Papers/Communications Historiques*, (1985), 117–31; and more generally G. R. Searle, *The Quest for National Efficiency: A Study in British Politics and British Political Thought, 1899–1914* (1971); Richard Soloway, 'Counting the Degenerates: The Statistics of Race Deterioration in Edwardian England', *Jour. Contem. Hist.*, 17 (1982), 137–64.

24 W. McAdam Eccles, 'Municipal Posters on Physical Deterioration and Alcoholism', *Brit. Jour. Inebriety*, 4 (1907), 195, 197–8, 200; E. Claude Taylor, 'The Teaching of Temperance' and V. H. Rutherford, 'Alcoholism and Legislation', T. N. Kelynack (ed.), *The Drink Problem in its Medico-Sociological Aspects* (1907), pp. 225–6, 243–4; *Temperance Record*, 5 (1907), pp. 34–6, 55–6; *Scottish Temperance League Register and Abstainers Almanac for 1907*, pp. 89–91. Poster's italics.

25 Eccles, 'Municipal Posters', p. 201; *Temperance Record*, 4 (1906), p. 292 and 5 (1907), p. 311.

and country brewers established the Fund, the Society and the League resolved their disputes, the LPDL lobbied on the trade's behalf and money spent on defence rose sharply. The peak of the trade's influence came in the 1890s, with the appointment of full-time agents, support from three large groups (shareholders, trade unions and friendly societies) and financial superiority over the UKA. In the Edwardian period, the trade's power steadily contracted for diverse reasons: incomes and membership in protective societies fell; friendly societies and trade unions became less reliable allies; and public opinion displayed growing hostility. Trade organization had become so defective that some publicans 'thought "Time Limit" meant the hours of opening and closing of public houses'.[26] Many of the trade's difficulties derived from heightened sectionalism, especially from bitter but inconclusive economic quarrels. These were crucial because brewers and retailers alike now faced declining profits and heavier taxes. Working-class men, less threatened by Liberal temperance proposals and more concerned about free trade, no longer found the retailer's propaganda persuasive when casting votes. For demoralized members of the trade increasingly saw solidarity replaced by sectional strife or stupor.

Threats of prohibition or sweeping licensing reduction without adequate compensation stimulated the trade into defending its interests. Seldom faced and never resolved was a fundamental conflict between sectionalism, based largely on self-interest, and centralized authority, committed to national unity and formidable political power. Despite the widely recognized need for cohesive national organization, geography, wealth, economic rivalry and a strong tradition of regional autonomy all fostered sectionalism. In seeking centralized power at the national level, trade leaders were repeatedly thwarted by regional organizations which pursued local priorities and grievances. What triumphed was debilitating sectionalism, the perpetrator of dissent, division and disunity and ultimately the destroyer of monolithic trade power.

---

[26] NTDA Home and S. Count. Min. Bk. 1, 16 Oct. 1907, p. 10.

APPENDIX 1

The largest contributors to the Fund, 1888 – 95

Firm	Location	(£) Donation
Courage & Co.[a]	London	1,550
Barclay, Perkins & Co.[a]	London	1,300
Charrington & Co.[a]	London[b]	1,300
Combe & Co.[a]	London	1,300
Watney & Co.[a]	London	1,300
Bass, Ratcliff & Gretton	Burton	1,050
Arthur Guinness, Son & Co.	Dublin	800
Samuel Allsopp & Co.	Burton	800
Mann, Crossman & Paulin[a]	London[b]	683
City of London Brewery[a]	London	678
Hoare & Co.[a]	London	650
Reid's Brewery Co.[a]	London	650
Truman, Hanbury, Buxton & Co.[a]	London[b]	650
Ind, Coope & Co.	Romford[b]	525
Peter Walker & Sons	Warrington[b]	525
Meux's Brewery Co.	London	515
Cannon Brewery Co.[a]	London	440
Lion Brewery Co.	London	420
H. & G. Simonds	Reading	325
Taylor, Walker & Co.	London	325
Seager, Evans & Co.[c]	London	315
Smith, Druce & Co.[c]	London	315
J. & W. Nicholson & Co.[c]	London	279
William Younger & Co.	Edinburgh	263
Cheltenham Original Brewery	Cheltenham	250
Newcastle Breweries	Newcastle	230

Firm	Location	(£) Donation
Greenall, Whitley & Co.	Warrington	200
Total		17,638

Source: Compiled from NTDF Cash Bk., Aug. 1888 – Sept. 1895.
[a] Member of Brewers' Co.
[b] Branch also located in Burton-on-Trent
[c] Distillery Co.

Select Bibliography

Place of publication, London, unless otherwise specified

Primary Sources

Manuscript Collections
Akers-Douglas Papers (Kent Archives Office)
Asquith Papers (Bodleian Library)
Balfour Papers (British Library)
Campbell-Bannerman Papers (British Library)
Cross Papers (British Library)
Davidson Papers (Lambeth Palace Library)
Fuller Papers (Wiltshire Record Office)
Herbert Gladstone Papers (British Library)
W. E. Gladstone Papers (British Library)
Kimberley Papers (National Library of Scotland)
Bonar Law Papers (House of Lords Record Office)
Rosebery Papers (National Library of Scotland)
Salisbury Papers (Hatfield House)
Sandars Papers (Bodleian Library)

Parliamentary Papers
Royal Commission Appointed to Inquire into the Operation of the Sunday Closing (Wales), Act, 1881, 1890, 40 (Cmnd. 5994 and 5994-I).

Royal Commission on Arsenical Poisoning, 1901–4, 9 (Cmnd. 1845).

Royal Commission on the Liquor Licensing Laws, 1897–9, 34–8 (Cmnd. 8355–6, 8523, 8693–6, 8821–2, 8979–80, 9075–6, 9379, 9379-I).

Select Committee on the Clubs Registration Bill, 1893 – 4, 10 (314).
Select Committee on Habitual Drunkards, 1872, 9 (242).
Select Committee on the Hop Industry, 1908, 8 (285).
Select Committee on Intemperance, 1877 – 9, 10 – 11, 14 (113, 171, 271, 338, 418).
Select Committee on Public Houses, 1852 – 3, 37 (855).
Select Committee on the Sale of Liquors on Sunday Bill, 1867 – 8, 14 (402).

Trade and Temperance Newspapers

Alliance News
Brewer and Publican
Brewers' Gazette
Brewers' Guardian
Brewers' Journal
Brewing Trade Gazette
Brewing Trade Review
Country Brewers' Gazette
Licensed Trade News
Licensee
Licensed Victuallers' Guardian
Licensing World and Licensed Trade Review
Liverpool Brewers' and Victuallers' Journal
Morning Advertiser
Northern Brewers' and Victuallers' Journal
Trade Paper

Trade Associations and Brewery Companies

Allied Brewery Traders' Association (London)
    Minute Books
Bradford and District Brewers' Association (Boston Spa, West Yorkshire)
    Minute Books
Brewers' Company (London)
    Minute and Scrap Books
Brewers' Society (London)
    Bedfordshire Brewers' Association Minute Books
    Brewers' Society Annual Reports and Minute Books
    Country Brewers' Society Annual Reports and Minute Books
    Hertfordshire Brewers' Association Annual Reports
    National Trade Defence Fund/Association Annual Reports, Minute Books and Cash Book (1888 – 95)
    National Trade Defence Association Eastern Counties District 1900 General Election
    Northumberland and Durham Brewers' Association Annual Reports
British Library of Political and Economic Science (London)

Liberty and Property Defence League Annual Reports and Pamphlets

East Midlands Brewers' Association (Nottingham)
Leicestershire and Rutland Brewers' Association Minute Book
Lincolnshire and Nottinghamshire Brewers' Association Minute Book
National Trade Defence Association Nottinghamshire, Lincolnshire, Rutland, and Peterborough District Minute Book

Guildhall Library (London)
Brewers' Company Court and Trade Minute Book, Ms. 5468

National Union of Licensed Victuallers (Farnham)
Licensed Victuallers' Protection Society of London Annual Reports and Minute Books
Licensed Victuallers' National Defence League Annual Reports and Minute Books
London and Provincial Licensed Victuallers' Defence League Minute Book

Northamptonshire Record Office (Delapre Abbey, Northampton)
Northamptonshire Brewers' Association Minute Book, SL 298

North East Brewers' Association (Newcastle upon Tyne)
National Trade Defence Association Northern District Annual Reports and Minute Books
Northumberland and Durham Brewers' Association Minute Books

Northern Home Counties Brewers' Association (London)
National Trade Defence Association, Eastern, Home and Southern Counties Districts Reports and Minute Books

South Eastern Brewers' Association (London)
Sussex Brewers' Association Minute Books

South Wales Brewers' Association (Cardiff)
National Trade Defence Association District 7 Minute Book
South Wales Brewers' Association Minute Book

Staffordshire Record Office (Stafford)
Birmingham and Midland Counties Wholesale Brewers' Association Minute Books and Correspondence
National Trade Defence Association Midland District Minute Books and Reports, D 3163/1/1/1 – 2/3/3

Suffolk Record Office (Ipswich)
Cobbold & Co., HA/231/1/3

University of Wisconsin (Madison, Wisconsin)
    Guy Hayler Temperance Collection
    United Kingdom Alliance Annual Reports
Western Counties Brewers' Association (Bristol)
    Berkshire Brewers' Union Minute Book
    Bristol and Thornbury Licensed Trade Electoral and
        Parliamentary Committee Minute Book
    Gloucestershire Brewers' Association Annual Reports and
        Minute Books
    National Trade Defence Association Western District
        Annual Reports and Minute Books
    Somersetshire Brewers' Association Minute Book
    Wiltshire Brewers' Association Minute Book
Yorkshire Brewers' Association (Boston Spa, West Yorkshire)
    Annual Reports

Secondary Sources

Drink and Temperance

Aldcroft, Derek H., 'Control of the Liquor Trade in Great
    Britain, 1914 – 21', W. H. Chaloner and Barrie M. Ratcliffe
    (eds.), *Trade and Transport: Essays in Economic History in
    Honour of T. W. Willan* (Manchester, 1977), pp. 242 – 57.
Backhouse, David W., *Home Brewed: A History of Brewing and
    Public Houses in North Wiltshire* (Swindon, 1984).
Bailey, Victor, 'Salvation Army Riots, the "Skeleton Army" and
    Legal Authority in the Provincial Town', A. P. Donajgrodzki
    (ed.), *Social Control in Nineteenth Century Britain* (1977), pp.
    231 – 53.
Ball, Mia, *The Worshipful Company of Brewers: A Short History*
    (1977).
Baxter, John, 'The Organisation of the Brewing Industry'
    (University of London Ph.D. dissertation, 1945).
Briggs, Asa, *Wine for Sale: Victoria Wine and the Liquor Trade,
    1860 – 1984* (Chicago, 1985).
Bristol, Edward, 'The Liberty and Property Defence League and
    Individualism', *Historical Journal*, 18 (1975), 761 – 89.
Brown, J. B., 'The Pig or the Stye: Drink and Poverty in Late
    Victorian England', *International Review of Social History*, 18
    (1973), 380 – 95.
—— 'The Temperance Career of Joseph Chamberlain, 1870 – 77:
    A Study in Political Frustration', *Albion*, 4 (1972), 29 – 44.

Brown, Jonathan, *Steeped in Tradition: The Malting Industry in England Since the Railway Age* (Reading, 1983).

Bruce, George, *Kimberley Ale: The Story of Hardys & Hansons, 1832 – 1982* (1982).

Carter, Henry, *The English Temperance Movement: A Study in Objectives* (1933).

Clark, Peter, *The English Alehouse: A Social History, 1200 – 1830* (1983).

Corley, T. A. B., 'Simonds' Brewery at Reading, 1760 – 1960', *Berkshire Archaeological Journal*, 68 (1978), 77 – 88.

Corran, H. S., *A History of Brewing* (1975).

Cowen, Frank, *A History of Chesters Brewery Company* (Manchester, 1982).

Crapster, Basil Long, ' "Our Trade, Our Politics": A Study of the Political Activity of the British Liquor Industry, 1868 – 1910' (Harvard University Ph.D. dissertation, 1949).

Crawford, Alan, Dunn, Michael and Thorne, Robert, *Birmingham Pubs, 1880 – 1939* (Oxford, 1986).

Crowe, A. J., *Inns, Taverns and Pubs of the London Borough of Sutton: Their History and Architecture* (1980).

Dingle, A. E., *The Campaign for Prohibition in Victorian England: The United Kingdom Alliance, 1872 – 95* (New Brunswick, New Jersey, 1980).

—— 'The Agitation for Prohibition in England, 1871 – 95' (Monash University Ph.D. dissertation, 1974).

—— 'Drink and Working-Class Living Standards in Britain, 1870 – 1914', *Economic History Review*, 25 (1972), 608 – 22.

—— 'The Rise and Fall of Temperance Economics', *Monash Papers in Economic History*, No. 3 (1977), 1 – 30.

—— and Harrison, B. H., 'Cardinal Manning as Temperance Reformer', *Historical Journal*, 12 (1969), 485 – 510.

Donnachie, Ian, 'Drink and Society, 1750 – 1850: Some Aspects of the Scottish Experience', *Journal of the Scottish Labour History Society*, 13 (1979), 5 – 22.

—— 'World War I and the Drink Question: State Control of the Drink Trade', *Journal of the Scottish Labour History Society*, 17 (1982), 19 – 26.

—— *A History of the Brewing Industry in Scotland* (Edinburgh, 1979).

Fahey, David M., 'Drink and the Meaning of Reform in Late Victorian and Edwardian England', *Cithara*, 13 (1974), 46 – 56.

—— 'The Politics of Drink: Pressure Groups and the British Liberal Party, 1883 – 1908', *Social Science*, 54 (1979), 76 – 85.

—— 'Temperance and the Liberal Party — Lord Peel's Report, 1899', *Journal of British Studies*, 10 (1971), 132 – 59.

—— 'Brewers, Publicans and Working-Class Drinkers: Pressure Group Politics in Late Victorian and Edwardian England', *Histoire Sociale/Social History*, 13 (1980), 85 – 103.

—— 'Drink in the United Kingdom: A Supplementary List of Works Appearing, 1932 – 82', *Alcohol & Temperance History Group Newsletter*, No. 6 (1983), 4 – 6.

—— (ed.) *The Collected Writings of Jessie Forsyth, 1847 – 1937: The Good Templars and Temperance Reform on Three Continents* (Lewiston, New York, 1988).

Gall, Alan, *Manchester Breweries of Times Gone By* (Swinton, 1982).

Girouard, Mark, *Victorian Pubs* (1975).

Gourvish, Terry, *Norfolk Beers from English Barley: A History of Steward & Patteson, 1793 – 1963* (Norwich, 1987).

—— and Wilson, R. G., 'Profitability in the Brewing Industry, 1885 – 1914', *Business History*, 27 (1985), 146 – 65.

Greenway, John R., 'Bishops, Brewers and the Liquor Question in England, 1880 – 1914', *Historical Magazine of the Protestant Episcopal Church*, 53 (1984), 61 – 75.

—— 'The Local Option Question and British Politics, 1864 – 1914' (University of Leeds Ph.D. dissertation, 1974).

Gutzke, David W., ' "The Cry of the Children": The Edwardian Medical Campaign Against Maternal Drinking', *British Journal of Addiction*, 79 (1984), 71 – 84.

—— 'The Social Status of Landed Brewers in Britain Since 1840', *Histoire Sociale/Social History*, 17 (1984), 93 – 113.

—— and Fahey, David M., 'Drink and Temperance in Britain', *Alcohol in History: A Multidisciplinary Newsletter*, No. 9 (1984), 3 – 5.

Hamer, D. A., *The Politics of Electoral Pressure: A Study in the History of Victorian Reform Agitations* (Hassocks, 1977).

Harrison, Brian, *Drink and the Victorians: The Temperance Question in England, 1815 – 72* (1971).

—— 'Pubs', H. J. Dyos and Michael Wolff (eds.), *The Victorian City: Images and Realities* (1973), 2: 161 – 90.

—— 'The British Prohibitionists, 1853 – 72: A Biographical Analysis', *International Review of Social History*, 15 (1970), 375 – 467.

—— ' "A World of Which We Had No Conception". Liberalism and the Temperance Press: 1830 – 72', *Victorian Studies*, 12 (1969), 125 – 58.

—— and Barrie Trinder, 'Drink and Sobriety in an Early Victorian Town: Banbury, 1830–60', *English Historical Review*, Supplement 4 (1969), 1–55.

Hawkins, Kevin, 'The Conduct and Development of the Brewing Industry in England and Wales, 1880–1938' (Univ. of Bradford Ph.D. dissertation, 1981).

—— and Pass, C. L., *The Brewing Industry: A Study in Industrial Organisation and Public Policy* (1979).

Jacobson, Michael, *The Cliff Brewery, 1723–1983* (n.p., 1973).

Janes, Hurford, *The Red Barrel: A History of Watney Mann* (1963).

Keir, David, *The Younger Centuries: The Story of William Younger & Co. Ltd., 1749–1949* (Edinburgh, 1951).

Kenna, Rudolph and Mooney, Anthony, *People's Palaces: Victorian and Edwardian Pubs of Scotland* (Edinburgh, 1983).

King, Elspeth, *Scotland Sober and Free: The Temperance Movement, 1829–1979* (Glasgow, 1979).

Knox, Diana M., 'The Development of the Tied House System in London', *Oxford Economic Papers*, 10 (1958), 66–83.

—— 'The Development of the London Brewing Industry, 1830–1914, with Special Reference to Messrs. Whitbread and Company' (Oxford University B. Litt. thesis, 1956).

Lambert, W. R., *Drink and Sobriety in Victorian Wales, c.1820–c.1895* (Cardiff, 1983).

—— 'The Welsh Sunday Closing Act, 1881', *Welsh History Review*, 6 (1972), 161–89.

—— 'Drink and Work-Discipline in Industrial Wales, c.1800–70', *Welsh History Review*, 7 (1978), 289–306.

Longmate, Norman, *The Waterdrinkers: A History of Temperance* (1968).

Luckett, Fred, Flint, Ken and Lee, Peter, *A History of Brewing in Warwickshire* (Warwick, n.d. [1982?]).

Lynch, Patrick and Vaizey, John, *Guinness's Brewery in the Irish Economy, 1759–1876* (Cambridge, 1960).

McCandless, Peter, ' "Curses of Civilization": Insanity and Drunkenness in Victorian Britain', *British Journal of Addiction*, 79 (1984), 49–58.

MacDonagh, Oliver, 'The Origins of Porter', *Economic History Review*, 16 (1964), 530–5.

MacLeod, Roy M., 'The Edge of Hope: Social Policy and Chronic Alcoholism, 1870–1900,' *Journal of the History of Medicine and Allied Science*, 22 (1967), 215–45.

Malcolm, Elizabeth, *'Ireland Sober, Ireland Free': Drink and Temperance in Nineteenth-Century Ireland* (Dublin, 1986).

Mathias, Peter, 'The Brewing Industry, Temperance and Politics', *Historical Journal*, 1 (1958), 97 – 114.
—— *The Brewing Industry in England, 1700 – 1830* (1959).
Maxwell, Sir Herbert E., *Half-a-Century of Successful Trade: Being a Sketch of the Rise and Development of W. & A. Gilbey, 1857 – 1907* (1907).
Monckton, H. A., *A History of the English Public House* (1969).
Nevile, Sydney O., *Seventy Rolling Years* (1958).
Newton, John, *W. S. Caine, MP: A Biography* (1907).
Olsen, Gerald Wayne, 'Pub and Parish — The Beginnings of Temperance Reform in the Church of England, 1835 – 75' (Univ. of Western Ontario Ph.D. dissertation, 1972).
—— 'The Church of England Temperance Magazine', *Victorian Periodicals Newsletter*, 11 (1978), 38 – 49.
—— 'Anglican Temperance Movements in England, 1859 – 73: An Example of Practical Ecumenism', *Study Sessions* (Canadian Catholic Historical Association), 40 (1973), 41 – 51.
Owen, C. C., *The Development of Industry in Burton upon Trent* (Chichester, 1978).
Page, Ken, *Greene King: Biggleswade Brewery, 1764 – 1984* (Sandy, Bedfordshire, 1984).
Parker, Hubert H., *The Hop Industry* (1934).
Parry, Dave, Parry, Don and Walker, Alan, *Bygone Breweries of Sheffield: A Summary of the Brewing Trade in the City 100 Years Ago* (Manchester, n.d. [1981]).
Payne, P. L., 'The Emergence of the Large-Scale Company in Great Britain, 1870 – 1914', *Economic History Review*, 20 (1967), 519 – 42.
Pruitt, Amy A., 'Approaches to Alcoholism in Mid-Victorian England', *Clio Medica*, 9 (1974), 93 – 101.
Pudney, John, *A Draught of Contentment: The Story of the Courage Group* (1971).
Richter, Donald, *Riotous Victorians* (Athens, Ohio, 1981).
Roberts, James S., *Drink, Temperance and the Working Class in Nineteenth-Century Germany* (Boston, 1984).
Robinson, P. W., 'The Emergence of the Common Brewer in the Halifax District', *Transactions of the Halifax Antiquarian Society*, (1981), 70 – 107.
Rowley, J. J., 'Drink and the Public House in Nottingham, 1830 – 1860', *Transactions of the Thoroton Society of Nottinghamshire*, 79 (1975), 72 – 83.
Russell, George W. E., *Sir Wilfrid Lawson: A Memoir* (1909).
Serocold, Walter Pearce, *The Story of Watneys* (St Albans, 1949).

Sheppard, Francis, *Brakspear's Brewery, Henley on Thames, 1779 – 1979* (Henley on Thames, 1979).

Shiman, Lilian Lewis, 'The Blue Ribbon Army: Gospel Temperance in England', *Historical Magazine of the Protestant Episcopal Church*, 50 (1980), 391 – 408.

—— 'The Church of England Temperance Society in the Nineteenth Century', *Historical Magazine of the Protestant Episcopal Church*, 41 (1972), 179 – 95.

—— 'Temperance and Class in Bradford: 1830 – 60', *Yorkshire Archaeological Journal*, 58 (1986), 173 – 8.

—— *Crusade Against Drink in Victorian England* (New York, 1988).

Sigsworth, E. M., *The Brewing Trade During the Industrial Revolution: The Case of Yorkshire* (York, 1967).

—— 'Science and the Brewing Industry, 1850 – 1900', *Economic History Review*, 17 (1965), 536 – 50.

Slater, J. Norman, *A Brewer's Tale: The Story of Greenall Whitley & Company Limited Through Two Centuries* (Warrington, 1980).

Soldon, N., 'Laissez-Faire as Dogma: The Liberty and Property Defence League, 1882 – 1914', Kenneth D. Brown (ed.), *Essays in Anti-Labour History: Responses to the Rise of Labour in Britain* (1974), pp. 208 – 33.

Spiller, Brian, *Victorian Public Houses* (1972).

Strong, L. A. G., *A Brewer's Progress, 1757 – 1957: A Survey of Charrington's Brewery on the Occasion of its Bicentenary* (1957).

Summerfield, Penelope, 'The Effingham Arms and the Empire: Deliberate Selection in the Evolution of Music Hall in London', Eileen and Stephen Yeo (eds.), *Popular Culture and Class Conflict, 1590 – 1914: Explorations in the History of Labour and Leisure* (Brighton, 1981), pp. 209 – 40.

Thorne, Robert, 'Places of Refreshment in the Nineteenth-Century City', Anthony D. King (ed.), *Building and Society: Essays on the Social Development of the Built Environment* (1980), pp. 228 – 53.

—— 'The Movement for Public House Reform, 1892 – 1914', Derek J. Oddy and Derek S. Miller (eds.), *Diet and Health in Modern Britain* (1985), pp. 231 – 54.

Turner, John, 'State Purchase of the Liquor Trade in the First World War', *Historical Journal*, 23 (1980), 589 – 615.

Vaizey, John, 'The Brewing Industry', P. Lesley Cook (ed.), *Effects of Mergers: Six Studies* (1958), pp. 397 – 422.

—— *The Brewing Industry, 1886 – 1951: An Economic Study* (1960).

Watts, H. D., 'Lager Brewing in Britain', *Geography*, 60 (1975), 139 – 45.

Waugh, Alec, *Merchants of Wine: Being a Centenary Account of the Fortunes of the House of Gilbey* (1957).

Weir, Ronald B., 'The Drink Trades', Roy Church (ed.), *The Dynamics of Victorian Business: Problems and Perspectives to the 1870s* (1980).

—— *The History of the Malt Distillers' Association of Scotland* (Elgin, n.d. [1975]).

—— 'The Distilling Industry in Scotland in the Nineteenth and Early Twentieth Centuries' (University of Edinburgh Ph.D. dissertation, 1974).

—— 'Obsessed with Moderation: The Drink Trades and the Drink Question , 1870 – 1930', *British Journal of Addiction*, 79 (1984), 93 – 107.

Williams, Gwylmor and Brake, George Thompson, *Drink in Great Britain, 1900 to 1979* (1980).

Wilson, George B., *Alcohol and the Nation: A Contribution to the Study of the Liquor Problem in the United Kingdom from 1800 to 1935* (1940).

Wilson, Richard G., *Greene King: A Business and Family History* (1983).

Winstanley, Michael, 'The Rural Publican and His Business in East Kent Before 1914', *Oral History*, 4 (1976), 63 – 78.

Wreglesworth, Paul, Richardson, Neil and Gall, Alan, *The Pubs and Breweries of Macclesfield* (n.p., 1981).

Wright, David Edwin, 'The British Liberal Party and the Liquor Licensing Question, 1895 – 1905' (McMaster University Ph.D. dissertation, 1972).

—— and Chorniawry, Cathy, 'Women and Drink in Edwardian England', *Historical Papers/Communications Historiques* (1985), 117 – 31.

Index

Showell's Brewery Co., 197 – 8
Sigsworth, E. M., 204
Simonds, Henry, 79 – 80,
    83 – 6, 93, 95, 103
Simonds, H. & G., 17, 246
Sims, George, 243 – 4
Skeleton Armies, 218 – 19
Smith, Druce & Co., 246
Smith, Henry, 90
Smith, W.H., 105
social class: drinking habits,
    2 – 4, 9, 12, 26, 32 – 9, 52 – 4,
    77, 164 – 6, 181, 193, 195 – 6,
    203 – 16, 241, 243; middle
    class, 3, 6 – 7, 9, 11, 26 – 7,
    30, 32 – 4, 36 – 40, 45 – 7, 51,
    119 – 20, 176, 203 – 4, 228,
    233, 237; upper class, 6, 11,
    25 – 7, 30, 32 – 3, 36, 51,
    80 – 1, 119 – 20, 176, 194,
    228, 233, 237; working class,
    3, 6 – 7, 9, 11, 26 – 7, 30,
    32 – 4, 36 – 40, 45 – 7, 51,
    52 – 4, 57, 93, 119 – 20, 127,
    130, 151, 164 – 6, 168, 176,
    192 – 6, 201, 203 – 16, 218,
    220 – 3, 229, 233, 235, 237,
    239 – 40, 245
South Wales Brewers'
    Association, 138
spirit merchants, 26 – 7
standard barrels, 165
Stansfeld, James, 62 – 3, 78, 119
Stansfeld & Co., 119
Steward, Fitzroy, 74
Steward, Patteson, Finch &
    Co., 17, 157
Stewart, Donald, 90
stout, 2 – 3, 12, 34
Sunday closing, 35, 74 – 7,
    80 – 2, 87, 91, 100 – 1, 106,
    124, 127, 141, 143 – 4, 147,
    184, 186, 189

Tamplin, William C., 90
Tanqueray, Andrew, 197
Taylor, Walker & Co., 246
temperance remedies: free
    trade in beer, 6, 14, 17, 30;

licensing reduction, 25, 30,
    46 – 8, 50 – 2, 54 – 9, 71,
    77 – 8, 87, 99 – 101, 104 – 6,
    122 – 4, 127 – 30, 132,
    153 – 7, 167, 173, 230, 235,
    245; moral suasion, 6, 30,
    54, 222 – 3; prohibition, 6,
    28 – 30, 35 – 8, 44 – 5, 48, 52,
    55 – 7, 59, 61 – 2, 68, 74,
    78 – 80, 82, 84 – 5, 87, 96 – 7,
    100, 106, 119 – 24, 126 – 9,
    133, 141, 143 – 5, 147 – 8,
    155, 161, 167, 176, 185 – 7,
    189, 200, 218, 220 – 1,
    223 – 4, 228 – 30, 233,
    235 – 7, 245; spirit
    abstention, 6, 30
Tetley, Joshua, 13
Thwaites, Daniel, 64
Tied House Tenants' League,
    185 – 7, 216
tied houses, 4 – 5, 7, 9, 11,
    13 – 26, 28, 47, 50, 55, 58,
    63, 77, 108, 115, 156 – 7, 163,
    170, 176, 181 – 92, 207 – 9,
    211, 216 – 17, 237, 239 – 40
time limit, 47 – 8, 55, 57 – 9, 81,
    119, 128, 132 – 4, 167, 224,
    226, 230, 235. See also com-
    pensation, monopoly value
trade electoral agents, 9, 96 – 7,
    104, 108 – 12, 116, 121 – 3,
    137, 149, 160 – 1, 176, 186,
    202, 210, 215 – 16, 219,
    221 – 2, 224 – 5, 228, 236,
    239, 245
trade influence, 1, 7 – 10,
    25 – 6, 51 – 2, 54, 60, 99,
    123 – 4, 127, 130, 163 – 4,
    169, 172, 174 – 5, 202,
    215 – 16, 229 – 45
trade MPs, see brewers'
    protective societies/
    parliamentary lobby
Trade Union and Labour
    Officials' Temperance
    Fellowship, 222 – 3
trade unions, 220, 222 – 3, 229,
    233, 236 – 7, 245

Tripp, Howard, 155
Truman, Hanbury, Buxton & Co., 12, 58, 63, 99, 113, 246
Turner, John, 8, 179, 241
Tweedmouth family, 243

United Kingdom Alliance, 55 – 6, 61, 64, 68 – 70, 87, 90, 97, 99 – 100, 104, 107 – 8, 111, 115, 121 – 3, 125, 127 – 9, 146 – 7, 151, 160 – 1, 189 – 90, 222, 228, 232 – 4, 236, 245. *See also* temperance remedies/ prohibition
United Parliamentary Council, 139 – 40, 142 – 5, 149 – 52, 199. *See also* retail protective societies

Vaizey, John, 8, 11, 19, 203, 205
Vincent, J. R., 28

Wadhams, Joseph, 68, 71
Walker, Charles, 129, 140, 142 – 4, 149 – 51
Walker family, 243
Walker, Peter & Sons, 13, 19, 185, 246
Watney, James, 94, 242
Watney & Co., 12, 63, 156, 162, 246
Weir, R. B., 8, 230
Wells, Edward, 64
Welsh Sunday closing act, 194 – 5
Wemyss, Earl, 80 – 2
West, Sir Algernon, 94
Wethered, Thomas, 62, 64, 83 – 6, 91, 95, 107

whisky, 39, 183
Whitbread, F. P., 177, 213 – 14
Whitbread, Samuel, 62, 92, 94, 131
Whitbread, Samuel & Co., 63, 99, 205, 208
Whitbread, Samuel H., 119, 123
Whitbread family, 242
White, John, 182, 209
Whiteley, George, 229
Whittaker, Thomas, 37 – 8, 52, 123, 130, 133
Whitworth, Robert, 35, 42
Wigan, James, 103
Wilson, Richard, 17, 156 – 7
Wiltshire Brewers' Association, 210
wine, 4, 14, 26 – 8, 32 – 3, 39
Wine and Spirit Association, 138
wine merchants, 7, 26 – 7, 122, 124, 131
Wodehouse, Armine, 132, 135, 146
women, 32 – 4, 36, 41, 50, 136, 150 – 1, 169, 195, 209, 243 – 4
Working Men's Club and Institute Union, 193 – 4, 199
Worthington, William, 90

Yorkshire Brewers' Association, 64 – 5, 90, 117, 158, 161
Younger, William & Co., 12, 246
Youngs, Crawshay & Youngs, 17